POMPEII

ITS LIFE AND ART

POMPEII

ITS LIFE AND ART

BY

AUGUST MAU

GERMAN ARCHAEOLOGICAL INSTITUTE IN ROME

Translated into English

By FRANCIS W. KELSEY

UNIVERSITY OF MICHIGAN

WITH NUMEROUS ILLUSTRATIONS FROM ORIGINAL
DRAWINGS AND PHOTOGRAPHS

New York

THE MACMILLAN COMPANY

LONDON : MACMILLAN & CO., LTD.

1899

Norwood Press
J. S. Cushing & Co. — Berwick & Smith
Norwood, Mass. U. S. A.

PREFACE

For twenty-five years Professor Mau has devoted himself to the study of Pompeii, spending his summers among the ruins and his winters in Rome, working up the new material. He holds a unique place among the scholars who have given attention to Pompeian antiquities, and his contributions to the literature of the subject have been numerous in both German and Italian. The present volume, however, is not a translation of one previously issued, but a new work first published in English, the liberality of the publishers having made it possible to secure assistance for the preparation of certain restorations and other drawings which Professor Mau desired to have made as illustrating his interpretation of the ruins.

In one respect there is an essential difference between the remains of Pompeii and those of the large and famous cities of antiquity, as Rome or Athens, which have associated with them the familiar names of historical characters. Mars' Hill is clothed with human interest, if for no other reason, because of its relation to the work of the Apostle Paul; while the Roman Forum and the Palatine, barren as they seem to-day, teem with life as there rise before the mind's eye the scenes presented in the pages of classical writers. But the Campanian city played an unimportant part in contemporary history; the name of not a single great Pompeian is recorded. The ruins, deprived of the interest arising from historical associations, must be interpreted with little help from literary sources, and repeopled with aggregate rather than individual life.

A few Pompeians, whose features have survived in herms or statues and whose names are known from the inscriptions, seem

v

near to us, — such are Caecilius Jucundus and the generous
priestess Eumachia; but the characters most commonly associated with the city are those of fiction. Here, in a greater
degree than in most places, the work of reconstruction involves
the handling of countless bits of evidence, which, when viewed
by themselves, often seem too minute to be of importance; the
blending of these into a complete and faithful picture is a task
of infinite painstaking, the difficulty of which will best be appreciated by one who has worked in this field.

It was at first proposed to place at the end of the book a
series of bibliographical notes on the different chapters, giving
references to the more important treatises and articles dealing
with the matters presented. But on fuller consideration it
seemed unnecessary thus to add to the bulk of the volume;
those who are interested in the study of a particular building
or aspect of Pompeian culture will naturally turn to the *Pom-
peianarum antiquitatum historia*, the reports in the *Notizie degli
Scavi*, the reports and articles by Professor Mau in the Roman
Mittheilungen of the German Archaeological Institute, the
Overbeck-Mau *Pompeji*, the Studies by Mau and by Nissen,
the commemorative volume issued in 1879 under the title
Pompei e la regione sotterrata dal Vesuvio, the catalogues of
the paintings by Helbig and Sogliano, together with Mau's
Geschichte der decorativen Wandmalerei in Pompeji, H. von
Rohden's *Terracotten von Pompeji*, and the older illustrated
works, as well as the beautiful volume, *Pompeji vor der Zer-
stoerung*, published in 1897 by Weichardt.

The titles of more than five hundred books and pamphlets
relating to Pompeii are given in Furchheim's *Bibliografia di
Pompei* (second edition, Naples, 1891). To this list should be
added an elaborate work on the temple of Isis, *Aedis Isidis
Pompeiana*, which is soon to appear. The copperplates for
the engravings were prepared at the expense of the old Accademia ercolanese, but only the first section of the work was
published; the plates, fortunately, have been preserved without

injury, and the publication has at last been undertaken by Professor Sogliano.

Professor Mau wishes to make grateful acknowledgment of obligation to Messrs. C. Bazzani, R. Koldewey, G. Randanini, and G. Tognetti for kind assistance in making ready for the engraver the drawings presenting restorations of buildings; to the authorities of the German Archaeological Institute for freely granting the use of a number of drawings in its collection; and to the photographer, Giacomo Brogi of Florence, for placing his collection of photographs at the author's disposal and making special prints for the use of the engraver. In addition to the photographs obtained from Brogi, a small number were furnished for the volume by the translator, and a few were derived from other sources.

The restorations are not fanciful. They were made with the help of careful measurements and of computations based upon the existing remains; occasionally also evidence derived from reliefs and wall paintings was utilized. Uncertain details are generally omitted.

It is due to Professor Mau to say that in preparing his manuscript for English readers I have, with his permission, made some changes. The order of presentation has occasionally been altered. In several chapters the German manuscript has been abridged, while in others, containing points in regard to which English readers might desire a somewhat fuller statement, I have made slight additions. The preparation of the English form of the volume, undertaken for reasons of friendship, has been less a task than a pleasure.

FRANCIS W. KELSEY.

ANN ARBOR, MICHIGAN,
October 25, 1899.

CONTENTS

INTRODUCTION

PART I

PUBLIC PLACES AND BUILDINGS

i

X CONTENTS

CONTENTS

PART III

TRADES AND OCCUPATIONS

PART IV

THE TOMBS

PART V

POMPEIAN ART

CONTENTS

PART VI

THE INSCRIPTIONS OF POMPEII

CONCLUSION

ILLUSTRATIONS

PLATES

PLANS

xiii

ILLUSTRATIONS IN THE TEXT

[1] From a drawing loaned by the German Archaeological Institute in Rome.

POMPEII

ITS LIFE AND ART

INTRODUCTION

CHAPTER I

THE SITUATION OF POMPEII

FROM Gaeta, where the south end of the Volscian range borders abruptly upon the sea, to the peninsula of Sorrento, a broad gulf stretched in remote ages, cutting its way far into the land. Its waves dashed upon the base of the mountains which now, rising with steep slope, mark the eastern boundary of the Campanian Plain — Mt. Tifata above Capua, Mt. Taburno back of Nola, and lying across the southeast corner, the huge mass of Monte Sant' Angelo, whose sharply defined line of elevation is continued in the heights of Sorrento.

This gulf was transformed by volcanic agencies into a fertile plain. Here two fissures in the earth's crust cross each other; each marked by a series of extinct or active volcanoes. One fissure runs in the direction of the Italian Peninsula; along it lie Monti Berici near Vicenza, Mt. Amiata below Chiusi, the lakes of Bolsena and Bracciano filling extinct craters, the Alban Mountains, and finally Stromboli and Aetna. The other runs from east to west; its direction is indicated by Mt. Vulture near Venosa, Mt. Epomeo on the island of Ischia, and the Ponza Islands.

At three places in the old sea basin the subterranean fires burst forth. Near the north shore rose the great volcano of Rocca Monfina, which added itself to the Volscian Mountains, and heaping the products of its eruptions upon Mons Massicus, — once an island, — formed with this the northern boundary of the plain. Toward the middle the numerous small vents of the Phlegraean Fields threw up the low heights, to which the north

shore of the Bay of Naples — Posilipo, Baiae, Misenum — is
indebted for its incomparable beauty of landscape. Finally,
near the south shore, at the intersection of the fissures, the
massive cone of Vesuvius rose, in complete isolation — the
only volcano on the continent of Europe still remaining active.
Its base on the southwest is washed by the sea, while on the
other sides a stretch of level country separates it from the

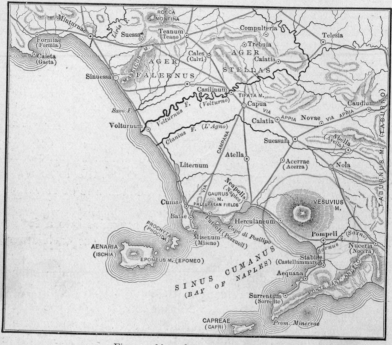

Fig. 1. — Map of Ancient Campania.

mountains that hem in the plain. On the side opposite from
the sea, however, Vesuvius comes so near to the mountains
that we may well say that it divides the Campanian plain into
two parts, of which the larger, on the northwest side, is drained
by the Volturno; the small southeast section is the plain of the
Sarno.

The Sarno, like the Umbrian Clitumnus, has no upper course.
At the foot of Mt. Taburno, bounding the plain on the north-

east, are five copious springs that soon unite to form a stream.
Since 1843 the river has been drawn off for purposes of irri-
gation into three channels, which are graded at different levels;
the distribution of water thus assured makes this part of Campania one of the most fertile districts in Italy.   In antiquity the
Sarno must have been confined to a single channel; according
to Strabo it was navigable for ships.

In Roman times three cities shared in the possession of the
Sarno plain.   Furthest inland, facing the pass in the mountains
that opens toward the Gulf of Salerno, lay Nuceria, now Nocera.
On the seashore, where the coast road to Sorrento branches off

Fig. 2. — Vesuvius as seen from Naples.

toward the southwest, was Stabiae, now Castellammare.   North
of Stabiae, at the foot of Vesuvius, Pompeii stood, on an elevation overlooking the Sarno, formed by the end of a stream of
lava that in some past age had flowed from Vesuvius down
toward the sea.   Pompeii thus united the advantages of an
easily fortified hill town with those of a maritime city.   "It
lies," says Strabo, "on the Sarnus, which accommodates a
traffic in both imports and exports; it is the seaport of Nola,
Nuceria, and Acerrae."

A glance at the map will show how conveniently situated
Pompeii was to serve as a seaport for Nola and Nuceria;
but it seems hardly credible that the inhabitants of Acerrae,
which lay much nearer Naples, should have preferred for their

marine traffic the circuitous route around Vesuvius to the Sarno. However that may have been, Pompeii was beyond doubt the most important town in the Sarno plain.

Pompeii formerly lay nearer the sea and nearer the river than at present. In the course of the centuries alluvial deposits have pushed the shore line further and further away. It is now about a mile and a quarter from the nearest point of the city to the sea; in antiquity it was less than a third of a mile. The line of the ancient coast can still be traced by means of a clearly marked depression, beyond which the stratification of the volcanic deposits thrown out in 79 does not reach. The Sarno, too, now flows nearly two thirds of a mile from Pompeii; in antiquity, according to all indications, it was not more than half so far away.

In point of climate and outlook, a fairer site for a city could scarcely have been chosen. The Pompeian, living in clear air, could look down upon the fogs which in the wet season frequently rose from the river and spread over the plain. And while in winter, Stabiae, lying on the northwest side of Monte Sant' Angelo, enjoyed the sun for only a few hours, the elevation on which Pompeii stood, sloping gently toward the east and south, more sharply toward the west, was bathed in sunlight during the entire day.

Winter at Pompeii is mild and short; spring and autumn are long. The heat of summer, moreover, is not extreme. In the early morning, it is true, the heat is at times oppressive. No breath of air stirs; and we look longingly off upon the expanse of sea where, far away on the horizon, in the direction of Capri, a dark line of rippling waves becomes visible. Nearer it comes, and nearer. About ten o'clock it reaches the shore. The leaves begin to rustle, and in a few moments the sea breeze sweeps over the city, strong, cool, and invigorating. The wind blows till just before sunset. The early hours of the evening are still; the pavements and the walls of the houses give out the heat which they have absorbed during the day. But soon — perhaps by nine o'clock — the tree tops again begin to murmur, and all night long, from the mountains of the interior, a gentle, refreshing stream of air flows down through the gardens, the roomy atriums and colonnades of the houses, the silent streets, and the buildings about the Forum, with an effect indescribably soothing.

How shall I undertake to convey to the reader who has not visited Pompeii, an impression of the beauty of its situation? Words are weak when confronted with the reality. Sea, mountains, and plain, — strong and pleasing background, — great

Fig. 3. — View from Pompeii, looking south.

masses and brilliant yet harmonious colors, splendid foreground effects and hazy vistas, undisturbed nature and the handiwork of man, all are blended into a landscape of the grand style, the like of which I should not know where else to look for.

If we turn toward the south, we have at our feet the level plain of the Sarno, in antiquity as now — we may suppose — not checkered with villages but dotted here and there with groups of farm buildings, surrounded with stately trees. Beyond the plain rises the lofty barrier of Monte Sant' Angelo, thickly wooded in places, its summit standing out against the sky in a long, beautiful profile, which, toward the right, breaks up into bold, rugged notches; the side of the mountain below is richly diversified with deep valleys, projecting ridges, and terraces that in the distance seem like steps, where among vineyards and olive orchards stand two villages fair to look on, Gragnano and Lettere, so near that individual houses can be clearly distinguished. Further west the plain before us opens out upon the sea, while the mountains are continued in the precipitous coast of the peninsula of Sorrento. Height crowds upon height, with villages wreathed in olive orchards lying between. Here the hills descend in terraces to the sea, covered with vegetation to the water's edge; there the covering of soil has been cast off from the steep slopes, exposing the naked rock, which shines in the afternoon sun with a reddish hue that wonderfully accords with the dark shades of the foliage and the brilliant blue of the sea. Further on the tints become duller, and the sight is blurred; only with effort can we distinguish Sorrento, resting on cliffs that rise almost perpendicularly from the line of the shore. Further still the outline of the peninsula sinks into the sea and gives place to Capri, island of fantastic shape, whose crags rising sheer from the water stand out sharply in the bright sunlight.

But we look toward the north, and the splendid variety of form and color vanishes; there stands only the vast, sombre mass of the great destroyer, Vesuvius, towering above the city and the plain. The sun as it nears the horizon veils the bare ashen cone with a mantle of deep violet, while the cloud of smoke that rises from the summit shines with a golden glow. Far above the base the sides are covered with vineyards, among which small groups of white houses can here and there be seen. West of us the outline of the mountain descends in a strong, simple curve to the sea. Just before it blends with the shore there rise behind it distant heights wrapped in blue haze, the first of moderate elevation, then others more prominent and further to the left. They are the heights along the north shore of the Bay of Naples — Gaurus crowned with the monastery of Camaldoli, famous for its magnificent view;

the cliffs of Baiae, the promontory of Misenum, and the lofty
cone of Epomeo on the island of Ischia. So the eye trav-
erses the whole expanse of the Bay; Naples itself, hidden
from our view, lies between those distant heights and the base
of Vesuvius.

But meanwhile the sun has set behind Misenum; its last rays
are lighting up the cloud of smoke above Vesuvius and the
summit of Monte Sant' Angelo. The brilliancy of coloring has
faded; the weary eye finds rest in the soft afterglow. We also
may take leave of these beautiful surroundings, and inquire into
the beginnings of the city which was founded here.

CHAPTER II

BEFORE 79

WHEN Pompeii was founded we do not know. It is more than likely that a site so well adapted for a city was occupied at an early date. The oldest building, the Doric temple in the Forum Triangulare, is of the style of the sixth century B.C.; we are safe in assuming that the city was then already in existence.[1] The founders were Oscans. They belonged to a widely scattered branch of the Italic stock, whose language, closely related with the Latin, has been imperfectly recovered from a considerable number of inscriptions, so imperfectly that in each of the longer inscriptions there still remain words the meaning of which is obscure or doubtful. From this language the name of the city came; for *pompe* in Oscan meant 'five.' The word does not, however, appear in its simple form; we have only the adjective derived from it, *pompaiians*, 'Pompeian.' If we are right in assuming that the name appeared in Oscan, as it does in Latin, in the plural form, it was probably applied first to a gens, or clan, and thence to the city; the Latin equivalent of Pompeii would be Quintii. Pompeii was thus the city of the clan of the Pompeys, as Tarquinii was the city of the Tarquins, and Veii the city of the Veian clan. The name Pompeius was common in Pompeii down to the destruction of the city, and in other Campanian towns, notably Puteoli, to much later times.

In order to follow the course of events at Pompeii, it will be necessary to pass briefly in review the main points in the history of Campania. The Campanian Oscans, sprung from a

[1] It seems strange that traces of other buildings of the same period have not been discovered; but, on the other hand, it is far from probable that the temple was first erected, and that the city afterward grew up around it, for in that case the temple must have been placed further west, on the highest point of the elevation, overlooking the sea.

8

rude and hardy race, became civilized from contact with the Greeks, who at an early period had settled in Cumae, in Dicaearchia, afterward Puteoli, and in Parthenope, later Naples; and the coast climate had an enervating effect upon them. When toward the end of the fifth century B.C. the Samnites, kinsmen of the Oscans, left their rugged mountain homes in the interior and pressed down toward the coast, the Oscans were unable to cope with them. In 424 B.C. the Samnites stormed and took Capua, in 420, Cumae; and Pompeii likewise fell into their hands. But they were no more successful than the Oscans had been in resisting the influence of Greek culture. How strong this influence was may be seen in the remains at Pompeii. The architecture of the period was Greek; Greek divinities were honored, as Apollo and Zeus Milichius; and the standard measures of the *mensa ponderaria* were inscribed with Greek names.

In less than a hundred years new strifes arose between the more cultured Samnites of the plain and their rough and warlike kinsmen in the mountains. But Rome took a part in the struggle, and in the Samnite Wars (343–290 B.C.) brought both the men of the mountains and the men of the plain under her dominion. Although the sovereignty of Rome took the form of a perpetual alliance, the cities in reality lost their independence. The complete subjugation and Romanizing of Campania, however, did not come till the time of the Social War (90–88 B.C.) and the supremacy of Sulla; the Samnites staked all on the success of the popular party, and lost.

In the narrative of these events Pompeii is not often mentioned. At the time of the Second Samnite War, in the year 310 B.C., we read that a Roman fleet under Publius Cornelius landed at the mouth of the Sarno, and that a pillaging expedition followed the course of the river as far as Nuceria; but the country folk fell on the marauders as they were returning, and forced them to give up their booty. We have no definite information regarding the attitude of the Pompeians after the battle of Cannae (216 B.C.); probably they joined the side of Hannibal, who, however, was defeated by Marcus Marcellus near Nola in the following year, and was obliged to leave Campania to the Romans.

In the Social War, when, in the summer of 90 B.C., the Samnite army marched into Campania, Pompeii allied itself with the insurgents; as a consequence, in 89, it was besieged by Sulla, but without success.   Two years later, Sulla went to Asia to conduct the war against Mithridates.   Returning victorious in the spring of 83 B.C., he led his army into Campania, where he spent the winter of 83–82; his soldiers, grown brutal in the Asiatic war and accustomed to every kind of license, may have proved unwelcome guests for the Pompeians.

The sequel came in the year 80, when a colony of Roman veterans was settled in Pompeii under the leadership of Publius Sulla, a nephew of the Dictator.   Cicero later made a speech in behalf of this Sulla, defending him against the charge that he had taken part in the conspiracy of Catiline and had tried to induce the old residents of Pompeii to join in the plot.   From this speech we learn that Sulla's reorganization of the city was accomplished with so great regard for the interests of the Pompeians, that they ever after held him in grateful remembrance.   We learn, also, that soon after the founding of the colony disputes arose between the old residents and the colonists, about the public walks (*ambulationes*) and matters connected with the voting; the arrangements for voting had probably been so made as to throw the decision always into the hands of the colonists.   The controversy was referred to the patrons of the colony, and settled by them.   From this time on, the life of Pompeii seems not to have differed from that of the other small cities of Italy.

As the harbor of Pompeii was on the Sarno, which flowed at some distance from the city, there must have been a small settlement at the landing place.   To this probably belonged a group of buildings, partly excavated in 1880–81, lying just across the Sarno canal (canale del Bottaro), about a third of a mile from the Stabian Gate.   Here were found many skeletons, and with them a quantity of gold jewellery, which was afterward placed in the Museum at Naples.   The most reasonable explanation of the discovery is, that the harbor was here, and that these persons, gathering up their valuables, fled from Pompeii at the time of the eruption either in order to escape by

sea or to take refuge in Stabiae. Flight in either case was cut
off. If ships were in the harbor, they must soon have been
filled with the volcanic deposits; if there was a bridge across
the river it was probably thrown down by the earthquake.

A second suburb sprang up near the sea, in connection with
the salt works (*salinae*) of the city. Our knowledge of the
inhabitants, the Salinenses, is derived from several inscriptions
painted upon walls, in which they recommend candidates for the
municipal offices, and from an inscription scratched upon the
plaster of a column in which a fuller by the name of Crescens
sends them a greeting: *Cresce[n]s fullo Saline[n]sibus salute[m]*.
From another inscription we learn that they had an assembly,
conventus, possibly judicial in its functions; for in connection
with a date, it speaks of a fine of twenty sesterces, which would
amount to about 3½ shillings, or 85 cents: *VII K. dec. Salinis
in conventu multa HS XX*, 'Fine of twenty sesterces; assembly at Salinae, November 25.' Still another inscription speaks
of attending such a meeting on November 19: *XIII K. dec.
in conventu veni.*

The suburb most frequently mentioned was at first called
Pagus Felix Suburbanus, but after the time of Augustus,
Pagus Augustus Felix Suburbanus. Its location is unknown.
As it evidently took the name of Felix from the Dictator Sulla,
who used this epithet as a surname, we may assume that its
origin dates from the establishment of the Roman colony; it
may have been founded to provide a place for those inhabitants
of Pompeii who had been forced to leave their homes in order
to make room for the colonists. The existence of a fourth
suburb is inferred from two painted inscriptions in which
candidates for office are recommended by the Campanienses;
this name would naturally be applied to the inhabitants of
a Pagus Campanus, who, perhaps, had originally come from
Capua.

Of the government of Pompeii in the earliest times, before
the Samnite conquest, nothing is known. The names of various
magistrates in the Samnite period, however, particularly the
period of alliance with Rome (290–90 B.C.), are learned from
inscriptions. Mention is made of a chief administrative officer

(*mediss, mediss tovtiks*); of quaestors, who, probably, like the
quaestors in Rome, were charged with the financial administration and let the contracts for public buildings; and of aediles,
to whom, no doubt, was intrusted the care of streets and build-

Fig. 4.— Venus Pompeiana.
From a wall painting.

ings, together with the policing of
the markets.   The Latin names of
the last two officials suggest that
their offices were introduced after
290.   There was also an assembly
called *kombenniom*, with which we
may compare the Latin *conventus;*
but whether it was an assembly of
the people or a city council cannot
now be determined.

After the establishment of the
Roman colony, Pompeii was named
Colonia Cornelia Veneria Pompeiano-
rum, from the gentile name of the
Dictator Sulla (Lucius Cornelius Sulla
Felix) and from the goddess to whom
he paid special honor, who now, as
Venus Pompeiana, became the tute-
lary divinity of the city.   This god-

dess is represented in wall paintings.   In that from which our
illustration is taken (Fig. 4), she appears in a blue mantle studded with golden stars, and wears a crown set with green stones.
Her left hand, which holds a sceptre, rests upon a rudder; in
her right is a twig of olive.   A Cupid stands upon a pedestal
beside her, holding up a mirror.

From this time the highest official body, as in Roman colonies everywhere, was the city council, composed of decurions.
The administration was placed in the hands of two pairs of
officials, the duumvirs with judiciary authority, *duumviri iuri*
dicundo, and two aediles, who were responsible for the care
of buildings and streets and the oversight of the markets.
When the duumvirs and the aediles joined in official acts they
were known as the Board of Four, *quattuorviri*.   Down to the
time of the Empire it appears that the aediles were not desig-

nated officially by that name, but by a title known to us only in an abbreviated form, *duumviri v. a. sacr. p. proc.* This prob ably stands for *duumviri viis, aedibus, sacris publicis procurandis*, 'duumvirs in charge of the streets, the temples, and the public religious festivals.' The title of aedile seems to have been avoided because it had been in use in the days of autonomy, and the authorities thought it prudent to suppress everything that would suggest the former state of independence. Nevertheless, the word retained its place in ordinary speech, as is shown by its use in the inscriptions painted on walls recommending candi- dates for office; thence it finally forced its way back into the official language. The duumvirs of every fifth year were called quinquennial duumvirs, *duumviri quinquennales*, and assumed functions corresponding with those of the censors at Rome; they gave attention to matters of finance, and revised the lists of decurions and of citizens.

All these officials were elected annually by popular vote. The candidates offered themselves beforehand. If none came forward, or there were too few, — for the city officials not only received no salary, but were under obligation to make generous contributions for public purposes, as theatrical representations, games, and buildings, — the magistrate who presided at the election named candidates for the vacancies; but each candi- date so named had the right to nominate a second for the same vacancy, the second in turn a third. The voting was by ballot; each voter threw his voting tablet into the urn of his precinct. No information has come down to us regarding the precincts (*curiae*) into which the city must have been divided for electoral purposes.

The election of a candidate was valid only in case he received the vote of an absolute majority of the precincts. If the result was indecisive for all or a part of the offices, the city council chose an extraordinary official who bore the title of prefect with judiciary authority, *praefectus iuri dicundo.* This prefect took the place of the duumvirs, not only when an election was inde- cisive, but also when vacancies arose in some other way, or when peculiar conditions seemed to make it desirable to have an officer of unusual powers, a kind of dictator; or finally, when the emperor had received the vote; in the last two cases, the prefect was undoubtedly appointed by the emperor. Thus, in the years 34 and 40 A.D., the Emperor Caligula was duumvir of Pompeii; but the duties of the office were discharged by a prefect. A law passed in Rome toward the end of the Republic on the motion of a certain Petronius contained provisions regarding the appointment of prefects; one chosen in accordance with them was called *praefectus ex lege Petronia,* 'prefect according to the law of Petronius.'

There were also in Pompeii priests supported by the city, but only a few of them are mentioned in the inscriptions. References are found to augurs and pontifices, to a priest of Mars, and to priests (*flamen, sacerdos*) of Augustus while he was still living; Nero had a priest even before he ascended the throne. Mention is made of priestesses, too, a priestess of Ceres and Venus, priestesses of Ceres, and others, the divinities of whom are not named.

The suburbs could scarcely have had a separate administration; they remained within the jurisdiction of the magistrates of the city. In the case of the Pagus Augustus Felix mention is made of a *magister,* 'director,' *ministri,* 'attendants,' and *pagani,* 'pagus officials'; but apparently these were all appointed for religious functions only, in connection with the worship of the emperor. The *magister* and the *pagani,* in part at least, were freedmen; the four *ministri,* first appointed in 7 B.C., were slaves.

Apart from commerce, an important source of income for the Pompeians lay in the fertility of the soil. In antiquity, as now, grapes were cultivated extensively on the ridge projecting from the foot of Vesuvius toward the south. The evidence afforded by the great number of wine jars, *amphorae* (Fig. 5), that have been brought to light would warrant this conclusion; and lately a wine press also has been discovered at Boscoreale, above Pompeii. Pliny makes frequent mention of the Pompeian wine, but adds that indulgence in it brings a headache that will last till noon of the following day. The olive too was cultivated, but only to a limited extent; this we infer from the small capacity of the press and other appliances for making oil found in the same villa in which the wine press was discovered. At the present time the making of oil is not carried on about Pompeii. In the plain below the city vegetables were raised ; the cabbage of Pompeii, frequently mentioned by ancient writers, was highly prized.

The working up of the products of the fisheries formed an important industry. The fish sauces which so tickled the palate of ancient epicures, *garum*, *liquamen*, and *muria*, were produced here of the finest quality. The making of them seems to have been practically a monopoly in the hands of a certain Umbricius Scaurus; a great number of earthen jars have been found with the mark of his ownership.

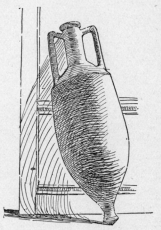

Fig. 5. — An amphora from Boscoreale.

The Pompeians turned to account, also, the volcanic products of Vesuvius. Pumice stone was an article of export. From the lava millstones were made for both grain mills and oil mills, which were apparently already in extensive use in the time of Cato the Elder; he mentions them in his treatise on farming. In Pompeii itself the millstones of the oldest period are of lava from Vesuvius; later it was found that the lava of Rocca Monfina was better adapted for the purpose, and millstones of that material were preferred. Small hand-mills of the lava from Vesuvius were in use at Pompeii down to 79 ; but the larger millstones of this material found in the bakeries had been put one side. In shape and finish the mills of local make were superior to the more carelessly worked stones from Rocca Monfina; the preference for the latter was due to the fact that they contained numerous crystals of leucite, which broke off as the mill wore away, and so kept the grinding surfaces always rough. Millstones from Rocca Monfina may be seen at different places in Rome, as in the Museum of the Baths of Diocletian.

To the sources of revenue which contributed to the prosperity of Pompeii we may add the presence of wealthy Romans,
who, attracted by the delightful climate, built country seats in
the vicinity.   Among them was Cicero, who often speaks of his
Pompeian villa (Pompeianum).   That the imperial family also had
a villa here is inferred from a curious accident.   We read that
Drusus, the young son of the Emperor Claudius, a few days
after his betrothal to the daughter of Sejanus, was choked to
death at Pompeii by a pear which he had thrown up into the air
and caught in his mouth.   These country seats, no doubt, lay
on the high ground back of Pompeii, toward Vesuvius; they
probably faced the sea.   But the identification of a villa excavated in the last century, and then filled up again, as the villa of
Cicero, is wholly without foundation.

Salve lucrum, 'Welcome, Gain!' Such is the inscription
which a Pompeian placed in the mosaic floor of his house.
Lucrum gaudium, 'Gain is pure joy,' we read on the threshold
of another house.   A thrifty Pompeian certainly did not lack
opportunity to acquire wealth.

How large a population Pompeii possessed at the time of the
destruction of the city it is impossible to determine.   A painstaking examination of all the houses excavated would afford
data for an approximate estimate; but the results thus far obtained by those who have given attention to the subject are
unsatisfactory.   Fiorelli assigned to Pompeii twelve thousand
inhabitants, Nissen twenty thousand.   Undoubtedly the second
estimate is nearer the truth than the first; according to all indication the population may very likely have exceeded twenty
thousand.

This population was by no means homogeneous.   The original Oscan stock had not yet lost its identity; inscriptions in the
Oscan dialect are found scratched on the plaster of walls decorated in the style prevalent after the earthquake of the year 63.
From the time when the Roman colony was founded no doubt
additions continued to be made to the population from various
parts of Italy.   The Greek element was particularly strong.
This is proved by the number of Greek names in the accounts
of Caecilius Jucundus, for example, and by the Greek inscrip-

tions that have been found on walls and on amphorae. The Greeks may have come from the neighboring towns; most of them were probably freedmen. In a seaport we should expect to find also Greeks from trans-marine cities; and, in fact, an Alexandrian appears in one of the receipts of Jucundus. There were Orientals, too, as we shall see when we come to the temple of Isis.

Thus far there has come to hand no trustworthy evidence for the presence of Christians at Pompeii; but traces of Jewish influence are not lacking. The words *Sodoma, Gomora,* are scratched in large letters on the wall of a house in Region IX (IX. i. 26). They must have been written by a Jew, or possibly a Christian; they seem like a prophecy of the fate of the city.

Fig. 6. — The Judgment of Solomon. Wall painting.

Another interesting bit of evidence is a wall painting, which appears to have as its subject the Judgment of Solomon (Fig. 6). On a tribunal at the right sits the king with two advisers; the pavilion is well guarded with soldiers. In front of the tribunal a soldier is about to cut a child in two with a cleaver. Two women are represented, one of whom stands at the block and is already taking hold of the half of the child assigned to her, while the other casts herself on her knees as a suppliant before the judges. It is not certain that the reference here is to Solomon; such tales pass from one country to another, and a somewhat similar story is told of the Egyptian king Bocchoris. The balance of probability is in favor of the view that we have here the Jewish version of the story, because this is consistent with other facts that point to the existence of a Jewish colony at Pompeii.

c

The names Maria and Martha appear in wall inscriptions. The assertion that Maria here is not the Hebrew name, but the feminine form of the Roman name Marius, is far astray. It appears in a list of female slaves who were working in a weaver's establishment, Vitalis, Florentina, Amaryllis, Januaria, Heracla, Maria, Lalage, Damalis, Doris. The Marian family was represented at Pompeii, but the Roman name Maria could not have been given to a slave. That we have here a Jewish name seems certain since the discovery of the name Martha.

In inscriptions upon wine jars we find mention of a certain M. Valerius Abinnerichus, a name which is certainly Jewish or Syrian; but whether Abinnerich was a dealer, or the owner of the estate on which the wine was produced, cannot be determined. In this connection it is worth while to note that vessels have been found with the inscribed labels, *garum castum* (for *casti-moniale?*), and *muria casta*. These fish sauces, prepared for fast days, were used especially by the Jews.

Some have thought that the word *Christianos* can be read in an inscription written with charcoal, and have fancied that they found a reference to the persecution of the Christians under Nero. But charcoal inscriptions, which will last for centuries when covered with earth, soon become illegible if exposed to the air; such an inscription, traced on a wall at the time of the persecutions under Nero, must have disappeared long before the destruction of the city. The inscription in question was indistinct when discovered, and has since entirely faded; the reading is quite uncertain. If it were proved that the word " Christians " appeared in it, we should be warranted only in the inference that Christians were known at Pompeii, not that they lived and worshipped there. According to Tertullian (Apol. 40) there were no Christians in Campania before 79.

CHAPTER III

THE CITY OVERWHELMED

PREVIOUS to the terrible eruption of 79, Vesuvius was considered an extinct volcano. "Above these places," says Strabo, writing in the time of Augustus, "lies Vesuvius, the sides of which are well cultivated, even to the summit. This is level, but quite unproductive. It has a cindery appearance; for the rock is porous and of a sooty color, the appearance suggesting that the whole summit may once have been on fire and have contained craters, the fires of which died out when there was no longer anything left to burn."

Earthquakes, however, were of common occurrence in Campania. An especially violent shock on the fifth of February, 63 A.D., gave warning of the reawakening of Vesuvius. Great damage was done throughout the region lying between Naples and Nuceria, but the shock was most severe at Pompeii, a large part of the buildings of the city being thrown down. The prosperous and enterprising inhabitants at once set about rebuilding. When the final catastrophe came, on the twenty-fourth of August, 79 A.D., most of the houses were in a good state of repair, and the rebuilding of at least two temples, those of Apollo and of Isis, had been completed. This renewing of the city, caused by the earthquake, may be looked upon as a fortunate circumstance for our studies.

Our chief source of information for the events of August 24–26, 79, is a couple of letters of the Younger Pliny to Tacitus, who purposed to make use of them in writing his history. Pliny was staying at Misenum with his uncle, the Elder Pliny, who was in command of the Roman fleet. In the first letter he tells of his uncle's fate. On the afternoon of the twenty-fourth, the admiral Pliny set out with ships to rescue from impending danger the people at the foot of Vesuvius, particularly in the vicinity

of Herculaneum.   He came too late; it was no longer possible
to effect a landing.   So he directed his course to Stabiae, where
he spent the night; and there on the following morning he died,
suffocated by the fumes that were exhaled from the earth.
The second letter gives an account of the writer's own experiences at Misenum.

To this testimony little is added by the narrative of Dion
Cassius, which was written a century and a half later and is
known to us only in abstract; Dion dwells at greater length on
the powerful impression which the terrible convulsion of nature
left upon those who were living at that time.   With the help
of the letters of Pliny, in connection with the facts established
by the excavations, it is possible to picture to ourselves the
progress of the eruption with a fair degree of clearness.

The subterranean fires of Vesuvius pressed upward to find
an outlet.   The accumulations of volcanic ash and pumice
stone that had been heaped up on the mountain by former
eruptions were again hurled to a great height, and came down
upon the surrounding country.   On the west side of Vesuvius
they mingled with torrents of rain, and flowed as a vast stream
of mud down over Herculaneum.   On the south side, driven
by a northwest wind as they descended from the upper air,
they spread out into a thick cloud, which covered Pompeii and
the plain of the Sarno.   Out of this cloud first broken fragments of pumice stone — the average size not larger than a
walnut — rained down to the depth of eight to ten feet; then
followed volcanic ash, wet as it fell by a downpour of water, to
the depth of six or seven feet.   With the storm of ashes came
successive shocks of earthquake.

Such was, in outline, the course of the eruption.   It must
have begun early in the morning of the twenty-fourth, and the
stream of mud must have commenced immediately to move in
the direction of Herculaneum; for shortly after one o'clock on
that day the admiral Pliny at Misenum received letters from
the region threatened, saying that the danger was imminent, and
that escape was possible only by sea.   Even then the Younger
Pliny saw, high above Vesuvius, the cloud, shaped like an um-
brella pine, which was to rain down destruction on Pompeii.

Toward evening, the ships off Herculaneum ran into the hail of pumice stone, which, during the night, reached Stabiae and so increased in violence that the admiral Pliny was obliged to leave his sleeping room from fear that the door would be blocked up by the falling masses.

Early in the morning of the twenty-fifth there was a severe shock of earthquake, which was felt as far as Misenum. Then the ashes began to fall, and a cloud of fearful blackness, pierced through and through with flashes of lightning, settled down over land and sea. At Misenum, even, it became dark; "not," says Pliny, "as on a cloudy night when there is no moon, but as in a room which has been completely closed."

How long the storm of ashes lasted we can only infer from this, that when it ceased the sun had not yet set. In Misenum, which the shower of pumice stone had not reached, everything was covered with a thick layer of ashes. Although the earthquake shocks continued, the inhabitants went back into their houses. But Pompeii and Stabiae had been covered so deep that only the roofs of the houses, where these had not fallen in, projected above the surface; and Herculaneum had wholly disappeared.

All the plain of the Sarno was buried, as were also the slopes of the mountains on the south. Stabiae, as we have seen, lay at the foot of the mountains, on the coast. It had been destroyed by Sulla in the Social War; its inhabitants, forced to scatter, settled in the surrounding country. In the years 1749–82 numerous buildings were excavated in the vicinity, in part luxurious country seats, in part plain farm buildings; but the excavations were afterward filled up again. The covering of Stabiae was like that of Pompeii, only not so deep.

Herculaneum was covered with the same materials; they were not, however, deposited in regular strata, but were mixed together, and being drenched with water, hardened into a kind of tufa which in places reaches a depth of sixty-five feet. Excavating at Herculaneum is in consequence extremely difficult; and the difficulty is further increased by the fact that a modern city, Resina, extends over the greater part of the ancient site. The excavations thus far attempted have in most cases been

conducted by means of underground passageways. The statement that Herculaneum was overflowed by a stream of lava,
though frequently repeated, is erroneous.

The woodwork of buildings in Pompeii has in many cases
been preserved, but in a completely charred condition. Frequently where walls were painted with yellow ochre it has
turned red, especially when brought immediately into contact
with the stratum of ashes — a change which this color under-
goes when it is exposed to heat. Nevertheless, the inference
would be unwarranted that the products of the eruption fell
upon the city red-hot and caused a general conflagration. The

Fig. 7. — Cast of a man.

fragments of pumice stone could scarcely have retained a great
degree of heat after having been so long in the air; it is evident
from Pliny's narrative that they were not hot.

With the ashes a copious rain must have fallen; for the
bodies of those who perished in the storm of ashes left perfect
moulds, into a number of which soft plaster of Paris has been
poured, making those casts of human figures which lend a
melancholy interest to the collections in the little Museum
at Pompeii (Fig. 7). The extraordinary freshness of these
figures, without any suggestion of the wasting away after death,
is explicable only on the supposition that the enveloping ashes
were damp, and so commenced immediately to harden into a

permanent shape. If the ashes had been dry and had packed down and hardened afterwards, we should be able to trace at least the beginnings of decay.

Neither the pumice stone nor the ashes, then, could have set wood on fire. The woodwork must have become charred gradually from the effect of moisture, as in the case of coal, and the change in the color of the yellow ochre must be due to some other cause than the presence of heat. This is all the more evident from the fact that vestiges of local conflagrations, confined within narrow limits, can here and there be traced, kindled by the masses of glowing slag which fell at the same time with the pumice stone, or by the fires left burning in the houses.

From the number of skeletons discovered in the past few decades, since an accurate record has been kept, it has been estimated that in Pompeii itself, about two thousand persons perished. As the city contained a population of twenty thousand or more, it is evident that the majority of the inhabitants fled; since the eruption commenced in the morning, while the hail of pumice stone did not begin till afternoon, those who appreciated the greatness of the danger had time to escape. It is, however, impossible to say how many fled when it was already too late, and lost their lives outside the city. Mention has already been made of some who perished at the harbor; others who went out earlier to the Sarno may have made good their escape. Of those who remained in the city part were buried in the houses — so with twenty persons whose skeletons were found in the cellar of the villa of Diomedes; others, as the hail of pumice stone ceased, ventured out into the streets, where they soon succumbed to the shower of ashes that immediately followed. As the bodies wasted away little except the bones was left in the hollows formed by the ashes that hardened around them, and the casts already referred to, which have been made from time to time since 1863, give in some cases a remarkably clear and sharp representation of the victims.

The Emperor Titus sent a commission of senators into Campania to report in what way help could best be rendered. A plan was formed to rebuild the cities that had been destroyed, and the property of those who died without heirs was set aside for this purpose. Nothing came of it, however, so far as our knowledge goes. Pompeii is indeed mentioned in the Peutinger Table, a map for travellers made in the third century, but the name was apparently given to a post station in memory of the former city. Conclusive evidence against the existence of a new city is the absence of any inscriptions referring to it.

CHAPTER IV

THE UNEARTHING OF THE CITY

THE first excavations at Pompeii were undertaken by the survivors shortly after the destruction of the city. As the upper parts of the houses that had not fallen in projected above the ashes, it was possible to locate the places under which objects of value were buried. Men dug down from the surface at certain points and tunnelled from room to room underneath, breaking through the intervening walls. This work was facilitated by the stratification of the volcanic deposits; the loose bits of pumice stone in the lower stratum were easily removed, while the stratum of ashes above was compact enough to furnish a fairly safe roof for narrow passageways. Only infrequently is a house discovered that was left undisturbed; from this we understand why comparatively little household furniture of value has been found. Not only were rich house furnishings in demand, — the excavators carried away valuable building materials as well. So eagerly were these sought after that large buildings, as those about the Forum, were almost completely stripped of their marble.

In the Middle Ages Pompeii was quite forgotten. Possibly some remains of the ancient buildings were yet to be seen; at any rate it seems to have been believed that a city once existed there, for the site was called La Civita.

In the years 1594–1600 Domenico Fontana was bringing water from one of the springs of the Sarno to Torre Annunziata, and in the course of the work ·cut an underground channel through the site of Pompeii and discovered two inscriptions; but no further investigations were made. The indifference of Fontana may be explained by the fact that the water channel was not dug out from above, like a railway cutting, and then covered over, but was carried as a tunnel

through the hill on which the city stood, so that the workmen came to the ancient surface at only a few points. In the
part now excavated, the original level was disturbed in but
one place, near the temple of Zeus Milichius; here the inscriptions were probably found.

The excavation of the buried Campanian towns began, not at
Pompeii, but at Herculaneum, where in 1719 the workmen of
the Austrian general, Count Elbeuf, sunk a shaft, reaching the
ancient level at the rear of the stage of the theatre. The
current statement that Elbeuf discovered the site of Herculaneum by accident, his workmen being engaged in digging a
well, is erroneous. The location of the city was already known,
and Elbeuf was searching for antiquities. The error probably
originated in a misunderstanding of the Italian word *pozzo*,
which has a double meaning, "shaft," and "well."

At first little was accomplished, but after 1738 excavations
were carried on by King Charles III in a more systematic
manner. The director of these excavations, Rocco Gioacchino
de Alcubierre, in March, 1748, had occasion to inspect the
water channel mentioned above, and learned that at the place
called La Civita — which he thought was Stabiae — objects of
antiquity were often found. He came to the conclusion
that this site was more promising than that of Herculaneum,
where the excavations just then were yielding little of value;
the result of his recommendation was that on the thirtieth of
the same month excavations were commenced at Pompeii, with
twelve workmen.

The first digging was done north of Nola Street, near the
Casa del Torello; then the men were set at work on the Street
of Tombs, near the Herculaneum Gate; and a part of the
Amphitheatre also was cleared. In 1750 the work was stopped,
because the results were thought to be unimportant.

Attention was again directed to Pompeii in 1754, when workmen engaged in constructing the highway that runs just south
of the city discovered a number of tombs. About the same
time, west of the Amphitheatre, the extensive establishment of
Julia Felix, arranged like a villa, and some buildings lying north
of it, were excavated; but they were all covered up again, as

was also the so-called villa of Cicero, which was more fully uncovered in 1763.

The parts excavated were not left clear until after 1763, when the discovery of the inscription of Suedius Clemens, on the Street of Tombs, had established the fact that the site was that of Pompeii. Important discoveries were made soon after. In the years immediately following 1764 the theatres, with the adjacent buildings, and the Street of Tombs, together with the villa of Diomedes, were laid bare. The excavations were conducted slowly and without system, yet with scientific interest fostered by the Herculaneum Academy (Accademia ercolanese), which had been founded in 1755.

Under Joseph Bonaparte and Murat, 1806–15, the work received larger appropriations, and was prosecuted with greater energy, particularly in the quarter lying between the Herculaneum Gate and the Forum. In the same period the Forum was approached from the south side also. In 1799, at the time of the Parthenopean Republic, the French general Championnet had excavated, south of the Basilica, the two houses which are still called by his name. From these, in 1813, the excavators made their way into the Basilica, whence, in November of the same year, they pushed forward into the Forum. However, the excavation of the Forum itself with the surrounding buildings, prosecuted less vigorously and with limited means in the period of the Restoration, was not completed till 1825; by this time the temple of Fortuna and the Baths north of the Forum had also been uncovered. The following years, to 1832, brought to light the beautiful houses on the north side of Nola Street — the houses of Pansa, of the Tragic Poet, and of the Faun — and those on Mercury Street; later came excavations south of Nola Street and in various parts of the city.

The disturbances of the period of Revolution caused a cessation of work for two years, from July 3, 1848, to September 27, 1850. During the next nine years effort was expended chiefly in clearing Stabian Street and the Stabian Baths.

The fall of the Bourbon dynasty and the passing over of Naples to the Kingdom of Italy caused another interruption, which lasted a year, from December 5, 1859, to December 20,

1860. On the last date the excavations were resumed under the direction of Guiseppe Fiorelli, a man of marked individuality, who left a permanent impress upon every part of the work. To him is due the present admirable system, excellent alike from the technical and from the administrative point of view. We owe it to him, that better provision is made now than formerly for the preservation and care of excavated buildings

Fig. 8.—An excavation. Atrium of the house of the Silver Wedding, cleared in the autumn of 1892.

and objects discovered; the earlier efforts in this direction naturally left room for improvement, and the painstaking of the present administration is especially worthy of commendation.

Fiorelli put an end to haphazard digging, to excavating here and there wherever the site seemed most promising. He first set about clearing the undisturbed places lying between the excavated portions; and when in this way the west part of the city had been laid bare, he commenced to work systematically from the excavated part toward the east. Since 1860 only one public building has been excavated — the baths at the corner of Stabian and Nola streets; but many private houses have been uncovered, some of which are of much interest. Fiorelli remained in charge of the excavations until 1875, when he was called to Rome to become General Director of Museums and Excavations; he died in 1896, at the age of seventy-two. His successors, first Michele Ruggiero, then Giulio de Petra, have worked according to his plans, and in full sympathy with his ideals.

Up to the present time about one half of Pompeii has been excavated. In 1872 Fiorelli made the calculation that if the excavations should continue at the rate then followed the whole city would be laid bare in sixty years. Since that time the work has progressed more slowly, partly in consequence of the greater care taken for the preservation of the remains. At the present rate of progress we may believe that the twentieth century will hardly witness the completion of the excavations.

Articles of furniture and objects of art that can easily be moved, as the statuettes often found in the gardens, are ordinarily taken to the Museum in Naples; a few things have been placed in the little Museum at Pompeii. Now and then small sculptures have been left in a house exactly as they were found; but the necessity of keeping such houses locked and of guarding them with especial care prevents the general adoption of this method of preservation.

In respect to the preservation of paintings the practice has varied at different periods. Generally, however, the best pictures have been cut from the walls and transferred to the Museum, while the decorative framework has been left undisturbed. It is keenly to be regretted that in this way the effect of the decorative system as a whole has been destroyed, for the picture forms the centre of a carefully elaborated scheme of decoration which needs to be viewed as an artistic whole in order to be fully appreciated; and the removal of a painting can hardly be accomplished without some damage to the parts of the wall immediately in contact with it. A far better method would be to leave intact all walls containing paintings or decorative work of interest, providing such means

of protection against the weather as may be necessary. A
good beginning in this respect has been made in the case
of the house of the Vettii, the beautiful and well preserved
paintings of which have been left on the walls and are preserved with the greatest care.

The treatment of a mosaic floor is an altogether different
problem. While the floor as a whole, with its ornamental
designs, is left in place, fine mosaics representing paintings,
which are delicate and easily destroyed, are wisely taken up
and placed in the Museum.

NOTES TO PLAN I

The Regions are given as they were laid out by Fiorelli (p. 34), the boundaries being marked by broken lines. The Insulae are designated by Arabic numerals.

Stabian Street, between Stabian and Vesuvius gates, separating Regións VIII, VII, and VI, from I, IX, and V, is often called Cardo, from analogy with the *cardo maximus* (the north and south line) of a Roman camp. Nola Street, leading from the Nola Gate, with its continuations (Strada della Fortuna, south of Insulae 10, 12, 13, and 14 of Region VI, and Strada della Terme, south of VI, 4, 6, 8), was for similar reasons designated as the Greater Decuman, *Decumanus Maior;* while the street running from the Water Gate to the Sarno Gate (Via Marina, Abbondanza Street, Strada dei Diadumeni) is called the Lesser Decuman, *Decumanus Minor*.

The only Regions wholly excavated are VII and VIII ; but only a small portion of Region VI remains covered.

The towers of the city wall are designated by numbers, as they are supposed to have been at the time of the siege of Sulla, in 89 B.C. (p. 234).

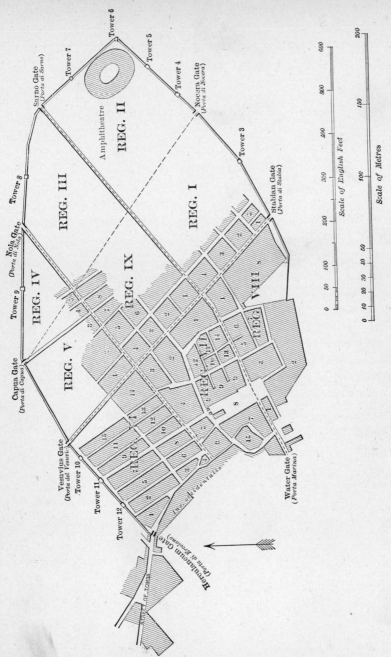

Sarno Gate
(Porta di Sarno)

Tower 7

Tower 5

Tower 4

Nocera Gate
(Porta di Nocera)

Amphitheatre

REG. II

Tower 3

Tower 8

REG. III

Stabian Gate
(Porta di Stabia)

Nola Gate
(Porta di Nola)

REG. I

REG. IV

REG. IX

REG. VIII

Tower 9

REG. V

REG. VI

Capua Gate
(Porta di Capua)

Vesuvius Gate
(Porta del Vesuvio)

Tower 10

Tower 11

Water Gate
(Porta Marina)

Via dell' Abbondanza

Tower 12

Herculaneum Gate
(Porta di Ercolano)

STREET OF TOMBS

Scale of English Feet

Scale of Metres

PLAN I. — OUTLINE PLAN OF POMPEII.

CHAPTER V

A BIRD'S-EYE VIEW

THE outline of Pompeii, with its network of streets, may be traced on the accompanying plan.

The city took its shape from the end of the old lava stream on which it lay, which ran southeast from Vesuvius. It formed an irregular oval a little less than four fifths of a mile (1200 metres) long and a little more than two fifths of a mile (720 metres) wide in its greatest dimensions. On three sides, west, south, and east, the wall of the city ran along the edge of the hill; on the northwest side, between the Herculaneum and Capua gates, it passed directly across the ridge formed by the lava.

The eight gates are known by the modern names given on our plan. Two of them, the Herculaneum and Capua gates, lie at the points where the wall comes to the edge of the lava bed on either side; the streets that led from them descended to the plain. At the Herculaneum Gate the much travelled highway from Naples, passing through Herculaneum, entered the city; the Capua Gate does not seem to have been built to accommodate a large traffic. Between these two lay the Vesuvius Gate, through which the Pompeians passed out upon the ridge toward Vesuvius.

From the Herculaneum Gate nearly to the Stabian Gate, on the south side, ran a bluff, with a sharp descent. Nevertheless, as a gate was needed on the side nearest the sea, the Water Gate, Porta Marina, was placed here; through it a steep road led to the Forum, so steep that it could not have been much used by vehicles; but that may have mattered little to the fishermen bringing their catches to the market.

The Stabian Gate lay in a depression at the end of the lava bed and afforded a more convenient means of access to the city; thence a road ran to the harbor on the Sarno, and to Stabiae.

At the left another road apparently branched off from this in the direction of Nuceria, which could be reached also from the conveniently located Nocera Gate further east; here also the slope of the hill was less pronounced. Two gates, finally, gave access to the city on the somewhat steeper east and northeast sides, the Sarno Gate, which takes its name, not from the river, but from the modern town of Sarno, and the Nola Gate; it is at least probable that the road passing through the latter led to Nola.

A glance at the plan will make it plain that the streets of Pompeii must have been laid out according to a definite system; an arrangement on the whole so regular and symmetrical would scarcely be found in a city that had developed gradually from a small beginning, in which the location of streets had been the result of accident.

Two wide streets that cross the city very nearly at right angles give the direction for the other streets running approximately north and south and east and west, Mercury Street with its continuations, and Nola Street. The former probably served as a base line in laying out the city; this we infer from the fact that while it is exceptionally broad, and the Forum lies on it, there is no gate at either end, and it could have been little used for traffic. Nola Street has a gate only at the east end; the west end opens into the Strada Consolare, which follows the line of the city wall and leads to the Herculaneum Gate at the northwest corner. That the other streets must have taken their direction from these two is clearly seen in the case of those in the northwest part of the city; on close examination it will be found that the arrangement of the rest also is in accordance with the same system, a fact which would perhaps be still more obvious if the unexcavated eastern portion of the city were laid bare.

In two instances, however, there is a deviation from this system. One is in the quarter near the Forum. For reasons which have not been satisfactorily explained, the Porta Marina was not placed on the prolongation of the street coming from the Sarno Gate, but further north. In order to reach this gate the street, as shown on the plan, makes a bend to the north which is reproduced in the other east and west streets lying south of Nola Street; west of the Forum, again, the streets converge in order to give access to this gate.

The other deviation, which affects Stabian Street, can be explained on grounds of convenience. This street, which runs from the Stabian to the Vesuvius Gate, abandoned the line of the north and south streets west of it in order to take advantage of a natural depression in the hill, by following which an easy grade could be established to the higher parts of the city; that the blocks along this important thoroughfare might not be too irregular in shape, the nearest parallel streets on the east were laid out in such a way as to follow the direction of Stabian Street. The street running south from the Capua Gate resumes, with slight variation, the north and south line of Mercury Street.

The public buildings of the city form two extensive groups. One group lies about the Forum (Plan II); with this we may reckon also the Baths in the block north of the Forum, and the temple of Fortuna Augusta. The nucleus of the other is formed by the two theatres and the large quadrangular colonnade which, designed originally to afford protection for theatre-goers against the rain, was later turned into barracks for the gladiators (Plan III). There are in addition only four public buildings that need to be mentioned. Two are bathing establishments, the Stabian Baths, and those at the corner of Stabian and Nola streets. The third is a small building near the Herculaneum Gate, consisting of a hall opening on the street, with a base for a statue near the rear wall; this on insufficient grounds has been called a customhouse. The fourth, the Amphitheatre, lies in the southern corner of the city.

As the public buildings were thus located in clearly defined groups, it is not probable that many yet remain in the portion of the city which has not been excavated. We may expect to find only bathing establishments, and perhaps one or two temples. There were priestesses of Ceres and of Venus, but the sanctuaries of these divinities have not been discovered. Mention is made also of a priest of Mars; but the temple of Mars, according to the precept of Vitruvius, would be outside the city.

A word should be added regarding the modern division of Pompeii into Regions, or wards, and Insulae. By an Insula is

D

meant — in accordance with ancient usage — a block of houses surrounded on all sides by streets. The division into Regions was introduced by Fiorelli, and rests upon a misconception which has been corrected by more recent excavations. Fiorelli thought that the Capua Gate and the Nocera Gate were connected by a street, and that the city was thus divided by four streets (the assumed street, Stabian Street, Nola Street, and Abbondanza Street with its continuations) into nine Regions, marked on our plan with the numerals I–IX.

In each Region every block, or Insula, has its number, and in the Insula a separate number is given to every door opening on a street. This arrangement is convenient because each house can be accurately designated by means of three numbers.

On the plans the Insulae are designated by Arabic numerals, but in the text small Roman numerals are used for the sake of clearness; thus, Ins. IX. i. 26, means the first Insula of Region IX, No. 26.

The names of several of the more important streets, as of the better known houses, are given in the text in the English form.

CHAPTER VI

BUILDING MATERIALS, CONSTRUCTION, AND ARCHITECTURAL PERIODS

Six centuries lie between the dates of the earliest and the latest buildings at Pompeii; and in order to understand any structure rightly we must first of all ascertain to what period it belongs. It is indeed rarely possible to fix dates with exactness for the earlier time; but certain periods are so clearly differentiated from one another, that in most cases there is no room for doubt to which of them a building is to be assigned. Before undertaking to characterize these periods, however, it will be necessary briefly to notice what building materials were used, and how they were turned to account in construction.

Exclusive of wood, which was more freely used in Pompeii than in Campanian towns to-day, the principal building materials were Sarno limestone, two kinds of tufa (gray and yellow), lava, a variety of limestone wrongly called travertine, marble, and brick.

The Sarno limestone (*pietra di Sarno*) is a deposit from the water of the Sarno, and is found in beds along the course of the river. It contains many impressions of the leaves and stems of plants, and varies greatly in compactness; it closely resembles the Roman travertine, except that it has a more decided yellowish tint.

Gray tufa is a volcanic ash which has been hardened by the presence of water into rock. It has a fine grain, and is easily worked; it was quarried in the vicinity of Nocera. The volcanic ash which formed the yellow tufa was thrown out in an earlier period, when the Sarno plain was still a part of the sea, and so hardened in salt water; it is more friable than the gray tufa, and not so durable.

The lava, which came originally from Vesuvius, was quarried

at Pompeii. Three varieties may be distinguished, differing in density according as they were taken from the lower or the upper strata: solid lava, or basalt, which, being heavy and extremely hard, was extensively used for pavements and thresholds; slag, like the scoriae found on the sides of Vesuvius to-day; and cruma, the foam of the lava stream, which is light and porous, but on account of its hardness has good resisting qualities.

The so-called travertine has a fine texture, without impressions of leaves, and is of a whitish color; it was to some extent employed as a substitute for marble. It was not quarried at Pompeii, and was not extensively used; the most important example of its use is in the later colonnade about the Forum. The white Carrara marble (*marmor lunense*) was preferred for columns, pilasters, and architraves; but colored marbles of many varieties, cut into thin slabs and blocks, were used as a veneering for walls and in the mosaic floors.

Bricks were used only for the corners of buildings, for doorposts, and in a few instances, as in the Basilica and the house of the Labyrinth, for columns; brick walls are not found in Pompeii. The bricks seen in corners and doorposts (Figs. 11, 90) are simply a facing for rubble work. They are ordinarily less than an inch thick; they have the shape of a right-angled triangle, and are so laid that the side representing the hypothenuse — about six inches long — appears in the surface of the wall. Sometimes fragments of roof tiles, more or less irregular in shape, were used instead. The bricks of the earlier time contain sea sand and have a granular surface, with a less uniform color; the later bricks are smooth and even in appearance.

The flat oblong roof tiles (*tegulae*), measuring ordinarily 24 by 19 or 20 inches, had flanges at the sides; over the joints where the flanges came together, joint tiles in the form of a half-cylinder (*imbrices*) were laid, like those in use at the present day (Figs. 109, 112).

The styles of masonry are characteristic and interesting. We may distinguish them as masonry with limestone framework, rubble work, reticulate work, quasi-reticulate work, ashlar work, and, in the case of columns and entablatures, massive construction.

The masonry with limestone framework dates from the earliest period. The walls were built without mortar, clay being used instead. Since this served only as a filling, without strength as a binding material, it was necessary to arrange the stones themselves in such a way that the wall would stand firm. This result was accomplished by using large, oblong blocks, not only for corners and doorposts, but also for a framework in the body of the wall; as shown in our illustration, alternate vertical

Fig. 9.— Wall with limestone framework.

and horizontal blocks were built up into pillars which would hold in place the courses of smaller stones that filled the intervening spaces. The material of the larger, hewn blocks, as well as of the smaller fragments, was Sarno limestone, with occasional pieces of cruma or slag.

The rubble work, *opus incertum*, consists of fragments irregular in shape, of the size of the fist and larger, laid in mortar. The material used in the earlier times was ordinarily lava; later, Sarno limestone. Corners and doorposts at first were built of hewn blocks; afterwards bricks and blocks of stone cut in the form of bricks were used for this purpose, and in the latest period frequently brick and stone combined, *opus mixtum* or *opus compositum* — a course of stone alternating with every two or three courses of brick. An example of the *opus mixtum* is seen in the entrances of the Herculaneum Gate (Fig. 108). Rubble work is the prevailing masonry at Pompeii; in comparison the other kinds described may be considered exceptional.

The reticulate work, *opus reticulatum*, formed the outer surface of a wall, the inner part of which was built up with rubble. It was composed of small four-sided pyramidal blocks, of which only the base, cut square and smooth, showed on the surface; the tapering part served as a key to bind the block into the wall. These blocks, which measured from three to four inches square at the base, were laid on their corners, so that the edges ran diagonally to the horizontal and vertical lines of the wall; the pattern thus formed had the appearance of a net, hence the name. The material was in most cases gray, occasionally yellow, tufa. The corners and doorposts were at first made of the same kind of stone cut in the shape of bricks; later of bricks. This style of masonry was in vogue at Rome, and apparently also at Pompeii, in the the time of Augustus (Fig. 12; see also the pedestal in the foreground of Plate I).

The quasi-reticulate work belongs to the early years of the Roman colony. In appearance it lies between rubble and reticulate work, differing from the latter in that the small blocks are less carefully finished and are laid with less regularity. The material is generally lava, but tufa and limestone are also found. The corners and doorposts are of brick, or of brick-shaped blocks of tufa or limestone (Fig. 11).

Ashlar work, of carefully hewn oblong blocks laid in courses, is found in the older portions of the city wall (Fig. 104) and in the walls of the Greek temple in the Forum Triangulare; it was used otherwise only for the fronts of houses (Fig. 10). The material in the earliest times was Sarno limestone, later gray tufa. With the coming of the Roman colony ashlar work went out of use, even for the corners of houses and doorposts.

In the construction of columns and many architraves large blocks were used. Previous to the time of the Roman colony these were of gray tufa, or, in rare instances, of limestone; a coating of white stucco was laid on the surface. From the advent of the colony to the time of the Early Empire, the so-called travertine was used; after that, Carrara marble.

Bearing in mind the styles of construction just described, we may now turn to the architectural history of Pompcii, which, as we shall see, falls naturally into six periods.

The first period is that to which the Doric temple in the Forum Triangulare and the city walls belong. From the style of the temple, we may safely conclude that it was built in the sixth century B.C.; the evidence is too scanty to enable us definitely to fix the date of the walls. The building materials used were the Sarno limestone and gray tufa.

The second period may be designated as the Period of the Limestone Atriums, so characterized from the peculiar construction of a number of houses found in different parts of the city. On the side facing the street these houses have walls of ashlar work of Sarno limestone (Fig. 10), but the inner walls are of limestone framework (Fig. 9).

Almost no ornamental forms belonging to this period have come down to us; so far only a single column has been found, built into the wall of a house. It is of the Doric style, and

Fig. 10. — Façade of Sarno limestone, house of the Surgeon.

once formed part of a portico that ran along the west side of the small open space at the northwest corner of Stabian and Nola streets; it is thus the sole remnant of a public building. In the only complete house that has survived from this period, the house of the Surgeon, there was a portico in front of the garden, but the roof was supported by square pillars, not by columns. There is no trace of wall painting.

Characteristic as the construction of the limestone atriums is, it is difficult to determine to what age they belong. The beginning of the period cannot be determined even approximately. The end, however, is fixed by the earlier limit of the next period, the Second Punic War. We may, therefore, assign the houses with the limestone atriums to a period just preceding this war; reckoning in round numbers, they were built before 200 B.C.

In the third, or Tufa Period, came the climax of the development of Pompeian architecture prior to the Roman domination. The favorite building material was the gray tufa.

With the exception of the Greek temple mentioned above, all the public buildings of Pompeii that do not belong to the time of the Roman colony have a homogeneous character; a list of them would include the colonnade about the Forum, the Basilica, the temples of Apollo and of Jupiter, the Large Theatre with the colonnades of the Forum Triangulare and the Barracks of the Gladiators, the Stabian Baths, the Palaestra, and the outer part of the Porta Marina with the inner parts of the other gates. Closely associated with these public edifices is a large number of private houses; as a specially characteristic example, we may mention the house of the Faun.

All these buildings are similar in style and construction; they evidently date from a period of great building activity. It must also have been a period of peace and prosperity; for the whole city, from the artistic and monumental point of view, underwent a transformation. Certain Oscan inscriptions, an early Latin monumental inscription, and a few words, dating from 78 B.C., scratched upon the plaster of the Basilica, oblige us to place the Tufa Period before the time of the Roman colony; yet not long before, for the next oldest buildings date from the first years of the colony. The time of peace that furnished the background for the period can only have been that between the Second Punic War and the Social War, about 200 to 90 B.C.; the Tufa Period was approximately the second century before Christ.

In marked contrast with the Period of the Limestone Atriums, the Tufa Period has a pronounced artistic character. It is preëminently a period of monumental construction. Buildings and public places are adorned with colonnades of the Doric, Ionic, and Corinthian orders. The simple and beautiful forms of the Greek architecture are used, sparingly indeed, but without petty detail and with evident fear of excessive ornamentation. Columns and architraves are white, with only slight suggestion of the earlier Greek polychrome decoration. A variety of color, however, is laid on the walls, and with this period the history of Pompeian wall decoration begins.

The Tufa Period coincides throughout with the time of the first style of decoration. This, known as the Incrustation Style, aimed to imitate in stucco the appearance of a wall veneered with colored marbles. Wall paintings are wholly lacking, but pictures, often of rare beauty, are found in the mosaics of the floors. In this period, we may truly say that Pompeian architecture was at its best. With it the pure Greek tradition dies out; all the buildings of later times bear the Roman stamp.

The buildings of the Tufa Period are easily recognized by the unobtrusiveness of the materials used in their construction. The rubble work is mostly of lava; but gray tufa was used exclusively, not only for ashlar work in façades, but also for columns and entablatures. The surface of the tufa was coated with a layer of fine white stucco, which gave it the appearance of marble. The use of marble for building purposes, however, is foreign to this period; and it speaks well for the culture of the Oscan Pompeians that they had pleasure in beauty of form above richness of material.

The fourth period covers the earlier decades of the Roman colony, from 80 B.C. to near the end of the Republic. According to inscriptions which are still extant, soon after the year 80 a wealthy colonist, Gaius Quinctius Valgus, when duumvir with Marcus Porcius as colleague, built the Small Theatre, and afterwards, when quinquennial duumvir with the same colleague, the Amphitheatre also. Both structures have the quasi-reticulate facing (Fig. 11); and several other buildings in which the same style of masonry is found without doubt belong to the same period — the Baths near the Forum, the temple of

Zeus Milichius, a building just inside the Porta Marina, and apparently the hall at the southeast corner of the Forum, which we shall identify as the Comitium; with these should be included also the original temple of Isis, which was destroyed by the earthquake of 63 A.D.   Few houses dating from this period have been discovered; the provision made by the pre-ceding period in this respect had been so generous that new houses were not needed.

From the aesthetic point of view the fourth period falls far below that just preceding; the exhaustion of resources and the decline of taste due to the long and terrible war are unmistaka-

Fig. 11.— Quasi-reticulate facing, with brick corner, at the entrance of the Small Theatre.

ble. Theatre, Amphitheatre, and Baths were alike built for imme-diate use, with crude and scanty ornamentation; and where richer ornament was applied, as in the case of the temple of Isis, it could not for a moment be compared with that of the Tufa Period in beauty and finish.

The wall decoration of the fourth period is of the second Pompeian style, which came into vogue just after the founding of the colony, and which we shall call the Architectural Style; for in part, as the first style, it imi-tated a veneering of marble, not however with the help of slabs or panels modelled in stucco, but by the use of color only, laid on walls finished to a plane surface; in part it made use of architectural designs which were painted either correctly or with at least some regard for proper proportions.

The fifth period extends from the last decades of the Repub-lic to the earthquake of the year 63 A.D.   In the entire period, covering more than a century, we are unable to distinguish a series of buildings which may be classed together in style and construction as constituting a homogeneous, representative group.   Here and there we can point out a piece of masonry which, from its similarity to that of the fourth period, may be assigned to the end of the Republic; again, walls with reticulate facing of tufa and corners of brick-shaped blocks of the same stone belong to the time of Augustus (Fig. 12), while reticulate work with corners of brick (Fig. 90) is of later date; but there is a total lack of those distinguishing characteristics which would serve to set off by themselves all the buildings belonging to a particular time. Consequently in the case of each structure it is necessary to take into account all the circumstances,

Fig. 12. — Reticulate facing, with corners of brick-shaped stone. The filled arch is probably to bear the weight of the wall over a sewer.

and then to form an independent judgment regarding its style and date.

The difficulty is further enhanced by the fact that three styles of wall decoration fall within the limits of the same period. The Architectural Style, already mentioned, remained in vogue to the time of Augustus; it then gave place to the third or Ornate Style, which is characterized by a freer use of ornament and the introduction of designs and scenes suggestive of an Egyptian origin. The fourth or Intricate Style came in about the year 50 A.D., and represents, with its involved and fantastic designs, the last stage in the development of Pompeian wall decoration. In the fifth period marble began to be employed as a building material; the earliest dated example of its use is the temple of Fortuna Augusta, erected about 3 B.C.

The sixteen years between the earthquake of 63 A.D. and the destruction of the city form the sixth period in the architectural history of Pompeii. The buildings belonging to it can be easily recognized, not only from their similarity in style and ornament, but also from certain external characteristics, as newness of appearance, unfinished condition, and the joining of new to broken walls. The only important building wholly new is the large bathing establishment, the Central Baths, at the corner of Stabian and Nola streets. For the rest, effort seems to have been directed toward restoring the ruined buildings as nearly as possible to their original condition. The wall decoration throughout is of the Intricate Style.

The measurements of buildings in the Roman Period conform to the scale of the Roman foot, while the dimensions of structures antedating the Roman colony in most cases reduce to the scale of the Oscan or old Italic foot. The Roman foot (296 mm.) may be roughly reckoned at 0.97 of the English foot (304.8 mm.); the Oscan foot (275 mm.) is considerably shorter. As the Roman standard is of Greek origin, we occasionally find a structure conforming to it that was designed by a Greek architect before the Roman Period.

KEY TO PLAN II

A. THE FORUM.
1. Pedestal of the statue of Augustus.
2. Pedestal of the statue of Claudius.
3. Pedestal of the statue of Agrippina.
4. Pedestal of the statue of Nero.
5. Pedestal of the statue of Caligula.
6. Pedestals of equestrian statues.
7. Pedestals of standing figures.
8. Pedestal for three equestrian statues.
9. Speaker's platform (p. 48).
10. Table of standard measures (p. 92).
11. Room of the supervisor of measures.

B. THE BASILICA.
a. Entrance court.
1. Corridor.
2. Main room.
3. Tribunal.
4-4. Rooms at the ends of the tribunal.

C. THE TEMPLE OF APOLLO.
1. Colonnade.
2. Podium.
3. Cella.
4. Altar.
5. Sundial.
6. Sacristan's room.
7-7. Rooms made from earlier colonnade.

D, D'. MARKET BUILDINGS.
E. LATRINA.
F, F. CITY TREASURY.

G. COMMEMORATIVE ARCH.
H. TEMPLE OF JUPITER.
I. ARCH OF TIBERIUS.
K. THE PROVISION MARKET — MACELLUM.
1. Portico.
2. Colonnade.
3-3. Market stalls.
4. Market for meat and fish.
5. Chapel of the imperial family.
6. Banquet room.
7. Round structure with water basin — Tholus.
8. Pen.

L. SANCTUARY OF THE CITY LARES.
1. Main room, unroofed, with an altar in the centre.
2. Apse, with shrine.
3. Recesses with pedestals.
4. Niche opening on the Forum.

M. TEMPLE OF VESPASIAN.
1. Colonnade.
2. Altar.
3. Cella.
4. Portico.

N. THE BUILDING OF EUMACHIA.
See plan on p. 110.

O. THE VOTING PLACE — COMITIUM.
1. Recess opening on the main room.
2. Recess opening on the Forum.

P-R. MUNICIPAL BUILDINGS.
P. Office of the duumvirs.
Q. Hall of the city council.
R. Office of the aediles.

S. FOUNTAIN.

PART I

PUBLIC PLACES AND BUILDINGS

CHAPTER VII

THE FORUM

THE Forum is usually approached from the west side by the short, steep street leading from the Porta Marina. Entering, we find ourselves near the lower end of an oblong open space (Plate I), at the upper end of which, toward Vesuvius, stands a high platform of masonry with the ruins of a temple — the temple of Jupiter; the remains of a colonnade are seen on each of the other three sides. Including the colonnade the Forum measures approximately 497 feet in length by 156 in breadth; without it the dimensions are 467 and 126 feet. The north side, at the left of the temple, is enclosed by a wall in which there are two openings, one at the end of the colonnade, the other between this and the temple; at the right the wall bounding the open space has been replaced by a stately commemorative arch, while the end of the colonnade is closed by a wall with a passageway. Another arch, of much simpler construction, stands at the left of the temple, in line with the façade; it cuts off the area between the temple and the colonnade from the rest of the Forum. A third arch once stood in a corresponding position at the right.

The colonnade is nowhere intersected by a street passable for vehicles. Even the entrances on the north side form no exception. At the left you descend to the area by several steps, at the right by one only; yet here the exclusion of carts and wagons was made doubly sure by placing three upright stones in the passageway. Only pedestrians could enter the Forum, and

45

they, too, could easily be shut out by means of gates in the
entrances; the places where the gates swung can still be seen
in the pavement, and one of them is shown in a painting
(Fig. 16). No private houses opened on this area; it was
wholly given up to the public life of the city and was surrounded by temples, markets, and buildings devoted to the
civic administration.

The colonnade was not uniform in character upon all the
three sides. As will be seen from our plan (Plan II), on the
south side, and on the adjoining portion of the east side as far
as Abbondanza Street, it was constructed with two rows of columns and had a double depth. On the east side north of this
street the porticos in front of four successive buildings (K, L,
M, N) took its place. For the greater part of its extent the colonnade was built in two stories, the lower of the Doric, the upper
of the Ionic order. The upper gallery was made accessible by
three stairways, at the southeast and southwest corners of the
Forum and at the middle of the west side; on the east side it
did not extend beyond Abbondanza Street.

The portico in front of the first of the four buildings referred
to, that of Eumachia, contained a double series of columns, one
above the other, corresponding in style and dimensions with
those of the colonnade; but there was no upper floor running
back from the intervening entablature. The arrangement in
front of the fourth building, the Macellum, was similar; as the
remains of the porticos in front of the two intervening buildings
have wholly disappeared, it is impossible to determine their
character.

The area of the Forum was paved with flags of the hard
limestone called travertine. In front of the colonnade, the
pavement of which was about twenty inches above that of the
open space, a broad shelf or ledge projected, covering a gutter
for rain water; the water found its way into the gutter through
semicircular openings in the outer edge of the shelf.

Of the many statues that once adorned the Forum not
one has been found. As may be seen from the pedestals
still in place, they were of three kinds, and varied greatly in
size.

First, statues of citizens who had rendered distinguished services were placed in front of the colonnade on the ledge over the gutter. Four pedestals that once supported statues of this sort may be seen on the west side.

Then equestrian statues of life size were set up in front of the ledge, these also in honor of dignitaries of the city (Fig. 17). On one of the pedestals the veneering of colored marble is still preserved, with an inscription showing that the person represented was Quintus Sallustius, " Duumvir, Quinquennial Duumvir, Patron of the Colony."

Finally, on the south side, the life size equestrian statues, which seem at the outset to have been arranged symmetrically, were almost all removed in order to make room for four much larger statues, the pedestals of which still remain (Fig. 51, p. 122). These must have represented emperors, or members of the imperial families. The pedestal in the middle, which is in the form of an arch almost square at the base, is much the oldest. Upon it was probably placed a colossal statue of Augustus. It is incredible that during the long and successful reign of the first emperor no statue in his honor should have been erected in Pompeii; and this is the most suitable place. The other three pedestals are similar in construction, and clearly belong together. The one at the right (2 on the plan) supported a colossal equestrian statue; that at the left (3) a colossal standing figure; on the third, further forward (4), was a smaller equestrian statue. Here stood, then, emperor, empress, and crown prince — Claudius, Agrippina, Nero.

A fifth pedestal, for an equestrian statue of the same size as that of Nero, is seen further to the north, in front of the temple of Jupiter (5). While unquestionably later than the time of Augustus, it must on the other hand be older than the pedestals of members of the Claudian family; for aside from himself, no one belonging to Nero's time can be taken into consideration, and after his death the Forum lay in ruins in consequence of the earthquake of the year 63. Who stood here, however, can scarcely be even conjectured. Not necessarily an emperor; the younger Drusus, for instance, Tiberius's son, or Germanicus might have been thus honored if they had in any way come

into relation with the Pompeians. But if an emperor, it mus'
have been Caligula; another place was provided for the statue
of Tiberius.

In the south side of the arch at the northeast corner of the
Forum are two niches. It is highly probable that statues of
the two oldest sons of Germanicus, Nero and Drusus, were
placed in them; a fragment of an inscription referring to the
former was found near by. These became presumptive heirs
to the throne after the death of Tiberius's son Drusus, in 23
A.D; but both afterwards fell victims to the morbid suspicions
of the emperor and the plots of Sejanus, Nero in 31 A.D.,
Drusus two years later.

On the top of the arch an equestrian statue of Tiberius probably stood. That such a statue was placed here seems clear
from analogy. North of this arch was another, almost in line
with it, at the end of Mercury Street where it opens into Nola
Street; and here the excavators found fragments of a bronze
equestrian statue which were put together and set up in the
Naples Museum. Whether this statue represented Caligula or
Nero has been a matter of dispute, but the former is really
excluded from consideration by the short, heavy figure, which is
better suited to Nero. There is no decided resemblance to
Nero either; but it is quite possible that, although as crown
prince he had been honored with a statue in the Forum, the
Pompeians thought it best to erect for him as emperor a more
imposing monument.

Before leaving the area we may raise the question whether it
contained a speakers' platform, like the Rostra in the Roman
Forum. If we have reference to a special structure, probably
not; no trace of a separate tribunal has been discovered. The
orator who wished to address the people, however, could mount
the broad platform in front of the temple of Jupiter, on which
once an altar stood; before him the audience could gather in
the open, on the only side of the Forum free from the colonnade. This place well suited the convenience of both speaker
and hearers. It is possible that we should also identify as a
tribune the platform in a recess at the southeast corner (p. 120).

On even a cursory inspection the Forum is seen to lack unity

n the details of its plan and in its architecture; the fact soon
becomes apparent that it reached its final form only as the
result of a long period of development. It will be worth while
briefly to trace this development, and to note at least the more
important changes which followed one another in the course of
the centuries.

In the earliest times the Forum was merely an open square
bounded by four streets.

The proof that this was the original form is in part based

Fig. 13.— North end of the Forum, with the Temple of Jupiter, restored.

upon the orientation of the temple of Apollo. The sides of
this temple have the same direction as the north and south
streets in the northern part of the city, and must have been
laid out parallel with a street that once ran between it and
the Forum. The temple is, therefore, older than the colonnade of the Forum, which shows a marked deviation from the
line of its axis; the divergence, as may be seen on our plan,
was in part concealed by making a difference in the thickness
of the pillars between the court of the temple and the Forum.
It is obvious that the colonnade on the west side takes the place
of an older street; the south side was probably defined by the
prolongation of Abbondanza Street toward the southwest.

E

Near the southeast corner an inscription was found : *V[ibius Popidius Ep[idii] f [ilius] q[aestor] porticus faciendas coeravi*
'Vibius Popidius, the son of Epidius, when quaestor caused thi colonnade to be erected.'   No clew to the date is given, but i must have been before the coming of the Roman colony, fo after that time there was no office of quaestor in Pompeii.   I must also have been before the Social War ; in those years o tumult an extensive colonnade would not have been built, and when the national spirit was so vehemently asserting itself, we should expect to find inscriptions upon public works in the Oscan language, certainly not in Latin.   But the use of Latin may very well date from the latter part of the period of alliance with Rome ; we may then with much probability assign the inscription to the second half of the second century B.C.

Remains of the colonnade of Popidius are still to be seen on the south side, and on the adjoining part of the east side, extending just across Abbondanza Street ; traces of it are found also on the west side, where it was afterward replaced by a new structure.   On the east side north of Abbondanza Street no traces remain ; the appearance of this part of the Forum was entirely changed when the four buildings (K, L, M, N) with their porticos were erected, but we can hardly doubt that the original colonnade extended here also.   Our illustration (Fig. 14) shows the arrangement of the Doric columns in the lower story ; of the Ionic columns above only scanty fragments have been recovered.   The appearance of the whole may be suggested by our restoration (Fig. 13).

In style and construction this colonnade belongs to the Tufa Period (p. 40).   While the forms are not those of the classical period, they nevertheless manifest Greek feeling.   The low ratio in the proportions of the Doric columns, of which the height is equal to five diameters, well accords with their use as a support for an upper gallery ; elsewhere in pre-Roman Pompeii more slender proportions are preferred, even for the Doric style. The shaft is well shaped, with a moderate swelling (*entasis*). Only the upper part is fluted ; as the sharp edges of the flutings near the bottom might easily be marred, the divisions of the surface on the lower third of the shaft were left flat.

The architrave is relatively low, the result of an interesting peculiarity in the method of construction. Blocks of tufa long enough to span the intercolumniations were too weak to sustain the weight of the rest of the entablature. To meet this difficulty a line of thick planks was placed in old Italic fashion above the capitals of the columns, and on these were laid short tufa blocks. Thus in our illustration (Fig. 14), while the upper of the two bands of the architrave is seen to be of stone, the lower shows the modern timber supplied in the place of the ancient. That the planks were in reality no thicker than has been

Fig. 14.— Remnant of the colonnade of Popidius, at the south end of the Forum.

assumed in the reconstruction is proved beyond question by the later colonnade on the west side, which, although entirely of stone, corresponds throughout in its proportions with the older one ; the architrave is equally narrow, and is likewise divided into two parts.

This explanation is curiously confirmed by an architectural painting on the garden wall of one of the finest houses of the Tufa Period, the house of the Faun. Here we find pilasters and entablature, except the architrave, painted white ; but the architrave is painted in two bands, of which the lower is yellow, as if to represent wood. Nothing would have been easier than to leave the architrave, moulded in stucco, of one color as if it were all of one material; but special effort was made apparently to indicate the appearance of a lower division of timber. From this we may infer that in actual construction no pains was taken to conceal the lack of uniformity in structural materials by laying a coat of white or colored stucco over wood and stone alike; on the contrary, the difference was not only recognized in the decoration, but even accentuated, as the timber, whether retaining its original color or painted with a suitable tint, presented a marked contrast with the stone the surface of which was covered with white stucco. If the strip of timber in the architrave had been perceptibly thicker than that of stone above it, the effect would not have been good; as the earlier Greek polychrome decoration was now no longer in vogue, the stripe of color above the capitals made a pleasing variation from the prevailing whiteness of the structure.

The Basilica at the southwest corner and the temple of Jupiter both conform to the same variation from the direction of the early north and south street that we have noticed in the case of the colonnade of Popidius; they belong, therefore, to the same remodelling of the Forum. It is quite possible that the erection of the temple, by limiting the area of the Forum on the north side, caused its extension toward the south beyond the earlier boundary. Originally the temple was isolated, the north end of the Forum on either side being left open; later, but still in the time of the Republic, a high boundary wall with passageways was built on both sides of it. Later still the two arches were erected in a line with its façade; afterwards, in the time of Tiberius, the wall at the right of the temple was replaced by the commemorative arch (I), and the smaller arch near the façade at the right was removed in order that there might be an unimpeded view of the great arch from the area.

The colonnade of Popidius may have stood for more than a century; the necessity of making thoroughgoing repairs no doubt became urgent. In the meantime, however, the taste of the Pompeians had undergone a change, and instead of repairing the old colonnade they began to replace it by a new one, a part of which is shown in Fig. 15. Better material, the so-called travertine, was used, and the construction was more substantial; the blocks of the entablature were fitted together so as to form a flat arch. Though the new colonnade followed closely the proportions of the old, effective details, such as the fluting of the columns, and the triglyphs with the guttae under-

Fig. 15.— Part of the new colonnade, near the southwest corner of the Forum.

neath, were omitted. The refined sense of form characteristic of the earlier time was no longer manifest; all is coarse and inartistic, the swelling on the shafts of the columns, for example, being carried too high.

The new colonnade had a second story of the Ionic order, of the columns of which (though not of the entablature) considerable fragments have been found. The stylobate on which the columns rested was renewed in limestone, and about the same time the Forum was paved and the ledge over the gutter was laid with flags of the same material.

This second remodelling of the Forum commenced in the early years of the Empire, the pavement having been laid before the pedestal of the monument to Augustus was built. It was never carried to completion. On the west side the new colonnade was almost finished when the earthquake of the year 63 threw it nearly all down. At the time of the eruption only the columns at the south end of this side, which had safely passed through the earthquake, were still standing with their entablature; they are shown in Fig. 15. The area was then strewn with blocks, which the stonecutters were engaged in making ready for the rebuilding.

The Forum of Pompeii, as of other ancient cities, was first of all a market place. Early in the morning the country folk gathered here with the products of the farm; here all day long tradespeople of every sort exhibited their wares. In later times the pressure of business led to the erection of separate buildings around the Forum to relieve the congestion; such were the Macellum, used as a provision market; the Eumachia building, erected to accommodate the clothing trade; the Basilica and the market house west of the temple of Jupiter, devoted to other branches of trade. Yet in a literal sense the Forum always remained the business centre of the city.

It served, too, as the favorite promenade and lounging place, where men met to discuss matters of mutual interest, or to indulge in gossip. Here idlers loitered and plied busier men with questions regarding public affairs, makers and dealers came together to talk over and settle points of difference, and young people pursued their romantic adventures. He can best form an idea of this bustling, ceaseless, varied activity who knows what the piazza means in the life of a modern Italian city, and stops to consider how much has been taken from the life of the piazza by the cafés and similar places of resort; modern squares, moreover, are usually not provided, as were the ancient, with inviting colonnades, affording protection against both sun and rain.

The life of the Forum seemed so interesting to one of the citizens of Pompeii that he devoted to the portrayal of it a series of paintings on the walls of a room. The pictures are

light and sketchy, but they give a vivid representation of
ancient life in a small city. First, in front of the equestrian
statues near the colonnade we see dealers of every kind and
description. There sits a seller of copper vessels and iron
utensils (Fig. 16), so lost in thought that a friend is calling
his attention to a possible purchaser who is just coming up.
Next come two shoemakers, one waiting on women, another
on men; then two cloth dealers. Further on a man is selling
portions of warm food from a kettle; then we see a woman
with fruit and vegetables, and a man selling bread. Another

Fig. 16. — Scene in the Forum.
In the foreground, at the left, dealer in utensils; at the right, shoemaker waiting on four
ladies. Wall painting.

dealer in utensils is engaged in eager bargaining, while his son,
squatting on the ground, mends a pot.

The scenes now change. A man sitting with a writing tablet
and stylus listens closely to the words of another who stands
near by; he reminds us of the scribes who, under the portico of
the theatre of San Carlo, at Naples, write letters for those that
have been denied the privilege of an education.

Then come men wearing tunics, engaged in some transaction,
in the course of which they seem to pass judgment on the contents of bottles which they hold in their hands; their business
perhaps involves the testing of wine. Beyond these, some men
are taking a walk; a woman is giving alms to a beggar; and

two children play hide and seek around a column. The following scene is not easy to understand, but apparently has reference
to some legal process; a woman leads a little girl with a small
tablet before her
breast into the pres-
ence of two seated
men who wear the
toga.

In the next scene
(Fig. 17) four men
are reading a notice
posted on a long
board, which is fast-
ened to the pedes-
tals of three eques-
trian statues. The
sketchy character of
the painting is espe-
cially obvious in the
representations of
the horses, which
are nevertheless life-
like. It is also inter-
esting to note that
the heads of the men
in these scenes are

Fig. 17. — Scene in the Forum.
Citizens reading a public notice. Wall painting.

uncovered; in stormy weather pointed hoods (shown in a tavern
scene, Fig. 224) were sometimes worn. The festoons suggest a
trimming of the colonnade for some festal occasion.

The last scene is from school life. A pupil is to receive
a flogging. He is mounted on the back of one of his school-
mates, while another holds him by the legs; a slave is about
to lay on the lash, and the teacher stands near by with an air
of composure. It would not be safe to infer from this, however, that there was a school in the Forum; the columns in
this scene are different from those in the others and are further
apart. Possibly a part of the small portico north of the court
of the temple of Apollo was at one time let to a schoolmaster.

The most important religious festivals were celebrated in the Forum. Here naturally festal honors were paid to the highest of the gods — the whole area enclosed by the colonnade was the court of his temple; but we learn from an inscription, mentioned below, that celebrations were held here in honor of Apollo also, whose temple adjoined the Forum, and was at first even more closely connected with it than in later times.

Vitruvius informs us that in Greek towns the market place, *agora*, was laid out in the form of a square (a statement which is not confirmed by modern excavations), but that in the cities of Italy, on account of the gladiatorial combats, the Forum should have an oblong shape, the breadth being two thirds of the length. The purpose in giving a lengthened form to the Forum, as also to the Amphitheatre, was no doubt to secure, at the middle of the sides, a greater number of good seats, from which a spectacle could be witnessed. In the Pompeian Forum, as may be seen from the dimensions given at the beginning of this chapter, the breadth is less than one third of the length. However, there can be little doubt that gladiatorial exhibitions were frequently held there before the building of the Amphitheatre, which dates from the earlier years of the Roman colony. After this time the Forum was still used for games and contests of a less dangerous character. The epitaph of a certain A. Clodius Flaccus, which is now lost, but was copied by a scholar in the seventeenth century, tells us at length how in his first, and again in his second, duumvirate (he was duumvir for the third time in 3 B.C.), in connection with the festival of Apollo, he not only gave gladiatorial exhibitions in the Amphitheatre, but also provided bullfights and other spectacles, as well as musical entertainments and pantomimes, in the Forum.

Speaking of the Forum as a place for gladiatorial combats, Vitruvius adds that the spaces between the columns should be wide, — that the view of spectators might be as little as possible impeded, — and that the upper story of the colonnade should be arranged with reference to the collection of an admission fee. The latter suggestion is of special interest. As we know from other sources, at public games certain places were reserved for the officials and for the friends of him who gave the spectacle; others were free to the public, while for still others an admission fee was charged. If the exhibition was held in a market place, with lower and upper colonnades, the former would be open to the people; the latter in part reserved, in part accessible on payment of the price of admission.

It would be interesting to know whether on such occasions at Pompeii the gates of the Forum itself were shut, so that admission even to the free space could be regulated; perhaps they were in earlier times when, as at Rome, slaves were forbidden to witness the games. However, Cicero speaks of this time-honored regulation as in his day already a thing of the past; and so in Roman Pompeii the gates of the Forum may have remained open even on the days of the games. Their most important use was probably in connection with the voting.

The Forum had a part also in spectacles which were not presented there. We are safe in assuming that, at least in the earlier times, whenever a gladiatorial combat was given in the Amphitheatre, or a play in the Theatre, the city officials, including especially the official providing the entertainment, formed in procession with their retinue and proceeded in festal attire to the place of amusement. These processions could scarcely have formed anywhere else than in the Forum, and thence they must have started out.

The fact that the Forum was not accessible for vehicles suggests a significant point of difference between the festal processions of the colony and those of the capital. In the latter, vehicles had a prominent place. Thus at Rome the official who gave the games in the Circus entered the edifice with his retinue in chariots in the imposing circus parade, *pompa circensis*, and a similar usage prevailed in the case of other processions; priests, too, and priestesses were on many occasions allowed to ride. But even in Rome carriages were always considered a matter of luxury; and the municipal regulations promulgated by Caesar prohibited the use of vehicles, except those required for religious and civic processions, on the streets of the city from sunrise till the tenth hour, that is, till four o'clock in the afternoon.

In Pompeii, and without doubt also in other cities of Italy and the provinces, the closing of the Forum to vehicles made it necessary that religious and other processions should proceed on foot. We have no evidence of any exception to this rule. We ought perhaps to recognize in it one of those devices by means of which Rome maintained a position of dignified superiority over the provincial towns; to her processions was allowed an element of display which to theirs was denied. It was not permitted to name the two chief executive officers of a municipality consuls, though their functions, within limits, corresponded with those of the consuls at Rome; nor could the city council be called a senate, though the Roman writers did not hesitate to apply this term to corresponding bodies in states and cities outside of Rome's jurisdiction. For like reasons, it would seem that on public occasions officials and priests of a provincial town were not permitted, as were those in Rome, to ride. Was this humiliating restriction laid upon the Pompeians when the Roman colony came, or previously when the city was in name the ally of Rome, but in reality already subject? The evidence is almost conclusive for the latter alternative; for the colonnade of Popidius, which as we have seen was erected in the period of autonomy, left no entrance for vehicles, though in other ways it added greatly to the attractiveness and convenience of the Forum as a place for civic and religious celebrations.

No record of events has survived to help us form a picture of the Forum as the seat of deliberative and judicial functions, the centre of the city's political life; yet stirring scenes present themselves to the imagination as we recall the critical periods in the history of the city.

In the Forum, about 400 B.C., the valiant Samnite mountaineers, having taken the city by storm, assembled and established their civic organization; here, in later times, without doubt amid conflicts similar to those at Rome, the polity was put to the test and underwent transformation. Fierce enough the strifes may have been during the Samnite wars, and again in the time of Hannibal, — after the battle of Cannae, — when the aristocrats who favored Rome contended with the national party for the mastery. Here, on the platform in front of the temple of Jupiter, the leaders of the national party stood in 90 B.C., and with flaming words roused the people to revolt, to join the movement which, starting in Asculum, had spread like wildfire over Southern Italy.

Then ten years of bloody war, — siege, campaigns, surrender, — and again the scene changes. Roman soldiers stand thick in serried ranks upon the area. They are the veterans of Sulla. An officer bearing a civil commission, the nephew of the Dictator, appears before them. Standing in front of the temple of Jupiter, he makes a proclamation regarding the founding and administration of the colony. The citizens crowd back timidly into the colonnade. Many of the best of the Pompeians have fallen in battle; of the rest, a part at least will be dispossessed of house and home to make room for the intruders, whose arrogance they will be compelled submissively to endure.

This is the last tragic act in the Pompeian Forum. After this time, there will be disputes regarding the rights of the old residents and the colonists, public questions of many kinds will call for settlement; the elections will come each year, and the ardent southern temperament may assert itself in violent scenes. Yet all these disturbances will be only as the ripples on the surface; the depths will remain undisturbed. The life of Pompeii has become an integral part of the life of the Roman world.

CHAPTER VIII

GENERAL VIEW OF THE BUILDINGS ABOUT THE FORUM — THE TEMPLE OF JUPITER

THE Forum was to the ancient city what the atrium was to the early Italic house; it was used for every purpose for which a special place was not provided elsewhere. And as sleeping rooms, dining rooms, and storerooms were grouped about the atrium and opened into it, so around the Forum lay the edifices which served the requirements of the public life, — the most important temples, the municipal buildings, and market houses or exchanges for different branches of business.

Three temples adjoined the Forum at Pompeii. In addition, there was a sanctuary of the City Lares; and the temple of Fortuna Augusta was but a short distance away. These religious edifices are representative of the different periods in the history of the city.

In very early times the Oscans of Pompeii received from the Greeks who had settled on the coast the cult of Apollo, and built for the Hellenic god a large, fine temple (C, in Plan II) adjoining the Forum on the west side.

Several centuries later, the divinities of the Capitol — Jupiter, Juno, and Minerva — were enthroned in the temple that on the north side towered above the area (H).

On the east or right side followed, in Roman times, the edifices erected for the worship of the emperors. The oldest is the unroofed building, with a broad, open front, dedicated to the Lares of the City and to the Genius of Augustus (L). Further north, in the first block at the right beyond the Forum, is the temple of Fortuna Augusta, the goddess who guarded the fortunes of Augustus, erected in 3 B.C. A chapel for the worship of Claudius and his family was placed in the Macellum

61

(K, 5); this seems to have sufficed also for the worship of
Nero. After Nero's death and after the brief Civil War,
a temple (M) was built close to the shrine of the Lares in
honor of Vespasian, the restorer of peace, the new Augustus.
This was the last temple erected in Pompeii; it was not entirely finished at the time of the eruption.

Three buildings at the south end of the Forum were used
for city offices (P–R). They were much alike, each containing
a single large hall. They were seemingly built in the early
years of the Empire, and repaired after the earthquake of the
year 63. There is also a structure at the southeast corner,
south of Abbondanza Street, which we may identify as the
voting place, the Comitium (O). At the northwest corner
was apparently the city treasury, built in the latest years of
Pompeii, perhaps on the site of an earlier structure of the
same kind (F).

At a comparatively early period the area was found to be
too small for the increasing volume of business; and the
demand for roofed space made itself felt. In the second
century B.C. the large and splendid Basilica (B), serving the
double purpose of a court and an exchange, was built at the
southwest corner.

Diagonally opposite, near the temple of Jupiter, a provision
market, the Macellum (K), was constructed; this also at an
early date. It was entirely rebuilt in the time of the Empire,
perhaps in the reign of Claudius. Previous to this rebuilding,
the priestess Eumachia had erected an exchange for the fullers
on the same side of the Forum, further south (N).

On the west side, from pre-Roman times, stood a small
colonnade in two stories, with its rear against the rear of
the colonnade on the north side of the court of the temple of
Apollo; only the first story, of the Doric order, has been preserved. Probably this structure and the small open space in
front were at first used as a market; later, in the imperial
period, shops (D′) were built upon the open space, and the
colonnade was made over into closed rooms, the purpose of
which, except in the case of one, is unknown (6, 7, 7). In the
last years of the city, a large market building (D) was erected

between this small place and the Forum. It was connected
both with the city treasury and with a latrina.

The temple of Jupiter dominates the Forum, and more than
any other structure gives it character. As we have seen, its
orientation accords with that of the colonnade of Popidius. It
probably dates from the pre-Roman period, the columns being
of tufa covered with white stucco. The earthquake of the year
63 left the temple in ruins, and at the time of the eruption the
work of rebuilding had not yet commenced. In the meantime,
it was used as a workshop for stonecutters. The journal of
the excavations reports the finding here of the torso of a colossal statue out of which a smaller statue was being carved. A
place for the worship of the divinities of the temple must temporarily have been provided elsewhere.

The temple stands on a podium 10 Roman feet high, and
including the steps, 125 Roman feet long (Fig. 18). Very
nearly a half of the whole length is given
to the cella ; of the other half, a little
more than two thirds is occupied by the portico, leaving about a third (20 Roman feet)
for the steps. The pediment was sustained by
six Corinthian columns about 28 feet high.
This arrangement — a deep portico in front
of the cella — is Etruscan, though the canon
of Vitruvius, that in Etruscan temples the
depth of the portico should equal that of the
cella, is violated. The high podium also,
with steps in front, is characteristic of Etrus-

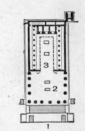

Fig. 18. — Plan of the
temple of Jupiter.
1. Speaker's platform.
2. Portico.
3. Cella.

can, or at least of early Italic religious architecture. On the
other hand, the architectural forms of the superstructure are
Greek, and these in turn have had their influence upon the
plan ; the intercolumniations are not wide, as in the Tuscan
style with its wooden architrave, but narrower, as in the Greek
orders. Vitruvius speaks of temples such as this, in which
Greek and Etruscan elements are united, at the end of his
directions for the building of temples ; they are a development
of Roman architecture.

The arrangement of the steps is peculiar. Above is a series of long steps reaching nearly across the front (Fig. 19); below are two narrow flights near the sides, and between them is the projecting front of the podium, used as a tribune, which has already been mentioned (p. 48).

That an altar stood at the middle of this platform is proved by a relief with a representation of the north side of the Forum, found on the base of a chapel of the Lares in the house of the wealthy Pompeian, L. Caecilius Jucundus. At the left we see the arch near the façade and a strip of wall connecting it with the temple; next a corner of the platform with an equestrian statue; then a flight of steps, and the

Fig. 19.— Ruins of the temple of Jupiter.

front of the platform with an altar at the middle; finally the other flight of steps and another equestrian statue in a position corresponding with that of the first. The columns shown in the relief do not agree in number or style with those of the façade of the temple, but such inaccuracies are common in ancient representations of buildings, and there can be no doubt that the temple of Jupiter is represented; the relief has, in fact, been used in making our restoration of the arch at the left (Fig. 13).

Both the portico and the cella no doubt had a coffered ceiling. Just in front of the doorway, which was fifteen Roman feet wide, are the large stones with holes for the pivots on which the massive double doors swung (indicated in Fig. 18); the doors here were not placed in the doorway, but in front of it, and were besides somewhat larger, so that the effect was rendered more imposing when they were shut.

The ornamentation of the cella was especially rich. A row of Ionic columns, about fifteen feet high, stood in front of each of the longer sides; the entablature above them probably served as a base for a similar row of Corinthian columns, the entablature of which in turn supported the ceiling. On the intermediate entablature, between the columns of the upper series, statues and votive offerings were doubtless placed. The floor about the sides was covered with white mosaic, of which scanty remains have been found; the marble pavement of the centre (inside of the dotted line, Fig. 18) has wholly disappeared.

A section of the wall decoration, in the second Pompeian style, is shown in Fig. 20. We notice here the characteristic elements — imitation of marble veneering, with large red central panels and a cornice above. The base with its simple dividing lines upon a black ground was painted over in the third style; originally it must have been more suggestive of real construction, with a narrow painted border along the upper edge.

Against the rear wall of the cella stands a large pedestal, three times as long as it is broad. It was originally divided by four pilasters — two at the corners and two on the front between them — into three parts. Later the pilasters and the entablature over them were removed, and the

Fig. 20. — Section of the wall decoration in the cella of the temple of Jupiter.

whole was covered with marble veneering. Inside were three small rooms, entered by separate doors from the cella. The pedestal was thus built for three images; three divinities were worshipped here, and in the little chambers underneath were

F

perhaps kept the trappings with which on festal occasions the images were decked.

A head of Jupiter, of which we shall speak later, was found in the cella, as was also an inscription of the year 37 A.D., containing a dedication to Jupiter Optimus Maximus, the ruling deity of the Capitol at Rome. It is thus proved beyond question that the Capitoline Jupiter was worshipped here; and it will not be difficult to ascertain what other divinities shared with him the honors of the temple.

As the Roman colonies strove in all things to be Rome in miniature, each thought it necessary to have a Capitolium — a temple for the worship of the gods of the Roman Capitol, Jupiter, Juno, and Minerva; and this naturally became the most important temple in the city. That the worship of the three divinities was established at Pompeii is evident from the discovery of three images representing them, in the little temple conjecturally assigned to Zeus Milichius. These are poor images of terra cotta, and the temple itself was altogether unworthy to be a place of worship for the great gods that shaped the destinies of Rome. We are warranted in the conclusion that the temple of Zeus Milichius was used temporarily for the worship of the three divinities of the large temple till the latter could be rebuilt; and that Juno and Minerva stood on the great pedestal beside the king of the gods.

It seems strange that the Pompeians should have erected a temple to the gods of the Capitol in the pre-Roman period. It must be remembered, however, that the worship of the three divinities was by no means limited to Rome and her colonies. The Etruscans, as Servius informs us in his commentary on Virgil, thought that a city was not properly founded unless it contained sanctuaries of Jupiter, Juno, and Minerva. Vitruvius, also, in his directions for laying out a city, makes the general statement that the most prominent site should be set aside for the temples of the same divinities. If we consider further that the opposition of the Italians to Rome found expression only in the Social War, and that previously they had looked upon the attainment of Roman citizenship as the highest object of ambition, the gradual adoption of Roman customs at Pompeii and the erection of a temple to the Capitoline divinities are seen to be less remarkable. The building of such a temple was a natural expression of political aspirations; it was in complete harmony with the use of Latin in the inscription of Popidius (p. 50).

There is, however, another possibility that may be stated. The remodelling of the Forum was certainly commenced in the pre-Roman period; but it is not impossible that the work was interrupted by the breaking out of the Social War and that the colonists completed it, dedicating the temple to the gods of the Capitol. The use of several brick-shaped blocks of stone, — such blocks are not found in other buildings of the pre-Roman time, — the lack of any trace of the wall decoration of the first style, the form of the egg-and-dart moulding on the capitals of the Ionic columns in the cella, and the correspondence of certain dimensions with the Roman scale of measurements may be alleged in favor of this hypothesis. The evidence at present does not warrant a positive decision against it.

The fact that we have here a Capitolium may explain the special prominence of the altar in front, which might just as well have been placed in the area of the Forum at the foot of the steps. In Rome the Capitol lay upon a summit of a hill; perhaps the aim in this case was to place not only the temple but also the altar upon an elevation so that here, as there, the priest should go up to offer sacrifice.

The podium of the temple contains vaulted rooms which can be entered from the Forum through a narrow door on the east side. Their use is unknown. We are reminded of the temple of Saturn in the Forum at Rome, the podium of which served as a treasury, *aerarium*. The vaults, *favissae*, may have been used as a place of safe keeping for treasure, or for furniture of the temple, or for discarded votive offerings.

The beautiful head of Jupiter found in the cella deserves more than a passing mention. In order to appreciate its character we may view it in contrast with the Otricoli Zeus, with which it is closely related. In both heads we feel the lack of that majestic simplicity, that ineffable and godlike calm, which rested on the features of the Zeus of Phidias. Here man has much more obviously made God in his own image; the face shows less of the ideal, with more of human energy and passion.

It is not for us to decide whether the Otricoli mask is from the school of Praxiteles, or shows more of the influence of Lysippus; it is sufficient here to notice that the type was developed in the

Fig. 21. — Bust of Zeus from Otricoli, now in the Vatican Museum. After Tafel 130 of the Brunn-Bruckmann Denkmaeler.

second half of the fourth century B.C., the century after Phidias. The similarity between these two examples of the type is apparent at first glance. The shape of the two heads is, in general, the same, and there is the same profusion of hair and beard, symbolic of power; but the differences in detail are striking.

In the Otricoli Zeus the peculiar shape of the forehead — prominent in the middle up to the roots of the hair and retreating at the sides — seems to suggest, not so much the power of a world-encompassing and lofty intellect, as absorption in great, unfathomable thoughts. In the lines of the massive face irresistible force of will is revealed, and the capability of fierce passion lurks beneath the projecting lower part of the forehead and uneven eyebrows, threatening like a thundercloud. But for the moment all is deep repose, and the lids seem partly closed over eyes that look downwards, as if not concerned with seeing. The sculptor has conceived of Zeus as the occult power of nature, alike the origin and law of all things, or as the personification of the heavens veiled by impenetrable mists.

Great force of will is seen also in the face of the Pompeian god; but it is will dominated by alert and all-embracing mind. The forehead expands in a broad arch; the eyes, wide open, look out with full vision under sharply cut brows. Here we have no secret brooding; a powerful yet clearly defined and comprehensible personality is stamped upon features carved in bold, free lines. And this personality is not lost in mystical self-contemplation; the god is following with closest attention the course of events in some far distant place, affairs that in the next moment may require his intervention; excitement and expectancy are seen in the raised upper lip. The ideal of this artist was the wise and powerful king,

Fig. 22. — Bust of Jupiter, found at Pompeii. Naples Museum.

whose watchful and all-protecting eye sees to the furthest limits of his kingdom. Surely this variation of the Otricoli type must have been conceived in a monarchical period, the period when the Greek world was ruled by the successors of Alexander.

The Pompeian god is more a sovereign; the Zeus of Otricoli is more poetic, more divine.

CHAPTER IX

THE BASILICA

THE Basilica, at the southwest corner of the Forum, was the most magnificent and architecturally the most interesting building at Pompeii. Its construction and decoration point to the pre-Roman time; and there is also an inscription scratched on the stucco of the wall, dating from almost the beginning of the Roman colony: *C. Pumidius Dipilus heic fuit a. d. v. nonas Octobreis M. Lepid. Q. Catul. cos.*, — 'C. Pumidius Dipilus was here on the fifth day before the nones of October in the consulship of Marcus Lepidus and Quintus Catulus,' that is October 3, 78 B.C.

The purpose of the building is clearly indicated not only by its plan and the details of its arrangement but also by the word *Bassilica* scratched a number of times by idlers on the stucco of the outer wall at the right of the south entrance. This sure identification lends to the edifice a special significance; it is without doubt the oldest example that we have of an important architectural type whose origin is lost in obscurity, but of which the derivative forms may still be recognized in the architecture of to-day. What the temple developed by the Greeks was to pagan antiquity, that the basilica became to the Christian Church — a type dominating a system of religious architecture. Pagan worship was individual, — a narrow chamber sufficed for the image of the god and the requirements of religious service; but Christian worship was social, and its functions demanded a larger room, in which a congregation could be assembled. The religious architecture of the Church therefore broke with the religious architecture of pagan antiquity, and turned for its model to the basilica.

Our knowledge of the history of the basilica begins with the erection of the Basilica Porcia in Rome by Cato the Elder, in

184 B.C.; other basilicas followed, and in Caesar's day a number stood about the Forum. Regarding its development prior to the time of Cato only conjectures can be offered. The name *basilica* (*basilike stoa*, 'the royal hall') points to a Greek origin; we should naturally look for the prototype of the Roman as well as the Pompeian structure in the capitals of the Alexandrian period and in the Greek colonies of Italy. But no ruin, no reference in literature comes to our aid. The supposition that the King's Hall (*basileios stoa*) in Athens, the official residence of the King Archon, was the prototype of all basilicas, has little to support it; our information in regard to the form of this building is quite inadequate, and the name alone warrants no positive conclusion. It is more probable that both the name and the architectural type came from the 'royal hall' of one of the successors of Alexander.

A basilica was a spacious hall which served as an extension of a market place, and was itself in a certain sense a covered market. It was not limited to a specific purpose; in general, whatever took place on the market square might take place in the basilica, the roof of which afforded protection against the weather. It was chiefly devoted, however, to business transactions and to the administration of justice. The form is known partly from the remains of the basilicas in Rome — Basilica Julia, Basilica Ulpia, the Basilica of Constantine — and in Africa, but more fully from the treatise of Vitruvius and the description of a basilica which he himself erected at Fano.

According to these sources the plan of a typical basilica is essentially that of the building before us (Fig. 23). An oblong space is divided by columns into a broad central hall and a corridor which runs around the four sides. The height of the columns, in the

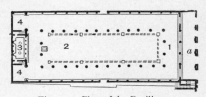

Fig. 23. — Plan of the Basilica.

a. Entrance court.   1. Corridor.
2. Main room.   3. Tribunal.
4. Rooms at the ends of the tribunal.

typical basilica, is equal to the width of the corridor, which is covered by a flat roof; the inner edge of this roof is carried by the entablature above the columns. The main room is higher than the corridor. Above the entablature is a low wall on which there is a second row of columns; these carry the main roof and form a clerestory, the light being admitted through the intercolumniations.

The main hall and the corridor were devoted to trade; the dealers perhaps occupied the former, while in the latter the throng of purchasers and idlers moved freely about. The place set aside for the administration of justice, the tribunal, was ordinarily an apse projecting from the rear end. In our Basilica, however, — and in some others as well, — it was a small oblong elevated room back of the central hall, toward which it opened in its whole length.

This ideal plan would answer very well for that of the early Christian basilicas, excepting in one respect; instead of a corridor on all four sides they have only aisles parallel with the nave, an arrangement which had already been adopted in some basilicas designed for markets. The Christian basilicas would give us a still truer idea of the arrangement and lighting of the pagan prototype if in most cases a part of the numerous windows had not been walled up, thus producing a dimness in keeping with a religious but not a secular edifice.

In pagan structures the ideal plan was by no means strictly followed. Vitruvius himself at Fano, and the architects of other basilicas the remains of which have been discovered, did not hesitate to depart from it. So the Basilica at Pompeii, as we shall see, presents a modification of the general plan in an important particular, the admission of light; and this deviation was carried out with finer artistic feeling than was displayed by Vitruvius in his building.

Our Basilica is undoubtedly of later date than the Basilica Porcia, but the Pompeians, who at the time when it was built were pupils of the Greeks in matters of art, found their model not in Rome but in a Greek city, perhaps Naples.

Five entrances, separated by tufa pillars, lead from the colonnade of the Forum into the east end of the basilica. First comes a narrow entrance court (*a*), extending across the entire building and open to the sky. On the walls, as also on the outside of the building, are remains of a simple stucco decoration;

below, a yellow base with a projecting red border along the upper edge; above, a plain white surface. At the left outside the entrance court is a cistern for rain water collected from the roof; the stairway close by (shown on the plan) had nothing to do with the Basilica, but was connected with the upper gallery of the colonnade about the Forum.

Mounting four steps of basalt we pass from the narrow court into the building. The five entrances here are separated by four columns. Those next to the two sides on the right and on

Fig. 24. — View of the Basilica, looking toward the tribunal.

the left were closed by a wall in which was a wide doorway; the three at the middle were left as open intercolumniations. The enclosed space before us measures $180\frac{1}{3}$ English feet (200 Oscan feet) in length, $78\frac{3}{4}$ feet in breadth. Twenty-eight massive brick columns, 4 Oscan feet in diameter, separate the great central hall from the broad corridor running about it; only the lower part of the columns, built of small bricks evidently made specially for this purpose, is preserved (Fig. 24). Attached half-columns, with a diameter a little more than three fourths that of the others, project from the walls; the wall decoration, which imitates in stucco a veneering of colored marbles, is of the first style (p. 41). The columns of the entrance and those at the rear have the same diameter as the half-columns; part of the Ionic capitals belonging to them have been found, but the capitals of the large columns have wholly disappeared.

There are only scanty remains of the floor, which consisted of bits of brick and tile mixed with fine mortar and pounded down (*opus Signinum*); it extended in a single level over the whole enclosed space, and from this level our estimates of height are reckoned. On three sides of the main hall at the base of the columns under the floor is a square water channel, indicated on our plan; eight rectangular basins lie along its course, but the purpose of it is not clear. The tribunal projects from the rear wall, its floor being six Oscan feet above that of the rest of the building.

The large columns about the main hall, with a diameter of more than $3\frac{1}{2}$ feet, must have been at least 32 or 33 feet high; the attached half-columns with the columns at the entrance and at the rear, including the Ionic capitals, were probably not more than 20 feet high. But since the roof of the corridor was flat, the walls must have been as high as the entablature of the large columns, and so must have extended above the entablature of the half-columns; considerable portions of this upper division of the walls remain.

Along the walls on the ground are to be seen a number of capitals, fragments of shafts and bases belonging to a series of smaller columns with a diameter of 1.74 feet, all found in the course of the excavations. They are of tufa, coated with white stucco; they can belong only here, and by the study of their forms — columns, half-columns, and peculiarly shaped three-quarter-columns — the upper division of the walls can be restored with some degree of certainty. Not to go into technical details, in the upper part of the side walls a section of wall containing a window alternated with a short series of columns in which the columns, for the sake of greater solidity, were set twice as close as the half-columns in the lower division of the wall, the intercolumniations being left entirely open (Fig. 25); over the entrances at the front the wall was continuous but was divided into sections by half-columns corresponding with the columns below, a window being placed between every two half-columns in order to conceal the difference in width between the sections of wall at the front and those at the sides. The arrangement was similar at the rear, on either side of the tribunal, as may be seen from the section (Fig. 27).

With this restoration of the outer walls completed we are able to form a clear idea of the appearance of the main hall. Whether or not the rafters could be seen from below is uncertain, but the probability is that, as assumed in our restoration (Fig. 26), they

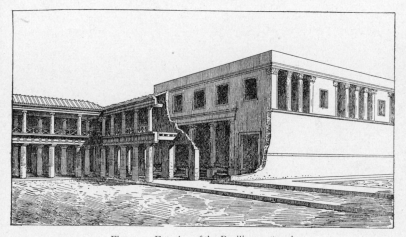

Fig. 25. — Exterior of the Basilica, restored.

were hidden by a coffered ceiling. The simple and beautiful interior abounded in fine spatial effects. The corridor and main room were almost as high as the main room was wide, that is between 35 and 40 feet. The light streaming in through the openings in the upper portion of the walls was evenly distributed throughout the hall; we may assume that when the sun became too hot on the south side it could be shut out by curtains.

In our Basilica, then, we notice a wide divergence from the ideal or normal plan. Instead of a clerestory above the main hall a proportionally greater height is given to the corridor. The normal height of a basilica corridor is represented by the

lower division of the walls with the attached half-columns and
their entablature; this, however, is here treated simply as a
lower member, and upon it, rather than upon the entablature
of the columns about the main hall, was placed an upper
division of wall admitting light and air through intercolumniations and windows.

The tribunal at the rear is the most prominent and architecturally the most effective portion of the building. The base is
treated in a bold, simple manner; upon it, at the front, stands a

Fig. 26.— Interior of the Basilica, looking toward the tribunal, restored.

row of columns the lower portions of which show traces of
latticework. The decoration of the walls, like that of the rest
of the interior, imitates a veneering of colored marbles. The
shape and comparatively narrow dimensions of the elevated
room indicate that we have here a tribunal in the strict sense, a
raised platform for the judge and his assistants; in the basilicas provided with apses the latter were large enough to make
room both for the judicial body and for the litigants. Here the
litigants stood on the floor in front of the tribunal, and when
court was in session the general public must have been excluded
from this part of the corridor. The arrangement in this respect

was far from convenient, but seemingly convenience was sacrificed to aesthetic considerations; the builders wished to treat the
projecting front of the tribunal as an ornament to the building.

Under the tribunal was a vaulted chamber half below the
level of the ground; two round holes, indicated on the plan,
opened into it from above. It could hardly have been designed
as a place for the confinement of prisoners; escape would have
been easy by means of two windows in the rear, especially
when help was ren-
dered from the out-
side. More likely it
was used, in connec-
tion with the business
of the court, as a
storeroom, in which
writing materials and
the like, or even doc-
uments, might be
kept; they could ea-
sily have been passed
up through the holes when needed. The second story of the
tribunal was not as completely open to the main hall as the
first. Its front, the remains of which have for the most part
been recovered, was divided off by half-columns corresponding
in number and arrangement with the columns of the first story,
but each half-column was flanked by narrow pilasters, while a
parapet of moderate height occupied the intervening spaces.
It was built apparently with a view to architectural effect rather
than practical use (Fig. 27).

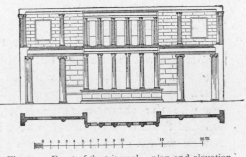

Fig. 27. — Front of the tribunal — plan and elevation.

At the right and the left of the tribunal are places for stairways. Each of these contains a landing on the same level with
the floor of the tribunal, from which it was cut off by a door;
the steps connecting with these landings, being of wood, have
disappeared. In both stair rooms, however, flights of stone
steps lead down to the vaulted chamber below, so that this
could not have been accessible if there were wooden steps on
both sides connecting the tribunal with the floor of the Basilica.
Probably on one side the wooden steps led from the tribunal

down to the floor, but on the other ascended from the corresponding landing to the second story, thus leaving the stairway to the lower room unobstructed on that side. At some later time the door at the left between the tribunal and the landing was walled up, perhaps because the gallery was no longer used; if still in use it could to all appearances have been reached only by a ladder.

The two open rooms at the rear on either side of the tribunal agree in their decoration with the entrance court except that the base with its border is higher, and the white surface above is moulded in stucco so as to give the appearance of slabs of white marble. They were no higher than the first division of the wall; the windows above the broad entrances opened into the outer air. Perhaps they were used as waiting rooms for litigants.

Opposite the north entrance between two columns stood a curb like those over the mouths of cisterns; only the foundation stone with a circular opening is preserved. The remains of a lead pipe, which brought the water to it, show that it must have been connected with an aqueduct. At the further end of the main hall was an equestrian statue of which no trace has been found.

The arrangement of the roof is a problem of much difficulty. Without wearying the reader by presenting various possibilities, it will be sufficient for our purposes to suggest the explanation which, on the whole, has the most in its favor. As assumed in our restoration, the roof of the main hall was carried by the entablature of the twenty-eight large columns. In other respects the arrangement corresponded fairly well with that of other basilicas except that, owing to the lack of a clerestory, the roof of the main hall was not raised high over that of the corridor. From the roof of the corridor, at least on the south side, the rain water flowed into the cistern near the front part of the building.

The five entrances opening from the Forum into the narrow court could be closed by latticed doors. Similar doors hung also on the wooden jambs of the north and south entrances. With such doors a complete safeguarding could not have been contemplated. Tradespeople using the Basilica must either have removed their wares at the close of business hours or have made the stalls sufficiently secure for protection. We can hardly doubt that ordinarily a night watchman was on duty about the building.

CHAPTER X

THE TEMPLE OF APOLLO

IN some respects the study of the large temple on the west side of the Forum is especially satisfactory. The building had been completely restored after the earthquake of 63, and was in good order at the time of its destruction. Though ancient excavators removed many objects of value, including the statue

Fig. 28.—Corner of mosaic floor, cella of the temple of Apollo.

of the divinity of the temple, much was left undisturbed, as the interesting series of statues in the court; in addition, a number of inscriptions have been recovered. On the whole, more complete information is at hand regarding this sanctuary than in reference to any other in Pompeii.

The identification of this as the temple of Apollo is certain. The accompanying illustration shows a corner of the floor laid over the greater part of the cella (3 on the plan); the parts along the inner walls were of black and white mosaic. This floor was composed of small, lozenge-shaped pieces of green and white marble and slate; of the two narrow stripes between the lozenge pattern and the bright mosaic fret along the border one is of slate, the other of red marble. In the slate stripe was an inscription. The letters were outlined by means of small holes filled with metal, every seven holes forming a vertical line, every four a horizontal. The inscription, which was in Oscan, stated that the quaestor O[ppius] Camp[anius], by order of the council and with money belonging to Apollo, had caused something to be made; [1] what this was cannot be determined, as the important word is missing, but apparently it was the floor. In the cella, moreover, stands a block of tufa, having the shape of half an egg; this is the Omphalos, the familiar symbol of Apollo. In the court on the first pilaster at the right as you enter a tripod is painted, too large for mere decoration, and explicable only as a symbol of the god. Lastly, in the design of the stucco ornamentation with which the entablature of the peristyle was adorned after the earthquake, the principal figures are griffins. The griffin was sacred to Apollo, and though it was often used as a purely decorative theme, in this case a reference to the divinity of the temple is unmistakable.

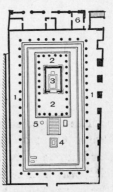

Fig. 29. — Plan of the temple of Apollo.

1. Colonnade.
2. Podium.
3. Cella.
4. Altar.
5. Sundial.
6. Sacristan's room.

As previously stated (p. 49), the deviation of the axis of this building from that of the Forum is undoubtedly due to the fact that it followed the direction of a street which bordered it on the east side before the colonnade of Popidius was built; this is therefore an evidence of the antiquity of the temple. The style of architecture, however, is in no essential particular different from that of the colonnade and of other buildings of the Tufa Period, and gives no indication of great age. The most probable explanation is that the temple was rebuilt in the Tufa Period on the site of an earlier structure, the orientation of which was preserved. The difference in direction is concealed by the increasing thickness, from south to north, of the pillars between the Forum and the court of the temple. The spaces between the pillars were originally left open. Later, at what time it is impossible to determine, they were all walled up except the three opposite the side of the temple; since the temple was excavated these also have been closed. In comparison with the entrances from the Forum, at first ten in number, the

[1] O · KAMP[aniìs . . . kva]ISSTUR · KOMBENNI[eìs tanginud] · APELLUNEÌS EÌTIU[vad . . . ops]ANNU · AAMAN[aff]ED.

G

one on the south side, opening on the street leading from
the Porta Marina, must have been considered unimportant.
Otherwise pains would have been taken to give to the colonnade on that side an even number of columns, so that the door
of the temple should face an intercolumniation; as it is the
number is uneven and the entrance to the court had to be put a
little to one side that it might not open upon a column.

The court is of oblong shape. The continuous colonnade
about the sides, the peristyle, was originally in two stories. At
the rear of the peristyle on the north side stood the small colonnade of the Doric order already mentioned (p. 62); one of the
rooms into which in later times this was divided (6) was connected with the court of the temple, and was probably occupied
by the sacristan (*aedituus*).

The temple stood upon a high podium, in front of which is a
broad flight of steps. The small cella was evidently intended
for but one statue. The columns at the sides of the deep portico, which in other respects follows the Etruscan plan (p. 63),
are continued in a colonnade which is carried completely around
the cella.

In Plate II and Fig. 30 we give a view of the ruins as they
are to-day; in Fig. 32 a view of the temple as it appeared
before the earthquake of 63. The height and diameter of the
Corinthian columns seen in the restoration can be calculated with
approximate correctness; of the entablature and parts above
nothing has been found except a large waterspout of terra cotta
in the form of a lion's head.

The colonnade about the court was built of tufa, and coated
with white stucco. It presents an odd mixture of styles, of
which other examples also are found at Pompeii; a Doric entablature with triglyphs was placed upon Ionic columns having
the four-sided capital known as Roman Ionic. Here, as in the
earlier colonnade about the Forum, the stone blocks of the
entablature were set upon beams; and in the blocks still in
place we may see the sockets made to receive the ends of the
joists of the second story floor. Evidently with the purpose of
supporting this second story, which was probably of the Corinthian order, the Ionic columns below were made relatively

short. No remains of an upper gallery, however, have been found; and it is quite possible that when the colonnade was restored, after the earthquake, the second story was omitted. The upper floor could be reached from the second story of the small colonnade north of the court, which was accessible by means of a stairway leading from the Forum.

When the restoration of the temple and its colonnade was

Fig. 30.— View of the temple of Apollo, looking toward Vesuvius.
At the left of the steps, the column on which was the sundial; in front of the steps, the altar.

undertaken, the feeling for the pure and simple forms of the Greek architecture was no longer present; the prevailing taste demanded gay and fantastic designs, with the use of brilliant colors. The Pompeians improved the opportunity afforded by the rebuilding to make the temple and its colonnade conform to the taste of the times.

First the projecting portions of the Ionic and Corinthian columns were cut off; then shaft and capital alike were covered with a thick layer of stucco. New capitals were moulded in the stucco, of a shape in general resembling the Corinthian, and were painted in red, blue, and yellow; the lower part of the shaft, unfluted, was also painted yellow. The entablature, at least in the case of the colonnade, was in like manner covered with stucco and ornamented with reliefs in the same colors. All this gaudy stucco has now fallen off; and our illustration (Fig. 31) is taken from Mazois, who made the drawing soon after the court was excavated. The later capitals and stucco ornamentation of the temple itself had wholly disappeared before the excavations were made.

The wall decoration of both the temple and the colonnade

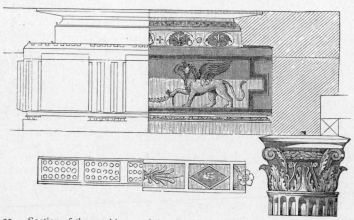

Fig. 31. — Section of the entablature of the temple of Apollo, showing the original form and the restoration after the earthquake.

was originally in the first style; a remnant of it may still be seen in the cella. After 63 it was modernized. The walls of the temple both within and without were done over in stucco, so as to resemble ashlar work of white marble; apparently it was the intention to give the appearance of real marble. The walls of the colonnade were painted in the latest Pompeian style, in bright colors, on a white ground. The decorative designs, to judge from the remains and from sketches, were not of special interest. There was a series of pictures representing scenes from the Trojan War, — the quarrel between Achilles and Agamemnon, the embassy of the Greeks to Achilles, the battle between Achilles and Hector (the subject of this, however, is doubtful), the dragging of Hector's body about the walls of

Troy, Priam making entreaty for the body of Hector, and the rape of the Palladium, — but they have long since perished and are known only from unsatisfactory drawings.

Long before this modernizing of the temple the west side of the court had undergone a complete transformation. The peculiar bend in the street at the northwest corner (shown in Plan II), the diagonal line with which the small colonnade north of the court ends, and the narrow, quite inaccessible space between the west wall of the court and the houses lying near it, cannot easily be explained as a part of an original plan, but must rather be the result of later changes. The north and south street which now ends abruptly at the northwest corner must originally have been continued through the west colonnade, the ends of which were left open; this colonnade was then a public thoroughfare, on which the windows of houses opened, and perhaps also doors.

We learn from an inscription that about the year 10 B.C. the city purchased from the residents whose property adjoined the colonnade, for the sum of 3000 sesterces (about $155), the right to build a wall in front of their windows; this explains how the narrow space between the wall on the north side of the court and the houses came to be cut off. The inscription reads : *M. Holconius Rufus d[uum] v[ir] i[uri] d[icundo] tert[ium], C. Egnatius Postumus d. v. i. d. iter[um] ex d[ecurionum] d[e-creto] ius luminum opstruendorum HS ∞ ∞ ∞ redemerunt, parietemque privatum Col[oniae] Ven[eriae] Cor[neliae] usque ad tegulas faciundum coerarunt,* — 'Marcus Holconius Rufus, duumvir with judiciary authority for the third time, and Gaius Egnatius Postumus, duumvir with judiciary authority for the second time, in accordance with a decree of the city council purchased for 3000 sesterces the right to shut off light (from adjoining buildings) and caused to be constructed a wall belonging to the colony of Pompeii to the height of the tiles,' that is, as high as the roofs of the houses.

The wall referred to was no doubt that on the west side of the court of the temple; when it was built the ends of the colonnade on that side must have been closed, so that this ceased to be a thoroughfare. Marcus Holconius was duumvir for the fourth time in the year 3–2 B.C.; as an interval of at least five years must intervene between two duumvirates, his third duumvirate must have been not far from 10 B.C.

The pedestal in the cella, on which the statue of Apollo stood, still remains, but no trace of the statue itself has been found.

Near the foot of the steps in front is a large altar of travertine, having the same inscription on both sides: *M. Porcius M. f., L. Sextilius L. f., Cn. Cornelius Cn. f., A. Cornelius A. f. IIII vir[i] d[e] d[ecurionum] s[ententia] f[aciundam] locar[uut]*, — 'Marcus Porcius the son of Marcus, Lucius Sextilius

Fig. 32. — Temple of Apollo, restored.

the son of Lucius, Gnaeus Cornelius the son of Gnaeus, and Aulus Cornelius the son of Aulus, the Board of Four, in accordance with the vote of the city council let the contract (for building this altar).' The names of the four officials who erected the altar, the two duumvirs and two aediles (for the title see p. 12), appear without surnames; this points to a relatively early time, at the latest the age of Augustus.

At the left of the steps is an Ionic column with the inscription: *L. Sepunius L. f. Sandilianus, M. Herennius A. f. Epidianus duovir[i] i[uri] d[icundo] d[e] s[ua] p[ecunia] f[aciundum] c[urarunt]*, — 'Lucius Sepunius Sandilianus the son of Lucius, and Marcus Herennius Epidianus the son of Aulus, duumvirs with judiciary authority, caused (this) to be erected at their own expense.' Old sketches, made soon after the court was excavated, represent the column with a sundial on the top. The probability that a sundial belonging to the column was actually found is increased by the fact that these same men placed one on the circular bench in the Forum Triangulare. Here, in front of the temple of the Sun-god, such a dial would certainly have been in place. At the right of the steps are some blocks of lava containing holes, in which, undoubtedly, the supports of a votive offering were once set, but the holes give no clew to the size or character of the offering.

Other divinities besides Apollo were honored in this sanctuary, which in the earlier time was evidently the most important in the city; statues and altars for their worship were placed in the court. The pedestals of the statues still remain where they were originally placed, on the step in front of the stylobate of the colonnade; the statues themselves, with one exception, have been taken to Naples. There were in all six of them, grouped in three related pairs. In front of the third column at the left of the entrance, stood Venus, at the right was a hermaphrodite—both marble figures of about one half life size. They belong to the pre-Roman period and were originally of good workmanship, but even in antiquity they had been repeatedly restored and worked over. As a work of art, the hermaphrodite is the more important.

An altar stands before the statue of Venus. In pre-Roman times this may have been the only shrine in the city at which worship was offered to Herentas; for by that name the goddess of love was known in the native speech. Venus as goddess of the Roman colony (Fig. 4), was represented in an altogether different guise, and must have had a special place of worship elsewhere.

Though the statues of Venus and of the hermaphrodite here form a pair, both artistically and in respect to arrangement, the latter belongs not to the cycle of Venus but to that of Bacchus; and in order to make this the more evident, the ears of a satyr were given to the figure. We may, perhaps, infer that the god of wine also was worshipped in this sanctuary. In the sacristan's room (6 on the plan) we find a painting in which Bacchus is represented as leaning upon Silenus who is playing the lyre, meanwhile allowing the panther to drink out of his cup. This seems strange enough in a temple of Apollo; still it cannot be considered conclusive evidence that Bacchus actually received worship here. Without doubt the Wine-god was honored in Pompeii, the region about which was rich in vines. He appears countless times in wall paintings, but no shrine dedicated to him has yet been found.

On the right side of the court, in front of the third column, was a statue of Apollo; on the left directly opposite stood Artemis, both life size figures in bronze. An altar stood before the statue of Artemis; the altar of Apollo was before the temple. Both statues were armed with the bow, and it is evident that they were not designed to stand facing each other, but side by side, or one behind the other; both may originally have belonged to a Niobe group. As works of art, they are not of high merit. We recognize a certain elegance and nicety of finish, but these qualities cannot compensate for superficiality in the treatment of the figure, want of expression in the faces, and lack of energy in the movement. We have no other evidence of the worship of Artemis in Pompeii.

Further on, in front of the fifth column on either side, is a marble herm. Both herms are of fine workmanship, and clearly belong to the pre-Roman period; they represent Mercury and Maia. The Mercury, on the right, is still in place, and is seen in Plate II. The god appears as a youth standing with his mantle drawn over the back of his head; the face, with a placid, serious, mild expression, is inclined a little forward. In this form Mercury was honored as the presiding divinity of the palaestra, the god of gymnastic exercises; we shall find him in the same guise later in the court of the Stabian Baths (p. 194). How this type of Hermes came to be chosen for the place of honor in athletic courts is by no means clear; it was certainly designed originally to represent him as a god of death, the Psychopompus, conductor of souls to the Underworld. The worship of Mercury here as a god of gymnastic exercises would not be in harmony with the surroundings; we should rather believe that the Pompeians, having placed him in such close

Marcus Holconius Rufus, duumvir with judiciary
the fourth time, Aulus Clodius Flaccus, duumvir
time, and of Publius Caesetius Postumus and
.tirius Rufus, duumvirs in charge of the streets,
public religious festivals (the official title of the
) in the thirteenth consulship of the Emperor
.stus), the other consul being Marcus Plautius

ficult to understand how the worship of Augustus
a place in this sanctuary. The divinities here
in close relation to him. Apollo was his tutelary
om he thought that he owed the victory at Actium,
honor he built the magnificent temple on the
nus, moreover, was revered as the ancestress of
iily; and finally Mercury was said to be incarnate
elf.

on found expression in one of the finest of
written in 28 B.C. Fearful portents, the
ing Rome; Jupiter with flaming right
his own temple on the Capitoline. To
for help — to Apollo, to Venus, or to
winged god, Maia's son, that even now
the form of a youth, the avenger of

            .utata iuvenem figura
          terris imitaris almae
        Maiae, patiens vocari
            Caesaris ultor.

        e that evidence of the worship of
     .as come to light also in Egypt. In an
    .derah we find *Helmîs Kaisar*, 'beloved of
    '; Helmîs Kaisar is apparently 'Hermes
in Egyptian inscriptions Augustus is not infre-
ed to as 'the beloved of Ptah and of Isis.'

relation with Apollo, god of the death-dealing
earth goddess, Maia, associated more serious i
image.

The herm on the opposite side of the court sh
of a goddess. The head is lacking; the one form
it, now removed, belonged to another figure. In
ogy, the mother of Hermes was Maia, the daugl
and this relationship, by a common confusion, was
the Italian Maia, who was originally goddess of t
gave her name to the month of May. The id
the figure as that of Maia rests upon a number
which establish the existence of a cult of Mercur
Pompeii. From the same source we learn that wi
of these two that of Augustus was intimately ass
are few better illustrations of the developmen
worship in the Early Empire.

These inscriptions were found in differe
them in their original location. They a
attached to votive offerings, of which one
by a college of priests, consisting of slav
the general direction of the city auth
of this college at first, certainly to 14 B.
Maiae, 'Servants of Mercury and M
indicates a low order of priesthood.
peror was then added, and the pries
Augustus, Mercury, and Maia.' S
2 B.C., the names of the two divinit
priests were designated simply as 'Se

The extant inscriptions of this series
40 A.D. As an example, we give that o
ministri Augusti first appear : *N. Veius Ph*
Moschus, T. Mescinius Amphio, Primus Arrun
Aug., ex d. d. iussu M. Holconii Rufi IV, A. Cl
d. v. i. d., P. Caeseti Postumi, N. Tintiri Rufi d.
Imp. Caesare XIII, M. Plautio Silvano cos, — 'N
Phylax, Numerius Popidius Moschus, Titus Mes
and Primus the slave of Marcus Arruntius, Servan
(set this up), in accordance with a decree of the c

f
                                                         ıs
                                                       ıa in
                                                       rship
                                                      there
                                                      peror

                              ent places, none of
                         ...re dedications once
                          : was set up each year
                    ves and freedmen, under
                    orities.   The official title
                c., was *Ministri Mercurii
            Iaia*' ; the word *minister*
            The worship of the em-
          sts were called 'Servants of
        till later, at least as early as
        ies were dropped, and the
        rvants of Augustus.'

          ; come down to the year
          f 2 B.C., in which the
          hylax, N. Popidius
          ti M. s., min.
          cci III
          s. p. p.
          Veius
          ıphio
          ıstus
          on

ca
hc
divin
and
Palat
the J
in Augustus hims

This last concepti
the odes of Horace,
poet says, are threaten
hand has even struck
what god shall we turn
Mars? or rather to thee,
doest walk the earth in
Caesar :—

Sive n
Ales i
Filius

It is interesting to not
Augustus as Mercury h
inscription from Den
Ptah and of Isi
Caesar,'
quently

CHAPTER XI

*THE BUILDINGS AT THE NORTHWEST CORNER OF THE
FORUM, AND THE TABLE OF STANDARD MEASURES*

THE large building at the northwest corner of the Forum
(Fig. 33, 1, 2, 3) was erected after the earthquake of the year
63. We do not know whether at the time of the eruption it
had yet been roofed; the inside at least was in an unfinished
state.

This building is divided into three parts, one of which, that
furthest north, at the corner, contains both lower and upper
rooms. Below, at the level of the Forum,
are two dark vaulted chambers, one at the
rear of the other. The front chamber is
dimly lighted by a slit in the ceiling and
was entered from the Forum by a narrow door; there are traces of a strong iron
grating in the doorway. It has been supposed, not without probability, that these
were the vaults of the city treasury, the
aerarium; if they had been built for
prison cells, they would naturally have
had separate entrances.

Above these chambers are two rooms
which open not on the Forum, but on the
street that runs past them on the north
(1, 1). They resemble shops and would

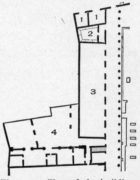

Fig. 33. — Plan of the buildings
at the northwest corner of the
Forum.

1. City treasury.
2. Latrina.
3, 4. Market buildings.

be classed as such without further question but for the fact that
the level of the floor is nearly five feet above the sidewalk, so
that they could have been reached only by means of steps. If
the identification of the chambers below as the vaults of the
city treasury is correct, these rooms must have been occupied

91

by the treasury officials, who could here transact business with the public without admitting the latter to their offices.

The middle room (2) was a public closet, with a small ante-room. As the doors to and from the anteroom were not placed opposite each other, the interior was not visible from the street. The room was not entirely finished; nevertheless, we can see the water channel running along three sides, and above it the stones on which the woodwork was to be placed; the inlet pipe was in position, as well as the outlet for carrying the water off into a sewer at the rear.

The last of the three parts of the building (3) is by far the largest. It was a high and spacious hall, with numerous entrances from the Forum. It was divided into two rooms by two short sections of wall projecting from the sides, and was evidently a market house, perhaps for vegetables and farm products.

The rooms formed by enclosing the small colonnade at the rear of the court of Apollo have already been mentioned (p. 62). At the left of the stairway leading to the second story (shown in Plan II) is a small room which opens in its entire breadth upon the Forum (11). Close by is a recess (10), also open toward the Forum, in the side of the first of the thick pillars which separate the Forum from the court of the temple.

In this recess stood the table of standard measures, *mensa ponderaria* (Fig. 34), which is now in the Naples Museum, unfortunately not entire; a part of it has disappeared. The part remaining consists of a large slab of limestone (a little over 8 feet long and 1.8, or 2 Oscan feet, wide), in which are nine bowl-shaped cavities with holes at the bottom through which the contents could be drawn off; this slab rested on two stone supports, and similar supports above it carried another slab, which is now lost, with three cavities. The table thus contained twelve standards of capacity for liquid and dry measure, but only ten are shown in the illustration, as two are too far back.

It is evident that the table has come down from the pre-Roman period. The names of the measures were orginally written in Oscan, beside the five largest cavities, and though

the letters were later erased, they are still in part legible.
Only one word, however, can be made out with certainty, beside
the next to the smallest cavity; that is *Kuiniks*, plainly the
same as the Greek
Choinix. We nat-
urally infer that in
the pre-Roman
time the Pompe-
ians used Greek
measures.

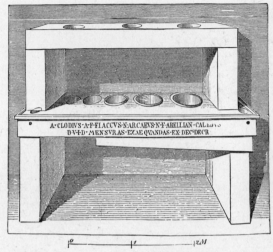

In the time of
Augustus, about 20
B.C., the cavities
were enlarged and
made to conform to
the Roman stand-
ard, but the new
names were not put
beside them. The
inscription on the

Fig. 34. — Table of standard measures, *mensa ponderaria*.

front of the larger slab has reference to these changes : ' Aulus
Clodius Flaccus, the son of Aulus, and Numerius Arcaeus
Arellianus Caledus, the son of Numerius, duumvirs with judiciary authority, in accordance with a decree of the city council,
caused the measures to be made equal ' to the Roman measures.

A similar adjustment of measures to the Roman standard is
indicated by the use of the phrase *mensuras exaequare* on a
table found at Minturnae.   The adoption of a uniform standard
was made a subject of imperial regulation by Augustus, who, by
this means, sought to promote the unification of the Empire.
Similar tables of measures have been found in various parts of
the Roman world, as at Selinunto in Sicily, in the Greek islands,
and at Bregenz on the Lake of Constance.

It is probable that an official charged with the oversight of
the measures had his office in the small room next to the stairway (11).

CHAPTER XII

THE MACELLUM

THE large building at the northeast corner of the Forum was a provision market, of the sort called *Macellum*. The name Pantheon, once applied to it, is now abandoned, and there is no longer the slightest doubt regarding its purpose, which is indicated by its general plan, the remains found in the course of the excavations, and the paintings upon the walls.

Such markets, where provisions, especially of the finer and more expensive kinds, were sold and in which a cook also might be secured, without doubt existed in the Greek cities after the time of Alexander; from the Greeks, as in the case of the basilica, the Romans took both the name and the architectural type.

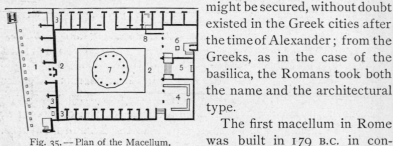

Fig. 35. — Plan of the Macellum.

1. Portico.
2. Colonnade.
3, 3, 3. Rows of market stalls.
4. Market room for meat and fish.
5. Chapel.
6. Banquet room.
7. Tholus.
8. Pen.

The first macellum in Rome was built in 179 B.C. in connection with the enlargement of a fish market. In later times, as we learn from inscriptions, others were constructed in Rome and in various cities of Italy and the provinces.

A macellum built by Nero is shown on one of the coins of this emperor. It agrees in essential points with our building, having stalls or shops of more than one story in height, and at the middle of the court a structure with a dome-like roof. The central structure, the *tholus*, is mentioned by Varro as an essential part of a macellum, but its use is known to us only from the remains found at Pompeii.

94

The plan of our building is simple. A court in the shape of a rectangle, slightly longer than it is broad, is surrounded by a deep colonnade on the four sides. In the middle twelve bases, arranged so as to form a dodecagon, supported an equal number of columns on which a roof rested; underneath was a rectangular basin in the pavement, from which a covered drain led toward the southeast corner. Under this roof the fish that had been sold were scaled, the scales being thrown into the basin, where

Fig. 36.—View of the Macellum.

In the foreground, part of the stylobate. In the middle ground, remains of the tholus. In the background, at the middle, walls and pedestal of the imperial chapel; at the right, market room; at the left, banquet room.

they were found in great quantity. Behind the colonnade on the south side, and opening into it, was a row of market stalls or small shops (3 on the plan). Above these were upper rooms, in front of which was a wooden gallery, but there was no stairway, and apparently the shopkeeper who wished to use his second story had to provide himself with a ladder.

There were shops also on the north side, but they opened upon the street bounding the Macellum on the north; a southern exposure for the shop fronts seems to have been avoided on account of the damage that the heat in summer might cause to the stock. In the shops on this street — whether in those belonging to the building or those on the opposite side is not stated — the excavators found charred figs, chestnuts, plums, grapes, fruit in glass vessels, lentils, grain, loaves of bread, and cakes. A few shops behind the portico in front faced toward the Forum.

A large market room (4) opened on the colonnade at the southeast corner, the entrance being divided by two columns. Along three sides runs a counter for meat and fish, the surface of which slopes toward the middle of the room. That fish were sold on the left side is plain from the special arrangement made to carry off the water; the floor behind the counter here was raised and sloped toward the rear, where a gutter ran under it, and passing across the room, led under the counter on the south side into the street.

In the little room or pen at the northeast corner of the colonnade (8) remains of skeletons of sheep were found. Such animals, then, were sold here alive; instead of buying the flesh of slaughtered animals, many purchasers no doubt preferred to obtain a victim which could be sacrificed as an offering to the household gods before it was used for food.

The paintings on the walls of the colonnade are among the best examples of the latest Pompeian style. Above the base are large black panels with a broad red border; between them, in the vertical spaces separating the border of one panel from that of the next, are light and fantastic architectural designs in yellow on a white ground, the parts designed to appear furthest from the eye being in green and red. In this way a rich development of architectural forms is united, in a consistent and effective decorative scheme, with large panels suitable for paintings.

Along the edges of the black panels run conventional plant designs; in the middle are paintings symmetrically arranged in a series in which a pair of floating figures alternates with a mythological scene enclosed in a painted frame. Among the mythological pictures are Ulysses before Penelope, who does not recognize him, Io guarded by Argus, and Medea plotting the murder of her children. The whole arrangement is in excellent taste, while the execution is careful and delicate.

The treatment of the upper part of the wall is especially worthy of note. Generally in walls of the fourth style the portion above the large panels is filled with airy architectural designs upon a white or at least a bright ground. In this instance the fantastic architectural forms in the spaces between the black panels are continued upwards to the ceiling, and in the midst of each group a standing figure is painted on a blue ground — a girl with utensils for sacrifice, a satyr playing the

Fig. 37. — The Macellum, restored.

flute; but the spaces above the panels are completely filled with representations of the things exposed for sale. Unfortunately only a few of these pictures remain. One contains birds, some alive, some killed and dressed; in another, different kinds of fish are seen; and a third presents a variety of vessels in which wine and other liquids could be kept. This departure from the usual style of decoration, unique in its way, can be explained only as having a direct reference to the purpose of the building.

In two small pictures in the black panels of the north entrance Cupids take the place of men. The Pompeians were very fond of the representation of Cupids as engaged in human occupations; it gave opportunity for the poetic treatment of everyday

H

life, which was thus carried over into fairyland. So in one picture sprightly, winged little figures are celebrating the festival of Vesta, the tutelary divinity of millers and bakers, who on this day, just as appears in the painting, wreathed with garlands their mills and much belabored asses that once a year were thus admitted to a share in the festal celebrations of their masters; the reference to trade in bread and flour is obvious.

In the other picture the Cupids are plaiting and selling wreaths; in view of the extensive use of garlands at banquets and on gala days the inference is warranted that they, too, were sold in this market. In the market room for meat and fish there is another interesting picture representing the local divinities of Pompeii — personifications of the Sarno, of the coast, and of the country round about, suggesting that here the products of the sea, the river, and the land might be obtained.

Fig. 38. — Statue of Octavia, sister of Augustus, found in the chapel of the Macellum. She is represented in an attitude of worship, with a libation saucer in her right hand, and offerings in her left.

Besides the rooms thus far considered, which served a practical end, we find in the Macellum two other rooms which gave to the building a religious character and placed it under the special protection of the imperial house. One, at the middle of the east end (5), is a chapel consecrated to the worship of the emperors. The floor is raised above that of the rest of the building, and the entrance is reached by five steps leading up from the rear of the colonnade. On a pedestal against the rear wall, and in four niches at the sides, were statues, of which only the two in the niches at the right have been found; these represent Octavia, the sister of Augustus (Fig. 38), and her son Marcellus, the hope of Augustus and of Rome, whose untimely death was lamented by Virgil in those touching verses in the sixth book of the Aeneid.   An arm with a globe was also found, doubtless belonging to the statue of an emperor that stood on the pedestal at the rear.   The chapel contains no altar ; sacrifice was probably offered on a portable bronze coal pan in the form of a tripod.   Several beautiful examples of these movable altars have been found, and there are numerous representations of them in reliefs and in wall paintings.

The Macellum in its present form was at the time of the eruption by no means an ancient building.   While finished and no doubt in use at the time of the earthquake of 63, it had been built not many years before, in the reign of Claudius or of Nero, in the place of an older structure which dated from the pre-Roman period.   The earlier Macellum, of which scanty but indubitable traces remain, could not have contained a chapel for the worship of the emperors ; this was probably introduced into the plan of the structure at the time of the rebuilding.   The most reasonable supposition is that the chapel was built in honor of Claudius, and that his statue with the globe as a symbol of world sovereignty stood on the pedestal at the rear, while in the niches at the left were his wife Agrippina and adopted son Nero.

We can hardly doubt that Claudius was worshipped in Pompeii during his lifetime ; it is known from inscriptions that even before the death of Claudius Nero was honored with the services of a special priest.   That Octavia and Marcellus, another mother with a son who was heir to the throne, should be placed opposite Agrippina and Nero, was quite natural. Claudius, who through his mother Antonia was the grandson of Octavia, had great pride in this relationship, through which alone he was connected with the family of Augustus ; and from Octavia, Agrippina and Nero also were descended, the former as a daughter of Germanicus, Claudius's brother, and the latter through his father Gnaeus Domitius, who was a son of the older daughter of Octavia, also called Antonia.   This thought was suggested by the grouping of Octavia and Marcellus with Agrippina and Nero : Octavia's descendants are now on the throne, as Augustus intended that they should be ; and Nero is the pride

and hope of the emperor and the Roman people, as once Marcellus was.

The room at the left of the imperial chapel, with a wide
entrance divided by two columns (6), was also consecrated to
the worship of the emperors. It contains a low altar (shown
on the plan) of peculiar shape. A slab of black stone rests on
two marble steps; it has a raised rim about the edge with a
hole in one corner. Evidently this is an altar for drink offerings;
in this room sacrificial meals were partaken of, at which the
long estrade at the right, like a counter, nearly three feet high,
was perhaps used as a serving table. Such meals had an important place among the functions of the Roman colleges of
priests, and some priesthood connected with the worship of the
emperors apparently had its place of meeting here; but whether
this was the college of the Seviri Augustales, composed of
freedmen, or a more aristocratic priesthood modelled after the
Sodales Augustales at Rome, cannot be determined. The purpose of the niche in the corner, with the platform in front of it
approached by steps, is unknown.

In this room, also, there are two pictures containing Cupids.
In one they are drinking wine and playing the lyre; in the
other they are represented as engaged in acts of worship —
both appropriate decorative subjects for a room intended for
sacrificial banquets.

The Macellum was entered from three sides. At the front,
facing the Forum, was a portico consisting of two orders of
white marble columns, one above the other, supporting a roof.
Fragments of the Ionic or Corinthian columns belonging to the
lower order, and of the well proportioned intermediate entablature, have been preserved. Statues stood at the foot of the
columns, as also at the ends of the party walls between the
shops at the rear of the portico, and beside the two columns
of the little vestibule at the entrance; between the two doors
was a small shrine, and here, too, was a statue.

The difference in direction between the front of the Macellum
and the side of the Forum is concealed by increasing the depth
of the shops from south to north, so that the depth of the
portico remained the same. The room at the extreme right,

being so shallow that it could not be used as a shop, was made
into a shrine; the image or images set up in it must have been
very small.   What divinities were worshipped here, unless the
Street Lares, cannot be conjectured.

There is another entrance on the north side, and a third
near the southeast corner.   In the latter are steps, and at the
left as you come in is a small niche under which two serpents
were painted.   This humble shrine was dedicated to the presiding divinity of the building, the Genius Macelli.

The colonnade of the Macellum was thrown down by the
earthquake of 63.   At the time of the eruption the stylobate
on which the columns rested, and the gutter in front of it, had
been renewed; but only the columns on the north side and a
part of those on the west side had been set up again.   Both
the columns and the entablature have entirely disappeared, in
consequence of excavations made in ancient times.

CHAPTER XIII

THE SANCTUARY OF THE CITY LARES

IN earlier times a street opened into the Forum south of the Macellum. Later, apparently in the time of Augustus, it was closed, and the end, together with adjoining space at the south, was occupied by a building which measures approximately sixty by seventy Roman feet.

In richness of material and architectural detail this was among the finest edifices at Pompeii. Its walls and floors were completely covered with marble. Now we see only rough masonry, stripped of its veneering, but enough vestiges remain to enable us to reconstruct the whole; in Figs. 40 and 41 both rear and side views of the interior are given.

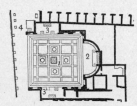

Fig. 39.—Plan of the sanctuary of the City Lares.

1. Main room, unroofed, with an altar in the centre.
2. Apse, with shrine.
3, 3. Recesses — alae.
4. Niche facing the Forum.

Opening into the main room at the rear is a large apse (Fig. 39, 2), which gives to the building a peculiar character. In the inner part of the apse is a broad foundation about six feet high, on which stood a shrine (*aedicula*), containing a pedestal for three statues of not more than life size; the foundation projects in front of the pedestal, forming a table for offerings. A base of the same height as the foundation of the shrine runs along the walls of the apse; it supported two columns and two attached half-columns on the right, and the same number on the left.

On either side of the main room is a recess, *ala*, containing a pedestal for a statue of more than life size. The two entrances were flanked by pilasters nearly two Roman feet square, while each entrance was divided into three parts by two columns. There were three niches about six feet above the floor in each

102

of the side walls of the main room, and two more at the rear;
all were originally flanked by small pilasters which rested on a
projecting base.   The remains of an altar may still be seen in
the middle of the room.

The height of both side and rear walls can be approximately
computed from the existing remains, the basis of computation
for the side walls being the thickness of the pilasters at the
entrance.   The rear part of the building was certainly not less
than 45 feet high, exclusive of the gable, while the sides could

Fig. 40. — Sanctuary of the City Lares, looking toward the rear, restored.

not have been more than 30 or at most 35.   This difference
in height, taken with other indications, obliges us to conclude
that the central room was treated as a paved court open to the
sky; only the apse and the wings were roofed.

It is evident that we have here a place of worship, yet not,
properly speaking, a temple.   The shrine in the apse, with its
broad pedestal for several relatively small images, presents a
striking analogy to the shrines of the Lares found in so many
private houses.   Cities, as well as households, had their guardian spirits.   The worship of these tutelary divinities was reorganized by Augustus, who ordered that, just as the Genius of

the master of the house was worshipped at the family shrine,
so his Genius should receive honor together with the Lares
of the different cities; thus in each city the emperor was to
be looked upon as a father, the head of the common household.   As the house had its shrine for the Lares, so also had
the city; that in Rome was near the spot on which the arch
of Titus was afterwards erected.

Undoubtedly we should recognize in this edifice the sanctuary
of the Lares of the city, *Lararium publicum*.   On the pedestal

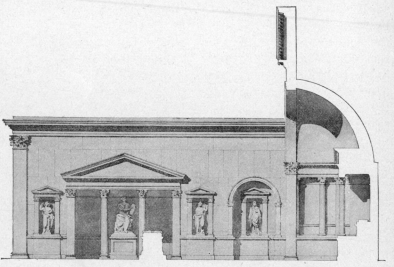

Fig. 41. — North side of the sanctuary of the City Lares, restored.

of the shrine in the apse the Genius of Augustus probably
stood, represented by a statue of the emperor himself, with his
toga drawn over the back of his head, offering a libation; on
his right and on his left were the two Lares, like those represented in paintings (p. 228) and in the little bronze images so
often found in house shrines.

In connection with the Lares the members of a family honored other gods, Penates, to whose special protection the head
of the household had committed himself and his interests.   As
we shall see later, in house shrines diminutive bronze figures
representing Hercules, Mercury, Fortuna, and other divinities

are often found together with those of the Lares. It is quite
possible that other gods were likewise associated with the Lares
of the city ; and perhaps here in the two chapels at the sides of
the main room images of Ceres and of Venus Pompeiana were
placed.   Regarding the statues that stood in the eight niches it
is better to refrain from conjecture.   On the outside of the
building, facing the Forum, was still another niche (4), the
raised floor of which was reached by steps.

At the edge of the Forum in front of the building are eight
square blocks of basalt, which still have traces of the iron clamps
by which marble veneering was fastened on.   These supported
the columns of a portico which was joined with the porticos of
the Macellum and the temple of Vespasian and took the place
of the Forum colonnade.   As the main room of the building was
open to the sky, the portico also must have been without a roof ;
there is no trace of any support for the ends of the rafters at the
rear.   The columns in front, probably of two orders one above
the other, were merely for ornament.   Possibly awnings were
at times stretched over the area of the portico as a protection
against sun and rain.

CHAPTER XIV

THE TEMPLE OF VESPASIAN

SOUTH of the sanctuary of the City Lares is another religious edifice of an entirely different character. Passing from the Forum across the open space once occupied by the portico — of which no remains have been found — we enter a wide doorway and find ourselves in a four-sided court somewhat irregular in shape (Fig. 42). The front part is occupied by a colonnade (1).

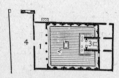

Fig. 42. — Plan of the temple of Vespasian.

1. Colonnade.
2. Altar.
3. Temple.
4. Portico, forming part of the colonnade of the Forum.

At the rear a small temple (3) stands upon a high podium which projects in front of the cella and is reached by two flights of steps. The pedestal for the image of the divinity is built against the rear wall.

In the middle of the court is an altar faced with marble and adorned on all four sides with reliefs of moderately good workmanship. The sacrificial scene shown in the accompanying illustration (Fig. 43) is on the front side, facing the entrance to the court. A priest with a toga drawn over his head in the manner prescribed for those offering sacrifice, pours a libation from a shallow bowl, *patera*, upon an altar having the form of a tripod. With him at the left are two lictors with their bundles of rods, a fluteplayer, two boys, *camilli*, carrying the utensils for the sacrifice, and an attendant; at the right a bull intended for sacrifice is being brought to the altar by the slayer, *victimarius*, and an assistant. In the background is a tetrastyle temple, doubtless the temple before us; the scene represents the dedicatory exercises. The middle intercolumniation of the portico, as indicated by the relief and shown in the plan, is wider than the other two.

On the sides of the altar some of the utensils and ceremonial objects used in sacrificing are represented: at the left the napkin (*mantele*), the augural staff (*lituus*), and the box in which the incense was kept (*acerra*); at the right the libation bowl (*patera*), a ladle (*simpulum*), and a pitcher.

The reliefs on the back of the altar, which consist simply of a wreath of oak leaves with a conventional laurel on either side, are of special significance and give a clew to the purpose of the

Fig. 43.— Front of the altar in the court of the temple of Vespasian.

edifice.   On the thirteenth of January, 27 B.C., the Senate voted that a civic crown — that is, one made of oak leaves, of the kind awarded to a soldier who had saved the life of a Roman citizen — should be placed above the door of the house in which Augustus lived, and that the doorposts should be wreathed with laurel.   From that time the civic crown and the laurel were recognized as attributes denoting imperial rank.   This temple, therefore, was built in honor of an emperor.   From the inscriptions of the Arval Brethren, we learn that in the case of a living em-

peror a bull was the suitable victim, but that an ox was sacrificed to an emperor who had been deified after death.   As the
victim on our altar is a bull, the temple must have been dedicated to an emperor during his lifetime.   With these facts in
mind it will not be difficult to ascertain to whose worship the
building was consecrated.

The coins of Augustus have both the civic crown and the
laurel, but those of his immediate successors have only the
former.   In the year 74 the laurel again appears with the crown
on the coins of Vespasian and Titus, and we may suppose that
the distinction formerly conferred on Augustus was about this

Fig. 44. — View of the temple of Vespasian.

time revived in honor of Vespasian.   It was indeed quite natural
that men should think of Vespasian and Augustus together.
Both restored peace and order after disastrous civil wars ; both
adopted severe repressive measures against luxury and immoral-
ity, and both adorned Rome with great public buildings.   The
temple of Jupiter on the Capitoline, which Augustus had repaired and made more magnificent, Vespasian rebuilt from the
foundation after it was burned in 69.

The Senate, which had suffered so seriously at the hands of

ing with the colonnade, and a third at the rear, entered from
the end of a passage leading up from Abbondanza Street (14),
the grade of which at this point is considerably below the pavement of the building (Fig. 48).

An inscription appears in large letters on the entablature of
the portico, and again on a marble tablet over the side entrance
in Abbondanza Street: *Eumachia L. f., sacerd[os] publ[ica],
nomine suo et M. Numistri Frontonis fili chalcidicum, cryptam,
porticus Concordiae Augustae Pietati sua pequnia fecit eademque
dedicavit,* — ' Eumachia, daughter of Lucius Eumachius, a city
priestess, in her own name and that of her son, Marcus Numis-
trius Fronto, built at her own expense the portico, the corridor
(*cryptam*, covered passage), and the colonnade, dedicating them
to Concordia Augusta and Pietas.'

The word *pietas*, in such connections, has no English equivalent, and is difficult to translate. It sums up in a single concept
the qualities of filial affection, conscientious devotion, and obedience to duty which in the Roman view characterized the
proper conduct of children toward their parents and grand-
parents. Here mother and son united in dedicating the building to personifications, or deifications, of the perfect harmony
and the regard for elders that prevailed in the imperial family.

The reference of the dedication can only be to the relation
between the Emperor Tiberius and his mother Livia; it cannot
apply to Nero and Agrippina, for the reason that the walls of
the building were decorated in the third Pompeian style, which
in Nero's time was no longer in vogue. In 22 A.D., when Livia
was very ill, the Senate voted to erect an altar to Pietas
Augusta. In the following year Drusus, the son of Tiberius,
gave expression to his regard for his grandmother by placing
her likeness upon his coins, with the word Pietas.

On the coins of colonies also — of Saragossa and another the
name of which is not known — the Pietas Augusta appears, apparently about the same time. Not long afterwards the harmonious relations between Tiberius and his mother gave place
to mutual suspicion and hostility; the dedication therefore
points to the earlier part of the reign of Tiberius, and in this
period the building was no doubt erected. The statue of

Concordia Augusta, a female figure with a gilded cornucopia, was found in the building; the head, which has not been preserved, probably bore the features of Livia. By this dedication the building of Eumachia, as the Macellum later, was placed under the protection of the imperial house.

While the parts are enumerated in the dedicatory inscription, neither the name of the building as a whole, nor the purpose, is mentioned. A hint of the latter, however, is found in another inscription. A broad niche (13) opens into the corridor at the rear, directly behind the largest apse. Here stood a marble statue of a beautiful woman (chap. 52), now replaced by a cast; the original is in Naples. Upon the pedestal we read: *Eumachiae L. f., sacerd* [*oti*] *publ* [*icae*], *fullones*, — 'Dedicated to Eumachia, daughter of Lucius Eumachius, a city priestess, by the fullers.'

This building, in which the fullers had set up, in a specially prominent place, a statue of the person who had erected it, must in some way have served the purposes of their trade. Clearly enough it was not a fullery; on the other hand, it was well adapted for a clothier's exchange, a bazaar for the sale of cloth and articles of clothing. Tables and other furniture for the convenience of dealers could be placed in the colonnade and the corridor; in the corridor, especially, goods exposed for sale in front of the open windows could be conveniently inspected by prospective buyers, — not only by those in the corridor itself, but also by those looking in from the colonnade. The small doors between the corridor and the colonnade could be securely closed, and the entrance from Abbondanza Street could be easily guarded; there was only a narrow door at the end of the passage opening into the corridor, and at the street entrance was a porter's room connected by doors both with the passage and with the street. This evidence of unusual precaution suggests that possibly the side entrance, from its close connection with the corridor, was intended especially for the conveyance of goods to and from the building, in order that the front entrance might be left for the exclusive use of purchasers and dealers.

On the assumption that the building was a cloth market, it is clear that the colonnade would naturally be open at all times, the corridor only during business hours; after business hours the corridor would be closed for the protection of the goods left there over night. The windows may have been closed with shutters as in the Oriental bazaars. Other peculiarities of arrangement also are cleared up by this explanation, but we cannot present them in detail. It is not possible, however, to make out what the purpose was of certain remains of masonry found on the south side of the court (18) which have now disappeared, or of two rectangular elevations at the rear (17), or, finally, of a large stone in the middle of the court in which a movable iron ring is fastened (15). Our information is so scanty that we are unable to determine in all particulars what the requirements of a fuller's exchange might have been.

At the time of the eruption men were still engaged in rebuilding the parts of the edifice that had suffered in the earthquake of 63. The front wall at the rear of the portico was finished and had received its veneering of marble; as shown by the existing remains, it conformed to the plan of the earlier structure. The columns and entablature of the portico had not yet been set in place; considerable portions of them were found in the area of the Forum. The wall at the rear of the court, with the three apses, had been rebuilt, and the workmen had begun to add the marble covering. The other walls had remained standing at the time of the earthquake; but the colonnade had been thrown down and was now in process of erection. The remains of the colonnade were removed in ancient times, probably soon after the destruction of the city; yet from the parts that remain, both of the old building and of the restorations, we can determine the architectural character with certainty. We give two reconstructions of the interior, one showing the front (Fig. 46), the other the rear (Fig. 47).

The colonnade and the portico were characterized by the same peculiarity of construction: they were in two stories, one above the other, but there was no upper floor corresponding with the intermediate entablature. In the case of the portico this is certain from the treatment of the wall at the rear, the ornamentation of which is carried without interruption high

I

above the level of the entablature. If the appearance of this building alone had been taken into account, it would have been simpler and more effective to place at the front of the portico a single order of large columns the height of which should correspond with that of the façade; but as the colonnade about the Forum was in two stories, the front of the portico was made to conform to it. The columns below were of the Doric, those above of the Ionic, order. The material — false travertine — was the same as that used in the new colonnade of the Forum. Nevertheless, by the skilful handling of details a certain individuality was given to the columns; while in general appearance they harmonized with those about the Forum, the portico as a whole stood out by itself as something distinct and characteristic.

The columns of the portico were left unfluted, as were those of the new Forum colonnade, and were of the same height; but

Fig. 46. — The building of Eumachia: front of the court, restored.

their proportions were more slender, their ornamental forms were slightly different, and they were set closer together. The pains and skill manifested in harmonizing the particular with the general architectural effect reflect much credit upon the Pompeian board of public works. Under the portico at the foot of each column was a statue, facing the front of the building; the pedestals, which still remain, assist in determining the places of the columns, of which only one was found in position. The spaces between the columns could be closed by latticed gates, as may be seen from traces of them remaining in the marble pavement at the south end of the portico; the pavement elsewhere has disappeared.

The wall at the rear of the portico, facing the Forum, was richly ornamented. The broad entrance in the middle (6) is bridged at the top by a lintel. At the ends are two large niches more than four feet above the pavement (5), both reached by flights of steps. Between each of these and the doorway is a large apsidal arched niche (4) extending down to the pavement. Lastly in the projecting portions of the wall are four smaller niches for statues. The whole façade was overlaid with various kinds of colored marbles.

None of the statues have been found, but the inscriptions belonging to the two that stood in the small niches at the left are extant and of special interest; the names of the persons represented, Aeneas and Romulus, are given, together with a short enumeration of their heroic deeds. These statues were evidently copies; the originals formed a part of a famous series in Rome.

Augustus set up in his Forum the statues of renowned Roman generals with inscriptions setting forth their services to the State; in this way, he said, the people might obtain a standard of comparison for himself and his successors. At the beginning of the series were Aeneas, the kings of Alba Longa, and Romulus. Not one of these statues has been preserved, but some of the inscriptions have been found in Rome, while others are known from copies discovered in Arezzo, where without doubt, as at Pompeii, they were set up with copies of the statues — a forcible illustration of the striving of the smaller cities to be like Rome. Two other statues, perhaps representing Julius Caesar and Augustus, stood in the niches at the right corresponding with those of Aeneas and Romulus; it is not probable that the rest of the series in Rome was duplicated here, because the remaining pedestals in the portico were all designed for figures of larger size.

The colonnade about the court was of marble. The front part, as one entered from the portico, was higher than that on the sides and rear (Fig. 46); it must have presented a fine architectural effect. The two series of Corinthian columns, one above the other, reached the height of 30 feet; the wall behind was diversified with niches and completely covered with marble. At the right and at the left one could pass down the sides under the colonnade, or through small doors into the corridor. The walls between the colonnade and the corridor, pierced with large windows, were decorated below with a dado of colored marbles and above with painting upon stucco, in the third style.

The two smaller apsidal niches at the rear were no higher than the colonnade, but the central apse projected above and terminated in a marble pediment (Fig. 47), fragments of which are still to be seen in the building. It was entered through three arched doorways, above which apparently there were windows. The image of Concordia Augusta, with the features of Livia, probably stood on the pedestal at the rear of the apse, while the statues of Tiberius and Drusus may have adorned the niches at the sides.

We can readily see why the colonnade was made so high, and in two stories, when a lower structure would have afforded better protection against sun and rain. Had it been limited to the usual height the corridor behind it would have been too dark; and if instead of a double series of small columns, one above the other, there had been a single series of large columns of the usual proportions, the thickness of the latter would have shut out much light

Fig. 47. — Rear of the court of the building of Eumachia, restored.

and have made the colonnade seem less roomy. The arrangement adopted had the further advantage that it harmonized the aspect of the colonnade with that of the portico, the character of which, as we have seen, was determined by that of the colonnade about the Forum.

The small rooms of irregular shape at the sides of the apse (11) were light courts, left open to the sky in order to furnish light to the corridor at the rear, which was shut off from the colonnade.

The corridor was about fourteen feet in height; its walls still have remains of decoration in the third style.

At the right of the broad niche (13), in which the statue of Eumachia was found, a door opened into the passage leading from Abbondanza Street; in the corresponding position at the left, where there was no entrance, a door was painted upon the wall. This is a folding door in three parts, of a kind quite common at Pompeii; the middle part is hung by means of hinges, like those on doors of the present day, fastened to one of the leaves at the sides, while these are represented as swinging on pivots at the top and the bottom.

A stairway at the southeast corner of the corridor, over the

Fig. 48. — Fountain of Concordia Augusta.
In the background, steps in the side entrance of the Eumachia building.

entrance from Abbondanza Street, led to an upper room. A similar stairway was placed in the last of the little rooms between the court and the portico, at the left of the front entrance. The upper rooms, difficult to reach, could hardly have been intended for salesrooms. They must have been low, probably no higher than the difference between the height of the colonnade and that of the corridor. They were most likely used as temporary storerooms for the goods of the dealers.

In front of the entrance from Abbondanza Street, is a fountain of the ordinary Pompeian form; as the material is travertine it is probably of later date than the other fountains, which are generally of basalt. As may be seen in our illustration

(Fig. 48), the inlet pipe was carried by a broad standard projecting above the edge of the basin, on the front of which a
bust of a female figure with a cornucopia is carved in relief.
The right side of the face has been worn away by eager drinkers pressing their mouths against the mouth of the figure,
whence the jet issued ; it reminds one of the attenuated right
foot of the famous bronze St. Peter in Rome.   Hands also have
worn deep, polished hollows in the stone on either side of the
standard.   The figure represents Concordia Augusta, but the
name Abundantia, given to it when first discovered, still lingers
in the Italian name for the street, which might more appropri-
ately have been called Strada della Concordia.

CHAPTER XVI

THE COMITIUM

THE last building on the east side of the Forum, south of Abbondanza Street, had undergone a complete transformation a short time before the destruction of the city. Before the rebuilding, a row of pillars separated the interior of the structure from the Forum and from the street. At the edge of the sidewalk along the latter are square holes opposite the pillars (shown on the plan, Fig. 49), evidently designed for the insertion of posts, so that a temporary barrier of some sort could be set up. The end of the space within the barrier where this came to the Forum, and of the rest of the street as well, could be shut off by latticed gates.

Fig. 49. — Plan of the Comitium.

1. Recess opening on the main room.
2. Recess opening on the Forum.

These arrangements suggest that the purpose of the building contemplated the presence of a moving crowd, which could pass from Abbondanza Street through the building into the Forum, or from the Forum in like manner to Abbondanza Street. After the rebuilding only two entrances from the Forum were left, and one from Abbondanza Street.

It is altogether unlikely that so large a building, of irregular shape and with pillars on two sides, was provided with a roof; we have here an open space rather, serving as an extension of the Forum. The walls were covered with marble and adorned with niches, in which, without doubt, statues were placed. On the south side is a large recess the floor of which, reached by a flight of steps, forms a kind of platform or tribune about four feet above the pavement of the enclosure (1). A small door at the right leads into a narrow room containing a similar platform opening on the colonnade of the Forum (2), and to all appearances once accessible from it by steps; afterwards both the steps and the tribune were walled up.

The purpose of these tribunes, and of the building as a whole, is far from clear. An analogy, however, suggests itself. On one side of the Roman Forum near the upper end was a small rectangular open space called the Comitium, used in early times as a voting place. Between the Forum and the Comitium was originally a speaker's platform, the Rostra, so placed that orators by turning toward one side could address an audience in the Comitium and facing about could harangue the Forum. Though the later changes have obscured the original form of our building, yet it is plain that at one time there must have been two connected tribunes, one facing the Forum, the other the enclosed open space; we may at least hazard the conjecture that the colonists of Sulla, taking the arrangements of the Capitol as their pattern in all things, designed this place as their Comitium.

The enclosure was too small to admit of its use for voting according to the ancient fashion, but general elections in the Comitium had long been a thing of the past; only the unimportant curiate elections were held there, at which each curia was represented by a lictor, and at other times the place was used for judicial proceedings. So our building was probably used, if not for elections, for formalities preliminary to the elections and for business connected with the courts.

CHAPTER XVII

THE MUNICIPAL BUILDINGS

At the south end of the Forum were three buildings similar in plan and closely connected. In front they presented a common façade, the narrow spaces between them being entered by low doors. The building at the right (Fig. 50, 3) was at the corner of the Forum, while the space separating the other two lay on a line dividing the Forum into two equal parts; east of the last building is the Strada delle Scuole.

The three buildings were erected after the earthquake of 63, on the site of older buildings of the same character. In the walls of that furthest east (1), considerable remains of the earlier walls are embodied; in that near the corner the original pavement is preserved, and in the middle building there are traces of the original pavement. Previous to this rebuilding the inner series of columns belonging to the colonnade about the Forum had in part been removed and a barrier set up, by which the space in front of the middle building and that at the left could be shut off (indicated

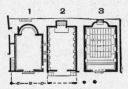

Fig. 50. — Plan of the Municipal Buildings.

1. Office of the duumvirs.
2. Hall of the city council.
3. Office of the aediles.

on the plan by broken lines). At the time of the eruption only the building at the left (1) was entirely finished. The others still lacked their decoration on both inner and outer walls.

These three spacious halls must have served the purposes of the city administration. The two at the right and the left are alike in having at the end opposite the entrance an apse large enough to accommodate one or more magistrates with their attendants; they were the official quarters of the aediles and the duumvirs, while the middle hall was the council chamber, *curia*, where the decurions met.

The middle room was obviously intended to be the most richly ornamented of the three, and was further distinguished from the others by the elevation of its floor, which was more than two feet above the pavement of the colonnade. In front of the entrance is a platform reached at either end by an approach hardly wide enough for two persons, thus suited for a select rather than a large attendance.

Along the sides within runs a ledge a little more than five feet above the floor, on which rested a double series of columns, one above the other, serving both as ornament and as a support for a flat roof like that on the temple of Jupiter.

Fig. 51. — View of the south end of the Forum.

In the background, the ruins of the municipal buildings; in front of these, the remains of the colonnade. In the middle ground the pedestals of the statues of the imperial family.

If we picture to ourselves the columns in place, the walls covered with marble, and a rich coffered ceiling above, we are led to form a favorable idea of the recuperative powers of the city which set about the construction of such costly and splendid buildings so soon after the terrible earthquake.

The recess at the rear was designed for a large shrine patterned after the small shrines of the Lares and Penates in private houses. The Penates of the city were above all the emperor and his family. If this shrine had been finished, figures representing Vespasian, Titus, and Domitian would probably have been placed in it, facing the three Capitoline divinities in the temple of Jupiter at the other end of the Forum.

The office of the aediles, situated at the corner of the colonnade and close to the Basilica, and with no barrier to prevent ready access, was particularly convenient for magistrates who, among other duties, were charged with the maintenance of order and the enforcement of regulations in the markets. One or perhaps both aediles sat in the apse; while the rear and middle parts of the room were reserved for those who had business with them. The front part, lower than the rest by two steps (shown on the plan), may have served as a waiting room. At the rear of the apse and in the walls at the sides were niches for the statues of members of the imperial family and of those who had rendered important services to the city.

As the duumvirs not only sat as judges but also had in their hands the financial administration of the city, we can see why the hall set aside for their use was the first to be rebuilt after the earthquake. The magistrates, of course, sat in the apse, along the wall of which was a ledge for statues. The strong front doors were fastened with iron bolts, and there was also a latticed gate on the step in front of the threshold; probably the archives of the duumviral office were kept within. The small side door at the right made it possible to enter and leave the building after business hours or at other times when the large doors were closed.

CHAPTER XVIII

THE TEMPLE OF FORTUNA AUGUSTA

PASSING out from the Forum under the arch at the northeast corner, we enter the broadest street in Pompeii. On the right a colonnade over the sidewalk runs along the front of the

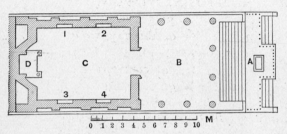

Fig. 52. — Plan of the temple of Fortuna Augusta.

A. Altar.   C. Cella.
B. Portico.   D. Shrine for the statue of the divinity.
1-4. Niches for statues.

first block, at the further corner of which, where Forum Street opens into Nola Street, stands the small temple of Fortuna Augusta. The front of the temple is in a line with the colonnade, which seems to have been designed as a continuation of the colonnade about the Forum; the builders apparently wished to have it appear that the temple was located on an extension of the Forum rather than on a street. The colonnade is certainly not older than the earlier years of the Empire, and the temple dates from the time of Augustus.

The divinity of the temple and the name of its builder are both known to us from an inscription on the architrave of the shrine at the rear of the cella: *M. Tullius M. f., d. v. i. d. ter., quinq[uennalis], augur, tr[ibunus] mil[itum] a pop[ulo], aedem Fortunae August[ae] solo et peq[unia] sua,* — 'Marcus Tullius the son of Marcus, duumvir with judiciary authority for the third time, quinquennial duumvir, augur, and military tribune by the choice of the people, (erected this) temple to Fortuna Augusta on his own ground and at his own expense.'

124

Such inscriptions were ordinarily placed on the entablature of the portico. The portico of this temple, however, had been thrown down by the earthquake of 63, and had not yet been rebuilt. The cella may have been damaged also, but in order that the worship might not be interrupted the shrine was restored; the inscription was temporarily placed over it.

The remains of the walls, columns, and entablature make it possible to reconstruct the edifice with certainty (Fig. 53). The

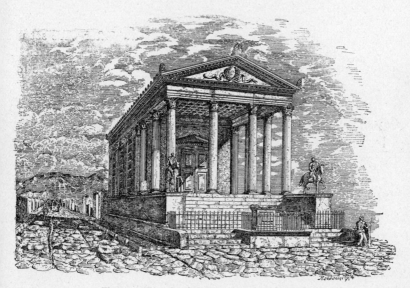

Fig. 53.— Temple of Fortuna Augusta, restored.

plan (Fig. 52) in several respects closely resembles that of the temple of Jupiter, from which the architect copied the projecting platform in front of the podium, with its altar and double series of steps. The eight columns sustaining the portico had Corinthian capitals. The walls of the cella were veneered with marble. In the shrine at the rear stood, without doubt, the image of Fortuna as guardian of the fortunes of Augustus and protectress of the imperial family (Fig. 54).

There were also in the walls of the cella four niches for statues, of which two have been found. The face of one, a female figure, had been sawed off in order to replace it with

another, which has not come to light; the features of the other
statue were said in the reports of the excavations to resemble
those of Cicero, but the resemblance is purely fanciful, suggested by the name Marcus Tullius in the dedicatory inscription. Both statues
were of persons con-
nected with the priest-
hood, not of members
of the imperial family.
Probably statues of
the latter were set up
elsewhere, so that the
cella was left free for
less important person-
ages.

Fig. 54.— Rear of the cella in the temple of Fortuna Augusta, with the statue of the goddess, restored.

The worship of
Fortuna Augusta was
in charge of a college
of priests, consisting
of four slaves and
freedmen, who were
called *Ministri For-
tunae Augustae*, —
'Servants of Fortuna
Augusta.' Our infor-
mation in regard to them is derived from five inscriptions, of
which two were found in the temple, the others in different
places; but none of them where they originally belonged.
These all relate to the small statues, *signa*, of which one was
set up by the college every year. One inscription, of the year
3 B.C., speaks of the 'first servants (*ministri primi*) of Fortuna
Augusta.' The priesthood was therefore established in that year,
and the temple was probably built only a short time before.

In donating the land for the temple Tullius retained the
ownership of a narrow strip of irregular shape at the right.
Here a rough block of basalt was set up with the inscription:
M. Tulli M. f. area privata, — 'Private property belonging to
Marcus Tullius, son of Marcus.'

KEY TO PLAN III

A. PORTICO AT THE ENTRANCE OF THE FORUM TRIANGULARE.

B. FORUM TRIANGULARE.
1, 1. Colonnade.
2. Promenade.
3. Doric temple.
4. Semicircular bench, with sundial.
5. Sepulchral enclosure.
6. Altars.
7. Well house.
8. Pedestal of the statue of Marcellus.

C. OPEN-AIR GYMNASIUM — PALAESTRA.
1. Colonnade.
2. Pedestal with steps behind it.
3, 3. Dressing rooms.

D. TANK FOR SAFFRON WATER.

E. LARGE THEATRE.
1. Dressing room.
2. Stage.
3. Orchestra.
4. Ima cavea.
5. Media cavea.
6. Summa cavea, over a corridor.
7, 7. Tribunals.

F. SMALL THEATRE.
1. Dressing room.
2. Stage.
3, 3. Tribunalia.

G. THEATRE COLONNADE, USED AS BARRACKS FOR GLADIATORS.
1. Passage leading from Stabian Street.
2. Entrance.
3. Doorkeeper's room.
4. Passage to the Large Theatre, walled up.
5. Stairway leading down from the Forum Triangulare.
6. Athletes' waiting room — Exedra.
7. Room with remains of weapons and cloth.
8. Guard room.
9. Stairs leading to overseer's rooms.
10. Kitchen.
11. Mess room.

H. TEMPLE OF ZEUS MILICHIUS.
1. Colonnade.
2. Altar.
3. Cella.
4. Sacristan's room.

I. TEMPLE OF ISIS.
1. Colonnade.
2. Cella.
3. Shrine of Harpocrates.
4. Purgatorium.
5. Hall of initiation.
6. Hall of the Mysteries.
7. Priest's residence.

K. CITY WALL.   L. FOUNDATIONS OF STEPS.

CHAPTER XIX

*GENERAL VIEW OF THE PUBLIC BUILDINGS NEAR THE
STABIAN GATE—THE FORUM TRIANGULARE AND THE
DORIC TEMPLE*

THE end of the old lava stream on which Pompeii lay runs
off into two points; in the depression between them, as we
have seen, was the Stabian Gate. On the edge of the spur at
the left a temple of the Doric style was built in very early
times. The descent here, toward the southwest, is so sharp
and the height so great that it was not necessary to add a
wall at the top as a means of defence.

The sides of the temple followed in general the direction of
the edge of the cliff. Raised upon a high foundation, it not
only dominated the plain below but was visible also from the
greater part of the city; glistening in the sun, it became a
landmark for mariners far out at sea, who from a distance
could offer greetings to the gods there enshrined.

In the second century B.C. the northwest corner of the
depression back of the Stabian Gate was selected as the site
for a large theatre (E on Plan III); previously, we may suppose, temporary wooden structures had answered the purpose.
This location was chosen, in accordance with the Greek custom,
because the places for the greater part of the seats for the
spectators could be easily cut in the natural slope, which here
had the shape of half a shallow saucer; a superstructure was
necessary only for the upper rows of seats. The architect, if
not a Greek, was certainly of Greek training.

South of the theatre an extensive colonnade (G) was erected.
It was intended as a shelter for theatre-goers, but was afterwards
turned into barracks for gladiators.

With a similar purpose, a colonnade of the Doric order
was built along two sides of the triangular level space about

the Greek temple (1). In front of the north end, where the
two arms of the colonnade meet, a high portico of the Ionic
order was erected (A) facing the street, thus forming a monumental entrance to the Theatre. The southwest side of
the area was left unobstructed, and the place, by reason of
its shape, is called the Forum Triangulare, 'Three-cornered
Forum.'

In connection with the building of the Theatre land had been
expropriated and cleared as far north as the first east and west
street. Here, near the entrance of the Forum Triangulare, a
Palaestra for gymnastic exercises (C) was built, with funds left
for public purposes by a benevolent citizen. Later, probably
not before the time of the Roman colony, a temple of Isis (I)
was erected, adjoining the Theatre on the northeast.

Early in the Roman Period, not long after 80 B.C., a small
roofed theatre (F) was constructed east of the stage of the
Large Theatre and of the area at the rear.

Stabian Street north and south of the Small Theatre was
lined with private houses. At the northeast corner of the block
was a temple of Zeus Milichius (H), seemingly of early date,
but entirely rebuilt about the time that the Small Theatre was
erected.

Part of the columns and entablature belonging to the beautiful portico at the entrance of the Forum Triangulare have
been set up again and are seen in our illustration (Fig. 55).
The brackets projecting from the rear wall were probably
designed for statuettes or vases. When the wall was rebuilt,
after the earthquake of 63, a change was made in at least one
particular. The small doorway at the middle, now at right
angles with the wall, formerly passed obliquely through it,
opening toward the end of the promenade which was laid out
in front of the colonnade at the left. This promenade (2 on
Plan III) was separated from the area of the Forum by a low
wall ; on sunny winter days it must have been the most frequented walk in the city.

Besides the small doorway, which was closed by a latticed
gate hung from a wooden jamb, there was at the left a massive

POMPEI·ANTIQVI·
TEMPLVM·GRAECVM·
FORMA·TRIANGVLARE·
CEPTVM

double door with strong bolts, inside of which was still a second
door. It seems odd that one entrance should be so securely
closed, while the fastenings of the other were so light. Ordinarily, the large doors must have been kept shut, while the
small entrance was left open for everyday use; but when there
was to be a play in the Theatre, and the magistrate who gave
the entertainment proceeded from the Forum with a retinue in
festal attire, then the great doors were swung back in honor of

Fig. 55. — Portico at the entrance of the Forum Triangulare.

the occasion, and the opening of them formed part of an impressive ceremony.

The colonnade within contained ninety-five Doric columns.
It was only one story in height, and the columns for this reason
are more slender than those of the same order in the Forum.
The entablature varies from the Doric type only in respect to
the architrave, which consists of two bands. The continuation
of the colonnade along the southwest side was prevented by
the nearness of the temple to the edge of the cliff. Here
the magnificent view over the plain to the mountains and
across the Bay was unimpeded; for the enjoyment of it, two
duumvirs in the early years of the Empire built near the west

K

corner of the temple a semicircular stone seat, *schola* (4 on Plan III), like those found in connection with tombs. On the back they placed a sundial with the inscription: *L. Sepunius L. f. Sandilianus, M. Herennius A. f. Epidianus duo vir*[*i*] *i. d. sco*[*lam*] *et horol*[*ogium*] *d. s. p. f. c.* (for *de sua pecunia faciundum curarunt*), — 'Lucius Sepunius Sandilianus the son of Lucius, and Marcus Herennius Epidianus the son of Aulus, duumvirs with judiciary authority, caused the seat and the sun-

Fig. 56. — View of the Forum Triangulare, looking toward Vesuvius.
At the left, remains of the Doric temple and of the altars and well house in front of it; at the right, exterior of the large theatre.

dial to be made at their own expense.' The same duumvirs, as we have seen, set up a sundial in the court of the temple of Apollo.

At the foot of the middle column at the north end of the colonnade stood a marble basin, of which only the finely proportioned, fluted standard remains; a jet of water fell into it from the end of a pipe which passed through the column above. A little further forward is a pedestal (8) veneered with marble on which is the inscription: *M. Claudio C. f. Marcello patrono*, — 'To Marcus Claudius Marcellus, the son of Gaius, patron.' Here stood a statue of Marcellus, the nephew of Augustus, a portrait statue of whom we have already found in the imperial chapel of the Macellum. The reason why he was honored with more than one statue is clear from the inscription before us : he was patron of the colony.

The surface of the Forum Triangulare was considerably higher than the top of the city wall (K) south of the barracks of the Gladiators. It seems likely that a flight of steps led down to the wall between the barracks and the long colonnade, as seen in Weichardt's restoration (Plate III). This explanation accounts for the existence of certain remains of walls (L on the plan), the purpose of which is otherwise obscure.

Of the ancient Doric temple but little remains : only the foundation, which was high for a Greek temple, with a flight of steps in front ; two stumps of columns and traces of a third ; four capitals, and portions of the right wall of the cella. The plan of the cella, however, has been traced by means of excavations.

The foundation, unlike the podiums of the other temples at Pompeii, was built up in a series of broad, high steps. The number of the columns, eleven on the sides and seven in front, as in the temple of Zeus at Agrigentum, has been calculated from the distances between the stumps. Of those in front two were opposite the corners of the cella, where the edges of the flight of steps come to the stylobate (Fig. 57). Only a narrow space was needed between the walls of the cella and the surrounding columns, but in order to make the outward appearance more imposing the columns were set as far out as they would

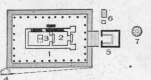

Fig. 57.—Plan of the Doric temple in the Forum Triangulare.

1. Colonnade.
2. Outer chamber of cella.
3. Inner chamber of cella.
4. Semicircular bench, with sundial.
5. Sepulchral enclosure.
6. Altars.
7. Well house.

have been if a second series had been placed within, between them and the cella ; according to the classification of Vitruvius the temple was a pseudodipteral. On account of the interval thus afforded between the entrance of the cella and the columns in front (a little over sixteen feet), it was thought proper to leave the number of columns uneven, so that one stood over against the middle of the doorway.

The temple was of mixed construction, part stone and part wood. The entablature must have been of stone, otherwise the intercolumniations would not have been so narrow. The space between the entablature and the cella, however, could only have been bridged by means of timbers. The stone used was the gray tufa, but the capitals were of the more durable Sarno limestone. The surface was coated with stucco, which in part at least was painted in bright colors. The projecting edge of the eaves trough, also covered with stucco, was painted red, yellow, and black, and ornamented with waterspouts in the shape of lions' heads alternating with rosettes.

The proportions of the columns (lower diameter 6.07 feet, upper diameter 3.12 feet) with their flaring capitals, and the

Fig. 58. — The Doric temple, restored.

narrow intercolumniations (Fig. 58), point to an early period; the archaic character of the capitals will be more fully appreciated if they are compared with those of the colonnade of the Forum Triangulare. In respect to age this temple ranks with the oldest of those at Selinunto; it must have been built in the sixth century B.C.

The cella, as our plan shows, was divided into two chambers. In the inner chamber (3) a large rectangular flag is embedded in the floor at one side so that a second (indicated on the plan by dotted lines) must have been near it; the supports of a stone table in front of the image of the divinity perhaps rested on them. On the long pedestal at the right of the cella stood a deer of terra cotta, above life size, of which some fragments have been found.

Directly in front of the temple, at the foot of the steps, we find a monument of an altogether unusual character. The respect with which it was regarded is evidenced by its location in the place ordinarily occupied by the principal altar. It consists of a small enclosure of peculiar shape, fenced in by an outer wall and a low inner wall. To judge from its form, it must have been a place of burial; we shall find a tomb later the plan of which is quite similar (Plan V, right side, 2), and it is said that human bones were found here. These walls are not earlier than the imperial period, but they must have taken the place of an older structure; for the altars were evidently put over near the east corner of the temple (6 on the plan), because the place which they would naturally have had was already occupied. For a time — how long it would be idle to conjecture — this was beyond doubt the most important temple of the city; the placing of the tomb in the most sacred spot in front of it suggests that the founder or founders of the city may have been buried here, and afterwards revered as heroes.

Instead of a single altar in front of the temple there are three, all made of blocks of tufa, two of them resting on a single foundation; the third is built on the ground without a foundation, and is of later date. One altar is larger than the other two, and its surface is divided into three parts.

Not far from the altars are the remains of a small round structure (7 on the plan, shown in Fig. 56) about twelve feet in diameter. The roof, supported by eight Doric columns, was over the mouth of a well, which had been driven down through the old lava bed till living water was found for cleaning the temple and for religious rites. According to the Oscan inscription on the architrave the well house was built by N. Trebius, chief administrative officer (*meddix tuticus*) of the city.

It is impossible to determine what divinities were worshipped here. The placing of two altars together, one being divided into three parts, and the addition of a third, seem to imply that three divinities received worship in common, and that besides these two other gods were honored in this sanctuary. The terra cotta deer furnishes a clew, but is not decisive evidence; deer were sacred to several divinities, among others to Apollo and

Artemis.   A marble torso of about half life size, found on the
declivity south of the temple, has been identified with some
degree of probability as belonging to a statue of Apollo.   Perhaps originally Apollo and Artemis were honored here, and
with them Leto ; but in an Oscan inscription discovered in 1897
the temple seems to be designated as belonging to Minerva
(p. 234).

At the time of the eruption the temple was in ruins.   It may
have been in this condition only since the earthquake of 63, or
for a longer time.   That the worship might not be abandoned a
poor shrine was built among the ruins, smaller than the old
cella and a little further to the right ; a drum of a column, set
up on the flag in the floor of the cella, served as a pedestal for
the image of the divinity.

CHAPTER XX

THE LARGE THEATRE

PERFORMANCES upon the stage were first given in Rome in the year 364 B.C.; a pestilence was raging, and the Romans thought to appease the gods by a new kind of celebration in their honor. The performers were brought from Etruria, and the exercises were limited to dancing, with an accompaniment on the flute. There was as yet no Latin drama. The first regular play was presented more than a century later, in 240 B.C., and the playwright was not a Roman but a Greek from Tarentum, Livius Andronicus, who translated both tragedies and comedies from his native tongue. The next dramatist was a Campanian, Gnaeus Naevius. The building of a theatre was not yet thought of; a temporary wooden platform was erected for the actors, and the spectators spread themselves out on the green slope of a hillside facing it.

When the censor Cassius Longinus in 154 B.C. commenced the erection of a theatre on the Palatine hill near the temple of Cybele, at whose festivals plays were given, the ex-consul Scipio Nasica rose in the Senate and in a speech full of feeling warned the Romans not to countenance this foreign amusement, on the ground that it would sap the foundations of the national character. His words produced so deep an impression that the Senate not only voted to pull down the part of the building already erected, and to refuse permission for the erection of similar buildings in the future, but even prohibited altogether the renting of seats at theatrical representations; Romans who wished to see a play must remain standing during a performance, or sit on the ground. Naturally so stringent measures could not long remain in force. Nine years later Mummius, the destroyer of Corinth, presented dramas in connection with his triumph, and put up wooden seats for the spectators. The first stone theatre in Rome was built by Pompey, the rival of Caesar, in 55 B.C. In Pompeii, on the contrary, a permanent theatre had been erected at least a hundred years earlier.

The Oscan culture was so completely merged in that of Rome that our knowledge of it as an independent development is extremely slight; and no information has come down to us regarding the history of the native drama. From literary sources we know only of a crude form of popular comedy in which, as in the Italian Commedia dell' arte, there were stock characters distinguished by their masks, — Maccus a buffoon, Bucco a voracious, talkative lout, Pappus an old man who is always cheated, and Dossennus a knave. The scene of these exhibitions was always Atella, the Gotham of Campania, whence they were called Atellan farces.

The Theatre at Pompeii, however, is a proof that as early as the second century B.C., in at least one Campanian city, dramatic representations of a high order were given. Here, perhaps, as at Athens, they were associated with the worship of Dionysus; for the satyrs were companions of the Wine-god, and the head of a satyr, carved in tufa, still projects from the keystone of the arch at the outer end of one of the vaulted passages leading to the orchestra. Greek verse, and native verse modelled after the Greek, must have gained a hearing at Pompeii, and the works of Oscan poets — not a line of which has come down to us — must have stirred the hearts of the people long before Livius Andronicus, and Naevius, who brought inspiration from his Campanian home, produced their dramas at Rome.

In describing the Theatre it will be best to take up in order the three main divisions common to Greek and Roman buildings of this class: the *cavea*, the large outer part shaped somewhat like half a funnel, containing seats for spectators; the orchestra, the small semicircular portion enclosed by the cavea, with an entrance, *parodos*, on either side; and the stage, facing the orchestra and the cavea. The accompanying illustrations give a plan (Fig. 59), and a view of the ruins in their present condition (Fig. 60); the exterior as seen from the south is shown in Fig. 56.

The cavea afforded seats for about five thousand persons. The greater part of it, from the orchestra to the vaulted corridor under the summa cavea (Fig. 59, 6), lies on the slope of the hill; the floor of the corridor is on a level with the Forum Triangulare.

The seats are arranged in three semicircular sections. The lowest, *ima cavea* (4), next to the orchestra, contains four broad ledges on which, as well as in the orchestra itself, the members of the city council, the decurions, could place their chairs, the 'seats of double width.'

The middle section, *media cavea* (5), was much deeper, extending from the ima cavea to the vaulted corridor. It contained twenty rows of marble seats arranged like steps, of which only a small portion is preserved. On a part of one of these, individual places, a little less than 16 inches wide, are marked off by vertical lines in front, and numbered; they probably belonged to some corporation which found it necessary, in order to avoid con-

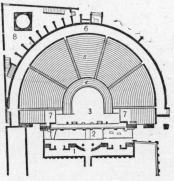

Fig. 59. — Plan of the Large Theatre.
1. Dressing room.   5. Media cavea.
2. Stage.   6. Summa cavea.
3. Orchestra.   7. Tribunalia.
4. Ima cavea.   8. Tank for saffron
                          water.

fusion, to assign places to its members by number. In Rome the fourteen rows nearest the bottom were reserved for the knights. Whether a similar arrangement prevailed in the municipalities and the colonies is not known, but if so the number reserved here must have been smaller.

The upper section, *summa cavea* (6), supported by the vault over the corridor, was too narrow to have contained more than four rows of seats.

The ima cavea was entered from the orchestra. The media cavea could be entered on the lower side from the passage (*diazoma, praecinctio*) between it and the ima cavea, which at the ends was connected by short flights of steps with the parodoi leading outside; on the upper side six doors opened into the media cavea from the corridor, from which flights of

steps descended dividing the seats into five wedgelike blocks,
cunei, with a small oblong block in addition on either side near
the end of the stage.

The corridor was accessible by four doors, one from the
Forum Triangulare, another from the open space between this
and the rounded exterior of the Theatre, a third at the end of
an alley east of the temple of Isis, and a fourth opening from a
steep passage leading up from Stabian Street. The summa
cavea, which for convenience we may call the gallery, was
entered by several doors (the exact number is uncertain) from
a narrow vaulted passage along the outside. This passage,
however, did not extend the whole length of the gallery, but
stopped where the outer wall of the Theatre joined that of the
Forum Triangulare. Here a stairway led to it; there was a
second stairway at the rear of the Palaestra, and a third leading
from the alley east of the temple of Isis; the three are shown
on Plan III. At the edge of the Forum Triangulare, a narrow stairway, built in the thick wall, led directly to the gallery
(Fig. 59).

The outer wall back of the gallery rose to a considerable
height above the last row of seats. On the inside near the top
were projecting blocks of basalt (seen in Fig. 60), containing
round holes in which strong wooden masts were set; from these
the great awning, *velum*, was stretched over the cavea and
orchestra to the roof of the stage, protecting the spectators
from the sun. This sort of covering for the theatre was a
Campanian invention, and here, where the cavea opened toward
the south, was especially necessary. In the Coliseum, and the
well preserved theatre at Orange, the arrangements for fasten-
ing the masts are on the outside of the wall. The upper part
of the wall of our Theatre has been rebuilt in modern times, and
it has been doubted whether the blocks of basalt and the pieces
of cornice above with corresponding incisions are ancient; the
latter surely are not modern, and their slightly wedged shape
shows that from the beginning they must have been on the
inside of the wall.

Near the front of the orchestra at the right and the left were
small rectangular platforms; one is shown in Fig. 60. They

were supported by the vaults over the entrances (7, 7), and
were reached by small stairways near the ends of the stage.
They were called tribunals, and here, as in Rome, were no
doubt reserved for the seats of those to whom special honor
was paid.   One was set aside for the use of the magistrate who
gave the play; in Rome the vestal virgins, in accordance with
a decree of Augustus, occupied the other, and in Pompeii their
place was very likely taken by the city priestesses.

Fig. 60. — View of the Large Theatre.

The shape of the orchestra is that of a semicircle enlarged
in the direction of tangents at right angles with the diameter;
a complete circle could be inscribed in the space.   It was
probably never used for a chorus, but was occupied by the seats
of prominent spectators, particularly the city officials and their
friends.   It was entered by means of the vaulted passages under
the tribunals.

The steps leading from the orchestra upon the stage (Fig. 60)
can be explained only on the supposition that even in the
Roman period, to which the steps in their present form belong,

actors who took the part of persons arriving from distant places
came upon the stage through the orchestra. In the niches in
front of the stage, as we learn from a wall painting, sat those
charged with the maintenance of order in the Theatre, two
perhaps in the rectangular niches, or one in the semicircular
niche in the middle.

The stage is long and narrow, measuring 120 by 24 Oscan
feet; the floor is a little more than three feet above the level
of the orchestra. The rear wall, as in ancient theatres generally, was built to represent the front of a palace, entered by
three doors, and adorned with columns and niches for statues.
In each of the short sections of wall at the ends of the stage is
a broad doorway, extending across almost the entire space.
The long narrow room behind the stage, used as a dressing
room (*postscaenium*), was entered by a door at the rear, which
was reached by an inclined approach. No trace of the roof
of the stage remains, but from the better preserved theatres at
Orange, in the south of France, and at Aspendus, in Asia
Minor, we infer that it sloped back toward the rear wall. The
floor was of wood.

The room underneath the stage was divided into several
parts. Between the front wall and that just back of it
(seen in Fig. 60) was the place for the curtain, which, as in
Roman theatres, was let down at the beginning of the play,
and raised at the end. The space between the parallel walls
must have been covered, leaving only a narrow slit for the curtain; otherwise it would not have been easy to go upon the
stage from the steps in the orchestra.

Underneath the place for the curtain was a low passage, in
the vaulted roof of which were two rows of holes, a little more
than a foot square, cut in blocks of basalt, and evidently
designed to hold upright timbers. This passage has in recent
years been entirely cleared. In the floor, directly under the
openings in the vaulted roof and corresponding with them, were
square holes. In those nearer the front of the stage were
remains of timbers and of square pieces of iron fitted to the
ends of these, a larger and a smaller piece for each hole. It
seems likely that, as Mazois suggested, hollow upright beams

were set in the holes, and in them smaller hollow beams were placed, in which were still smaller poles or iron rods; by the sliding of these up and down, the long horizontal pole on which the curtain was hung could be raised or lowered. The use of the inner row of holes has not been satisfactorily explained.

The room under the right of the stage is so low, about three feet, that it could not have been available for any purpose, but that at the left is higher, and was used for theatrical machinery, the scanty remains of which arouse our curiosity without satisfying it. In the floor are set two oblong blocks of travertine, about four feet in length. Each has in its upper surface a round hole, between two and three inches deep, with an iron socket, in which there are still remains of an iron cap once fitted to the lower end of a vertical wooden shaft that turned in it; the upper end of the shaft — assuming that the blocks are in their original position — must have revolved in a socket fixed in one of the joists of the stage floor. There is besides on the upper surface of each block a rectangular depression, and on either side a shallow incision; the purpose is altogether obscure. A third stone, similar to these two, is set in the side of the wall at the right end of the place for the curtain, and opposite it was fitted another; here, then, a horizontal shaft turned; there is a similar pair of stones in the walls at the other end. These arrangements suggest the crane-like machine by which floating figures were brought upon the stage, as Medea in the play of Euripides riding in a chariot drawn by dragons, and the familiar *deus ex machina;* such machinery, according to Pollux, was placed on the left side of the stage.

When plays were presented, the front of the palace at the back of the stage was concealed by painted scenery. As several pieces might be produced one after the other, it was necessary to arrange for the shifting of scenes. This was accomplished by drawing one set of decorations off to the sides, thus bringing the next set into view (*scaena ductilis*); the ends were changed by turning the *periactae*, huge three-sided prisms, each side of which was suited to a different scene (*scaena versilis*). In spite of the clumsiness of the arrangements, as contrasted with those of the best modern theatres, the mount-

ing of plays was artistic and impressive, and compares favorably
with that of Shakespeare's time.

The only allusions to matters connected with theatrical representations at Pompeii are in inscriptions relating to actors, as
Sorex (p. 170). A number of graffiti scratched on walls in
various parts of the city mention an Actius Anicetus, whose
name is given in full in an inscription found at Puteoli,
C. Ummidius Actius Anicetus. He seems to have been a very
popular actor of pantomime, at the head of a troupe. One of
the inscriptions reads: *Acti, a*[*mor*] *populi, cito redi,* — 'Actius,
darling of the people, come back quickly!'

The theatre in antiquity was by no means reserved for scenic
representations alone. It was a convenient place for bringing the
people together, and was used for public gatherings of the
most varied character. In the theatre at Tarentum the memo-
rable assembly met which heaped insults upon the Roman
ambassadors and precipitated war with Rome. At Pergamos
King Mithridates was to be crowned in the theatre by a descending Victory, but by some mishap the wreath fell to the
floor, an omen of evil. When the Ephesians, stirred up by
Demetrius the silversmith, wished to take measures against
Paul and his companions, "They rushed with one accord into
the theatre." On such occasions we may suppose that the
front of the palace at the rear of the stage served as a background without other decoration. This use of the theatre for
general purposes was a Greek rather than a Roman custom,
but the theatre itself in Italy was an importation from Greece;
and we may suppose that the theatre at Pompeii was on more
than one occasion the scene of notable demonstrations.

Our Theatre, as is evident from the character of the construction, in its original form belonged to the Tufa Period, but
was rebuilt in Roman times. Some particulars in regard to the
rebuilding are given in an inscription: *M. M. Holconii Rufus
et Celer cryptam, tribunalia, theatrum,* — 'Marcus Holconius
Rufus and Marcus Holconius Celer (built) the crypt, the tribunals, and the part designed for spectators,' that is, the vaulted
corridor under the gallery, the platforms over the entrances to
the orchestra, and the cavea.

The two Holconii lived in the time of Augustus. The elder, Rufus, was duumvir for the fourth term in 3--2 B.C. The work on the Theatre was probably done about that time; for soon afterwards, before his fifth duumvirate, a statue in his honor was erected in the Theatre, as we learn from an inscription. Later, in 13–14 A.D., the younger Holconius also, when he had been chosen quinquennial duumvir, was honored with a statue. The masonry of the corridor and of the exterior arches support-ing it, as well as of the tribunals, well agrees with that in vogue in the Augustan Age; we find brick-shaped blocks of tufa and reticulate work. The marble seats in the cavea may be assigned to the same period; in the original structure the benches must have been of tufa. About the same time the present wall at the back of the stage was built, in the place of an older and much simpler façade, but not by the Holconii; if this also had been rebuilt by them, it would have been mentioned in the inscription.

Possibly the tribunals were an addition due to the Hol-conii. The corridor under the gallery, however, must have been built in the place of an earlier corridor, for the piers on the outside rest on foundations similar in character to the oldest parts of the building. As these piers served no other purpose than to sustain the passage opening into the section of seats above the corridor, this must have formed a part of the original plan.

The statues of both the Holconii probably stood in niches in the wall at the back of the stage. Holconius Rufus was further honored with a monument of some sort in the cavea. The lowest seat of the media cavea had at the middle, directly opposite the stage, a double width for a distance of about five feet, gained by removing a portion of the next seat above. Here was an inscription in bronze letters: *M. Holconio M. f. Rufo, II. v. i. d. quinquiens, iter[um] quinq[uennali], trib[uno] mil[itum] a p[opulo], flamini Aug[usti], patr[ono] colo[niae], d[ecurionum] d[ecreto]*, — ' [Dedicated] in accordance with a decree of the city council to Marcus Holconius Rufus the son of Marcus, five times duumvir with judiciary authority, twice quinquennial duumvir, military tribune by the choice of the

people, priest of Augustus, and patron of the colony.' The
object placed here was of bronze, and was made secure by
fastenings set in twelve holes; what it was is altogether uncertain. The ancients had the custom of conferring lasting
honor upon a deserving man after death by placing in the
theatre a seat inscribed with his name. We should be glad to
believe that a 'seat of double width,' *bisellium*, the use of
which was allowed to members of the city council, was placed
here, but the arrangement of the twelve holes is difficult to
reconcile with this explanation.

The architect employed by the Holconii, a freedman, was
not honored with a statue, but his name was transmitted to
posterity in an inscription placed in the outer wall near the
east entrance to the orchestra: *M. Artorius M. l[ibertus]
Primus, architectus,* — 'Marcus Artorius Primus, freedman of
Marcus, architect.'

The plan of the Theatre could not have been taken from a
Roman model; it conforms, as we should have expected, to the
Greek type. In the Roman theatre the orchestra was in the
form of a semicircle, of which the diameter was represented
by the stage. In Greek theatres, on the contrary, the stage
according to Vitruvius was laid out on one side of a square inscribed in the circle of the orchestra; the orchestra, as shown
by existing remains, in most cases was either a complete circle
or was so extended by tangents at the sides that a circle could
be inscribed in it. The latter is the case in our Theatre, of
which the orchestra has essentially the same form as that of
the theatre of Dionysus at Athens.

The stage falls under the limit of height, — five feet, —
allowed by Vitruvius for the stage of the Roman theatre, not
to mention the height of ten to twelve feet specified for that
of the Greek type. The reason assigned for the moderate elevation of the Roman stage is that the orchestra was occupied by the seats of senators, whose view would be obstructed
if more than a moderate elevation should be given to the front
of the stage. The orchestra of our Theatre was apparently
from the beginning intended for the use of spectators, not
for a chorus.

The conclusions reached by Dr. William Doerpfeld in regard to the stage of the Greek theatre, if borne out by the facts, would necessitate a complete abandonment of previous views on the subject. His theory, in brief, is, that not only the chorus but also the actors went through their parts not on the stage but in the orchestra, which had the form of a circle, and that what we are accustomed to consider the front wall of the stage was rather the rear wall of the platform in the orchestra on which the actors and chorus stood, this wall being laid out on a tangent of the circle and having a height of twelve feet, as we may understand from Vitruvius and from the remains of the theatre at Epidaurus.

The main reasons advanced in support of this theory are that the platform currently regarded as the stage, which according to Vitruvius and the existing remains was hardly more than ten feet wide, must have been too narrow to allow free movement on the part of the actors, and that the height above the orchestra was too great to admit of the close relation between the actors and the chorus, of which there is abundant evidence in the extant dramas. According to Dr. Doerpfeld, the stage came into existence in Italy first, and in the Roman period, when there was no longer any chorus; a platform five feet high was built for the actors, extending to the middle of the orchestra, so that this now took the form of a semicircle and could be used for the seats of spectators.

To undertake the examination of Dr. Doerpfeld's theory in detail would not be pertinent here; yet we cannot bring our description of the Theatre at Pompeii to a close without inquiring whether this structure, which is perhaps a century older than the oldest Roman theatre, shows any trace of the arrangement which the theory assumes. We may answer positively that it does not. This theatre was never used without a stage — that previously described, or one essentially like it. For while the façade at the rear of the stage owes its present form to a rebuilding, the entrances at both ends, and the walls of the room behind the stage, belong to the original structure.

On the supposition that this was a Greek theatre, Dr. Doerpfeld's theory would require us to believe that originally

L

the orchestra was on a level with the top of the present stage, and that the broad ledges of the lowest part of the cavea were not yet laid; the orchestra, moreover, must have been so much larger that the rear wall of the stage lay on a tangent of it, while the present entrances at the end of the stage, which belong to the oldest part of the building, were entrances to the orchestra, the parodoi. We are therefore led to the impossible conclusion that the orchestra had two entrances on each side : one opening directly upon the place occupied by the actors, the present stage entrances ; and the other on a lower level further back near the foot of the cavea, the present entrances to the orchestra; for these also were a part of the original structure.

In opposition to Doerpfeld's view Puchstein and Koldewey have recently expressed the opinion that the Theatre was originally of the Greek type described by Vitruvius, with a narrow stage 3 or 4 feet higher than now, and that then the stage was separated from the rest of the structure by unroofed parodoi. The last assumption is clearly incorrect, because the vaulted entrances of the parodoi belong to the oldest parts of the building. The assumption of a higher stage also involves serious difficulties, but they are of too technical a character to be discussed here.

In the open space between the Theatre, the Forum Triangulare, and the Palaestra there is a small reservoir for water (D), square on the outside and round within. It was evidently used for the sprinklings, *sparsiones*, with saffron-colored water, by which on summer days the heat of the Theatre was mollified. That such sprinklings were in vogue in Pompeii is known from announcements of gladiatorial combats, painted on walls, in which they are advertised together with an awning as part of the attraction, — *sparsiones, vela erunt.*

CHAPTER XXI

THE SMALL THEATRE

THE names of the builders of the Small Theatre are known
from an inscription which is found in duplicate in different parts
of the building: *C. Quinctius C. f. Valg[us], M. Porcius M. f.
duovir[i] dec[urionum] de[creto] theatrum tectum fac[iundum]
locar[unt] eidemq[ue] prob[arunt]*, — 'Gaius Quinctius Valgus
the son of Gaius and Marcus Porcius the son of Marcus, duumvirs, in accordance with a decree of the city council let the contract for building the covered theatre, and approved the work.'
Later the same officials, when, after the customary interval, they
had been elected quinquennial duumvirs, built the Amphitheatre
'at their own expense' (p. 206).

When two magistrates set up an inscription in duplicate, ordinarily the name of one appears first in one copy, while that of
the second is put first in the other. In all
four inscriptions, however, two at the Small
Theatre and two at the Amphitheatre, Valgus
has the first place. The reason in the case of
the Amphitheatre is not far to seek: Valgus
was the man of means, who furnished the
money for the building, but allowed his colleague and friend to share in the honor. We
may also believe that, while the Small Theatre was erected 'in accordance with a decree
of the city council,' and hence presumably at

Fig. 61. — Plan of the
Small Theatre.

1. Dressing room.
2. Stage.
3, 3. Tribunals.

public expense, a part of the funds was contributed by Valgus, who
on this account received honor above his less opulent colleague.

The son-in-law of this Valgus, Publius Servilius Rullus, has
been undeservedly immortalized by a speech of Cicero in opposition to a bill brought forward by him in regard to the division
of the public lands. From the same oration we learn that Val-

gus, a man without scruples, had taken advantage of the reign
of terror instituted by Sulla to acquire vast wealth, particularly
in the way of landed property. Among his estates was one in
the country of the Hirpini, near the city of Aeclanum (south of
Beneventum), which made him its patron and for which, as
shown by an inscription, he repaired the walls destroyed in the
Civil War. He was undoubtedly one of the leading men in the
colony founded by Sulla at Pompeii, and very likely sought by

Fig. 62. — View of the Small Theatre.

large public benefactions to cast his former life into oblivion.
The Small Theatre must have been built in the early years of
the Roman colony, not long after 80 B.C.

A covered auditorium in the immediate vicinity of a large
unroofed theatre was not uncommon. About the time of the
destruction of Pompeii the poet Statius, praising the magnifi-
cence of his native city Naples, speaks of ‘twin theatres in a single structure, one open and one roofed,’ — *geminam molem nudi
tectique theatri.* Our only clew to the special use of such a

building, however, is derived from the one erected at Athens by
Herodes Atticus, in the reign of Hadrian. This was called an
Odeum, that is, according to the derivation of the word, a room
for singing; musical entertainments were held there, especially,
we may assume, those musical contests which had so important
a place in ancient festivals. The purpose of the roof was doubtless to add to the acoustic effect.

The plan of the Large Theatre has been discussed at so great
length that a few words will suffice in relation to that of the
smaller structure (Fig. 61). That it might be possible to cover
the enclosed space with a roof, the upper rows of seats were
reduced in length, and the whole building — cavea, orchestra,
and stage — was brought into an oblong shape; only the orchestra and the lower rows of seats in the cavea form a complete
semicircle. The pyramidal roof was supported by a wall on all
four sides; in the upper part of the wall, between the roof and
the highest row of seats, there were probably windows.

The seating capacity of the building was about fifteen hundred.
The lowest section of the cavea, as in the Large Theatre, consisted of four low, broad ledges on which
the chairs of the decurions could be placed.
Above these is a parapet, behind which
is a passage accessible at either end by
semicircular steps. The broad range of
seats above was divided into five wedge-
shaped blocks by flights of steps; only two

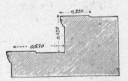

Fig. 63. — Section of a seat
in the Small Theatre.

of these, however, extended as far as the passage running along
the upper side, which could be reached from the alley at the rear
of the building by means of stairways connecting with outside
doors.

The seats were of masonry capped with slabs of tufa about
seven inches thick. They had depressions in the side and in
the top, as may be seen in the accompanying section (Fig. 63).
They were thus made somewhat more comfortable, the person
in front being less subject to disturbance from the feet of one
sitting on the next seat behind; a saving of room was also
effected — an important consideration in the construction of
a small auditorium.

The tribunals (3, 3) differed from those in the Large Theatre in that they were shut off entirely from the seats of the cavea by a sharply inclined wall, and were entered only from the stage,

by means of narrow stairways; in this way the exclusive character of the seats was made still more prominent. Besides the platform itself, measuring only about 8 by 9 feet, three seats above each tribunal were set off with it by the same division wall and were available for the occupants. The sloping wall between the tribunal and the cavea on each side ends with a kneeling Atlas

Fig. 64.— An Atlas. (Fig. 64); large vases probably stood on the two brackets supported by these figures. The end of the parapet on either side is embellished with a lion's foot of tufa (Fig. 65). These rather coarse sculptures illustrate the character of the art that was brought to Pompeii by the Roman colony. The workmanship is by no means fine, yet the muscles of the figures are well rendered, and the effect is pleasing.

The pavement of the orchestra (seen in Fig. 62) consists of small flags of colored marble. An inscription in bronze letters informs us that it was laid by the duumvir Marcus Oculatius Verus *pro ludis*, that is instead of the games which he would otherwise have been expected to provide.

Fig. 65.— Ornament at the ends of the parapet.

At the ends of the stage, as in the case of the Large Theatre, there were two broad entrances. The wall at the rear, which was veneered with marble, had the customary three doors, and in addition two small doors, one near each end. The long dressing room behind the stage had likewise two broad entrances at the ends, besides four at the rear. Apparently the two narrow doors near the ends of the wall at the rear of the stage, and the two doors corresponding with them at the back of the dressing room, were for the use of those who had seats on the tribunals; they could thus enter and leave their places even when the large side doors of both stage and dressing room had been shut —as undoubtedly happened immediately after the procession (*pompa*) had passed across the stage.

CHAPTER XXII

THE THEATRE COLONNADE, USED AS BARRACKS FOR GLADIATORS

'BEHIND the stage,' says Vitruvius, speaking of the arrangements of the theatre, 'colonnades should be built, that shelter may be afforded to spectators in case of rain and a place provided for making preparations for the stage.'

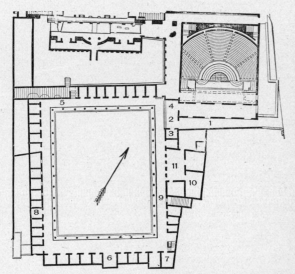

Fig. 66.— Plan of the Theatre Colonnade, showing its relation to the two theatres.

1. Passage leading from Stabian Street.
2. Entrance.
3. Doorkeeper's room.
4. Passage to Large Theatre, walled up.
5. Stairway from the Forum Triangulare.
6. Exedra — athletes' waiting room.
7. Room with remains of costumes.
8. Guard room.
9. Stairway to overseer's rooms.
10. Kitchen.
11. Mess room.

This maxim of ancient architects was applied at Pompeii in a generous way; in connection with the theatres there was an extensive system of colonnades. To understand their use it will be necessary first to view them as they were in the earlier time, and then to take account of later changes.

In the Oscan Period, and afterwards to the end of the Re-

public, when a performance in the Large Theatre was interrupted by a shower, the spectators in the upper seats could
take refuge under the colonnade of the Forum Triangulare;
those below found shelter under the rectangular colonnade
at the rear, which was obviously built for the purpose, and
may be called, by way of distinction, the Theatre Colonnade (Fig. 66). It contained seventy-four Ionic columns,
and enclosed a large open area. The main entrance (2) was
near the northeast corner. The entrance hall on the side of the
colonnade was supported by four Doric columns. It was connected at the north end with a short colonnade on the east side
of the area back of the stage of the Theatre; this led to the
large door at the east end of the stage and the corresponding
parodos of the orchestra; the wall at 4 on our plan is a later
addition. The Theatre Colonnade must have been used also
as a promenade on days when there was no performance; it
was connected by a broad passage (1) with Stabian Street.

This colonnade seems too far away to have served as a place
for making preparations for the stage; another was erected for
that purpose. At the northwest corner a broad stairway leads
down from the Forum Triangulare, from the foot of which you
pass by a small and inconvenient flight of steps into the area
at the rear of the stage. In a line with the stairway is a series
of small rooms opening toward the south. These do not belong
to the original structure. In their place there was once a colonnade, which faced the north and connected the large stairway
with the short colonnade, the remains of which are still to be
seen on the east side of the area; the back of it was at the
same time the back of the north division of the Theatre Colonnade. There was thus a covered passage extending from the
foot of the stairway along two sides of the area to the east
entrance of the stage and of the orchestra, which would answer
very well to the second part of Vitruvius's dictum; but it had
also another important use.

The portico of the Forum Triangulare, as we have seen, was
at the same time the monumental entrance of the Theatre, and
the large doorway at the left was used only for the ceremonious
admission of the city officials, who with their retinue formed a

procession in the Forum and wended their way hither in festal attire in order to open the performance — a formality that may be compared with the parade with which the Roman games were opened at Rome.

The route of such a procession, after entering the Forum Triangulare, is now clear. It passed along under the colonnade adjoining the Theatre, beyond the entrances to the upper portion of the cavea; turned and descended the broad stairway (5), proceeded under the colonnade along the south and east sides of the area behind the stage, and finally came upon the stage through the wide doorway at the east end. It was indeed possible to pass beyond the stage entrance and proceed through the parodos directly to the seats of the orchestra and the lowest section of the cavea; but it is more in accordance with the fondness of the ancients for display to suppose that the procession moved across the stage, receiving as it passed the plaudits of the great audience, and emerged from the entrance opposite that by which it came in, disbanding in the court, whence the members could go to their respective seats. This explanation assumes that the triangular side screens, the periactae, were not set in place till after the procession had left the stage; but there is no reason to suppose that this may not have been the case.

When the colonnade on the south side of the court had been replaced by rooms, and the Theatre Colonnade itself had been transformed into barracks, this route of the processions was blocked. They could still pass down the street in front of the temple of Isis, turn into Stabian Street, and reach the stage through the passage at the rear of the Small Theatre; but it does not seem probable that they followed this course, for the reason that there are three large stepping stones in the street before one comes to the entrance of the passage; these would have proved a serious obstruction, and would undoubtedly have been removed had the processions gone this way.

We may rather believe that before the usual route was closed the processions themselves had been given up. They were still in vogue, however, when the Small Theatre was built; otherwise the purpose of the wide entrances at the ends of the stage and of the room back of it is not clear. Moreover the sidewalk

in front of the Small Theatre, on Stabian Street, is of an altogether unusual width, and was apparently covered by a portico.
We infer that the procession to this theatre entered at the west
end of the stage, and passed out at the east end; since it could
not disperse on the street, it would turn where the sidewalk was
broadest, go back through the room at the rear of the stage
into the court, and there disband.

The discontinuance of the processions must then be assigned
to the period between the building of the Small Theatre and
the changing over of the Theatre Colonnade into barracks, which,
to judge from the masonry and the remains of the decoration,
did not take place till the time of the Empire. The processions
were abandoned either in the troubled period of the Civil Wars,
or in the early years of the Empire; if in the latter period, their
discontinuance may have been due to legislation connected with
the reorganization of the Empire under Augustus, or to the
overshadowing of them by more imposing ceremonies introduced in connection with the religious festivals.

Our information in regard to the later use of the Theatre
Colonnade is indeed meagre; not a single inscription bearing
upon it has been found. Yet when we take into account the
changes that were made in it, and the objects found there, the
supposition that it was turned into barracks for gladiators in
the time of the Early Empire, and so used till the destruction of
the city, is seen to harmonize with almost all the facts.

First, rooms were built on all sides behind the colonnade; on
the north side they took the place of the south arm of the colonnade in the area back of the stage. They were in two series,
one above the other; the upper rooms were entered from a low
wooden gallery accessible by three stairways. They could not
have been intended for shops; they were too small, measuring
on the average hardly more than twelve feet square, and the
doors were too narrow. There were no doors opening from one
room into the other. Both lower and upper rooms, we may
conclude, were used for men's quarters.

In the middle of the south side a large room was left, with
the front open toward the area, an exedra (6). On the east
side was a still larger room the front of which is divided off

by pillars; other rooms open from it, and among them is one
(10) with several hearths, evidently intended for a mess kitchen.
Over these rooms was a second story, reached by a broad stairway (9).

The immediate connection of the colonnade with the area
behind the stage was now cut off by a wall (4); there was left
only a small door in the corner, which could be readily fastened.
The entrance from the passage leading to Stabian Street (2)
was provided with doors and placed under the control of a
guard, for whom a special room was built at one side (3).
There was a third entrance, narrow and easily closed, at the
northwest corner, where a flight of steps connected the foot of
the broad stairway (5) with the landing of the stairs leading to
the wooden gallery.

Thus a complete transformation was effected. The promenade for theatre-goers had become barracks, with a great number
of cell-like rooms, a mess kitchen, and narrow, guarded entrances.
Soldiers, however, could not have been kept here; in the period
to which the rebuilding belongs, garrisons were not stationed in
the cities of Italy except the Capital. On the other hand, gladiatorial combats in Pompeii were so frequent, and on so large a
scale, that a special building for the housing and guarding of
gladiators would seem to have been a necessity; such a building
would naturally have been erected by the city and placed at the
disposal of those who gave the games. As early as the time of
Augustus, Aulus Clodius Flaccus brought forward forty pairs
of gladiators in a single day, and on various occasions afterwards
as many as thirty pairs were engaged. How well the colonnade
was now suited for gladiators' quarters may be seen from a
glance at the plan. The area would serve as a practice court,
the exedra on the south side (6), protected from the sun, as the
station for the trainers and lounging room for men awaiting their
turn; the mess room would be the large apartment adjoining the
kitchen (11), while the quarters of the chief trainer, *lanista*, and
his assistants, would be in the second story, reached by the broad
stairway (9).

The small rooms were poorly decorated, in the fourth style.
There were better paintings only in the exedra. On the rear

wall of this room was the oft repeated group of Mars and Venus;
on the side walls, gladiatorial weapons were represented, piled
up in heaps, after the manner of trophies, about eight feet high.
The reference to the purpose of the building, as in the case of
the paintings in the Macellum, is obvious. The columns about
the area were originally white; after the rebuilding the unfluted
lower part was painted red, the upper part yellow. Four columns, however, two at the middle of the east side, and the two
opposite them on the west side, were painted blue, probably to
serve as bounds in marking off the area for athletic exercises.

The objects found in the barracks are recorded in the journal
of the excavations. They indicate that at the time of the eruption the rooms were occupied. Everything
of value was removed from those on the north
side by the survivors, but the south half was
apparently left undisturbed, and has yielded
a rich harvest.

In ten rooms the excavators found a great
quantity of weapons of the kinds used by
gladiators, including fifteen helmets, a number of greaves (Fig. 67), several broad belts
trimmed with metal, and a couple of armlets;
there were more than a hundred scales of bone
belonging to a coat of mail, and a half dozen
shoulder protectors, *galeri*, which the net
fighter, *retiarius*, who carried no shield and
was armed only with a net and a trident, wore
on his left shoulder. The weapons were
mostly for defence, but remains of a few
offensive weapons were found, as the head
of a lance, a sword, and a couple of daggers.

Fig. 67. — A gladiator's greave.

In the same room with the daggers and the
sword (perhaps 7) were the remains of two
wooden chests containing cloth with gold thread; this may have
been used in gladiators' costumes.

The helmets are characteristic (Fig. 68). They are furnished
with a visor, and part of them have a broad rim, richly ornamented with reliefs; their shape corresponds exactly with that

of the helmets seen in paintings and reliefs representing gladiatorial combats. The shields, which are round and only a little
more than a foot in diameter, would have been quite useless in
military service. In a room under the stairs the skeleton of a
horse was found, with remains of trappings richly mounted with
bronze; one class of gladiators, the equites, fought on horseback.

One of the small rooms on the west side (8) was used as
a guard room. Here were the stocks, the remains of which are
shown in Fig. 69; they were fastened
to a board. At one end of the under
piece was a lock, by which the bar
passed through the rings could be
made secure. The men confined had
the choice of lying down or sitting in
an uncomfortable position. The four
persons whose skeletons were found
in this room, however, were not in
the stocks at the time of the eruption. That such means of discipline
should be employed in a training
school for gladiators is entirely consistent with ancient methods.

Fig. 68.—A gladiator's helmet.

Besides these finds, there were others not so easily explained.
In the two rooms in which the spearhead and the other offensive weapons were found, there were eighteen skeletons, among
them that of a woman richly adorned with gold jewellery; she

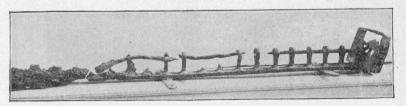

Fig. 69.—Remains of stocks found in the guard room of the barracks.

had a necklace with emeralds, earrings, and two armbands, besides rings and other ornaments, and in a casket a cameo, the
elaborate setting of which is in part preserved. In a room near

the southwest corner the bones of a new-born infant were found in an earthen jar. A number of weights also were discovered, and vessels of terra cotta and glass; in three rooms there were more than six dozen small saucers. Were the barracks wholly given up to gladiators at the time of the eruption, or were some other persons allowed to have quarters here, perhaps some of those whose houses had been destroyed by the earthquake of 63 and had not been rebuilt? A certain conclusion cannot be reached.

CHAPTER XXIII

THE PALAESTRA

THE oblong court north of the Large Theatre, between the entrance of the Forum Triangulare and the temple of Isis, is the Palaestra. Originally, the enclosed area was entirely surrounded by a colonnade, with ten columns on the sides and five at each end; but at a comparatively late period, probably after the earthquake of 63, the columns at the east end were removed and the space thus gained was added to the temple of Isis.

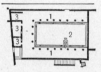

Fig. 70. — Plan of the Palaestra.

1. Colonnade.
2. Pedestal.
3. Dressing rooms.

A number of the columns on the other three sides are still standing. They are Doric but of slender proportions, the height, $10\frac{1}{2}$ feet, being equal to eight diameters, while the intercolumniations measure about nine feet. It is doubtful whether the columns carried a complete entablature; more likely the roof rested directly on a wooden architrave.

The building clearly dates from the pre-Roman period. The columns are of tufa coated with stucco, the dimensions of the colonnade (90 by 36 Oscan feet) reduce to the early standard of measurement; and an Oscan inscription was found here which says that the building was erected by the Quaestor Vibius Vinicius, with money which Vibius Adiranus had left by will to the Pompeian youth. The translation of the word *vereiiai*, ' to the youth,' otherwise doubtful, is confirmed by various facts which indicate that the building was intended as a small palaestra or open-air gymnasium for boys.

While the Palaestra had its original length, the entrance, which is now nearer the east end, was at the middle of the north side. Opposite it, near the colonnade on the south side, is a pedestal of tufa, before which stands a small table of the

same stone (Fig. 71). The pedestal is reached by narrow
steps. Here stood a statue of the patron divinity of the Palaestra. When an athletic contest was held, the wreath intended
for the victor was laid on the stone table before the god; after
the award had been made, the successful contestant took up the
wreath and dedicated it to the divinity by mounting the steps
and placing it on the head of the statue. It is evident from the
height of the steps that the contestants were boys, not men.

Fig. 71. — View of the Palaestra, with the pedestal, table, and steps.

We should have expected to find on the pedestal an image of
Hermes, who was everywhere worshipped as the god of athletes;
but for local reasons a different divinity seems to have had this
place of honor.

There was another statue in the Palaestra, standing at the
foot of one of the columns on the south side, which should
perhaps be restored as a Hermes. This is the one shown in
Fig. 72, now in the Naples Museum; it has been restored as a

copy of a famous original by Polyclitus, representing a youth with a spear over his left shoulder — the doryphorus. It could not have belonged to the pedestal because the depression in the upper surface of the latter is too small for the plinth. A replica

of the doryphorus as an ideal of youthful strength and beauty would have been appropriate in a palaestra; but this statue should have on the left shoulder a herald's staff with entwined snakes, *caduceus*, rather than a spear. In the palaestra of the Stabian Baths Hermes was honored with an image of an altogether different type.

Fig. 72. — Hermes (?) wrongly restored as doryphorus. Statue found in the Palaestra.

At the west end of the court were dressing rooms where the boys, before exercising, could anoint themselves and afterwards could remove the oil and dirt with the strigil; such a dressing room in connection with a bath was called a destrictarium. Water was brought into the court by a lead pipe, which passed through one of the columns at the right of the entrance and threw a jet either into a basin standing below or into the gutter in front of the colonnade.

It would be of interest to know what athletic exercises were practised in the Palaestra; but apart from the pedestal with its steps and table no characteristic remains were found here. The exercises in the Roman period undoubtedly differed somewhat from those practised at the time when the building was erected, when the Greek system was everywhere in vogue.

M

CHAPTER XXIV

THE TEMPLE OF ISIS

THE loftiest and purest religious conceptions of the ancient Egyptians were embodied in the myth of Isis and Osiris, which in the third millennium B.C. had already become the basis of a firmly established cult. These conceptions approached the monotheistic idea of an omnipresent god, and with them was associated a belief in a blessed immortality. Isis was the goddess of heaven, and Osiris was the Sun-god, her brother and husband, who is slain at evening by his brother Set, — the Greek Typhon, — ruler of darkness. Their child Horus, also called Harpocrates, born after the father's death, is the fresh sun of the new day, the successor and avenger of his father, the conqueror of Set; he becomes a new Osiris, while the father, ever blessed, rules in the realm of the dead, the kingdom of the West. Man, the followers of Isis taught, is an incarnation of deity, whose destiny is also his. He is himself an Osiris, and will enter upon a better state of existence beyond the grave if a favorable judgment is passed upon him in the trial given to the dead.

The worship of Isis, associated with Mysteries from an early period, was reorganized by the first Ptolemy with the help of Manetho, an Egyptian priest, and Timotheus, a Greek skilled in the Eleusinian Mysteries. The purpose of the king was to unite his Egyptian and Greek subjects in one faith, and the effort was more successful than might have been anticipated. In its new Alexandrian form the worship of Isis and Osiris, or Serapis, as the latter divinity was now called, spread, not only over all Egypt, but also over the other countries in the East into which Greek culture had penetrated, and soon made its way to Italy and the West.

Various causes contributed to the rapid extension of the cult.

It had the charm of something foreign and full of mystery. Its doctrine, supported by the prestige of immemorial antiquity, successfully opposed the mutually destructive opinions of the philosophers, while at the same time its conception of deity was by no means inconsistent with philosophic thought; and it brought to the initiated that expectation of a future life to which the Eleusinian Mysteries owed their attractive power. The ascetic side of the worship, too, with its fastings and abstinence from the pleasures of sense, that the soul might lose itself in the mystical contemplation of deity, had a fascination for natures that were religiously susceptible; and the celebration of the Mysteries, the representation of the myth of Isis in pantomime with a musical accompaniment, appealed powerfully to the imagination. The cult also possessed elements that brought it nearer to the needs of the multitude. The activities of the Egyptian divinities were not confined to the other world; their help might be sought in the concerns of this life. Thus the chief priest could say to Apuleius that Isis summoned her elect to consecrate themselves to her service only when the term of life allotted to them had really expired, and that she lengthened their tale of years, so that all of life remaining was a direct gift from the hands of the goddess. The priests of Isis were looked upon as experts in astrology, the interpretation of dreams, and the conjuring of spirits.

A college of the Servants of Isis, Pastophori, was founded in Rome in the time of Sulla, about 80 B.C. In vain the authorities tried to drive out the worship of the Egyptian gods. Three times their temple, in the midst of the city, was destroyed by order of the consuls, in 58, 50, and 48 B.C. But after Caesar's death, in 44 B.C., the triumvirs built a temple in honor of Isis and Osiris; and a few decades later, perhaps in the reign of Caligula, their festival was recognized in the public Calendar. In Campania the Alexandrian cult gained a foothold earlier than in Rome. An inscription of the year 105 B.C., found at Puteoli, proves that a temple of Serapis was then standing in that enterprising city, which had close commercial relations with Egypt and the East. Soon after this date the earlier temple of Isis at Pompeii must have been built.

The entrance to the court of the temple (Fig. 73) is from the north. Above the door is an inscription which informs us that after an earthquake (that of the year 63) Numerius Popidius Celsinus, at his own expense, rebuilt the temple of Isis from the

foundation, and that in recognition of his generosity, though he was only six years of age, the members of the city council, the decurions, admitted him without cost to their rank: *N[umerius] Popidius N[umerii] f[ilius] Celsinus aedem Isidis terrae motu conlapsam a fundamento p[ecunia] s[ua] restituit; hunc decuriones ob liberalitatem, cum esset annorum sexs, ordini suo gratis adlegerunt.* The temple evidently belonged to the city; and the places for statues in the court, as the inscriptions show, were assigned by vote of the city council.

Fig. 73.— Plan of the temple of Isis.

1. Portico.
2. Cella.
3. Shrine of Harpocrates.
4. Purgatorium.
5. Hall of initiation.
6. Hall of the Mysteries.
7, 8, 9. Dwelling of priest.
a. Colonnade.

b. Pit for the refuse of sacrifices.
c. Niche for statue of Bacchus.
d, d. Niches at the sides of the cella.
e. Large altar.

Other inscriptions give information in regard to the family of the child Celsinus. His father was Numerius Popidius Ampliatus, his mother Corelia Celsa; a brother bore the same name as the father. The real rebuilders were of course the parents; by associating their munificence with the name of their son, they opened the way for him to the city offices, for which the father, a freedman, was not eligible. Ampliatus perpetuated his own name by setting up a statue of Bacchus in a niche in the outside of the rear wall of the temple (at *c* on the plan), with the inscription: *N. Popidius Ampliatus pater p. s.*, 'Numerius Popidius Ampliatus the father (set up this statue) at his own expense.' The names of the two sons appear with that of their mother in the mosaic floor of the large room (6) behind the colonnade at the rear.

Though the rebuilding of Celsinus was 'from the foundation,' remains of the old temple were utilized, as shafts of columns and Corinthian capitals coated with white stucco ; and the plan of the new building was very nearly the same as that of the old. The stylobate of the colonnade belongs to the earlier structure, but the columns originally stood nearer together, eight instead of seven at the ends, and ten on the sides.

The architectural forms and the workmanship of these remains point to a time just after the founding of the Roman colony ; nevertheless the dimensions of the colonnade, approximately fifty by sixty Oscan feet, reduce to the pre-Roman standard of measurement, and the building may have been commenced earlier. In later times the increasing number of the worshippers of Isis made necessary an enlargement of the sanctuary. The two rooms at the west end (5 and 6) were added at the expense of the Palaestra, probably at the time of the rebuilding.

In the middle of the court, which is surrounded by the colonnade, is the temple, consisting of an oblong cella (2), the east side of which is treated as a front, with a portico borne by six columns (1). A pit for the refuse of sacrifices, enclosed by a wall (b) stands in the corner of the court near the entrance from the street ; in the opposite corner there is a larger enclosure having the appearance of a small temple (4). Near this are two altars ; a third altar stands close to the temple, and there are five others, somewhat smaller, between the columns. On the south side, between the colonnade and the Theatre, is a small area of irregular shape, east of which is a dwelling containing five rooms (7, 8, 9).

The accompanying illustrations show the temple as it is to-day (Fig. 74) and as it was before the eruption (Fig. 75). It has architecturally nothing suggestive of the Egyptian style. Yet the plan presents a marked deviation from ordinary types, as if the builders, erecting an edifice for the worship of foreign gods, strove with set purpose to produce a bizarre effect ; at the right and the left of the front of the cella is a large niche, projecting beyond the sides of the portico, and inorganically connected with the main part of the temple by a pilaster. In the ornamentation of this temple, as in that of the temple of Apollo, the simple and chaste forms of the Greek architecture were replaced by gaudy stucco ornaments more in harmony with the prevailing taste.

Besides the broad flight of steps in front, a narrow stairway at the left of the temple led to a side door opening into the cella. A base of masonry about six feet high extends across the rear of the cella, on which were two pedestals of tufa, about sixteen inches square, for the statues of Isis and Osiris. In the

Fig. 74. — View of the temple of Isis.

two large niches outside other divinities stood, perhaps Anubis and Harpocrates. The latter was apparently worshipped also at the shrine in the wall on the east side of the court (3), facing the doorway of the cella. A painting from this shrine, now in the Naples Museum, represents a statue of Harpocrates of the familiar type — a boy with his finger in his mouth holding a cornucopia, with a lotus blossom resting on his forehead; before him stands a priest in a long white robe, holding a candlestick in each hand, while in the background is a temple surrounded by a colonnade, evidently intended for a free representation of the temple before us. In front of the shrine were the charred remains of a wooden bench.

No statue was found in the cella or in the two niches in front. We may suppose that the images of the four divinities, being of relatively small size, were carried off by the priests at the time of the eruption; had they been removed afterwards, the excavators would have taken also the other objects in the cella used in the services of the temple. Among these were two skulls, probably made use of in the ceremonies attending ini-

Fig. 75.— The temple of Isis, restored. In the background, the Large Theatre.

tiation into the Mysteries, and a marble hand, about four inches long, but whether a right or a left hand, the journal of the excavations does not say. A left hand was carried in the procession in honor of Isis, described by Apuleius; as the weaker of the two, and so less ready to do evil, it symbolized the even justice (*aequitas*) with which the deity governs the world. There were also two wooden caskets, one of which contained a diminutive gold cup, measuring less than an inch across the top, a glass vessel a trifle over an inch and a half in height, and a statuette of a god about half as high; in the other were two

bronze candlesticks about ten inches high, the use of which
may be inferred from the painting described above, and a
bronze lamp with places for two wicks.

The walls of the colonnade were painted in bright colors on
a deep red ground. The lower part of the columns was red,
but above they were white; the temple also was white, the
purpose obviously being to give the appearance of marble.
Nevertheless the same decorative framework appears both in
the white stucco of the temple and the painted decoration of
the colonnade: a division of the body of the wall into large
panels, with a continuous garland of conventional plant forms
above. In the colonnade there was a yellow base, treated as
a projecting architectural member; above it large red panels
alternated with light, fantastic architectural designs in yellow
on a red ground. The frieze was black, with garlands in strong
contrast — green, blue, and yellow — enlivened with all sorts
of animal forms. In the middle of each of the large panels
was a priest of Isis; in the lower part of the intervening architectural designs were marine pictures, — galleys maneuvring,
and seafights. Similar pictures are found in other buildings,
as the Macellum, but marine views were especially appropriate
here, because Isis was a patron divinity of seamen. Apuleius
gives an interesting description of the spring festival, by which
the navigation of the opening season was committed to her
guardian care.

Opposite the entrance of the temple the colonnade presents
an interesting peculiarity of construction, which is found also in
other buildings at Pompeii, as the Stabian Baths. The place
of the three middle columns on that side is taken by two large
pillars, higher than the rest of the colonnade, each of which is
backed by an attached half-column. This arrangement made
the approach to the temple more imposing, and also furnished
an appropriate setting for the shrine of Harpocrates against
the wall.

The principal altar, on which sacrifice was offered to the
divinities worshipped in the temple, is that near the foot of
the steps in front (e). The officiating priest stood on a block
of stone at the side of it, with the temple at his right; on this

altar were found ashes and fragments of calcined bones. The two smaller altars near by were probably consecrated to the gods whose images were placed in the exterior niches.

Two rectangular pits were used as receptacles for the refuse of sacrifices. One was quite small, and no trace of it can now be found; it was near the large altar, and contained remains of burnt figs, pine kernels and cones, nuts, and dates, with frag-ments of two statuettes representing divinities. The wall about the other (*b*), when excavated, was built up at each end in the form of a gable, and evidently once supported a wooden roof; in this pit also were charred remains of fruits. What divinities were worshipped at the altars between the columns, it is impos-sible to determine. The small base standing against the corner column near the entrance (seen in Fig. 74) was probably a pedestal, not an altar.

At the left of the steps leading up to the temple, and facing the large altar, is a small pillar of masonry fifteen inches square and nearly two and a half feet high. A similar pillar, which formerly stood at the right, had thin slabs of stone on three sides. One of these, facing in the direction of the altar (now in the Naples Museum), was covered with hieroglyphics. It is a memorial tablet, which Hat, 'the writer of the divine word,' *hierogrammateus*, set up in honor of his parents and grand-parents; it contains symbolic representations in three divisions, one above the other. In the upper division Hat, his brother and colleague Meran, their father and grandfather, are praying to Osiris, 'Lord of the Kingdom of the Dead'; below, Hat is bringing to his parents and grandparents offerings for the dead, while in the lower division Meran and two sisters unite with him in prayer to Osiris. The tablet could hardly have been designed for a temple, but still, by reason of its contents, it was considered appropriate for this place. It was doubtless in-tended that a similar tablet should be affixed to the pillar at the left, but perhaps none happened to be available; statuettes of divinities were probably placed on the pillars.

The presence of a statue of Bacchus in the niche in the rear wall of the cella is easily explained; this divinity was identified with Osiris. Two ears are moulded in the stucco of the niche, symbolic of the listening of the god to the prayers of his worshippers.

Against the west wall of the colonnade, near the corners, were two pedestals, with statues of female divinities about one half life size. At the right was Isis, in archaic Greek costume, with the inscription: *L. Caecilius Phoebus posuit l[oco] d[ato] d[ecurionum] d[ecreto]*, 'Set up by Lucius Caecilius Phoebus, in a place granted by a decree of the city council'; the name indicates that the donor was a freedman. The other statue, at the left, represents Venus drying her hair after the bath; it is of a common type and possesses small value as a work of art, yet is of interest because of the well preserved painting and gilding. Venus, as many other goddesses, was identified with Isis.

In the same corner with the statue of Venus, against the south wall, stood the herm of Gaius Norbanus Sorex, a marble pillar with a bronze head. According to the inscription, he was an actor who played the second part (*secundarum, sc. partium*), and was also magister of the suburb Pagus Augustus Felix. He was probably a generous supporter of the temple. A duplicate of the herm is found in the Eumachia building, to which also he may have made a contribution. The low social standing of the various benefactors of the temple is noteworthy; it indicates in what circles the worship of the Egyptian divinities found its adherents. As yet this was by no means an aristocratic cult, although it became such later, especially after the time of Hadrian.

While the Greek and Roman gods were honored chiefly at their festivals, the Egyptian divinities demanded worship every day, indeed several times a day. The early service, the 'opening of the temple,' is described for us by Apuleius, who was admitted to the college of the Servants of Isis in Rome in the time of the Antonines, and wrote not far from 160 A.D. Before daybreak the priest went into the temple by the side entrance and threw back the great doors, which were fastened on the inside. White linen curtains were hung across the doorway, shielding the interior from view. Now the street gate of the court was opened; the thronging multitude of the devout streamed in and took their places in front of the temple. The curtains were drawn aside and the image of the goddess was presented to the gaze of her worshippers, who greeted her with prayers and shaking of the sistrum, a musical rattle, the use of which was characteristic of the worship of the Egyptian gods. For a time

Fig. 76. — Scene from the worship of Isis — the adoration of the holy water. Wall painting from Herculaneum.

they remained sitting, engaged in prayer and in the contemplation of the divinity; an hour after daybreak the service was closed with an invocation to the newly risen sun. This description throws light on the purpose of the bench in front of the shrine of Harpocrates.

The second service was held at two o'clock in the afternoon, but we do not possess exact information in regard to it. It is,

perhaps, depicted in a fresco painting from Herculaneum (Fig.
76), the subject of which is a solemn act in the worship of Isis,
the adoration of the holy water. In the portico of the temple,
above the steps, two priests and a priestess are standing. The
priest in the middle holds in front of him, in the folds of his
robe, a vessel containing the holy water, which was supposed to
be from the Nile; his two associates are shaking the sistrum.
There is an altar at the foot of the steps; a priest is fanning
the fire into flame. On the right and the left of the altar
are the worshippers, with other priests, part of whom are shaking the sistrum, while a fluteplayer sits in the foreground at
the right.

Another painting, the counterpart of that just described,
seems to portray the celebration of a festival; the surroundings
correspond fairly well with those of our temple. The doors are
thrown back; a dark-visaged man, wearing a wreath, is dancing
in the doorway. Behind him, within the temple, are the musicians, among whom can be distinguished a girl striking the
cymbals and a woman with a tambourine. About the steps are
priests and other worshippers, shaking the sistrum and offering
prayer; in front stands a burning altar. An important festival
of Isis occurred in November. It commenced with an impas-
sioned lamentation over the death of Osiris and the search for
his body. On the third day, November 12, the finding of the
body by Isis was celebrated with great rejoicing. So, perhaps,
in this painting the dance is a manifestation of the joy with
which the festival ended, the whole picture being a scene from
the observance of the Egyptian Easter.

In such celebrations use would be made of the small brazier
of bronze found in the court in front of our temple, on which
incense could be burned. The ablutions, which played so
important a part in Egyptian rites, were performed in the rear
of the court, where stood a cylindrical leaden vessel, adorned
with Egyptian figures in relief; a jet fell into it from a lead
pipe connected with the city aqueduct.

The small building at the southeast corner of the court, which
we may call the Purgatorium, was open to the sky. It was
made to look like a roofed structure by the addition of gables

at the ends.   On the inside, at the rear, a flight of steps leads
down toward the right to a vaulted underground chamber, about
five feet wide and six and a half feet long.   The inner part of
the chamber, divided off by a low wall, was evidently intended
for a tank.   In one of the corners in the front part is a low
base, on which a jar could be set while it was being filled.
Here the holy Nile water — more or less genuine — was kept
for use in the sacred rites.

The purpose of the tank is suggested by certain of the stucco
reliefs on the outside of the enclosing wall.   In the gable, above
the entrance, is a vase, standing out from a blue ground, with a
kneeling figure on either side.   The frieze contains Egyptian
priests and priestesses, also on
a blue ground, with their faces
turned toward the vessel (Fig.
77).   The figures are all wor-
shipping the sacred water in
the vase.

Of the other figures in relief,
only the two goddesses in the
panels at the sides of the entrance have an Egyptian character.   Under each of them
was a small altar of tufa, attached to the wall; the figure
at the left (Fig. 77) is plainly
Isis.

The side walls are decorated
with reliefs in Greco-Roman
style.   They are divided into
a large middle panel, containing
two figures, and two side panels,
each with a Cupid.   In the
middle panel, on the right side,

Fig. 77.— Part of the façade of the Purgatorium.

Mars and Venus are represented; in that at the left, Perseus
rescuing Andromeda (Fig. 78).

The dwelling back of the colonnade, on the south side, consists of a kitchen (8), a dining room (7), a sleeping apartment (9),

and two small rooms at the rear, under the stairway leading to
the highest seats of the Large Theatre.   The ritual of the
Egyptian gods was so exacting, and the services of worship
were so numerous, that it was necessary for one or more priests
to reside within the precincts of the temple.   These rooms were
the habitation of a priest.

One of the rooms on the west side (6) is oblong in shape,
with five broad, arched entrances opening from the colonnade.
The walls were richly decorated in the last Pompeian style.
There were seven large paintings, five of which were land-

Fig. 78. — Decoration of the east side of the Purgatorium — Perseus rescuing Andromeda.
At the right and the left floating Cupids, the one at the left bearing a box of incense.

scapes with shrines, part being Egyptian landscapes; the other
two represent Io watched by Argus, with Hermes coming to
rescue her, and Io in Egypt, received by Isis.   Against the rear
wall is a pedestal, on which probably stood the female figure,
above life size, the remains of which were found in one of the
entrances.   Only the head, the hands, and the front parts of
the feet were of marble; the rest was of wood, no doubt concealed by drapery.   The priests seemingly had started to carry
the statue with them when they fled, but abandoned the attempt
at the doorway.   In the same room a marble table, a sistrum,
two pots of terra cotta, three small glass bottles, and a glass
cup were found.   We may safely conclude that here the common

meals were served, of which, as we learn from Apuleius, the
devotees of the cult partook. And when, in connection with
the great festivals, the Mysteries were celebrated with a presentation of the myth of Isis and Osiris in pantomime, this large
room was well adapted for the sacred exhibitions.

The adjoining room, at the southwest corner of the colonnade
(5), is irregular in shape and of an entirely different character.
It seems to have been regarded as a sacred place, and to have
been used for secret ceremonies. It was entered from the colonnade by a narrow door, which could be securely fastened.
Large, sketchy pictures of gods were painted on the walls on a
white ground, — Isis, Osiris, Typhon, — with sacred animals
and symbols relating to the myth which to us are unintelligible.
The excavators found here the remains of four wooden statues
with marble heads, hands, and feet, one of a male figure, the
other three female; there were besides a statuette of an Egyptian god made of green stone, on which were hieroglyphics; a
statuette of white clay, covered with a green glaze; a sphinx of
terra cotta, fragments of terra cotta statuettes of Egyptian
figures, different kinds of vessels of clay, glass, and lead, and a
bronze knife, evidently intended for use in sacrifices. At the
left near the entrance is a small reservoir, reached by three
steps. On the north side is a niche that apparently formed
part of a small shrine.

A kind of alcove opens off from the southeast corner of this
room, the entrance to which could be closed by a curtain. From
this a few steps and a door led into a storeroom, in which were
found about three dozen vessels of various shapes, an iron tripod,
and no less than fifty-eight earthen lamps. The lamps were in
part provided with iron rings, so that they could be suspended;
there were also iron rods, which the excavators supposed to
be lamp holders. A rear door connected the storeroom with
the small area of irregular shape between the Palaestra and the
Theatre.

These arrangements suggest the celebration of secret rites
by night; we may well believe that novices were here initiated
into the order of the Servants of Isis. Obscure hints in regard
to the ceremonies connected with the consecration to the ser-

vice of the goddess are thrown out by Apuleius. 'The initiation,' said the priest to him, 'is conducted under the image of
a voluntary death, with the renewing of life as a gift from the
deity.' Of his own experience he says merely: 'I came to
the borders of death, I trod the threshold of Proserpina, then
came back through all the stages to life. In the middle of the
night I saw the sun shine brightly; I entered into the immediate presence of the gods above and the gods below, and worshipped them face to face.'

Renunciation of past life, and a second birth to a new and
purified existence, were the main ideas underlying the ceremonies, which as presented here must have been far less
splendid and impressive than in Rome, where they were
witnessed by Apuleius.

CHAPTER XXV

THE TEMPLE OF ZEUS MILICHIUS

THE small temple near the northeast corner of the block containing the theatres is entered from Stabian Street. The court (Fig. 79, 2), like that of the temple of Vespasian, has a colonnade across the front; only the foundation and a Doric capital of lava are preserved.

At the end of the colonnade on the right is the room of the sacristan (4). The large altar (Fig. 241) stands close to the foot of the steps leading up to the temple. It is of tufa, and its construction — blocks of hewn stone with bevelled edges and a frieze of triglyphs — is in conformity with the first style of decoration.

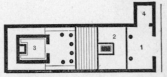

Fig. 79. — Plan of the temple of Zeus Milichius.

1. Colonnade.
2. Court, with large altar.
3. Cella.
4. Sacristan's room.

The steps extend across the front of the temple, the unusual elevation of which is explained by the inequality of the ground. Of the six columns in the tetrastyle portico no remains have been found, but three capitals of pilasters are preserved, two belonging to those at the corners of the cella, and one, considerably smaller, to a doorpost; they are of tufa, and were once covered with white stucco.

The excellent proportions and fine workmanship of the capitals point to the period of the first style of decoration; there was formerly a remnant of that style on the north wall of the cella, copied by Gau in 1837. Nevertheless the quasi-reticulate masonry of the cella, closely resembling that of the Small Theatre, dates from the early years of the Roman colony. In this period the temple in its present form was built, perhaps with the help of native Pompeian masons.

Attached to the rear wall of the cella was an oblong pedestal
on which were placed two statues, representing Jupiter and
Juno, together with a bust of Minerva, all of terra cotta and of
poor workmanship. The suggestion at once presents itself that
this was the Capitolium, erected by the Roman colonists soon
after they settled in Pompeii. It is incredible, however, that
colonists who had the means to erect monumental buildings,
such as the Amphitheatre and the Small Theatre, should have
housed the great gods of the Capitol in so modest a temple,
in so inconspicuous a spot, and should not have provided more
costly images.

All the evidence is in favor of the explanation, already
proposed (p. 66), that after the earthquake the worship of
the gods of the Capitol was
transferred hither temporarily
from the temple in the Forum,
until that should be rebuilt.

Fig. 80. — Capital of pilaster with the
face of Zeus Milichius.

What divinity thus became
the host of the Roman gods?
It would be impossible to say
but for the fortunate recovery
of an Oscan inscription, which
was set up in the passage of
the Stabian Gate. This com-
memorates the work of two
aediles, M. Sittius and N. Pontius, who improved the street
leading out from the Stabian Gate 'as far as the Stabian
Bridge, and the Via Pompeiana as far as the temple of Zeus
Milichius; these streets, as well as the Via Jovia (and another,
the name of which cannot be made out) they placed in perfect
repair.'

It is natural to suppose that the Via Pompeiana, mentioned
in immediate connection with the road leading to Stabiae, was
the continuation of the latter within the city, or Stabian Street.
This, then, led to the temple named in the inscription, and as
there is no other temple on the street, the small sanctuary in
which the images of the Capitoline divinities were placed was
the temple of Zeus Milichius.

This building, however, is not old enough to have been mentioned in an Oscan inscription.   It probably stands in the place
of a much earlier edifice.   The masonry of the wall on the south
side of the court is different from that of the other walls, and
older; as it shows no trace of a cross wall, it must always have
stood at the side of an open space, such as that of the present
court.   To the earlier building the capitals belong, the style of
which, as remarked above, is pre-Roman.

In view of this explanation, we should probably recognize in
the head carved on the smallest of the pilaster capitals (Fig. 80)
a representation of Zeus Milichius, a divinity honored in many
parts of Greece, especially by the farmers; Zeus the Gracious,
the patron of tillers of the soil.   The serious, kindly face, bearded
and with long locks, was more than a mere ornament; it was the
god himself looking down upon the worshipper who entered his
sanctuary.

CHAPTER XXVI

THE BATHS AT POMPEII.— THE STABIAN BATHS

In comparison with the great bathing establishments of Rome, the baths at Pompeii are of moderate size. They have, however, a special interest, due in part to their excellent preservation, in part to the certainty with which the purpose of the various rooms can be determined; and their remains enable us to trace the development of the public bath in a single city during a period of almost two hundred years. From this source, moreover, most of our knowledge of the arrangements of the ancient bath is derived, without which the imposing but barren remains of Rome itself would be for the most part unintelligible. It is not easy for one living under present conditions to understand how important a place the baths occupied in the life of antiquity, particularly of the Romans under the Empire; they offered, within a single enclosure, opportunities for physical care and comfort and leisurely intercourse with others, not unlike those afforded in the cities of modern Europe by the club, the café, and the promenade.

Though the Roman baths differed greatly in size and in details of arrangement, the essential parts were everywhere the same. First there was a court, *palaestra*, surrounded by a colonnade. This was devoted to gymnastic exercises, and connected with it in most cases was an open-air swimming tank. The dressing room, *apodyterium*, was usually entered from the court through a passageway or anteroom. A basin for cold baths was sometimes placed in the dressing room; in large establishments a separate apartment was set aside for this purpose, the *frigidarium*. To avoid too sudden a change of temperature for the bathers, a room moderately heated, *tepidarium*, was placed between the dressing room and the *caldarium*, in which hot baths were given. At one end of the caldarium was

180

a bath basin of masonry, *alveus ;* at the other was ordinarily a semicircular niche, *schola*, in which stood the *labrum*, a large, shallow, circular vessel resting upon a support of masonry, and supplied with lukewarm water by a pipe leading from a tank back of the furnace. The more extensive establishments, as the Central Baths at Pompeii, contained also a round room, called *Laconicum* from its Spartan origin, for sweating baths in dry air. In describing baths it is more convenient to use the ancient names.

In earlier times the rooms were heated by means of braziers, and in one of the Pompeian baths the tepidarium was warmed in this way to the last. A more satisfactory method was devised near the beginning of the first century B.C. by Sergius Orata, a famous epicure, whose surname is said to have been given to him because of his fondness for golden trout (*auratae*). He was the first to plant artificial oyster beds in the Lucrine Lake, and the experiment was so successful that he derived a large income from them ; we may assume that he turned an honest penny also by his invention of the 'hanging baths,' *balneae pensiles*, with which his name has ever since been associated. These were built with a hollow space under the floor, the space being secured by making the floor of tiles, two feet square, supported at the corners by small brick pillars (Fig. 83); into this space hot air was introduced from the furnace, and as the floor became warm, the temperature of the room above was evenly modified.

This improved method of heating was not long restricted to the floors. As early as the Republican period, the hollow space was extended to the walls by means of small quadrangular flues and by the use of nipple tiles, *tegulae mammatae*, large rectangular tiles with conical projections, about two inches high, at each corner ; these were laid on their edges, with the projections pressed against the wall, thus leaving an air space on the inside.

In bathing establishments designed for both men and women, the two caldariums were placed near together. There was a single furnace, *hypocausis*, where the water for the baths was warmed ; from this also hot air was conveyed through broad flues under the floors of both caldariums, thence circulating through the walls. Through similar flues underneath, the warm air, already considerably cooled, was conveyed from the hollow spaces of the caldariums into those of the tepidariums. In order to maintain a draft strong enough to draw the hot air from the furnace under the floors, the air spaces of the walls had vents above, remains of which may still be seen in some baths. These vents were no doubt sufficient to keep up the draft after the rooms had once been heated; but in order to warm them at the outset a draft fire was needed, — that is, a small fire under the floor at some point a considerable distance from the furnace and near the vents, through which it would cause the escape of warm air, and so start a hot current from the furnace. The place of the draft fire has been found under two rooms of the Pompeian baths; and a similar arrangement has been noted in the case of Roman baths excavated in Germany.

The use of the baths varied according to individual taste and medical advice. In general, however, bathers availed themselves of one of three methods.

The most common form of the bath was that taken after exercise in the palaestra, — ball playing was a favorite means of exercise, — use being made of all the rooms. The bather undressed in the apodyterium, or perhaps in the tepidarium, where he was rubbed with unguents; then he took a sweat in the caldarium, following it with a warm bath. Returning to the apodyterium, he gave himself a cold bath either in this room or in the frigidarium; he then passed into the Laconicum, or, if there was no Laconicum, went back into the caldarium for a second sweat; lastly, before going out, he was thoroughly rubbed with unguents, as a safeguard against taking cold.

Some bathers omitted the warm bath. They passed through the tepidarium directly into the Laconicum or caldarium, where they had a sweat; they then took a cold bath, or had cold water poured over them, and were rubbed with unguents.

In the simplest form of the bath the main rooms were not used at all. The bathers heated themselves with exercise in the palaestra, then removed the dirt and oil with scrapers, *strigiles*, and bathed in the swimming tank.

Up to the present time three public baths have been excavated in Pompeii, two for both men and women, one for men only. Besides these there are two private establishments in the eighth Region (VIII. ii. 17 and 23), perhaps one for men, the other for women; and another, apparently for men, was discovered in the last century near the Amphitheatre and covered up again, being a part of the villa of Julia Felix. It is quite possible that two or three more bathing establishments yet await excavation; one at least, connected with a warm spring, is known to us from an inscription — that of M. Crassus Frugi. About a dozen houses also contain complete baths for private use.

The largest and oldest bathing establishment at Pompeii is that to which the name Stabian Baths has been given, from its location on Stabian Street. It was built in the second century B.C., but was remodelled in the early days of the Roman colony, and afterwards underwent extensive repairs. It is of irregular shape, and occupies a large part of a block, having streets on three sides; on the north side it is bounded by the house of Siricus. Opening upon two of the streets are shops, which have nothing to do with the baths and are not numbered on the plan (Fig. 81).

Entering from the south through the broad doorway at A, we find ourselves in the palaestra, C, which has a colonnade on three sides. On the west side the place of the colonnade is taken by a strip of smooth pavement with a raised margin; two heavy stone balls were found here, which were obviously used in a game resembling the modern ninepins; at the further end is the room for the players, K. Close to the bowling course, at the middle of the west side, is the swimming tank, F, with rooms (E, G) adjoining it at either end. At the corner near the further room, G, is a side entrance, L; J is the office of the director or superintendent in charge of the building.

On the east side of the court are the men's baths, rooms I–VIII; north of these are the women's baths, rooms 1–6, with the furnace room, IX, between them. In the northwest corner of the building were small rooms (e–e) intended for private baths. They had not been provided with the improved heating arrangements, and were not in use at the time of the catastrophe. The larger room adjoining (*k*) was a closet.

The anteroom of the men's baths (IV), opens at one end into the dressing room or apodyterium (VI), as seen in Plate V. It has a vaulted ceiling, richly decorated.

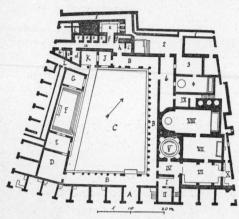

Fig. 81.— Plan of the Stabian Baths.

A. Main entrance.
B. Colonnade.
I-VIII. Men's baths.
　IV. Anteroom.
　V. Frigidarium.
　VI. Apodyterium.
　VII. Tepidarium.
　VIII. Caldarium.

C. Palaestra.
F. Swimming tank.
IX. Furnace room.
1-6. Women's baths.
　1, 5. Entrances.
　2. Apodyterium.
　3. Tepidarium.
　4. Caldarium.

A door at the left leads into the frigidarium (V), and another at the right into a servants' waiting room (I), which is accessible from the court. This room was formerly entered also from the street, through a passage (III), which was later closed; on one side of it is a bench of masonry for the slaves in attendance upon their masters. Similar benches are found in the waiting room at the other end of the apodyterium (X).

The apodyterium also was provided with benches of the same sort, as indicated on the plan; they are shown in Plate V. Along the walls at the sides, just under the edge of the vaulted ceiling, was a row of small niches, the use of which corresponded with that of the lockers in a modern gymnasium. These niches are about $5\frac{3}{4}$ feet above the floor, while those in the other dressing room (2) are a little less than five feet; from this difference in height it has been rightly inferred that the smaller and simpler division of the baths was set aside for women. The floor is paved with rectangular flags of gray marble, with blocks of basalt next to the walls. While the walls were left simply white, with a red base, the ceiling was elaborately decorated with stucco reliefs in the style prevalent shortly before the destruction of the city; there are vestiges of similar decoration in the tepidarium. In octagonal, hexagonal, and quadrangular panels are rosettes, Cupids, trophies, and bacchic figures. The lunettes are adorned with fantastic architectural designs, in which we see bacchic figures standing on pedestals, and Cupids riding on dolphins; the sides of the two arches supporting the ceiling (one of them is seen in Plate V) are decorated with female figures mounted on dolphins, which run out into arabesques. The frequent suggestion of water in these motives is in harmony with the purpose of the room.

Even more effective is the decoration of the small round frigidarium. Light is admitted, as in the Pantheon at Rome, through a round hole in the apex of the domed ceiling. At the edge of the circular bath basin, lined with white marble, is a narrow strip of marble floor, which is extended into the four semicircular niches. Wall and niches alike are painted to represent a beautiful garden, with a blue sky above (Fig. 82). The eye

Fig. 82.— Stabian Baths : interior of the frigidarium, restored.

wanders among trees and shrubs, catching glimpses of birds overhead, of statues and vases here and there in the midst of the green foliage, and of jets of water falling into circular basins. The blue dome is studded with stars. The bather could scarcely feel the narrowness of a room, the decoration of which was so suggestive of expanse and open air. A jet of water fell into the basin from a small niche in the upper part of the wall; and remains of an overflow pipe are still to be seen.

The tepidarium (VII) and caldarium (VIII) were heated by means of hollow floors and walls. The former is much the smaller, as we should have expected from its use as an intermediate room, in which the bathers would ordinarily not tarry so

long as in the caldarium. The large bath basin at the east end
(indicated on the plan) is unusual; it was seemingly a later
addition, and was probably made to accommodate those who in
the winter shrank from using the frigidarium, but wished nevertheless to take a moderately cold bath. Near the bottom of the
wall back of this basin, a hole had been made so that underneath
a fire could be kindled from the outside (in X), not in order to
heat the basin, which could be supplied with warm water by
means of a pipe, but to start the circulation of hot air from the
furnace; at the top of the wall above were two vents opening
from the warm air chamber. There was a place for another
draft fire under the women's caldarium.

One of the fragments of stucco relief still remaining in the
tepidarium presents the figure of a man reading from a roll of
manuscript. It suggests the standing complaint of the ancients
in regard to the trials of bathers, who could not escape the ever-
present poet declaiming his latest production.

At one end of the caldarium we find the bath basin, alveus;
at the other is the support of the labrum, which has disappeared.
In the niche above the latter are two vents for the draft, and
above the niche is a round window. This room, as most of the
others, was dimly lighted. The little round window of the anteroom is shown in our plate. There were two similar windows
in the lunette of the apodyterium, above the roof of the anteroom; they are not seen in our plate, having at one time been entirely covered up by the construction of a wall to support the
roof. A similar window was very likely placed at the end of
the tepidarium, over the roof of the frigidarium; and perhaps
these were supplemented by holes in the crown of the arched
ceilings, as in the women's apodyterium.

The women's baths are entered from the court through a long
anteroom (6); the dressing room is connected also with the two
side streets by means of corridors (1, 5). Originally there was no
communication between the women's baths and the palaestra.

The apodyterium (2) is the best preserved room of the entire
building, and also the most ancient. It shows almost no traces
of the catastrophe. The vaulted ceiling is intact. The smooth,
white stucco on the walls and the simple cornice at the base of

the lunettes date from the time of the first builders. Now, as then, light is admitted only through two small openings in the crown of the vault and a window in the west lunette. To a modern visitor the interior seems gloomy. The pavement, of lozenge-shaped, reddish glazed tiles, belongs to the same early period. There is a strip of basaltic flags connecting the door of one of the corridors (1) with that of the tepidarium. This much travelled path seems to indicate that many ladies — particularly, we may assume, in the winter — went at once into the more comfortable tepidarium without stopping in the dressing room. Along the walls were benches, and above them niches, as in the men's apodyterium. In the time of the Empire the fronts of the niches, finely carved in tufa, were overlaid with a thick coating of stucco, the upper part being ornamented with designs in relief.

The women had no frigidarium. A large basin for cold baths was built at the west end of the dressing room, but this also is a later addition ; before it was made, those who wished for cold baths must have contented themselves with portable bath tubs.

The tepidarium (3) and caldarium (4) are in a better state of preservation than those of the men's baths, which they so closely resemble in all their arrangements that a detailed description is unnecessary. In their present form they are not so ancient as the apodyterium, and the decoration is less elaborate than that of the corresponding rooms on the other side.

The labrum is intact, a round, shallow basin of white marble resting on a support of masonry ; it has here no separate niche. The bath basin in the caldarium also retains its veneering of white marble, with an overflow pipe of bronze at the upper edge ; it is about two feet deep. In such basins the bathers leaned against the sloping back, which for this reason was called a cushion (*pulvinus*) by Vitruvius. This alveus would accommodate eight bathers, that in the men's caldarium perhaps ten. Places were probably assigned in numerical order, each bather awaiting his turn. Those who did not wish to wait, or preferred to bathe by themselves, might use individual bath tubs of bronze. Remains of such a tub, as well as of bronze benches, were found in this room. Near the bottom of the alveus in front is an opening, through which the water could be let out ; when it was emptied, the water ran over the white mosaic floor, which was thus cleaned.

In the time of the Early Empire it became the fashion to bathe with very warm water. 'People want to be parboiled,' Seneca exclaims. The construction of the alveus, however, was not well adapted to conserve the heat, and an ingenious contrivance was devised to remedy the difficulty, which may best be explained with the help of our illustration, showing the arrangement of the bath basin in room 4 (Fig. 83). A large hot air flue, D, led directly from the furnace to the hollow space, C, under the alveus, A. Above this flue was a long bronze heater, B, in the form of a

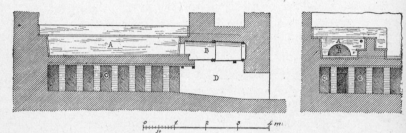

Fig. 83. — The bath basin in the women's caldarium — longitudinal and transverse sections, showing the arrangement for heating the water.

A. Bath basin, alveus.   C. Hot air chamber under the floor.
B. Bronze heater.   D. Hot air flue.

half cylinder, with one end opening into the end of the alveus. As the bottom of the heater was six inches lower than that of the alveus, the cooler water from the basin would flow down into it and be heated again, a circulation being thus maintained.

A similar arrangement (called *testudo alvei* by Vitruvius) probably existed for the alveus in the caldarium on the other side ; but that part of the men's baths has been destroyed. Only one other heater of this kind has been found, — and that is of lead, — in a villa at Boscoreale, recently excavated ; but the semicircular opening made for the heater above the hot air flue may be seen in the Central Baths, in a private establishment at Pompeii, and generally in the remains of Roman public baths.

In the furnace room (*praefurnium*, IX) between the two caldariums, stood three large cylindrical tanks. They have disappeared, but their outlines can still be seen in the masonry of the foundations, and are shown in our plan. The one furthest east was for hot water. It was directly over the fire, and connected with the bath basins of the two caldariums. The next, for lukewarm water, stood over a hollow space opening into the furnace. A lead pipe leading from it to the labrum of the women's caldarium is still to be seen; the water bubbled up in the middle of the labrum. The third and largest reservoir, for cold water, was placed on a foundation of solid masonry.

The more important alterations made in the baths during the two centuries that they were in use had to do with the arrangements for heating, and may briefly be considered here before we proceed to another part of the building. It will be best not to weary the reader with details, but to present a brief summary of conclusions, which will perhaps be found of interest, not only as casting light on the gradual development of these baths, but also as illustrating that adjustment of public buildings to the needs and tastes of successive generations, which was as characteristic of ancient as it is of modern life.

For the extensive changes made in the earlier part of the first century B.C. we have the evidence of an inscription, which had been cast aside and was found in one of the smaller rooms. It reads, *C. Uulius C. f., P. Aninius C. f., II v. i. d., Laconicum et destrictarium faciund. et porticus et palaestr[am] reficiunda locarunt ex d[ecurionum] d[ecreto] ex ea pequnia quod eos e lege in ludos aut in monumento consumere oportuit faciund. coerarunt eidemque probaru[nt]*. The form of the letters and the spelling point to the time of Sulla as the period in which the inscription was cut. The syntax is confused, but the meaning is clear: a Laconicum and *destrictarium* were built, the colonnade and palæstra repaired, by the duumvirs Gaius Ulius and Publius Aninius, in accordance with a vote of the city council; and they furnished the means for this work in fulfilment of their obligation, incurred by the acceptance of the duumviral office, to spend a certain sum upon either games or buildings.

The destrictarium — a room for removing dirt and oil with the strigil after gymnastic exercises — is easily identified (D), as are also the palaestra and colonnade; but in our survey of the baths, we have found no separate chamber to which the term Laconicum could properly be applied. In order to arrive at a solution of the difficulty, we must note the successive steps by which, as shown by an examination of the remains of the masonry, the heating arrangements were extended and improved.

At first, in the Baths as originally constructed, there were neither hollow walls nor hollow floors. The heating was done by means of braziers; and there were niches or lockers in the walls of the caldariums and tepidariums similar to those now found in the dressing rooms, but in double rows, the upper niches being larger, the lower smaller.

Later, a hollow floor was built in the men's caldarium. Later still, this room was provided with hollow walls, which were extended to the crown of the ceilings and the lunettes, the tepidarium being still heated with braziers.

Finally, a hollow floor and hollow walls were constructed at the same time in the men's tepidarium, but the hot air chamber was not carried up into the ceiling or the lunettes.

A similar transformation was gradually accomplished in the women's apartments; but owing, it would seem, to a desire for greater warmth in the tepidarium, the hot air chamber here, as in the caldarium, was extended to the lunettes and the ceiling.

Since the method of heating by means of hollow floors only came into vogue about 100 B.C., and since the duumvirate of Ulius and Aninius must have occurred soon after 80 B.C., we are probably safe in supposing that they built the hollow floors of the two caldariums, and that the new heating arrangement was loosely called a Laconicum. At least a partial warrant for this interpretation is found in a passage of Dion Cassius (LIII. xxvii. i), in which he says that Agrippa built the 'Spartan sweating bath,' τὸ πυριατήριον τὸ Λακωνικόν. Agrippa, however, built, not a Laconicum in the narrow sense, but a complete bathing establishment, and Dion, doubtless following some earlier writer, uses the word as generally applicable to a system of warm baths. In default of a better explanation, we must accept a meaning equally loose for our inscription.

It is not possible to date, even approximately, the other

changes by which the baths were conformed to the increasing desire for warmth and comfort; but the decoration of the greater part of the building, with its complicated designs and stucco reliefs, was clearly applied to the walls not many decades before the destruction of the city.

The unroofed swimming tank, F, was separated from the court by a barrier of masonry about two feet high, which was extended also in front of the rooms at the ends, E and G. On either side was a step, both the steps and the barrier being veneered with white marble. The tank was supplied by a pipe entering from the northeast; the overflow pipe, at the southeast corner, is indicated on the plan.

The rooms E and G, opening both on the swimming tank and on the court with high arched doorways, were roofed shallow basins where the athletes could give themselves a preliminary cleaning before going into the tank. The walls are veneered with marble to a height of $6\frac{1}{2}$ feet; above are painted plants, birds, statues, and nymphs, one of whom holds a shell to catch a jet of water; over these the blue sky. Here, as in the frigidarium, the artist strove to convey the impression of being in the open air, in a beautiful garden, adorned with sculptures. A jet of water spurted from the rear wall just above the marble dado; above it is a large oblong niche, apparently for a statue.

After a time the basin in G was filled up, and covered with a mosaic floor of the same height as the threshold; when one cleaning room was found to be adequate, that was retained which had a separate dressing room, D. On the white walls of the dressing room are traces of the wooden wardrobes that once stood against them. In this room, the destrictarium, the athletes disrobed, and rubbed themselves with oil before engaging in gymnastic exercises, and to it they returned from the palaestra, in order to scrape themselves (*se destringere*); then they washed themselves in the next room, E, and finally plunged into the tank.

The room of the official in charge of the baths, J, had windows opening on the court and into the bowlers' room, K. A large bronze brazier was found here, presented, according to an inscription on it, by Marcus Nigidius Vaccula, who, as a

symbol of his name, had the figure of a cow (*vacca*) stamped
in relief on the brazier. We find a similar brazier, together
with benches, in the tepidarium of the baths near the Forum,
which had no other means of heating; we naturally infer that
the furniture here was intended for one of the tepidariums, and
used there before the improved method of heating was introduced.   A Nasennius Nigidius Vaccula, who died before 54
A.D., is known to us from the receipts of Caecilius Jucundus.
If he was the donor, and made the gift when he was a young
man, the change of the system of heating in the tepidarium
may have been made as late as 20 A.D.

The colonnade was originally uniform on all the three sides.
The Doric columns were of tufa, coated with fine white stucco.

They were of slender
proportions, the height
being a trifle over nine
feet, with a diameter of
only   sixteen   inches.
They were edged, not
fluted, and doubtless carried an entablature with
triglyphs, of which no
trace remains.   In the
time of the Empire,
apparently before the
earthquake of 63, the
colonnade was remod-

Fig. 84.—Colonnade of the Stabian Baths: capital
with section of entablature, restored.

elled in accordance with the prevailing taste.   The columns received a thick coating of stucco, incised lines taking the place
of flutings; the lower third of the shaft was painted red, the
upper portion being left white.   Over the capitals, moulded
in stucco, was an entablature resting on thick planks, and ornamented with light-colored stucco reliefs.   The general effect may
be seen from our illustration (Fig. 84).

In this reconstruction the sameness of the earlier colonnade
was varied with pleasing irregularities.   Thus in front of the
main entrance (A), and in a corresponding position on the
opposite side of the court, the place of four columns was taken

by two broad pillars flanked by half-columns, and carrying a
roof more than five feet higher than that of the rest of the
colonnade.   A similar arrangement has already been noted in
the colonnade of the temple of Isis (p. 168).

The wall decoration of the court has been particularly well
preserved on the outer wall of the rooms D and E (Fig. 85).
The surface is diversified by fantastic architectural designs in
two stories, made up of slender columns with their entablatures,

Fig. 85. — Stabian Baths : southwest corner of the palaestra, showing part of the colonnade and wall decorated with stucco reliefs.

open doorways with steps leading up to them, and glimpses of
interiors.   In the panels thus outlined, figures of all kinds stand
out in white relief on a bright red or blue ground.   Above the
arched doorway Jupiter sits, resting his right hand on his
sceptre ; near by, on a pillar, is the eagle.   Further to the left
a satyr offers Hercules a drinking horn.   Another relief, not so
well preserved, has a motive suggestive of the purpose of the
building — Hylas at the spring seized by the nymphs.   With
this we may associate two designs having reference to the exer-

o

cises of the palaestra : a boxer, at the left of the doorway of E,
and at the right a man scraping himself with a strigil. On
the outer wall of G is Daedalus, making wings for himself and
Icarus.

Under the colonnade at the rear, a herm stands close to the
wall, having the features of a youth with a garment drawn over
his head and covering the upper part of the body. For the
explanation of it we are indebted to Pausanias. 'In the gymnasium at Phigalia, in Arcadia,' says this writer, 'is an image
of Hermes. It has the appearance of a man wrapped in a
cloak, and terminates below in a square pillar in the place of
feet.' This is Hermes, the god of the Palaestra, here, as in
Phigalia, in a guise suggestive of his function of Psychopompus,
the conductor of departed souls. We have already met with
an example of the same type in the court of the temple of
Apollo.

A sundial stood on the roof of the frigidarium and men's
caldarium, supported by a foundation of masonry still visible.
It bore an Oscan inscription, from which we learn that it was
set up by the Quaestor Maras Atinius, in accordance with a
decree of the council, the money for the expenditure being
derived from fines. The fines were very likely collected here,
by the official in charge of the building. Sundials were erected
also in the other baths at Pompeii. They were a necessity, for
all such establishments were conducted on a schedule of hours.
Hadrian ordered that the baths in Rome should be open from
the eighth hour, that is, after two o'clock in the afternoon ; and
a regulation in regard to the time of opening, if not of closing,
was probably in force at Pompeii.

A motley and tumultuous life once filled the barren court, the
rooms now ruined and deserted. The scene is well pictured by
Seneca (Ep. 56): 'Quiet is by no means so necessary for study
as men commonly believe,' the philosopher gravely argues.
'I am living near a bath : sounds are heard on all sides. Just
imagine for yourself every conceivable kind of noise that can
offend the ear. The men of more sturdy muscle go through
their exercises, and swing their hands heavily weighted with
lead : I hear their groans when they strain themselves, or the

whistling of labored breath when they breathe out after having held in. If one is rather lazy, and merely has himself rubbed with unguents, I hear the blows of the hand slapping his shoulders, the sound varying according as the massagist strikes with flat or hollow palm. If a ballplayer begins to play and to count his throws, it's all up for the time being. Meanwhile there is a sudden brawl, or a thief is caught, or there is some one in the bath who loves to hear the sound of his own voice; and the bathers plunge into the swimming tank with loud splashing. These noises, however, are not without some semblance of excuse; but the hair plucker from time to time raises his thin, shrill voice in order to attract attention, and is only still himself when he is forcing cries of pain from some one else, from whose armpits he plucks the hairs. And over all the din you hear the cries of those who are selling cakes, sausages, and sweetmeats.'

Such were the distractions of a Roman bath.

CHAPTER XXVII

THE BATHS NEAR THE FORUM

THE bathing establishment in the block north of the Forum is smaller and simpler in its arrangements than that described in the last chapter, but the parts are essentially the same. Here also we find a court, with a colonnade on three sides ; a system of baths for men, comprising a dressing room (I) with a small round frigidarium (II) opening off from it, a tepidarium (III), and a caldarium (IV) ; a similar system for women, the place of the frigidarium being taken by a tank for cold baths (2) in the dressing room ; and a long narrow furnace room between the two baths (V). On three sides of the establishment are shops, in connection with which are several inns.

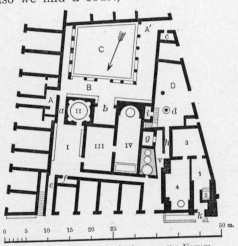

Fig. 86. — Plan of the baths near the Forum.

A, A'. Street entrances to court.
B. Colonnade.
C. Area.
D. Court back of women's baths.
I-IV. Men's baths.
    I. Apodyterium.
    II. Frigidarium.
    III. Tepidarium.
    IV. Caldarium.
V. Furnace room.
1-4. Women's baths.
    1. Apodyterium.
    2. Basin for cold baths.
    3. Tepidarium.
    4. Caldarium.
d. Sundial.

These baths were built shortly after 80 B.C., about the time that Ulius and Aninius repaired the Stabian Baths ; the characteristic masonry, with quasi-reticulate facing, is similar to that of the Small Theatre and the Amphitheatre. The names of the builders are known from an inscription found in duplicate : *L. Caesius*

C. f. d[uum] v[ir] i[uri] d[icundo], C. Occius M. f., L. Ni-
raemius A. f. II v[iri] d[e] d[ecurionum] s[ententia] ex
peq[unia] publ[ica] fac[iundum] curar[unt] prob[arunt]
q[ue]. Thus we see that the contract for the building was
let and the work approved by Lucius Caesius, duumvir with
judiciary authority, — his colleague had probably died since
election and the vacancy had not yet been filled, — and the two
aediles, Occius and Niraemius, who are here styled 'duumvirs,'
for reasons already explained (p. 12); the cost was defrayed
by an appropriation from the public treasury.   Though these
Baths are of later construction than the Stabian Baths, they
seem more ancient because fewer changes were made in them.

The court here was not a palaestra; it was small for gymnastic exercises, and was not provided with a swimming tank
and dressing rooms.   The open space was occupied by a garden.

The colonnade on the north and west sides of the court had
slender columns standing far apart, with a low and simple
entablature; on the east side the columns were replaced by
pillars carrying low arches, which served as a support for
a gallery affording a pleasant view of the garden.   This
gallery was accessible from the upper rooms of several
inns along the street leading north from the Forum, whose
guests no doubt found diversion in watching what was going
on below — an advantage that may have been taken into
account by the city officials in fixing the rent.   There are
benches on the north side of the court, and at the middle a
deep recess, or exedra (*b*), making a pleasant retreat for quiet
conversation.   The entrance from the frequented street at the
left (A) is so arranged that passers-by could not look in; near
the entrance from the street on the opposite side (A') is a
closet (*c*).   The decoration of the court was extremely simple.
Columns and walls were unpainted; on the lower parts, stucco
with bits of brick in it; above, white plaster.

From the court a corridor (*a*) led into the men's apodyterium,
which could be entered also on the north side from the Strada
delle Terme.   This room contained benches, as shown on the
plan; but there were no niches, as in the dressing rooms of
the Stabian Baths, and wooden shelves or lockers may have

been used instead.   The small dark chamber at the north end
(*f*) may have been used as a storeroom for unguents, such as
the Greeks called *elaeothesium*.   It seems to have been thought
necessary here to connect the dressing room with the furnace
room (V) by a separate passage.

Light was admitted to the dressing room through a window
in the lunette at the south end, closed by a pane of glass half
an inch thick, set in a bronze frame that turned on two pivots.

Fig. 87. — Baths near the Forum : interior of the men's tepidarium.

On either side of the window are huge Tritons in stucco relief,
with vases on their shoulders, surrounded by dolphins ; underneath is a mask of Oceanus, and in the same wall is a niche
for a lamp, similar to that seen in Fig. 87, blackened by the soot.

The frigidarium is well preserved.   In all its arrangements
it is almost an exact counterpart of the one in the Stabian
Baths, but the scheme of decoration, suggestive of a garden,
is less realistically carried out, the ground being yellow ; and
the round window at the apex of the domed ceiling has a

rectangular extension toward the south in order to admit as
much sunlight as possible.

The tepidarium, as will be seen from our illustration (Fig. 87),
is in the condition of the tepidariums of the Stabian Baths
before the improved arrangements for heating were introduced.
There were no warm air chambers in the walls or the floor.
At one end we see the remains of the large bronze brazier and
benches (the iron grating is modern) presented by Vaccula, to
which reference has already been made (p. 191). The feet of
the benches are modelled to represent hoofs, each with a cow's
head above.

There are niches in the walls, as formerly in the tepidariums
of the Stabian Baths, but several of them for some reason have

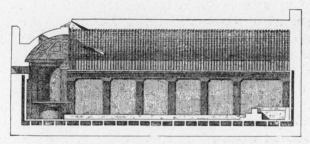

Fig. 88.— Longitudinal section of the men's caldarium.

been walled up. Wild-visaged, muscular Atlantes stand out
in bold projection on the front of the partitions between the
niches, sustaining a cornice upon their uplifted hands. The
window, seen in the illustration above the lamp niche, was
closed, as that in the dressing room, by a pane of glass in a
bronze frame.

The decoration of the ceiling, unfortunately only in part
preserved, is well designed. Along the lower edge are arabesques, interwoven in a scroll pattern, in white stucco on a
white background. Above these are panels of different sizes,
in which raised white ornaments and figures appear on a white,
blue, or violet ground ; among the motives are Cupid leaning on
his bow, Apollo riding on a griffin, Ganymede with the eagle,
and Cupids on sea horses.

The caldarium is well preserved ; only a part of the vaulted

ceiling has been destroyed. The hollow space for hot air in
the floor and walls is indicated in our section (Fig. 88). Here
we see at the right, the bath basin, lined with white marble,
with its sloping back affording a comfortable support for the
bathers; at the other end is the apsidal niche (*schola*) with the
labrum. The direction of Vitruvius, that the labrum should be
placed under a window in such a way that the shadows of those
standing around should not fall on it, is here literally observed.
There were two other small windows at the same end of the
room, and a niche for a lamp.

We learn from an inscription on the labrum, in bronze letters,
that it was made under the direction of Gnaeus Melissaeus Aper
and Marcus Staius Rufus, who were duumvirs in 3–4 A.D., at
a cost of 5250 sesterces, not far from \$270. This room seems
to have received its final form before the new method of heating the water in the alveus came into vogue; there is no trace
of a bronze heater, such as that found in connection with the
bath basin of the women's caldarium at the Stabian Baths. The
simple decoration is in marked contrast with the usual ornamentation of the later styles. Above a low marble base are
yellow walls divided by dark red pilasters, shown in Fig. 88.
These support a projecting flat cornice of dark red, whose surface is richly ornamented with stucco reliefs. The ceiling is
moulded in flutings running up to the crown of the vault; only
in the ceiling of the schola do we find raised figures.

The rooms of the women's baths are small, their arrangement
being determined in part by the irregular shape of the corner
of the building in which they are placed; but the system of
heating is more complete than in the men's baths, for both the
tepidarium (3) and the caldarium (4) were provided with hollow
floors and hot air spaces in the walls extending to the lunettes
and the ceiling. The vaulted ceilings of both of these rooms, as
well as of the apodyterium, are preserved; but the caldarium
has lost its hollow floor and walls, together with the bath basin,
which was placed in a large niche at the right as one entered;
only the base of the labrum remains. The condition of this
room may be due to the earthquake of the year 63, the necessary repairs not having been made before the eruption. There

was no connection between the women's baths and the court at the rear (D), which had a separate entrance from the street. At the women's entrance there was a narrow waiting room for attendants, separated from the street by a thin wall and protected by a roof.

The furnace room could be entered at one end from the street. The three cylindrical tanks for hot, lukewarm, and cold water were arranged as in the Stabian Baths. Beyond the tanks is a cistern (*g*), which was supplied in part by rain water from the roof, in part by a feed pipe connected with the water system of the city. The raised walk (*h*) on the right side of the furnace room is continued to the small court (D) in the corner of which is a stairway leading to the flat roof of the men's caldarium. From this point of vantage, the view over the landscape and the sea must have been beautiful in antiquity, as it is to-day.

A sundial doubtless stood on the larger of the two pillars in the court (*d*), which is about sixteen feet high and nearly five feet thick at the base; the purpose of the smaller pillar is not clear.

CHAPTER XXVIII

THE CENTRAL BATHS

SENECA in an entertaining letter (Ep. 86) gives an account of a visit about 60 A.D. to the villa at Liternum in which the Elder Scipio had lived in the years immediately preceding his death, in 183 B.C. The philosopher was particularly struck with the bath, the simplicity of which he contrasts forcibly with the luxurious appointments of his own time. We cannot follow him through the extended disquisition — he speaks of various refinements of luxury of which we find no traces at Pompeii; but he mentions as the most striking difference the lack of light in the old bath, with its small apertures more like chinks than windows, while in his day the baths were provided with large windows protected by glass, and people 'wanted to be parboiled in full daylight,' besides having the enjoyment meanwhile of a beautiful view. Some such feeling as this we have in turning from the two older baths at Pompeii — one of pre-Roman origin, the other dating from the time of Sulla — to the Central Baths, which were in process of construction at the time of the eruption, and had been designed in accordance with the prevailing mode of life.

This extensive establishment, at the corner of Stabian and Nola streets, occupied the whole of a block; but a large part of the frontage on the two streets mentioned was utilized for shops. Notwithstanding the size of the building, it had only a single series of apartments, which were laid out on a correspondingly large scale. It was doubtless built for men, although the use of it at certain hours by women may possibly have been contemplated, in case the women's baths at the two other establishments should be overcrowded.

Entrances from three streets lead to the ample palaestra, from which the remains of the houses demolished to make room

The tepidarium (q) — here, as usual, relatively small — is connected with the apodyterium by two doors, and similarly with the caldarium. The latter room has a bath basin at each end, thus affording accommodations for twenty-six or twenty-eight bathers at once; at the middle of the southeast side was a smaller basin that took the place of the labrum. The hot air flues leading from the furnaces under the bath basins were already built, and above them openings were left for semi-cylindrical heaters like that in the women's caldarium of the Stabian Baths.

The round sweating room, Laconicum, was made more ample by means of four semicircular niches, and lighted by three small round windows just above the cornice of the domed ceiling. There was probably another round opening at the apex, designed for a bronze shutter, which could be opened or closed from below by means of a chain, so as to regulate the temperature. Doors led into the Laconicum from both the tepidarium and the caldarium.

The oblong court between the bath rooms and the street on the northeast side was apparently to be laid out as a garden. At the north end the workmen had begun to build pillars for a short colonnade. A large square foundation for a sundial stands near the opposite corner.

CHAPTER XXIX

THE AMPHITHEATRE

In the southeast corner of the city, at a distance from the other excavations, lies the Amphitheatre, the scene of gladiatorial combats. The Pompeians called it 'the show,' *spectacula*, as in the inscription, preserved in two copies, that gives us the names of the builders: *C. Quinctius C. f. Valgus, M. Porcius M. fi[lius] duo vir[i] quinq[uennales] coloniai honoris caussa spectacula de sua peq[unia] fac[iunda] coer[arunt] et coloneis locum in perpetuom deder[unt].* According to this, the Amphitheatre was built by the same men, Valgus and Porcius, who are already known to us as the builders of the Small Theatre (p. 147); and they presented it to the city in recognition of the honor conferred upon them by their reëlection as duumvirs. The Amphitheatre may thus have been finished half a decade later than the Theatre, but in any case it belongs to the earliest years of the Roman colony, — as might be inferred, in default of other evidence, from the archaic spelling of the inscription and the character of the masonry, which is like that of the Small Theatre and the baths north of the Forum (p. 45).

The colonists, however, did not receive from Rome their impulse to erect such a building. The passion for gladiatorial combats was developed in Campania earlier, and manifested itself more strongly, than in Latium. Strabo's statement that gladiators were brought forward at Campanian banquets, in larger or smaller numbers according to the rank of the guests, has reference to the period before the Second Punic War; but it was considered a noteworthy event in Rome when, in 264 B.C., three pairs of gladiators fought in the Forum Boarium in celebration of funeral rites, as also when, on a similar occasion in 216 B.C., twenty-two pairs engaged in combat. Buildings were

erected for gladiatorial shows in Campanian towns earlier than
at the Capital. As late as the year 46 B.C. the spectators who
witnessed the games given by Julius Caesar sat on wooden seats
supported by temporary staging; and the first stone amphitheatre in Rome was built by Statilius Taurus in 29 B.C., almost
half a century after the quinquennial duumvirate of Valgus and
Porcius. The Amphitheatre at Pompeii is the oldest known
to us from either literary or monumental sources.

In comparison with later and more imposing structures, our
Amphitheatre seems indeed unpretentious. Its exterior elevation is relatively low (Fig. 91); as our section shows (Fig. 94),
the arena and the lower ranges of seats are in a great hollow

Fig. 91. — The Amphitheatre, seen from the west side.

excavated for the purpose below the level of the ground.
The dimensions (length 444 feet, breadth 342) are small when
compared with those of the Coliseum (615 and 510 feet, respec-
tively) or even the amphitheatres at Capua or Pozzuoli; and
the lack of artistic form is noteworthy.

The exhibitions held here must also have been on a modest
scale. There were no underground chambers, below the arena,
with devices by means of which wild beasts could be lifted up
into view and the sand suddenly covered with new combatants.
The limited means of this small city were not adequate to make
provision for the elaborate equipment and costly decoration
found in the amphitheatres of larger towns.

The arena, a view of which is given in Plate VI, is surrounded by a wall about 6½ feet high. This wall was covered
with frescoes which, still fresh at the time of excavation, are

now known to us only from copies in the Naples Museum.
They consisted of alternate broad and narrow panels, the latter
containing each a herm between two columns, while the larger
spaces presented alternately a conventional pattern and a
scene connected with the games.   One of the scenes gives an
interesting glimpse of the preparations for the combat (Fig. 92).
In the middle we see the overseer marking out with a long staff
the ring within which the combatants must fight.   At the right
a gladiator stands, partly armed; two attendants are bringing
him a helmet and a sword.   A hornblower, also partly armed,
stands at the left; and behind him two companions, squatting

Fig. 92. — Preparations for the combat.   Wall painting, from the Amphitheatre.

on the ground, make ready his helmet and shield.   At either
end of the scene, in the background, is an image of a Winged
Victory with a wreath and palm.

The travertine coping of the wall about the arena shows
traces of iron in the joints between the blocks, apparently
remains of a grating designed to protect the spectators from
attacks by the infuriated wild beasts.   The traces are not visible
all the way around, but this may be accounted for on the supposition that repairs were in progress at the time of the eruption.

Two broad corridors (3, 3A) connect the ends of the arena
with the outside of the building.   The one at the north end,
toward Vesuvius, follows a straight line; the other bends
sharply to the right in order to avoid the city wall, which bounds
the structure on the south and east sides.   By these corridors
the gladiators entered the arena, first in festal array, passing

in stately procession across the sand from one entrance to
the other, then coming forth in pairs as they were summoned
to mortal combat.

At the middle of the west side there is a third passage,
narrow and low (*e*); this is the grewsome corridor through

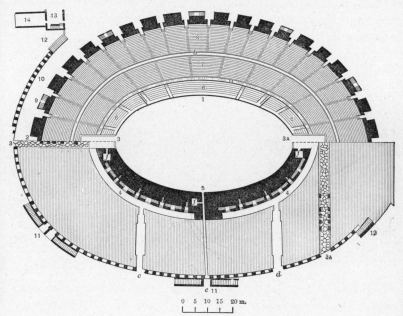

Fig. 93.— Plan of the Amphitheatre at different levels showing, above, the arrangement
     of the seats; below, the arrangement of the vaulted passages under the seats.

1. Podium.	11, 11. Outer double stairways to terrace.
2. Gallery.	12, 12. Single stairways to terrace.
3, 3A. Entrances to arena.	13. Tower of city wall.
4, 4. Vaulted corridor.	14. City wall.
5. Passage to death gate.	*a*. First praecinctio.
6. Ima cavea.	*b*. Second praecinctio.
7. Media cavea.	*c, d*. Side entrances.
8. Summa cavea.	*e*. Death Gate.
9. Stairs of balcony.	*f, f, f*. Dens.
10. Terrace.	

which the bodies of the dead were dragged by means of hooks,
its entrance being the Porta Libitinensis, 'Death Gate.' Near
the inner end of each of the three corridors is a small, dark
chamber (*f*) the purpose of which is unknown. It has been

P

suggested that wild animals may have been confined here, but larger and more easily accessible rooms would have been required for this purpose. They may have been storerooms for appliances of various kinds required for the exhibitions.

The seats, of which there are thirty-five rows, have the same form as those in the Small Theatre, and are of the same material, gray tufa. They are arranged in three divisions, — the lowest, *ima cavea*, having five rows; the middle division, *media cavea*, twelve; and the highest, *summa cavea*, eighteen (Figs. 93, 94). In the middle section of the ima cavea on each side the place of the seats is taken by four low, broad ledges, set aside for members of the city council, who could place upon them the seats of honor, *bisellia*, to the use of which they were entitled. At the middle of the east side the second ledge is interrupted for a distance of ten feet (the break is shown in Plate VI), a double width being thus given to the lowest. This place was designed for seats of special honor, and was, no doubt, reserved for the official who provided the games, and his associates. On the same side the ledges are extended into the next section on the south, the continuity of the seats being interrupted by a low barrier. This supplementary section was, perhaps, intended for certain freedmen, as the Augustales (p. 100), who had the right to use bisellia, but who nevertheless could not become members of the city council, and were not ranked on a social equality with the occupants of the middle section.

The seats of the ima cavea and media cavea were reached through a vaulted passage (4), which, in accordance with ancient usage, we may call a crypt. It ran under the first seats of the second range, and stairs led from it to both divisions. It might be entered either from the two broad corridors leading to the arena, or directly from the west side by means of two separate passages (*c, d*, on the plan). It is, however, interrupted at the middle on each side of the Amphitheatre. On the west side the prolongation of the crypt would have interfered with the use of the corridor leading to the Death Gate; but as no such reason existed for blocking the east branch, it is probable that the designers of the Amphitheatre interrupted both branches of the crypt in order to force the spectators who had seats in

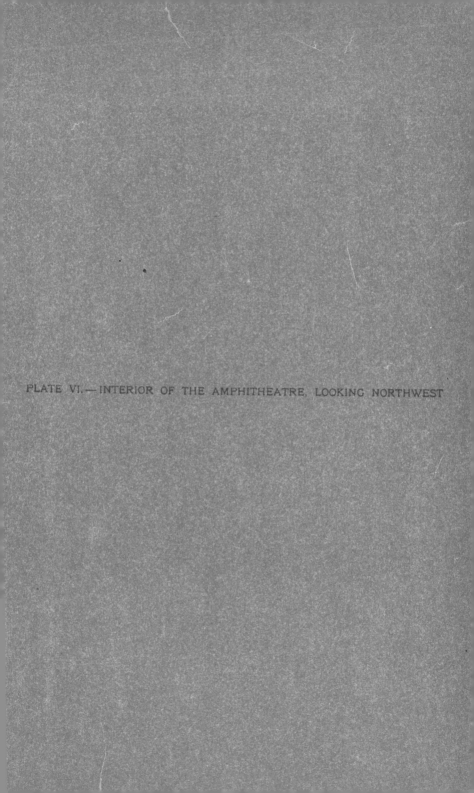

PLATE VI. — INTERIOR OF THE AMPHITHEATRE, LOOKING NORTHWEST

the lower and middle divisions of the south half of the structure to enter and leave by the somewhat inconvenient south
entrances, which are situated in an angle of the city wall. Had
the crypt been carried completely around, the crowd would
always have pressed into the building through the north entrances, which opened toward the city, thus causing confusion,
if not danger, on occasions of special interest.

In the corridor leading from the north entrance, as may be
seen on the plan, a row of stones with square holes in them
were placed in the pavement near the left wall. In these stakes
could be set and connected by ropes, thus making a narrow passageway along the side. The purpose of the arrangement is
not difficult to understand. Through the north corridor the
gladiators entered and left the building, and the wild beasts.

Fig. 94. — Transverse section of the Amphitheatre.

▓▓▓▓t in ; so provision had to be made to give them a
▓▓▓▓▓▓parate from that used by the spectators. Before the
commencement of an exhibition the whole entrance was accessible to the populace, which eagerly crowded forward to secure
seats in good season. When they had for the most part found
their places, the barrier was set up, and only a narrow alley
was left along the east wall for belated spectators who wished
to pass into the crypt on that side ; the rest of the passage was
reserved for the gladiators, and the spectators whose seats were
reached from the opposite branches of the crypt were obliged to
use the side entrance (c).

The middle division was separated from the summa cavea (8)
by a low parapet with a narrow passage (*praecinctio*, b) on the
upper side. The seats of the summa cavea could be reached in
two ways, by passing through the crypt and up the long flights
of stairs that led through the middle division to the top (best
seen in Fig. 94), or by mounting the stairs on the outside of the

building to the terrace (10), which has the same level as the highest rows of seats; it is also of the same height as the city wall, with which it is merged on the south and east sides. The terrace was no doubt the principal means of access; ample provision was made for the crowd by building two large double stairways (11), with smaller single flights at the corners where the terrace joined the city wall (12).

Between the terrace and the seats of the summa cavea was an elevated gallery, divided up into small boxes, about four feet square; under the row of boxes were vaulted vomitoria, making the seats of the summa cavea accessible from the terrace. A passage ran along the outside of the boxes, with steps leading from the terrace; only every third box was connected with this passage, however, the other two of the group being entered from a narrow ramp along the front (Fig. 95).

Fig. 95.— Plan of the gallery.

1. Steps.   2. Boxes.

The Amphitheatre had a seating capacity of about twenty thousand persons. We have no information in regard to the distribution of seats, but it may safely be assumed, from the arrangements known to have existed elsewhere, that the lowest division was reserved for the city officials with t' and other prominent people; that an admission fee w for the seats of the middle division; and that the s upper division were free. The gallery was doubtless set aside for women, who were permitted by a regulation promulgated in the reign of Augustus to have a place only in the upper portion of the Amphitheatre.

Besides the inscription giving the names of the builders (p. 206) there are several others of interest in connection with the building. Four of them, cut in large letters in the travertine coping of the wall about the arena, commemorate the construction of seats. One reads: *L. Saginius II vir i. d. pr[o] lu[dis] lu[minibus] ex d[ecurionum] d[ecreto] cun[eum]*, — 'Lucius Saginius, duumvir with judiciary authority, in accordance with a resolution of the city council (constructed) a section of seats in the place of the games and illumination,' that otherwise he would have been required to provide. Another of the series is even more abbreviated, but the meaning is clear: MAG · PAG · AUG · F ·

the lower and middle divisions of the south half of the structure to enter and leave by the somewhat inconvenient south entrances, which are situated in an angle of the city wall. Had the crypt been carried completely around, the crowd would always have pressed into the building through the north entrances, which opened toward the city, thus causing confusion, if not danger, on occasions of special interest.

In the corridor leading from the north entrance, as may be seen on the plan, a row of stones with square holes in them were placed in the pavement near the left wall. In these stakes could be set and connected by ropes, thus making a narrow passageway along the side. The purpose of the arrangement is not difficult to understand. Through the north corridor the gladiators entered and left the building, and the wild beasts.

Fig. 94. — Transverse section of the Amphitheatre.

was charged in ; so provision had to be made to give them a seats of the parate from that used by the spectators. Before the commencement of an exhibition the whole entrance was accessible to the populace, which eagerly crowded forward to secure seats in good season. When they had for the most part found their places, the barrier was set up, and only a narrow alley was left along the east wall for belated spectators who wished to pass into the crypt on that side ; the rest of the passage was reserved for the gladiators, and the spectators whose seats were reached from the opposite branches of the crypt were obliged to use the side entrance (*c*).

The middle division was separated from the summa cavea (8) by a low parapet with a narrow passage (*praecinctio*, *b*) on the upper side. The seats of the summa cavea could be reached in two ways, by passing through the crypt and up the long flights of stairs that led through the middle division to the top (best seen in Fig. 94), or by mounting the stairs on the outside of the building to the terrace (10), which has the same level as the highest rows of seats; it is also of the same height as the city wall, with which it is merged on the south and east sides. The terrace was no doubt the principal means of access; ample provision was made for the crowd by building two large double stairways (11), with smaller single flights at the corners where the terrace joined the city wall (12).

Between the terrace and the seats of the summa cavea was an elevated gallery, divided up into small boxes, about four feet square; under the row of boxes were vaulted vomitoria, making the seats of the summa cavea accessible from the terrace. A passage ran along the outside of the boxes, with steps leading from the terrace; only every third box was connected with this passage, however, the other two of the group being entered from a narrow ramp along the front (Fig. 95).

Fig. 95.—Plan of the gallery.
1. Steps. 2. Boxes.

The Amphitheatre had a seating capacity of about twenty thousand persons. We have no information in regard to the distribution of seats, but it may safely be assumed, from the arrangements known to have existed elsewhere, that the lowest division was reserved for the city officials with t' and other prominent people; that an admission fee v for the seats of the middle division; and that the s upper division were free. The gallery was doubtles. for women, who were permitted by a regulation promulgated in the reign of Augustus to have a place only in the upper portion of the Amphitheatre.

Besides the inscription giving the names of the builders (p. 206) there are several others of interest in connection with the building. Four of them, cut in large letters in the travertine coping of the wall about the arena, commemorate the construction of seats. One reads: *L. Saginius II vir i. d. pr*[*o*] *lu*[*dis*] *lu*[*minibus*] *ex d*[*ecurionum*] *d*[*ecreto*] *cun*[*eum*], — 'Lucius Saginius, duumvir with judiciary authority, in accordance with a resolution of the city council (constructed) a section of seats in the place of the games and illumination,' that otherwise he would have been required to provide. Another of the series is even more abbreviated, but the meaning is clear: MAG · PAG · AUG · F ·

S · PRO · LUD · EX · D · D, that is, *Magistri Pagi Augusti Felicis Suburbani pro ludis ex decurionum decreto,* — ' The officials of the suburb Pagus Augustus Felix by authority of a resolution of the city council (constructed a section of seats) in the place of providing games.'

From an inscription in the Stabian Baths, to which reference has already been made (p. 189), it is clear that some freedom of choice was permitted to the city officials regarding the disposition of the sum which they were required to contribute for public purposes in recognition of the honor conferred upon them by their election. The Amphitheatre was not provided with seats at the beginning, and one wedge-shaped section (*cuneus*) after another was added until the divisions were complete; meanwhile the spectators made themselves as comfortable as they could on the sloping ground. As the organization of the Pagus Augustus Felix did not take place till 7 B.C., the construction of the seats could not at that time have been completed; but they were all finished long before the overwhelming of the city, as shown by the signs of use.

The north entrance to the arena was adorned with two portrait statues of Gaius Cuspius Pansa, father and son, placed in niches in the walls facing each other. The statues have disappeared, but the inscriptions underneath are still in place. What services the Pansas had rendered in connection with the Amphitheatre to merit this distinction, we do not know; but the father, as the inscription indicates, was ' prefect in accordance with the law of Petronius' (p. 14); that is, he was appointed by the city council to exercise the functions of the two duumvirs when no valid election occurred. Bulwer Lytton, by a natural error, makes Pansa a commissioner to secure the execution of an altogether different *Lex Petronia*, which forbade the giving of slaves to wild beasts unless judicial sentence had been previously passed upon them.

The attraction of the gladiatorial exhibitions, together with the ample seating capacity of the building, stimulated attendance from neighboring cities, and on one occasion unfortunate results followed. In the year 59 A.D. a Roman senator, Livineius Regulus, who had been expelled from the Senate, and had apparently taken up his residence at Pompeii, gave an exhibition that attracted a great concourse. Among those who came to witness the combats were many inhabitants of Nuceria. The people of the two towns may not have been on the best of terms previously; whatever the cause, the Pompeians and Nucerians commenced with mutual bantering and recriminations, then resorted to stone-throwing, and finally engaged in a free fight with weapons.

The Nucerians, as can easily be understood, fared the worse, having many killed and wounded. They carried the matter to Rome, lodging a complaint with Nero; the emperor referred the case to the Senate, which decreed that Regulus and the leaders of the disturbance should be sent into exile, that the Pompeians should not be permitted to hold any gladiatorial exhibitions for the space of ten years, and that the illegal societies at Pompeii — in regard to which, unfortunately, we have no further information — should be dissolved. From the receipts of Caecilius Jucundus we learn, further, that the duumvirs of the year 59 were removed from office, and that with the new duumvirs, elected in their places, a magistrate with extraordinary powers, *praefectus iuri dicundo*, was associated — measures that indicate how serious the disturbance of public order must have been.

Reminiscences of this bloody fray are found in several inscriptions scratched on walls; and a lively idea of it is given by a wall painting found in 1869 in a house near the theatres, now in the Naples Museum (Fig. 96). The picture is of special interest as throwing light on the surroundings of the Amphitheatre and some of its arrangements. The open space with the trees in the foreground, among which are various booths, remind one of a park; at the right is a single house. It is clear from the painting that the women's boxes, in the gallery, were arched in front; and we see how the great awning, *velum*, was stretched over the south end to protect the audience from the sun. It was carried by the two towers of the city wall (one of them is indicated on the plan, 13) and by masts that stood in the passage behind the women's boxes, where several of the perforated stones in which they were set may still be seen.

That the sports of the Amphitheatre had at all times the keenest interest for the Pompeians is evident, not only from the number of notices having to do with the games, which we see painted in red on walls along the streets or on tombs by the roadside, but also from the countless graffiti in both houses and public places having reference to combats and favorite gladiators. The limits of space do not permit us to describe

Fig. 96. — Conflict between the Pompeians and the Nucerians. Wall painting.

the gladiatorial exhibitions as they took place at Pompeii and other Roman cities; but the inscriptions bring so near to us the scenes and excitement of those days that it seems worth while to quote and interpret a few typical examples.

On a tomb near the Nuceria Gate, excavated in 1886, is the following notice, painted in red letters: *Glad[iatorum] par[ia] XX Q. Monni Rufi pug[nabunt] Nola K[alendis] Mais, VI. V. Nonas Maias, et venatio erit,* — 'Twenty pairs of gladiators, furnished by Quintus Monnius Rufus, will fight at Nola May 1,

2, and 3, and there will be a hunt.' The forms of the letters
and the numerous ligatures point to a comparatively early
period, perhaps antedating the reign of Augustus. The 'hunt,'
venatio, was an exhibition of wild beasts, which sometimes
were pitted against one another, sometimes fought with men.
Another tomb close by bears a notice of a gladiatorial combat
to take place at Nuceria.

A still larger number of gladiators is announced in this notice :
*Cn. Allei Nigidi Mai quinq[uennalis] gl[adiatorum] par[ia]
XXX et eor[um] supp[ositicii] pugn[abunt] Pompeis VIII
VII VI Kalendas Dec[embres]. Ven[atio] erit. Maio quin-
[quennali] feliciter. Paris va[le]*, — 'Thirty pairs of gladiators
furnished by Cn. Alleius Nigidius Maius, quinquennial duumvir,
together with their substitutes, will fight at Pompeii November
24, 25, 26. There will be a hunt. Hurrah for Maius the quinquennial! Bravo, Paris!' The substitutes were to take the
place of the killed or wounded, that the sport might not suffer
interruption. Nigidius Maius appears to have been a rich
Pompeian of the time of Claudius. In another painted inscription, he advertises a considerable property for rent (chap.
55). His daughter, as we know from an inscription belonging
to a statue erected in her honor, was a priestess of Venus and
Ceres. Paris was probably a popular gladiator.

Other officials besides duumvirs provided exhibitions. Thus
an aedile : *A. Suetti Certi aedilis familia gladiatoria pugnab[it]
Pompeis pr[idie] K[alendas] Iunias ; venatio et vela erunt,* —
'The gladiatorial troop of the aedile Aulus Suettius Certus will
fight at Pompeii May 31 ; there will be a hunt, and awnings
will be provided.'

The following notice can be dated, approximately : *D. Lucreti
Satri Valentis flaminis Neronis Caesaris Aug[usti] fili perpetui
gladiatorum paria XX, et D. Lucreti Valentis fili glad[iatorum]
paria X pug[nabunt] Pompeis VI V IV III pr[idie] Idus
Apr[iles]. Venatio legitima et vela erunt. Scr[ipsit] Aemilius Celer sing[ulus] ad luna[m]*, — 'Twenty pairs of gladiators
furnished by Decimus Lucretius Satrius Valens, permanent
priest of Nero, son of the emperor, and ten pairs of gladiators
furnished by Decimus Lucretius Valens his son, will fight at

Pompeii April 8, 9, 10, 11, and 12. There will be a big hunt, and awnings. Aemilius Celer wrote this, all alone by the light of the moon.' The reference to Nero as the son of the emperor, shows that the inscription was written after he was adopted by Claudius, in 50 A.D., and before Claudius's death, in 54. Celer was an enterprising painter of notices, whose name appears elsewhere in a similar connection.

Besides the general announcement of a gladiatorial exhibition, a detailed programme, *libellus*, was prepared in advance, of which copies were sold. No such copy has come down to us, but the character of the contents of a programme may be inferred from the order of events which a Pompeian with waste time on his hands scratched on a wall; the memorandum covers two exhibitions, which came near together in the early part of May, the result of each combat being carefully noted. Unfortunately the letters have now become almost illegible; but we give the superscription and the first three of the nine pairs of combatants mentioned in the second programme, which is the better preserved of the two, adding in a separate column the full forms of the abbreviated words; the figures indicate the number of combats in which the different gladiators had taken part: —

MUNUS · N . . . . IV · III		Munus N . . . . IV. III.
PRID · IDUS · IDIBUS · MAIS		pridie Idus, Idibus Mais
T M		Threx, Myrmillo
v.	PUGNAX · NER · III	*vicit.* Pugnax, Neronianus, III
p.	MURRANUS · NER · III	*periit.* Murranus, Neronianus, III
O T		Hoplomachus, Threx
v.	CYCNUS · IUL · VIII	*vicit.* Cycnus, Iulianus, VIII
m.	ATTICUS · IUL · XIV	*missus.* Atticus, Iulianus, XIV
ESS		Essedarii
m.	P · OSTORIUS · LI	*missus.* Publius Ostorius, LI.
v.	SCYLAX · IUL · XXVI	*vicit.* Scylax, Iulianus, XXVI

The name of the official who gave the exhibition (*munus*) is obliterated. The contests extended over four days, May 12–15.

In the first pair of gladiators Pugnax, equipped with Thracian weapons — a small, round shield and short, curved sword or dagger — was matched with the Myrmillo Murranus, who bore arms of the Gallic fashion, with the image of a fish on his helmet. Both were *Neroniani;* that is, from the training school for gladiators founded by Nero, apparently at Capua. Pugnax and Murranus had both been through three contests previously. The name of a gladiator entering a combat for the first time was not followed by a number, but by the letter T, standing for *tiro,* 'novice.' At the left we see the record added to the programme by the writer in order to give the result of the combat. Pugnax was the victor, Murranus was killed.

In the second pair Cycnus, in heavy armor, was pitted against Atticus, who had the Thracian arms. Both were from the training school founded by Julius Caesar, probably at Capua, and hence are called *Iuliani.* Cycnus won, but the audience had compassion on Atticus, and his life was spared. The same term was applied to a defeated gladiator permitted to leave the arena as to a soldier having an honorable discharge — *missus,* 'let go.'

The third pair fought in chariots, being dressed in British costume. Scylax was from the Julian school. Such establishments let out gladiators to those who gave exhibitions, and obtained in this way a considerable income. But Publius Ostorius, as his name implies, was a freeman; presumably he was a gladiator, who, having served a full term, had secured his freedom, and was now fighting on his own account. Though beaten, he was permitted to live, perhaps on account of his creditable record; he had engaged in fifty-one combats.

The combatants from the schools of Caesar and Nero were especially popular, and were generally victorious; but gladiators belonging to other proprietors are mentioned, as in the inscriptions of a house on Nola Street, which will be mentioned again presently. Here we find gladiators who were evidently freemen named with others who were slaves of different masters. In only one of these inscriptions, however, do we find the name of an owner that is known to us : *Essedarius Auriolus Sisen[nae].* The chariot fighter Auriolus belonged to a Sisenna, seemingly either the Sisenna Statilius Taurus, who was consul in 16 A.D., or his son of the same name. As we have seen, it was a Statilius Taurus who built the first permanent amphitheatre in Rome, in 29 B.C. The control of this building remained in the hands of the family. In the columbarium in which the ashes of their slaves and freedmen were placed, we find inscriptions of a 'guard of the amphitheatre,' and of a 'doorkeeper' — *custos de amphitheatro, ostiarius ab amphitheatro.* It is highly probable that the family — the first in Rome after the imperial house — possessed a training school, and derived an income from furnishing gladiators to those who gave exhibitions.

In view of these facts, we must suppose that the 'troop' (*familia gladiatoria*) of Suettius Certus, for example, was simply a band of gladiators brought together for a particular engagement, not a permanent organization. The giver of an exhibition would make a contract for the gladiators that he might need. At the close of the combats the dead would be counted, the surviving freemen paid off and dismissed, and the surviving slaves returned to their masters, 'the troop' thus going out of existence.

Occasionally the individual who provided the combats would erect a monument to the fallen, by way of perpetuating the memory of his munificence. A familiar example is the memorial set up by Gaius Salvius Capito at Venosa, of which the inscription is extant. The names are given of the gladiators who were killed, together with the number of their previous combats and victories. They were slaves of different masters, only one of them, Optatus, being owned by Capito himself. Optatus was a tiro, who fell thus in his first contest. Possibly his master had obliged him, on account of some misdemeanor, to enter the arena with little previous training.

Besides the classes of inscriptions of which examples have been presented, all sorts of scratches upon the plastered walls bear witness to the general enthusiasm for gladiatorial sports. Sometimes there is simply the name of a gladiator, with his school and the number of combats, as *Auctus, Iul*[*ianus*], *XXXXX;* sometimes we find a rough outline of a figure with a boastful legend, as *Hermaïscus invictus hac,* 'Here's the unconquered Hermaïscus.'

There are also memoranda in regard to particular combats,

illustrated by rude sketches. Thus on a wall in the house of
the Centenary we find a drawing of a gladiator in flight, pursued by another, with the note : *Officiosus fugit VIII Idus
Nov[embres] Druso Caesare M. Iunio Silano cos.*, — ' Officiosus
fled on November 6, in the year 15 A.D.' A similar sketch has
been found in another house, with these words written beside
the fleeing gladiator, *Q. P[e]tronius O[c]ta[v]us XXXIII,
m[issus]* ; beside the pursuer, *Severus lib[ertus], XXXXXV,
v[icit]*. Severus was thus a gladiator who had been a slave,
and had gained his freedom : he had fought fifty-five combats.
Petronius Octavus may have been a freeman, who had fought
on his own account from the beginning. In taverns a painting
of a gladiator with an inscription like the record of a programme was a favorite subject of decoration.

Athletes in all ages have won the admiration of the gentler
sex ; and it would be surprising if among so many gladiatorial
graffiti there were not some containing references to female
admirers. In the peristyle of a house on Nola Street (V. v. 3)
the names of about thirty gladiators are found ; the kinds of
weapons and the owners are designated, and the number of
previous combats given, as in the programmes, while records
of the results of the combats are usually lacking. Terms of
endearment are lavished upon two, Celadus, Threx, and Crescens, net fighter ; Celadus is *suspirium puellarum*, ' maidens'
sigh,' and *puellarum decus*, ' glory of girls ' ; while Crescens is
puparum dominus, ' lord o' lassies,' and *puparum medicus*, 'the
darlings' doctor.'

Another graffito informs us that at one time — before the year
63 — a gladiator lived in this house : *Samus I Ↄ I m[urmillo],
idem eq[ues], hic hab[itat]*, — ' Samus, who has fought once,
and once conquered (Ↄ is for *corona*, ' crown '), Myrmillo, and
at the same time fighter on horseback, lives here.' Other
gladiators, no doubt, shared the dwelling with him ; and the
amatory graffiti may have been written by one and another
miles gloriosus, referring to conquests outside the arena, or by
companions in bitter scorn.

CHAPTER XXX

STREETS, WATER SYSTEM, AND WAYSIDE SHRINES

THE streets of Pompeii vary greatly in width. The widest is Mercury Street, the continuation of which near the Forum

Fig. 97. — View of Abbondanza Street, looking east.
At the left, fountain of Concordia Augusta, and side entrance of the Eumachia building.
In the pavement, three stepping stones.

has a breadth of nearly 32 feet. Next come Abbondanza and Nola streets, the greatest width of which is about 28 feet; the other streets and thoroughfares vary from 10 to 20 feet. With unimportant exceptions, broad and narrow streets alike are paved with polygonal blocks of basalt, which in laying were fitted to one another with great care; on both sides are raised sidewalks, with basalt or tufa curbing. The sidewalks in some places are paved with small stones, elsewhere are laid with concrete, or left with a surface of beaten earth. As there is no uniformity, the sidewalk varying in front of adjoining houses, it is clear that the choice of materials was left to individual owners of abutting property. The limits of ownership are often designated by boundary stones, laid in the surface of the walk.

Broad ruts, worn by wheels, are seen in the pavement, shallower in places where the basalt flags, cut from the lowest stratum of the stream of lava, are particularly hard; deeper wherever there are blocks quarried nearer the surface. Only the principal streets were wide enough to allow wagons to meet and pass; elsewhere drivers must have waited at a corner for a coming team to go by. It seems likely that driving on the streets of the city was forbidden, wheeled vehicles being used only for traffic; people who wished to ride availed themselves of litters.

At various places along the thoroughfares, but particularly at the corners, large oblong stepping stones with rounded corners were set in the pavement at convenient distances for those wishing to cross, the surface being on a level with the sidewalk. The number varied according to the width of the pavement; in the broadest streets as many as five were used. They were arranged always in such a way as to leave places for the wagon wheels. It is not difficult to understand how Pompeian drivers guided their teams past them; draft animals were attached to the wagon by means of a yoke fastened to the end of the pole, and, as there were no tugs or whippletrees, they had a greater freedom of movement than is allowed to modern teams.

It is not to be supposed that so complete a system of paving existed from the beginning of the city. Some light is thrown on the period of its laying by two inscriptions, — one, EX · K · QUI, cut in the edge of the sidewalk west of Insula IX. iii; the other, K · Q, in the pavement between the second and third Insulae of Region VII. Both are evidently dates, and in full would read *ex Kalendis Quinctilibus*, 'from the first day of July,' and *Kalendis Quinctilibus*, 'July 1.' Apparently they relate to the laying of the pavement; this was in place, even in the unimportant side street of Region VII, when the inscriptions were cut, and so must go back to the time before the name of the month *Quinctilis* was changed to *Iulius*, our July. Pompeii was paved, therefore, before 44 B.C.

The stepping stones were particularly useful when there was a heavy rain; for the water then flowed in torrents down the streets, as it does to-day in Catania, where the inhabitants have light bridges which they throw over the crossings after a storm. There were covered conduits to carry off the surface drainage of the Forum, one of which runs under the Strada delle Scuole to the south, the other under the Via Marina to the west. Elsewhere the water rushed down the streets till it came near the city walls, where it was collected and carried off by large storm sewers. These are still in successful operation, as are also the conduits at the Forum. One is at the west end of the Via dei Soprastanti, another at the west end of Nola Street; and a third leads from Abbondanza Street, nearly opposite the entrance of the Stabian Baths, toward the south.

There were other sewers in the city, but they were of small dimensions and have not been fully investigated. They seem generally to have been under sidewalks. They were not designed to receive surface water, but the drainage of houses. They cannot have served this purpose fully, however, for most of the closets were connected, not with the sewers, but with cesspools.

After the lapse of more than eighteen centuries, the visitor at Pompeii will distinguish at a glance the business streets from those less frequented. The sides of the former are lined with shops; along the latter are blank walls, broken only by house doors, with now and then a small window high above the pavement. The greatest volume of business was transacted on the two main thoroughfares, Stabian and Nola streets; next in importance were Abbondanza Street, leading from the Forum toward the Sarno Gate, and the continuation of Augustales Street from the north end of the Forum toward the east. First in the list of quiet thoroughfares is the broad Mercury Street, along which were many homes of wealth; the north end of it is closed by the city wall.

There were many fountains along the streets of Pompeii, most of them at the corners. They were fed by pipes connecting with the water system of the city. The construction is simple. A deep basin was made by placing on their edges four large slabs of basalt, held together at the corners by iron clamps. Above one of the longer sides, usually near the middle, is a short, thick standard, of the same stone, pierced for the lead feed pipe, which threw a jet of water forward into the basin below; on the opposite side is a depression through which the superfluous water ran off into the street. Most of these standards are ornamented with reliefs, roughly carved but effective, — an eagle with a hare in its beak, a calf's head, a bust of Mercury, a head of Medusa, a drunken Silenus (Fig. 98), or some other suitable design, arranged so that the water would spurt from the mouth of the figure or from an amphora.

Occasionally we find a fountain of finer material. That of Concordia Augusta, of travertine, has already been mentioned (p. 117). In the neighborhood of the Porta Marina there is a fountain of white marble with a relief showing a cock that has tipped over a jar, from the mouth of which the water flowed. Both these more costly fountains were probably the gift of private individuals, one presented to the city by Eumachia, the other by the owner of the nearest house, at VII. xv. 1–2. All the fountains bear witness to long use by the depressions worn in the stone by the hands of those leaning forward to drink.

Water towers stand at the sides of the streets, small pillars of masonry preserved ordinarily to the height of 20 feet. Usually on one side there is a deep perpendicular groove (shown in Fig. 98) in which ran the pipe that carried the water to the top of the tower, where it was received by a small open reservoir, presumably of metal, and distributed through numerous small pipes leading to the fountains and to private houses. The sides of the towers are often covered with incrustations of lime deposited from the water, in which the impressions of the lead pipes are still to be seen; in the case of one tower, at the northeast corner of Insula VI. xiii, a number of the pipes have been preserved. A reservoir was placed also on the top of the commemorative arch at the lower end of Mercury Street, on which stood the bronze statue of Nero or Caligula (p. 48); the traces of the pipes leading from it are clearly seen on the surface of the arch. Similar water towers are in use now in Constantinople and Palermo, having been introduced into the latter city, it would seem, by the Saracens, who very likely took their water system from that of the Turkish capital.

In consequence of these arrangements, Pompeii was well supplied with water. There were flowing jets in all houses except the poorest, and in some the amount used must have been large. In the house of the Vettii there were no less than

Fig. 98. — Fountain, water tower, and street shrine, corner of Stabian and Nola streets.

sixteen jets, in the house of the Silver Wedding, seven; and an equally generous distribution is found in many other of the more extensive private establishments. Large quantities of water were used also in the public baths. The water pipes were made of sheet lead folded together, a transverse section showing the shape of a pear. They were of all sizes, according to the pressure; the flow of water was regulated by means of stopcocks, much like those in use to-day.

Across the street from the Baths near the Forum, on the west, is a large reservoir, of which we give the plan (Fig. 99). It is built partly below the level of the sidewalk, and measures 55 feet in length, the height being $13\frac{1}{2}$ feet to the crown of the

Q

vault. In the south end is a window (*c*), reached from one of
the stairways; when the reservoir was filled to the bottom of the
window, it contained not far from ninety-five thousand gallons.
There were two outlets. One was at the level of the floor,
closed by means of a bronze slide; the grooves in which the
slide worked are preserved. This must have been used only when
the reservoir was cleaned. The other outlet was placed about
three feet above the floor, so that the water could be drawn
off without disturbing the bottom. On the flat roof were rooms
the arrangement of which cannot be determined.

Similar reservoirs are found in Constantinople, designed to
furnish a supply of water in case of siege. Such may have
been the purpose of our structure, which seems to have been
built in the early years of
the Roman colony. The residents, remembering the hard-
ships of the siege of Sulla,
may have thought it necessary to make provision against
a similar strait in the future.

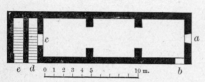

Fig. 99. — Plan of reservoir, west of the
Baths near the Forum.

a, b. Outlets.   *c.* Window.   *d, e.* Stairs.

The source from which the
city received its water supply
has not been discovered. Evidently it did not draw upon the
sources of the Sarno; the water channel constructed by Fontana (p. 25) runs through the city at a height of less than sixty
feet above the level of the sea, while the ancient aqueduct that
supplied Pompeii had so great a head that in the highest parts
of the city, more than 130 feet above the sea, it forced the
water to the top of the water towers, at least twenty feet more.
Copious springs can never have existed on the sides of Vesuvius; water must have been brought to the city from the more
distant mountains bounding the Campanian plain on the east.

We can hardly believe that the construction of a water channel for so great a distance lay within the resources of so small
a town. We find, however, the remains of a great aqueduct
which, starting near Avellino, a dozen miles east of Nola,
skirted the base of Vesuvius on the north and extended westward, furnishing water not only to Naples but also to Puteoli,

Baiae, and Misenum. This ancient structure drew from the same springs, and followed substantially the same route, as the new aqueduct which since 1885 has been bringing water to Naples. No inscription in regard to it has been found, and there is no reference to it in ancient books. The remains — of which the longest section, known as Ponti Rossi, 'Red Bridges,' may be seen near Naples — seem to indicate two styles of construction, extensive repairs having been made after the aqueduct had been partly destroyed; but up to the present time it has not been possible to determine the period to which they belong.

The water system of Pompeii goes back to the time before the founding of the Roman colony. This is evident, not only from the arrangements of the older baths, which comtemplated a freer use of water than could well have been provided by cisterns, but also from the existence of three marble supports for fountain basins, which, as shown by their style of workmanship, the use of Oscan letters as mason's marks, and their location in pre-Roman buildings — the temple of Apollo, the Forum Triangulare, and the house of the Faun — belonged to the earlier period. If we may ascribe the building of the great aqueduct to the time of peace and prosperity in Campania between the Second Punic War and the Social War, and suppose that Pompeii, joining with other towns in its construction, was supplied by a branch from it, we have a simple and highly probable solution of the problem. Nothing in the character of the masonry requires us to assign the aqueduct to a later date.

The shrines along the streets, with few exceptions, were dedicated to the guardian deities presiding over thoroughfares, particularly the gods of street crossings, *Lares Compitales*. The worship of these divinities in Rome was reorganized by Augustus and placed in charge of the precinct wardens, *vicorum magistri*, who were to see that the worship of his guardian spirit, Genius, was associated with that of the Lares at each shrine. The arrangements at the Capital were naturally followed by the colonies and other cities under Roman rule.

At Pompeii the shrines of the street gods differ greatly in size and character. Sometimes there is a small altar against the side of a building, with two large serpents, personifications of the Genius of the place, painted on the wall near it; one of the serpents, with a conspicuous crest, represents a male, the other, a female.

Frequently the place of the altar is taken by a niche, in which the passer-by could deposit his offering. In our illustration (Fig. 100) we see an ancient street altar which was carefully preserved when the Central Baths were built, a niche being made over it in the new wall.

Fig. 100. — Ancient altar in new wall, southeast corner of the Central Baths.

Sometimes a large altar is found, and the Lares, with their offerings, are painted on a wall above it. Such a shrine may be seen at the northwest corner of Stabian and Nola streets, between the fountain and the water tower (Fig. 98). Back of the altar is a wall terminating in a gable (the tiles are modern) on which is a painted altar with four worshippers clad in togas, and a fluteplayer, the inseparable accompaniment of a Roman sacrificial scene; at the sides are the two Lares, represented as youths, in loose tunics confined by a girdle, holding in one hand, high uplifted, a drinking horn (*rhyton*), from which a jet of wine flows into a small pail (*situla*) in the other hand. It is remarkable that we do not find in this or similar paintings at Pompeii,

any figure representing the Genius of the emperor, while in
private houses the Genius of the proprietor often has a place
with the Lares, and sometimes the Genius of the emperor also;
in theory at least, as already remarked (p. 104), the emperor
stood to all men in the relation that the master of a house bore
to the household.

There is also a small chapel for the worship of the street
gods on the west side of Stabian Street, near
Abbondanza Street. As may be seen from
the accompanying plan (Fig. 101), at the left
as you enter is a bench of masonry (1), at the
rear a long altar (2).   In the wall at the right
is a niche for the bronze or terra cotta figures
of the Lares and the Genius, while the surface
of the altar is divided into two parts, for the
separate worship of the same divinities.   A
similar chapel is situated on the west side of

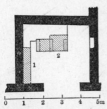

Fig. 101.— Plan of a
chapel of the Lares
Compitales.

Mercury Street (VI. viii. 14).   Here also we find a bench of
masonry, with two niches above it, and in the middle a block
of travertine which may have been used as an altar.   At the
rear is a door leading into a small back room.   This chapel was
formerly thought to be a barber shop.

It has been customary to assign to the street gods all of the
shrines at the side of the street.   Occasionally, however, other
divinities were thus honored; and the only street altar found
with an inscription is consecrated to a different deity.   This
altar is near Nola Street, on the east side of Insula IX. vii.   On
the wall above two cornucopias are painted the words *Salutei
sacrum*, 'Sacred to Salus'; the goddess of health was worshipped here.

Near the upper end of the Forum, on the north side of Insula
VII. vii, is another altar, above which is a stucco relief representing a sacrifice; at the sides of the relief are pilasters, and
over it a gable, in which an eagle is seen.   This indicates that
the shrine was dedicated to Jupiter.

The largest of the street altars, of tufa, stands free in a vaulted
niche on the north side of Insula VIII. ii, but no traces of painting are to be seen near it (Fig. 102).

Various divinities are painted on the outside of houses. The largest picture of this kind is at the corner of Abbondanza Street, on the east side of Insula VIII. iii. It contains figures of the twelve gods, distinguished by their attributes — Vesta, Diana, Apollo, Ceres, Minerva, Jupiter, Juno, Vulcan, Venus Pompeiana, Mars, Neptune, and Mercury. Underneath are the two serpents, facing each other, on either side of a painted altar; near the altar are other figures that cannot be plainly distinguished, probably of men offering sacrifice. This is not a shrine — there is no place for the offerings. The owner of the property (house of the Boar), desired to place his household under the protection of these gods, perhaps also to preserve the corner from defilement. We often find roughly sketched figures of single gods, to the guardian care of whom the master of a house wished to commit his interests — most frequently Mercury, the patron divinity of traders, and Bacchus; but also Jupiter, Minerva, and Hercules.

Fig. 102. — Large street altar.

Sometimes merely a pair of serpents are painted on a wall, in order to give a religious association to the place, as a means of protection. In one case (east side of Insula VI. xi) an explicit warning is scratched on the plaster beside them: *Otiosis locus hic non est; discede, morator,* — 'No place for loafers here; move along!'

CHAPTER XXXI

THE DEFENCES OF THE CITY

FROM the military point of view, Pompeii at the time of the eruption did not possess a system of defences. For many years previously the city wall had been kept in repair only as a convenience in matters of civil administration, and the gates had long since lost all appearance of preparedness to resist attack. The fortifications are not, however, without interest. They form a massive and conspicuous portion of the ruins, and as a survival from an earlier period they have recorded many evidences of the successive changes through which the city passed.

The relation of the wall to the configuration of the height on which Pompeii stood was pointed out in connection with our general survey of the city (p. 31). Along the southwest side, at the time of the eruption, it had almost completely disappeared. Here, where the slope was steepest and the city best defended by nature, the wall had been removed, and its place occupied by houses, at a comparatively early date, probably in the second century B.C.; enough fragments remain, however, to enable us to determine its location with certainty. Elsewhere the greater part of the wall is in a fair state of preservation. The towers did not belong to the original structure, and one of the gates in its present form is of still more recent origin.

The construction of the wall will be readily understood with the help of the accompanying illustrations.

First, two parallel stone walls were built, about 15 feet apart and 28 inches thick; both walls were strengthened on the side toward the city by numerous buttresses, the inner wall being further supported by massive abutments projecting into the space between (Fig. 103). This space was filled with earth.

When the desired height, 26 or 28 feet, was reached, a breast-work of parapets was constructed on the outer wall; the inner wall was carried up about 16 feet above the broad passageway on the top (Fig. 105) as a shield against the weapons of the enemy, preventing the missiles from going over into the town and causing them to fall where the garrison could easily pick them up to hurl back again. Rain water falling on the top flowed toward the outside, and was carried beyond the face of the masonry by stone waterspouts.

For additional strength there was heaped against the inner wall an embankment of earth, which still remains on the north side, between the tenth and twelfth towers. At the right of the Herculaneum Gate the place of the embankment and of the inner wall was taken by a massive stairway (E in Fig. 103) leading to the top. Originally, the stairs extended east about 270 feet, but afterwards they were demolished for the greater part of the distance, and houses were built close to the wall. There is a smaller stairway of the same kind east of the Stabian Gate (Fig. 106).

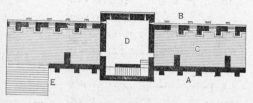

Fig. 103. — Plan of a section of the city wall.

A. Inner wall with buttresses and abutments.
B. Outer wall.
C. Filling of earth between the stone walls.
D. Tower.
E. Stairs leading to the top of the wall.

In the original structure both outer and inner walls were built of hewn blocks of tufa and limestone; but we find portions of the outer wall, and all the towers, of lava rubble, the surface of which was covered with stucco. The towers were already standing, as shown by inscriptions, at the time of the Social War. We are therefore safe in believing that in the period of peace following the Second Punic War the walls were not kept in repair, some parts of the outer wall being utilized as a quarry for building stone; that with the advent of the Social War they were hastily repaired on the north, east, and south sides, and strengthened by towers, but that no attempt was made to renew the fortifications on the steep southwest side, between the Her-

culaneum Gate and the Forum Triangulare, where the line of
the old wall was covered with buildings.

When the towers were added — probably not long before

Fig. 104. — View of the city wall, inside, where the embankment has been removed. The
door in the tower at the left marks the height of the embankment.

90 B.C. — they were not distributed evenly along the wall, but
were placed where they seemed to be most needed. The
western portion of the ridge between the Herculaneum and

Capua Gates was particularly favorable for the approach of
an enemy; hence three towers were built near together here,
numbered 10, 11, and 12 on Plan I.   Another part of the
wall especially exposed was on the southeast side, where
the height covered by the city slopes gradually down to the
plain; and we find five towers within a comparatively short
distance, two east of the Amphitheatre, the other three further
south.   On the north side, between the Capua and Sarno
gates, the slope is steeper and two towers were thought to be
sufficient.

That there were once two additional towers, besides the ten
that have been enumerated, is evident from several Oscan
inscriptions, painted in red letters on the street walls of houses.
One of them, near the southwest corner of the house of the
Faun, reads thus: 'This way leads between Towers 10 and 11,
where Titus Fisanius is in command.'   The street referred to
runs between the tenth and twelfth Insulae of Region VI, direct
to the city wall.   Two others refer to a 'Tower 12' near the
Herculaneum Gate, this part of the fortifications being in charge
of Maras Adirius.

In a fourth inscription we read: 'This way leads between
the houses of Maras Castricius and of Maras Spurnius, where
Vibius Seximbrius is in command.'   In 1897, a fifth inscription
became visible on the north side of Insula VIII. v–vi, where it
had been concealed by a coat of plaster: 'This way leads to
the city building (and) to Minerva.'   The street referred to is
seemingly the blind alley which formerly ran through the insula
(Plan I).   If this is correct, the sanctuary of Minerva is the
Doric temple in the Forum Triangulare; but the 'city building'
cannot be identified.

The five inscriptions evidently date from the siege of Sulla;
they were intended for the information of the soldiers, belonging to the army of the Allies, who were quartered in the city to
assist in its defence.   At this time there must have been twelve
towers, that near the Herculaneum Gate being reckoned last in
the enumeration, as in Plan I; but the location of the two that
have disappeared has not been determined.   Another suggestive reminder of the same siege is the name L · SULA,

scratched by a soldier in the stucco on the inside of Tower 10, near a loophole.

The towers, which measure approximately 31 by 25 feet, were built in two stories, with strong vaulted ceilings. The floor of the second story was on a level with the top of the wall, and over this story was a terrace with battlements, as shown in Fig. 105; the roof seen on the two towers in Fig. 96 was a later addition, made when the city walls were no longer needed as a means

Fig. 105. — Tower of the city wall, restored.

of defence. Stairways on the inside gave ready access to the lower part of the towers, which could be entered from the city by a door (Fig. 104) opening on the enbankment. On the outside were loopholes. Below, at the right, was a sally port, placed thus in order that the soldiers when rushing forth might present their shields to the enemy, leaving the right hand free to use with offensive weapons; when returning to the wall they would, if possible, cut their way to the sally port in the next tower to the right, so as to avoid the danger of exposing their right sides to the enemy.

Four of the gates have been excavated, the Porta Marina and the Stabian, Nola and Herculaneum gates; two others, the Vesuvius and Sarno gates, have been partly exposed to view. The remaining two are still completely covered. All bear evidence of extensive repairs, and one of them, the Herculaneum Gate, was entirely rebuilt at a comparatively late period; with this exception, however, they seem to have assumed their present form in the Tufa Period. Three of them still retain traces of decoration of the first style on the inner parts. The different gateways enter the walls at various angles.

The Stabian Gate may be taken as typical. Entering from the outside, at A, one came through a vaulted passage, B, about twelve feet wide, to a broad middle passage, or vantage court, open to the sky, into which missiles and boiling pitch could be hurled from above upon the heads of an enemy attempting to force the gates; then followed a second vaulted passage, a little wider than the other, in which were hung the heavy double doors, opening outward. The projecting posts of the doors

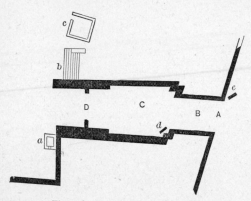

Fig. 106. — Plan of the Stabian Gate.

B. Outer passage.   b. Steps leading to the top of the wall.
C. Vantage court.   c. Gatekeeper's lodge.
D. Doors.   d. Oscan inscription.
a. Well.   e. Latin inscription.

are preserved, as are also the stones on which they rested when they were swung back against the wall; but the vaulting has fallen in. The gateway was paved throughout, with a raised walk on the right side. On one side of the inner entrance is a well (a), the Gorgon's head upon the curb reminding one of the protectress of the gate; on the other, the flight of steps already mentioned (b) leads to the top of the wall. Just beyond the steps are the remains of a small building, perhaps the lodge of the gate keeper (c).

The patron divinity of city gates, Minerva, was probably honored with a small statue in the niche still to be seen in the wall of the vantage court. Two inscriptions commemorate the making of repairs on the thoroughfare passing under the gateway. One of them (at d) is the Oscan inscription recording the work of the aediles Sittius and Pontius, to which reference has already been made (p. 178). The other (at e) is in Latin, and of much later date. It informs us that the duumvirs L.

Avianius Flaccus and Q. Spedius Firmus at their own expense
paved the road 'from the milestone,' which must have been
near the gate, 'to the station of the gig drivers (*cisiarios*), at
the limits of the territory of the Pompeians.' The Roman gigs,
cisia, were very light, and adapted for rapid travelling; they
were drawn by horses or mules, and were kept for hire at
stations along the highways. The site of the station between
Pompeii and Stabiae is not known.

The Nola Gate, and the partially excavated Vesuvius and
Sarno gates, follow the plan just described in all essential particulars. The inner keystone of the Nola Gate, facing the city,
is ornamented with a helmeted head of Minerva, in high relief,
which being of tufa has suffered from exposure to the weather.
There was once an Oscan inscription near by, which stated that
the chief executive officer of the city, Vibius Popidius, let the
contract for building this gate, and accepted the structure from
the contractor.

The front of the Porta
Marina has the appearance
of a tower projecting from
the wall. The gateway
consists simply of two
vaulted entrances, of un-
equal width; one for vehicles, the other, at the left,
for pedestrians. Both were
closed by doors. In the
niche at the right of the
narrow passage the lower

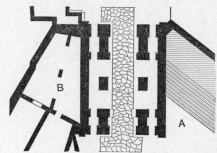

Fig. 107. — Plan of the Herculaneum Gate.
A. Steps leading to the top of the city wall.
B. Room belonging to the house at the left of the Gate.

part of a terra cotta statue of Minerva was found. There was
no vantage court, no inner passage; but in the early years of
the Roman colony the steep lower end of the Via Marina for a
distance of 70 feet was covered with a vaulted roof, which still
remains. Opening into this corridor on the right is a long
narrow room, the original purpose of which is not clear; it is
now used as the local Museum.

This gate in its present form could hardly have been intended for defence; it was adapted rather for administrative

purposes, and must have been built — probably in the place of
an earlier structure — in a period when the possibility of war
seemed remote.   Such a time, as previously remarked, was the
second century B.C., particularly the latter half, after the destruction of Carthage.

A still more peaceful aspect is presented by the Herculaneum
Gate.   The style of masonry — rubble work with *opus mixtum*
at the corners — points to the end of the Republic, rather than

Fig. 108. — Herculaneum Gate, looking down the Street of Tombs.
The corners of the entrances are opus mixtum, a course of brick-shaped blocks of stone
alternating with three courses of bricks.

to the Empire, as the period of construction.   Here we find
three vaulted passages, the middle one for vehicles, those on
either side for pedestrians.   The vaulting over the greater part
of the gate has disappeared ; but according to appearances a vantage court was left here, in the middle passage, if not in those at
the sides ; at the inner end of this court the gates were placed.
The greater part of the structure served no purpose of utility ; it
was obviously designed as a monumental entrance to the city.

PART II

THE HOUSES

CHAPTER XXXII

THE POMPEIAN HOUSE

OUR chief sources of information regarding the domestic architecture of ancient Italy are two, — the treatise of Vitruvius, and the remains found at Pompeii. The Pompeian houses present many variations from the plan described by the Roman architect; yet in essential particulars there is no disagreement, and it is not difficult to form a clear conception of their arrangements.

The houses of Greco-Roman antiquity differed from those of modern times in several respects. They took their light and air from the inside, the apartments being grouped about a court or about a large central room which ordinarily had an opening in the ceiling; the distribution of space being thus made on a different principle, the large rooms were often larger, the small rooms smaller and more numerous than in modern dwellings of corresponding size; and in the better houses the decoration of both walls and floors was more permanent than is usual in our day. The ancient houses were relatively low, in most cases, if we except the crowded tenements of imperial Rome, not exceeding two stories. The windows in the outside walls were generally few and small, and the external appearance was not unlike that of Oriental houses of the present time. In the city house the large front entrance was frequently ornamented with carved posts and lintel.

The development of the Italic house can be traced at Pompeii over a period of almost four hundred years. The earlier form consisted of a single series of apartments, — a central room, *atrium*, with smaller rooms opening into it, and a garden at the rear; an example is the house of the Surgeon (p. 274). A restoration of such a house with its high atrium, wide front door, and garden is shown in Fig. 109.

Fig. 109. — Early Pompeian house, restored.

Later, under Greek influence, a court with a colonnade and surrounding rooms was added. This was called *peristylium*, 'peristyle'; it is simply the more elaborate inner part of the Greek house, *adronitis*, joined to the dwelling of Italic origin. We find the union of atrium and peristyle with their respective groups of apartments fully accomplished in the second century B.C., the Tufa Period; the type of dwelling thus developed remained in vogue during Roman times and is often called the Roman house.

The double origin is clearly indicated by the names of the rooms. Those of the front part are designated by Latin words, — *atrium, fauces, ala, tablinum ;* but the apartments at the rear bear Greek names, — *peristylium, triclinium, oecus, exedra.* In large houses both atrium and peristyle were sometimes duplicated.

The houses of Pompeii impress the visitor as having been designed primarily for summer use. The arrangements contemplate the spending of much time in the open air, and pains was taken to furnish protection from the heat, not from the cold. The greater part of the area is taken up by colonnades, gardens, and courts; from this point of view the atrium may be classed as a court. The living rooms had high ceilings. In summer

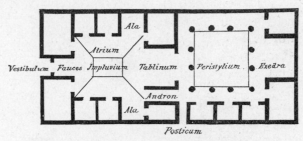

Fig. 110. — Plan of a Pompeian house.

they were cool and airy, in winter difficult to heat; they were dark and close when the door was shut, cold when it was open.

With a single exception the arrangements for heating so often met with in the remains of houses discovered in northern countries are found at Pompeii only in connection with bath-rooms; the cold was ineffectively combated by means of braziers. We are led to believe that the Pompeians were extremely sensitive to heat, but endured cold with great patience. One who makes himself familiar with the arrangements of Italian houses to-day will receive a similar impression, although the peculiarity is perhaps less obvious than in the case of the ancient dwellings.

In describing the Pompeian houses it is more convenient to designate the principal rooms by the ancient names. In Fig. 110 we present an ideal plan; in it the names are given to the parts of the house, the relative location of which is subject to compara-

R

tively little variation. These parts will first be discussed; then those will be taken up which present a greater diversity in their arrangements.

I. Vestibule, Fauces, and Front Door

The *vestibulum* was the space between the front door and the street. The derivation of the word (*ve-* + the root of *stare*, 'to stand aside') suggests the purpose; the vestibule was a place where one could step aside from the bustle and confusion of the street. In many houses there was no vestibule, the front door opening directly on the sidewalk; and where vestibules did exist at Pompeii, they were much more modest than those belonging to the houses of wealthy Romans, to which reference is so frequently made in classical writers. Roman vestibules were often supported by columns of costly marbles, and adorned with statues and other works of art. Only one vestibule at Pompeii was treated as a portico, that of the house of the Vestals near the Herculaneum Gate. This was once as wide as the atrium, the roof being carried by four columns; but before the destruction of the city two partitions were built parallel with the sides dividing it into three parts, a narrow vestibule of the ordinary type, with a shop at the right and at the left.

The passage inside the front door was called *fauces*, or *prothyron*. According to Vitruvius the width of it in the case of large atriums should be half, in smaller atriums two thirds, that of the tablinum; at Pompeii the width is generally less than half. In the houses of the Tufa Period the corners of the fauces where it opens into the atrium were ornamented with pilasters connected at the top by an entablature.

The vestibule and fauces were ordinarily of the same width, and were separated by projecting doorposts with a slightly raised threshold (Fig. 111) and heavy double doors. Sometimes, as in the house of Epidius Rufus, there was in addition a small door at the side of the vestibule opening into a narrow passage connecting with the fauces (Fig. 143). In such cases the folding doors, which on account of their size and the method of hanging must always have been hard to open, were generally kept shut.

They would be thrown back early in the morning for the reception of clients, and on special occasions; at other times the more convenient small door would be used.

In several instances the volcanic ash so hardened about the lower part of a front door that it has been possible to make a cast by pouring soft plaster of Paris into the cavity left by the crumbling away of the wood; there are several of these casts in the little Museum at Pompeii. With their help, and with the

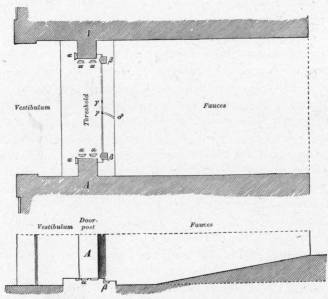

Fig. 111.— Plan and section of the vestibule, threshold, and fauces of the house of Pansa.

well preserved stone thresholds before us, it is possible to picture to ourselves the appearance of the doorway.

The doorposts were protected by wooden casings, *antepagmenta*, which were made fast at the bottom by means of holes in the threshold (*a, a* in Fig. 111).

The folding doors swung on pivots, which were fitted into sockets in the threshold (*β, β*) and in the lintel. The pivots were of wood, but were provided — at least the lower ones — with a cylindrical cap of iron or bronze, and the socket had a protective lining of the same metal. Both caps and sockets,

especially those of bronze, are found in the thresholds in a
good state of preservation. It seems strange that ancient
builders did not use smaller pivots of solid metal, on which the
doors would have turned much more easily ; but a conservative
tradition in this regard prevailed against innovation.

The fastenings were elaborate. Near the inner edge of each
door was a vertical bolt, which shot into a hole in the threshold
(γ, γ); there was probably a corresponding bolt at the top,
as in the case of large modern doors. Sometimes there was a
heavy iron lock, turned with a key, and also an iron bar which
was fastened across the crack in such a way as to tie the two folds
together. In many houses there are holes in the walls of the
fauces, just back of the door, in which at night a strong wooden
bar, *sera*, was placed ; hardly less often we find a hole in the
floor a few feet back, in which one end of a slanting prop was
set, the other end being braced against the middle of the door.
These arrangements bring to mind Juvenal's vivid picture of the
disturbances and dangers of the streets of Rome at night.

II. The Atrium

An atrium completely covered by a roof was extremely rare.
With few exceptions, there was a large rectangular opening
over the middle, *compluvium*, toward which the roof sloped
from all sides (Figs. 109, 113). In the floor, directly under the
compluvium, was a shallow basin, *impluvium*, into which the
rain water fell (*h* in Fig. 113). The impluvium had two outlets.
One was connected with the cistern ; a round cistern mouth,
puteal, ornamented with carving, often stood near the edge of
the basin, as in the house of the Tragic Poet (Fig. 146). The
other outlet led under the floor to the street in front, carrying
off the overflow when the cistern was full, and also the water
used in cleaning the floor. In the better houses a fountain was
often placed in the middle of the impluvium.

Vitruvius mentions five kinds of atriums, the basis of classification being the construction of the roof—Tuscan, tetrastyle,
Corinthian, displuviate, and tortoise atriums. The first three
are well illustrated at Pompeii.

The Tuscan atrium, supposed by the Romans to have been derived from the Etruscans, was apparently the native Italic form. Two heavy girders were placed across the room, above the ends of the impluvium (Fig. 112, *b*). On these, two shorter crossbeams were laid (*c*), over the sides of the impluvium. The corners of the rectangular frame thus made were connected with the walls at the corners of the atrium by four strong slanting beams (Figs. 112, 113, *e*). On these and on the frame were placed the lower ends of the sloping rafters (Fig. 112, *f*), carrying the tiles, the arrangement of which can be seen in Figs. 109, 112, and 113. This was the most common arrangement of the roof at Pompeii.

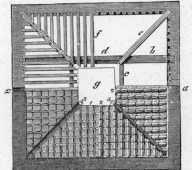

Fig. 112. — A Tuscan atrium: plan of the roof.

a, a. Side walls.
b. One of the two girders supporting the roof.
c. Crossbeam, resting on the two girders.
d. Short beam of the thickness of *c*.
e. Corner beam.
f. Rafters, sloping toward the inside.
g. Compluvium.
1. Flat tiles, *tegulae.*
2. Semicylindrical tiles for covering the joints, *imbrices.*
3. Gutter tiles.

The edge of the compluvium was frequently ornamented with terra cotta waterspouts, representing the heads of animals. In a house near the Porta Marina the projecting foreparts of dogs and lions were used in place of the heads; the remains of a part of the compluvium have been put together again, and are seen in Fig. 114. The lions were placed over the larger spouts at the four corners; the under side of the spouts surmounted by the dogs and lions was ornamented with acanthus leaves in relief. The same illustration presents an example of the antefixes sometimes found.

The tetrastyle atrium differed from the Tuscan in only one respect: there were four columns supporting the roof, one at each corner of the impluvium. In most cases these supports, which interfered with the view of the interior, can hardly have been intended primarily for ornament; they simplified the construction, making the ceiling and roof firm without the use of the heavy and expensive girders.

The Corinthian atrium had a larger compluvium than the other kinds, the roof being supported by a number of columns standing along the edge of the impluvium. There is a good example in the house of Epidius Rufus, where there are sixteen columns.

The roof of the displuviate atrium sloped from the middle toward the sides, the water being carried off by lead pipes. The aperture for the admission of light and air was relatively

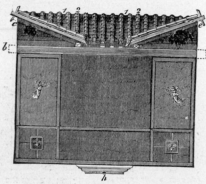

Fig. 113.—A Tuscan atrium: section.

b. Girder.   1. Flat tiles.
e. Corner rafter. 2. Semicylindrical tiles.
h. Impluvium.

much higher above the floor than in the kinds previously described. No example of this type has been found at Pompeii.

The tortoise atrium, *atrium testudinatum*, was small and without a compluvium. The roof had a pyramidal shape. There were possibly a few examples at Pompeii, as we may infer from the occasional absence of an impluvium; in the only instance, however, in which it is possible to determine the form of the roof (V. v. 1–2), this must have been very different from that referred to by the Roman writer.

Vitruvius says further that the atrium should have an oblong shape, the width being three fifths or two thirds of the length, or measured on the side of a square, the hypothenuse of which is taken for the length. The design was obviously to bring the sides nearer together, thus lessening the strain on the two girders which in the commonest form were used to sustain the roof. The height, to the frame of the compluvium, should be three fourths of the width.

In the case of the tetrastyle and Corinthian atriums at Pompeii the height is indicated by that of the columns, but there are rarely adequate data for determining the height of the others with exactness. In regard to length and breadth the proportions harmonize fairly well with those recommended by Vitruvius; but the height, in the cases in which it can be ascertained, is often greater than that contemplated by the rules of the architect.

Looking at the Pompeian atriums in their present condition (Plate VII, Figs. 116, 146) one might easily receive the impression that they were primarily courts rather than rooms. In this respect the restorations of Roman houses in the older books are often at fault, the atrium being generally represented as too low in comparison with the rooms around it.

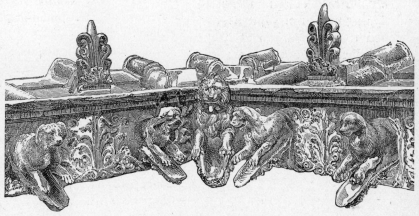

Fig. 114. — Corner of a compluvium with waterspouts and antefixes, reconstructed.

The references in the ancient writers uniformly point to this as the principal room of the house. In the earliest times the hearth stood here; a hole in the roof served as a chimney. The accumulation of soot on the ceiling and the walls suggested the characteristic name 'black room'; for *atrium* comes from *ater*, 'black.' Here the household gathered at mealtime; here they worked, or rested from their labors. In the atrium Lucretia sat with her maids spinning late at night when her husband entered unexpectedly with his friends.

Such the atrium remained in farmhouses to the latest times. The name meanwhile was transferred to the corresponding apartment of elegant city homes, while in the country it went out of use, being replaced by *culina*, 'kitchen,' on account of

the presence of the hearth. In such a room in his Sabine villa
Horace loved to dine, conversing on topics grave or gay with
his rustic neighbors, and partaking of the simple fare with
relish; while his slaves, freed from the restraints of city life,
were permitted to eat at the same time, sitting at a separate
table. The remains of an atrium of this kind, with its hearth
and niche for the images of the household gods, may be seen in
the villa recently excavated at Boscoreale.

Without doubt some houses of the ancient type might be
found in cities, even in Rome, as late as the end of the Republic. We read of one in Cicero's time in the atrium of which
spinning was done. But at Pompeii the hearth had been ban-
ished from the atrium at a comparatively early date, in the
Tufa Period if not before; and the room was made uncomfortable to sit in, for a considerable part of the year, by the
broad opening of the compluvium.

From the architectural point of view, however, the atrium
never lost its significance as the central apartment. In all its
dimensions, but particularly in height, it presents so great a
contrast with the rooms around it as to remind us of the relation of a Roman Catholic church to the chapels at the sides.
The impression of spaciousness was perhaps deepened when
the atrium was provided with a ceiling. Few traces of such
ceilings are found at Pompeii, and in the smaller houses the
inside of the roof seems generally to have been visible.

The atrium of the Corinthian type most nearly resembled a
court, on account of the size of the opening to the sky and the
use of many columns. A suggestion of the un-Italic character
of this type appears in the name; for one can scarcely suppose
that atriums in the strict sense existed at Corinth.

Although the Pompeian atriums, with few exceptions, show no
traces of a hearth, there is a reminiscence of the ancient arrangement in the *gartibulum*, a table which we frequently find at the
rear of the impluvium. Varro says that since his boyhood these
tables, on which vessels of bronze were placed, had gone out
of use; at Pompeii they remained in fashion much longer. The
gartibulum with its bronze vases may symbolize the ancient
hearth with the cooking utensils. Possibly, however, it repre-

sents the kitchen table near the hearth on which the dishes were washed; that it may have served a similar purpose in later times is evident from the fact that in front of it a marble pedestal was often placed for a statuette which threw a jet of water into a marble basin at the edge of the impluvium. This group of table, fountain figure, and basin appears in many Pompeian atriums. In Plate VII we see the gartibulum and the supports of the marble basin, but the base of the fountain figure has disappeared.

The strong box of the master of the house, *arca*, often stood in the atrium, usually against one of the side walls. It was sometimes adorned with reliefs, as the one shown in Fig. 115, which is now in the Naples Museum. It stood on a heavy block of stone, or low foundation of masonry, to which it was attached by an iron rod passing down through the bottom. A wealthy Pompeian sometimes had more than one of these chests.

Fig. 115.—A Pompeian's strong box, *arca*.

In three atriums the herm of the proprietor stands at the rear. One, with the portrait of Cornelius Rufus, is shown in Fig. 116.

When there were two atriums in a house, the larger was more elaborately furnished than the other, and was set aside for the public or official life of the proprietor; the smaller one was used for domestic purposes. Typical examples are found in the houses of the Faun and of the Labyrinth. In the former the principal atrium is of the Tuscan type, the other tetrastyle; in the latter the large atrium is tetrastyle, the smaller Tuscan.

III. The Tablinum

The tablinum was a large room at the rear of the atrium, opening into the latter with its whole width; the connection of the two rooms is clearly shown in Plate VII and Fig. 116.

According to Vitruvius, when the atrium was 30 to 40 feet
in width — as in the larger Pompeian houses — the tablinum
should be half as wide; when the atrium was smaller, the width
of the tablinum should be two thirds that of the atrium, while
the height at the entrance should be nine eighths, and inside
four thirds of the width. These proportions will not hold

Fig. 116. — Atrium of the house of Cornelius Rufus, looking through the tablinum and
andron into the peristyle.

In the foreground, the impluvium, with the carved supports of a marble table; at the left,
between the entrances to the andron and the tablinum, the herm of Rufus.

good for Pompeii, where the tablinum is generally narrower
and higher.

The posts at the entrance were usually treated as pilasters,
joined above by a cornice; architecturally the front of this room
formed the most impressive feature of the atrium. Between the
pilasters hung portières, which might be drawn back and fastened at the sides. In the house of the Silver Wedding the
fastenings were found in place, — bronze disks from which a
ship's beak projected, attached to the pilasters.

In early times the tablinum ordinarily had an opening at the rear also, but this was not so high as that in front, and could be closed by broad folding doors. In winter the doors were probably kept shut. In summer they were left open and the room, cool and airy, served as a dining room, as we infer from a passage of Varro which explains the derivation of the name. "In the olden time," says this writer, " people used to take their meals in the winter by the hearth; in summer they ate out of doors, country folk in the court, city people in the *tabulinum*, which we understand to have been a summer house built of boards." The derivation of *tabulinum*, of which *tablinum* is a shortened form, from *tabula*, 'a board,' is obvious.

The period to which Varro refers antedates that of the oldest houses at Pompeii. The room which we call tablinum was then a deep recess at the rear of the atrium, open at the front, as now, but enclosed by a wall at the rear; against this wall was a veranda opening into the garden, toward which the board roof sloped. People took their meals in the veranda in summer, and to it the name tablinum was naturally applied. In the recess at the rear of the atrium, corresponding to the later tablinum, was the bed of the master of the house, called *lectus adversus* because 'facing' one who entered the front door. As late as the reign of Augustus, long after it became the custom to set aside a closed apartment for the family room, a reminiscence of the ancient arrangement still remained in the couch which stood at the rear of the atrium or in the tablinum, which was called *lectus adversus*, or even *lectus genialis*.

The removal of the hearth and the bed from the atrium must have taken place when the small hole in the roof was replaced by the compluvium. A broad opening was made in the rear wall, and the place where the bed had been was turned into a light, airy room; this was now used as a summer room instead of the veranda, the name of which was in consequence transferred to it.

Even in later times, when the houses were extended by the addition, at the rear, of a peristyle with its group of apartments, the tablinum may often have been used as a summer dining room; but the tendency now was to withdraw the family life

into the more secluded rooms about the peristyle. The tablinum, lying between the front and the rear of the house, was
used as a reception room for guests who were not admitted into
the privacy of the home ; and here undoubtedly the master of
the house received his clients.

In the house of the Vettii the tablinum is omitted on account
of the abundance of room ; but at the rear of the atrium there
are wide openings into the peristyle (Fig. 151).

IV. The Alae

The alae, the 'wings' of the atrium, were two deep recesses
in the sides (Fig. 110). They were ordinarily at the rear, but
were sometimes placed at the middle, as in the house of Epidius
Rufus (Fig. 143). Vitruvius says that where the atrium is from
30 to 40 feet long, one third of the length should be taken for
the breadth of the alae ; in the case of larger atriums the breadth
of these rooms should be proportionally less, being fixed at one
fifth of the length for atriums from 80 to 100 feet long ; the
height at the entrance should be equal to the breadth.

At Pompeii the alae, as the tablinum, are narrower and higher
than required by these proportions. In the Tufa Period the
entrances were ornamented with pilasters, and treated like the
broad entrance of the tablinum.

With reference to the purpose and uses of these rooms we
have no information beyond a remark of Vitruvius in regard to
placing the images of ancestors in them. This throws no light
upon their origin ; for only a few noble families could have possessed a sufficiently large number of ancestral busts or masks to
make it necessary to provide a special place for these, while the
alae form an essential and characteristic part of the Pompeian
house. Now and then an ala was used as a dining room ; more
frequently, perhaps, one was utilized for a wardrobe, as may
be seen from the traces of the woodwork. A careful study of
the remains only deepens the impression that at Pompeii the
alae served no definite purpose, but were a survival from a previous period, in which they responded to different conditions of
life.

An interesting parallel presents itself in the arrangements of a type of peasants' house found in Lower Saxony. The main entrance, as in the early Italic house, leads into a large and high central room; at the sides of this and of the main entrance are the living rooms and stalls. At the back the central room is widened by two recesses corresponding with the alae; the hearth stands against the rear wall. In the side walls, at the rear of each recess, are a window and a door. The two windows admit light to the part of the central room furthest from the entrance; the doors open into the farmyard and the garden.

The Italic house in the beginning was not a city residence shut in by party walls, but the isolated habitation of a countryman. The design of the alae, as of the recesses in the Low Saxon farmhouse, was to furnish light to the atrium, which, as we have seen, was completely covered by a roof, there being only a small hole to let out the smoke. The large windows in the rear of the alae of the house of Sallust may be looked upon as a survival; but in city houses generally light could not be taken in this way from the sides. After the compluvium had come into general use, a conservative tradition still retained the alae whenever possible, though they no longer answered their original purpose.

V. The Rooms about the Atrium. The Andron

In front there were rooms at either side of the entrance, ordinarily fitted up as shops and opening on the street, but sometimes used as dining rooms or sleeping rooms, or for other domestic purposes.

On each side of the atrium were two or three small sleeping rooms; in narrow houses these, as well as one or both of the alae, were occasionally omitted.

At the rear were one or two rooms of the same depth as the tablinum, used in most cases as dining rooms. They frequently had a single broad entrance on the side of the peristyle or the garden (Fig. 129, 22), but were sometimes entered by a door from the atrium or from one of the alae (Figs. 110, 116). The door on the side of the atrium seems generally to have been

made when the house was built; if the owner did not wish to
use it, it was walled up and treated as a blind door, an ornament of the atrium.

The rooms about the atrium in the pre-Roman period were
made high, those in front and at the sides often measuring fifteen
feet to the edge of the ceiling, which had the form of a groined
vault. The rear rooms were still higher, the crown of the vaults
being as far above the floor as the flat ceiling of the tablinum.
A corresponding height was given to the doors; those in the
house of the Faun measure nearly fourteen feet. The upper
part of the doorway was doubtless pierced for the admission of
light in the manner indicated by wall paintings, and shown in
our restoration of one side of the atrium in the house of Sallust
(Figs. 250, 251).

The andron was a passage at the right or the left of the tablinum, connecting the atrium with the peristyle (Figs. 110, 116).
The name was used originally to designate an apartment in the
Greek house, but was applied by the Romans to a corridor. In
modern times the passage has often been erroneously called
fauces.

The andron is lacking only in small houses, or in those in
which a different connection is made between the front and
rear portions by means of a second atrium, or other rooms.

VI. Garden, Peristyle, and Rooms about the Peristyle

A few Pompeian houses, like those of the olden time, are
without a peristyle, having a garden at the rear. In such cases
there is a colonnade at the back of the house, facing the garden; this is the arrangement in the houses of the Surgeon, of
Sallust, and of Epidius Rufus. In the large house of Pansa
(Fig. 172), we find both a peristyle and a garden, the latter
being at the rear of the peristyle; and in many houses a small
garden was placed wherever available space could be found.

The peristyle is a garden enclosed by a colonnade, or having
a colonnade on two or three sides. When this was higher on
the north side than on the other three, as in the house of the
Silver Wedding, the peristyle was called Rhodian. In the Tufa

TE VII.—INTERIOR OF A HOUSE, LOOKING FROM THE MIDDLE OF THE ATRIUM
TOWARD THE REAR

Period the colonnade was frequently in two stories, on all four sides or on the front alone. Fragments of columns belonging to the second story have been found in many houses, but in only one instance, that of the house of the Centenary, are they of such a character as to enable us to make an accurate restoration; here the double series of columns extended only across the front.

A separate entrance, *posticum* (Fig. 110), usually connected the peristyle with a side street. At the rear there was often a broad, deep recess, *exedra*, corresponding with the tablinum. The location of the other rooms in this part of the house is determined by so many conditions, and manifests so great a diversity that it may be spoken of more conveniently in connection with their use.

VII. SLEEPING ROOMS

The small, high rooms about the atrium were in the earlier times used as bedrooms; and such they remained in some houses, as that of the Faun, down to the destruction of the city.

The sleeping rooms about the peristyle were much lower, and the front opened by means of a broad door in its whole, or almost its whole, width upon the colonnade. These rooms could frequently be entered also through a small side door from a dining room, or a narrow recess opening on the peristyle (Fig. 141, *x*). The design of the arrangement is obvious. In summer the inconvenient large door could be left open day and night, a curtain being stretched across the space; in winter it would be opened only for airing and cleaning, the small door being used at other times.

The place for the bed was sometimes indicated in the plan of the room. In a bedroom of the house of the Centaur, of which an end view is given in Fig. 117, a narrow alcove was made for the bed at the left side; the floor of the alcove is slightly raised, and the ceiling, as often, is in the form of a vault, while the ceiling of the room is higher and only slightly arched. A similar arrangement is found in several other rooms decorated in the first style. In the house of Apollo there is a sleeping room with alcoves for two beds.

In bedrooms with a mosaic floor the place for the bed is ordinarily white, being separated from the rest of the room by a stripe suggestive of a threshold. A similar division is often indicated in the wall decoration, particularly that of the second style; the part designated for the bed is set off by pilasters on the end walls, and differently treated both in respect to the decorative design and in the arrangement of colors.

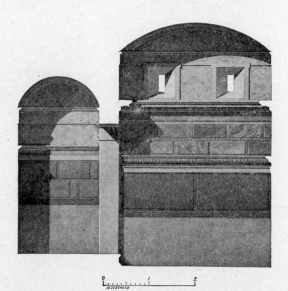

Fig. 117. — End of a bedroom in the house of the Centaur, decorated in the first style. At the left, alcove for the bed; above, two windows.

VIII. DINING ROOMS

As long as it was customary to sit at meals any fair-sized apartment could be used as a dining room. When the early Italic house was extended by the addition of a peristyle, and the Greek custom of reclining at table was introduced, it became necessary to provide a special apartment, and the Greek name for such a room with the three couches, *triclinium*, came into use. For convenience in serving, the length of a dining room, according to Vitruvius, should be twice the width. At Pompeii, however, the dimensions are less generous; with an average width of 12 or 13 feet the length rarely exceeds 20 feet. In many cases one end of the room opened on the peristyle, but could be closed by means of broad doors or shutters.

The plan of a typical dining room is given in Fig. 118. The couch at the right of the table was called the upper couch; that at the left, the lower; and that between, the middle couch. With few exceptions each couch was made to accommodate three persons; the diner rested on his left arm on a cushion at the side nearer the table, and stretched his feet out toward the right. Hence, the first on the upper couch had what was called 'the highest place.' The one next was said to recline 'below' him, because lying on the side toward which the first person extended his feet; the man at the outer end of the lower couch was said to be 'at the foot,' *imus*.

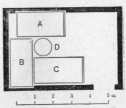

Fig. 118.— Plan of a dining room with three couches.

A. Upper couch, *lectus summus*.
B. Middle couch, *lectus medius*.
C. Lower couch, *lectus imus*.
D. Table, *mensa*.

When in the Gospel of John we read of a disciple "lying on Jesus' breast," the meaning is easily explained by reference to Roman usage ; John was reclining in the place next below the Master. This arrangement makes clear to us the reason why the couches were so placed that the lower one projected further beyond the table than the upper one; the feet of those on the lower couch were extended toward the end furthest from the table.

To the couches grouped in the manner indicated the same name was applied as to the dining room, triclinium. Of those in the dining rooms only scanty remains are found. In summer the Pompeians, as the Italians of to-day, were fond of dining in the open air. In order to save the trouble of moving heavy furniture couches of masonry were not infrequently constructed in the garden, and have been preserved; such a triclinium is that in the garden of the tannery (p. 390). The arrangement is in most cases precisely that indicated in Fig. 118, the outer end of the lower couch projecting beyond the corresponding

S

end of the upper one. In the middle stands the base of the table, also of masonry; the top is rarely preserved. Near by is a little altar for the offerings made in connection with each meal. The appearance of such a triclinium may be inferred from that of the triclinium funebre shown in Fig. 235, which has a square table and round altar.

In many gardens we find about the triclinium the remains of four or six columns. These supported a frame of timber or

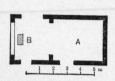

lattice-work, upon which vines were trained, making a shady bower, as in the garden of the tavern in the first Region, referred to below (p. 396).

Fig. 119. — Plan of a dining room with an ante-
room containing an
altar for libations.

A. Room for the table and
couches.
B. Anteroom with altar.

The couches were ordinarily not provided with backs, but the outer ends of the upper and lower couches sometimes had a frame to hold the cushions, as indicated in Fig. 118 and shown more clearly in our restoration, Fig. 180. In the dining rooms small movable altars must have been used for the offer-
ings, such as those of terra cotta or bronze not infrequently met with in the course of excavation. A fixed altar has been found in only one instance, in a small dining room in the eighth Region (VIII. v–vi. 16). Here, as our plan (Fig. 119) shows, the front of the apartment is set off as an anteroom, and in this was placed an altar of tufa.

In accordance with an ancient custom the children, even those of the imperial family, sat on low stools at a table of their own on the open side of the large table. In an open-air triclinium in the ninth Region (IX. v. 11) the children's seat is preserved, a low bench of masonry about five feet long connected with the projecting arm of the lower couch.

The inner part of the dining room, designed for the table and couches, was often distinguished from the free space in the same way that the place for the bed was indicated in bedrooms, sometimes by a difference in the design of the mosaic floor, more frequently by the division of the wall decoration and the arrangement of the ceiling. In the third and fourth decorative styles the division is less plainly marked than in the second; but often

the side walls back of the couches and the inner end of the room have each a single large panel with a small panel at the right and left, while on each side wall in front are only two panels, of the same size.

In one respect the ordinary dining room was far from convenient; those who had the inner places could not leave the table or return to it in the course of a meal without disturbing one or more of those reclining nearer the outside. Large rooms, in which an open space was left between the couches and the wall, or in which several tables with their sets of couches could be placed, were unknown in pre-Roman Pompeii. In the time of the Empire a few of these large dining rooms were built in older houses. There is one measuring about 25 by 33 feet in the house of Pansa; another, of which the dimensions are 23 by 30 feet, in the house of Castor and Pollux; and a third, 36 feet long, in the house of the Citharist.

In a number of houses we find a large, fine apartment — designated by the Greek word *oecus* — which seems often to have been used for a dining room, especially on notable occasions. A particularly elegant form was the Corinthian oecus, which had a row of columns about the sides a short distance from the walls, the room being thus divided into a main part with a vaulted ceiling and a corridor with a flat ceiling. The couches would be placed in the main part; the guests could pass to their places along the corridor, behind the columns. The remains of such an oecus may be seen in the houses of Meleager and of the Labyrinth.

A specially interesting example — unfortunately not yet wholly excavated — is in the house of the Silver Wedding. In this case only the inner part, designed for the couches, is set off by columns. We may assume that there was a vaulted ceiling over the middle, resting on the entablature of the columns; that the ceiling of the corridor between the columns and the wall was flat, and of the same height as the entablature; and that the front part of the room had a flat or slightly arched ceiling of the same height as the crown of the vault over the middle.

In the more pretentious Roman houses there was sometimes a dining room for each season of the year; when Trimalchio in

Petronius's novel boasts that he has four dining rooms, we are to understand that he had one each for winter, summer, autumn, and spring. In the case of the Pompeian houses we are warranted in assuming that dining rooms opening toward the south were for winter use, those toward the north for use in summer. Other airy apartments, with a large window in addition to the wide door, may well have been intended for summer triclinia. Further than this it is hardly possible to classify Pompeian dining rooms according to the seasons.

IX. The Kitchen, the Bath, and the Storerooms

In the Pompeian house the kitchen had no fixed location. It was generally a small room, and was placed wherever it would least interfere with the arrangement of the rest of the house.

The most important part of the kitchen was the hearth. This was built of masonry, against one of the walls. It was oblong, and the fire was made on the top. The cooking utensils sometimes rested on rectangular projections of masonry, as in the kitchen of the house of Pansa, sometimes on small iron tripods, as in the house of the Vettii (Fig. 120). The hearth of the latter house was found undisturbed, with a vessel in place ready to be heated. In one house the place of an iron tripod was taken by three pointed ends of amphorae set upright on the hearth. Underneath there was often a hollow place, like that shown in our illustration, in which fuel was kept, as in similar openings under the hearths of Campanian kitchens to-day.

Sometimes we find near the hearth a bake oven, not large enough to have been used for bread, and evidently intended for pastry; bread must ordinarily have been obtained from the bakers. In one of the cellars of the house of the Centenary there is a larger oven, which may have been used to bake coarse bread for the slaves; the heat was utilized in warming a bath above.

Over the hearth was a small window to carry off the smoke. As the kitchen was ordinarily high there may have been a hole in the roof also, but the upper parts have been destroyed, and their arrangement cannot be determined. From the small size of the kitchens and of the hearths in even the largest and finest houses, we may infer that the luxury of the table prevalent in the Early Empire had made only slight progress at Pompeii.

Close by the kitchen, frequently forming a part of it and next to the hearth, was the closet; a separate closet of good size is found in the houses of the Faun and of Castor and Pollux.

In many large houses there is a bath, generally too small to have been used by more than one person at a time. These baths ordinarily include only a tepidarium and a caldarium, but occasionally there is an apodyterium, less frequently still a small

Fig. 120. — Hearth of the kitchen in the house of the Vettii.
The arched place underneath is for the storage of fuel.

frigidarium ; in most cases a basin in the apodyterium or tepidarium must have been used for the cold bath. The heating arrangements are similar to those found in the public baths, and more or less complete according to the period in which the bath was fitted up, and the taste of the proprietor ; a progressive refinement in the appointments of the private baths can be traced similar to that which we have already noted in the case of the Stabian Baths. The close relation generally existing between the bathrooms and the kitchen is well illustrated in the houses of the Faun and of the Silver Wedding.

In connection with this group of rooms we may mention the

storerooms, which are found in various parts of the houses and may be identified by the traces of the shelves that were fastened to the walls.

Comparatively few houses were provided with cellars. In the house of the Centenary, however, there are two. One, entered from the atrium by a stairway, extends under the tablinum and the front colonnade of the peristyle; the other is accessible from a side atrium and is divided into several rooms, in one of which is the oven mentioned above. The cellar belonging to the house of Caecilius Jucundus is under the garden; that of the villa of Diomedes will be described later.

X. The Shrine of the Household Gods

In ancient Italy each household worshipped its guardian spirits and tutelary divinities, which formed a triple group, the Lares, the Penates, and the Genius. In Pompeii the remains associated with domestic worship are numerous and important.

Many Pompeians painted representations of the household gods upon an inner wall, often upon a wall of the kitchen, near the hearth. There was usually a painted altar underneath, with a serpent on either side coming to partake of the offerings.

In a large number of houses a small niche was made in the wall, in which were placed little images of the gods, the Lares and the Genius being also painted on the back of the cavity or on the wall at the sides or below. Such a niche may be seen in a corner of the kitchen in the house of Apollo (Fig. 121); the pictures of the gods are almost obliterated, but that of the serpent — in this case there is but one — and of the altar can be clearly seen. In front is a small altar of masonry; the ferns and grasses with which the floor is carpeted make this kitchen in summer an attractive nook. Sometimes the niches were ornamented with diminutive half-columns or pilasters at the sides and a pediment above.

Frequently a more elaborate shrine was provided, a diminutive temple raised on a foundation, placed against a wall of the atrium or of the garden. An example is the one at the rear of the peristyle in the house of the Tragic Poet (Fig. 146).

In rare instances a small, separate chapel was devoted to the domestic worship, as in the house of the Centenary. In a house of the ninth Region (IX. viii. 7) there is such a chapel in the garden, a niche for the images being placed in the wall.

The Lares are the guardian spirits of the household. Originally but one was worshipped in each house; they began to be honored in plurality after the time of Cicero, and at Pompeii we invariably find them in pairs. They are represented as youths clad in a short tunic confined by a girdle (Fig. 122), stepping lightly or dancing, with one hand high uplifted in which a drinking horn, *rhyton*, is seen; from the end of the horn a jet of wine spurts in a graceful curve, falling into a small pail, *situla*, or into a libation saucer, *patera*, held in the other hand.

Fig. 121. — Niche for the images of the household gods, in a corner of the kitchen in the house of Apollo. Underneath, a painted serpent represented as about to take offerings from a round altar. In front is a square altar for the domestic worship.

Simple offerings were made to these beneficent spirits, — fruits, sacrificial cakes, garlands, and incense, — and at every meal a portion was set aside for them in little dishes. When a sacrifice was offered to the Lares, the victim was a pig.

With the worship of the Lares was associated that of the Genius, the tutelary divinity of the master of the house. He is represented as a standing figure, the face being a portrait of the master. The toga is drawn over his head, after the manner of one sacrificing; in the left hand there is usually a cornucopia, sometimes a box of incense, *acerra ;* with the right hand he pours a drink offering from a patera.

Very rarely we find a representation of the Genius of the mistress of the house. In one painting she appears with the attributes of Juno; the Genius of a woman was often called Juno, as in the inscription on the bust stone of Tyche, the slave of Julia Augusta (p. 410). As a man might swear in the name of his Genius, so a woman's oath might be ' By my Juno.'

The Lares and the Genius are often found together both in the hearth paintings, and in the groups of little bronze images frequently placed in the shrines. They are associated also in an inscription on the shrine in the house of Epidius Rufus : *Genio M[arci] n[ostri] et Laribus duo Diadumeni liberti,* — ' To the Genius of our Marcus and the Lares; (dedicated by) his two freedmen with the name of Diadumenus.' Marcus was the first name of the head of the household.

In a few cases the Genius of the emperor seems to have been revered at a house shrine. Horace (Od. IV. v. 34) speaks distinctly of the worship of the tutelary divinity of Augustus in connection with that of the Lares, — *et Laribus tuum Miscet numen.* On the rear wall of a little chapel in a garden is a painted altar at the right of which stands Jupiter, at the left a Genius, each pouring a libation. We can scarcely believe that the Genius of an ordinary man would thus be placed as it were on an equality with the ruler of heaven; more likely the Genius of an emperor is represented, perhaps that of Claudius. The face is not unlike the face of Claudius, and the painting is on a wall decorated in the third style.

In another house (IX. viii. 13) two Genii are painted, and under one of them is scratched in large letters *EX SC,* undoubtedly for *ex senatus consulto,* — ' in accordance with a decree of the Senate.' We are probably safe in assuming that the decree referred to is that of the reign of Augustus, by which the worship of the Lares was regulated; if so, the figure is intended to represent the Genius of that emperor.

Fig. 122. — Shrine in the house of the Vettii.

In the middle the Genius, with libation saucer and box of incense; at the sides, the two
Lares, each with a drinking horn and pail; below, a crested serpent about to partake
of the offerings.

265

The face of the Genius in the house of the Vettii (Fig. 122)
bears a decided resemblance to that of Nero. Here the shrine
was placed in the rear wall of the smaller atrium. It consists
of a broad, shallow niche, the front of which is elaborately
ornamented to give the appearance of a little temple, while on
the back are painted the household divinities. The Genius
stands with veiled head between the two Lares, holding in his
left hand a box of incense and pouring a libation with the right.
In the original painting the features were unusually distinct.

The Penates were the protecting divinities of the provisions
or stores, *penus*, and the storerooms of the house; under this
name were included various gods to whom the master and the
household offered special worship. At Pompeii the Penates, as
the Lares and the Genius, appear in paintings, and are also represented by bronze images placed in the shrines. In the shrine
of the house of Lucretius were diminutive bronze figures of the
Genius and of Jupiter, Hercules, Fortuna, and another divinity
that has not been identified. Statuettes of Apollo, Aesculapius,
Hercules, and Mercury were found, together with those of the
two Lares, in another house; in a third, Fortuna alone with the
Lares.

Jupiter and Fortuna are frequently met with in shrine paintings, as well as Venus Pompeiana (Fig. 4), Hercules, Mars, and
Vulcan as a personification of the hearth fire; Vesta, the patron
goddess of bakers, usually appears in the hearth paintings of
bake shops.

Underneath the representations of the Lares and Penates
ordinarily are painted two serpents, one on either side of an
altar, which they are approaching in order to partake of the
offerings; these consist of fruits, in the midst of which an egg
or a pine cone can usually be distinguished. As early as the
beginning of the Empire the significance of the serpent in the
Roman worship had ceased to be clearly understood; Virgil
represents Aeneas as in doubt whether the serpent which came
out from the tomb of Anchises was the spirit of his father or
the Genius of the place.

In the Pompeian paintings, when a pair of serpents occurs,
one may usually be recognized as a male by the prominent

crest. They were undoubtedly looked upon as personifications of the Genii of the master and mistress of the house. When a single crested serpent appears, as in the shrine paintings of both the house of the Vettii (Fig. 122) and the house of Apollo (Fig. 121), we are to understand that the head of the household was unmarried.

XI. Second Story Rooms

With few exceptions the houses of pre-Roman Pompeii were built in only one story; where the peristyle was in two stories, there must have been rooms opening upon the upper colonnade. In Roman times, as the population of the city increased and more space was needed, it became a common practice to make the rooms about the atrium lower and build chambers over them. A complete second story was rare; small rooms were added here and there, frequently at different levels and reached by different stairways. Sometimes the second story on the front side projected a few feet over the street; an example may be seen in a house in the seventh Region (casa del Balcone Pensile), the front of which, with the part projecting over the sidewalk, has been carefully rebuilt by replacing the charred remains of the ancient beams with new timbers.

Houses with three stories were quite exceptional, and the rooms of the third floor must have been unimportant. Along the steep slope of the hill, on the west and southwest sides of the city, a number of houses are found that present the appearance of several stories; they are not properly classed with those just mentioned, however, for the reason that the floors are on terraces, the highest at the level of the street, the others lower down and further back, being adjusted to the descent of the ground.

From the time of Plautus, second story rooms were designated as 'dining rooms,' *cenacula*. Varro says that after it became customary to dine upstairs, all upper rooms were called cenacula. This explanation is not altogether satisfactory, because other literary evidence for the prevalence of such a custom is lacking. Perhaps in early times, when, on account

of the introduction of the compluvium and impluvium, the
atrium ceased to be convenient and comfortable for the serving
of meals, a dining room was frequently constructed on an upper
floor, and, being the principal second story apartment, gave its
name to the rest.   In some places the ancient custom may still
have lingered in the time of the Early Empire.

The upper parts of the Pompeian houses in most cases have

Fig. 123. — Interior of a house with a second story dining room opening on the atrium,
restored.

been completely destroyed ; in three, however, there are traces
of a second story apartment that was probably used as a dining
room.

One of these houses is in Insula xv of Region VII, near the
temple of Apollo.   It is painted in the second style, and dates
apparently from the end of the Republic.   At the rear of the
atrium are two rooms and a passageway leading to the back of
the house.   Over these was a single large apartment, closed at

the sides and rear, but opening on the atrium in its entire length; along the front, as seen in our restoration (Fig. 123), ran a balustrade connecting the pilasters — ornamented with half-columns — which supported the roof.

In a corner of the atrium at the rear a narrow stairway led to the second floor. At the right, as our section shows (Fig. 124), was a narrow gallery resting on brackets, which connected the upper room at the rear with one in the front of the house.

The large upper room was so well fitted for a dining room, especially in summer, that we can hardly resist the conclusion that it was designed for this purpose. There is no trace of a kitchen on the ground floor; and for greater convenience this

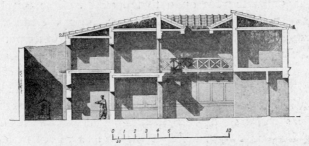

Fig. 124. — Longitudinal section of the house with a second story dining room.

At the right, vestibule, door, and fauces, with front room above; then the atrium, with the gallery connecting the front room with the dining room; lastly, the apartments at the rear of the house. In this house there was no peristyle.

also was probably placed in the second story, behind the dining room.

In the fifth Region there was a small dwelling, which afterwards became a part of the house of the Silver Wedding; the arrangement of the two stories at the rear of the atrium was similar to that just described, except that columns were used in place of the pilasters, and there was only the one upper room in the back part of the house. In such cases as this 'dining room' and 'upper story' might easily have come to be used as synonymous terms.

Where there was a large upper room at the rear of the atrium, no place was left for the high tablinum; in a house in the seventh Region (casa dell' Amore Punito, VII. ii. 23) the cenaculum was in front. On the front wall of the atrium one may still see part of the carefully hewn stones on which the columns of the second story rested, and fragments of these columns were found on the floor below.

XII. The Shops

The outer parts of the houses fronting on the principal thoroughfares were utilized as shops. On the more retired side streets there were fewer shops; and we often find a façade of masonry unbroken except for the front door and an occasional window.

The shop fronts were open to the street. The counter, frequently of masonry, has in most cases the shape indicated on our plan (Fig. 125, 2), being so arranged that customers could make their purchases, if they wished, without going inside the

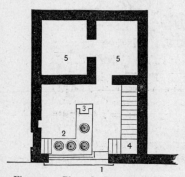

Fig. 125. — Plan of a Pompeian shop.

1. Entrance. 3. Place for a fire.
2. Counter. 4. Stairway to upper floor.
5, 5. Back rooms.

shop. Large jars were often set in it, to serve as receptacles for the wares and edibles exposed for sale. Sometimes on the end next to the wall there are little steps, on which, as seen in our restoration (Fig. 126), measuring cups and other small vessels were placed. At the inner end we see now and then a depression (3) over which a vessel could be heated, a fire being kindled underneath as on a hearth. In the wineshops a separate hearth is sometimes found, and occasionally a leaden vessel for heating water.

In the houses of the Tufa Period the shops, as the front doors and the rooms about the atrium, were relatively high. Those of the house of Caecilius Jucundus measured nearly 16 feet; those of the house of the Faun, 19 feet; the appearance of the latter may be suggested by our restoration (Fig. 134). The height was divided by an upper floor, *pergula*, about 12 feet above the ground, along the open front of which was a balustrade; the stairs leading to it were inside the shop. On such a pergula Apelles, according to Pliny (N. H. xxxv. 84), was accustomed to display his paintings; and in the Digest reference is more than once made to cases in which a person passing along the street was injured by an object falling upon him from the second story of a shop. 'Shops with their upper floors'

Fig. 126. — A shop for the sale of edibles, restored.

are advertised for rent in one of the painted inscriptions found at Pompeii (p. 479).

In Roman times the shops, as the inner rooms of the house, were built lower, and over them small closed rooms were made, which were called by the same name as the open floor, pergula. These rooms were frequently accessible from the street by a stairway, and in such cases could be rented separately. In colloquial language, a man whose early life had been passed amid unfavorable surroundings was said to have been 'born in a room over a shop,' — *natus in pergula.*

Shops were entered by means of small doors; the front was closed with shutters. These consisted of overlapping boards set upright in narrow grooves at the top and the bottom   A separate set of shutters was provided for the open pergula.

XIII. Walls, Floors, and Windows

The walls were covered with a thick layer of plaster and painted; the preparation of the stucco, the processes employed in painting, and the styles of decoration are reserved for discussion in a later chapter.

The floors were frequently made of an inexpensive concrete, consisting of bits of lava or other stone pounded down into common mortar. A much better floor was the Signia pavement, *opus Signinum*, so named from a town in Latium. This was composed of very small fragments of brick or tile pounded into fine mortar. The surface was carefully finished, and was sometimes ornamented with geometrical or other patterns traced in outline by means of small bits of white stone.

In the Tufa Period a floor was often made by fitting together small pieces of stone or marble, and bedding them well in mortar. The colors are white and black, — slate is used in the floor of the atrium in the house of the Faun; sometimes also violet, yellow, green, and red appear with white and black. Pavements of square or lozenge-shaped and triangular pieces of colored marble and slate, like that in the cella of the temple of Apollo (Fig. 28), are occasionally found in houses. In the time of the Early Empire floors paved with larger slabs were not uncommon.

The mosaics of the Pompeian floors — using the term mosaic in a restricted sense — may be divided into two classes, coarse and fine. In the former the cubes, *tesserae*, are on the average a little less than half an inch square. The patterns are sometimes shown in black on a white surface, sometimes worked in colors. The finer variety, in which the pictures appear, is not often extended over a whole room, but is usually confined to a rectangular section in the middle, coarse mosaic being used for the rest of the floor.

The windows at the front of the house, as we have seen, were ordinarily few and small. From the Tufa Period, however, large windows were often made in the rooms around the peristyle; in the house of the Faun they range in width from 10 to 23 feet, and are so low that one sitting inside could look out through them. Upper rooms, also, were provided with windows of good size, sometimes measuring $2\frac{1}{2}$ by 4 feet; but the remains are scanty. In later times occasionally a lower window opening on the street was made almost as large, and was protected by an iron grating.

Windows were ordinarily closed by means of wooden shutters. Small panes of glass were found in the openings of the Baths near the Forum; had the Central Baths been finished, glass would undoubtedly have been used for the windows of the caldarium. Four panes were found in the villa of Diomedes (p. 351); in the other houses a pane of glass is rarely seen, and then ordinarily set in masonry; movable frames like those in use to-day were not yet invented.

T

CHAPTER XXXIII

THE HOUSE OF THE SURGEON

The house of the Surgeon (casa del Chirurgo) is the oldest of the Pompeian houses that retained to the last, with but slight modifications, its original plan and appearance. It lies at the right of the Strada Consolare (VI. i. 10), about fifty paces inside the Herculaneum Gate. The name was suggested by the discovery of several surgical instruments in one of the rooms.

This house was undoubtedly built before 200 B.C. The façade (Fig. 10) and the walls of the atrium are of large hewn blocks of Sarno limestone; other inner walls are of limestone framework (p. 37). The plan conforms to the simple Italic type, before the addition of the peristyle; yet it does not illustrate the oldest form of the native house, for the tablinum (Fig. 127, 7) has already displaced the recess for the bed opposite the front door. The measurements of the rooms are according to the Oscan standard (p. 44), the atrium being about 30 by 35 Oscan feet.

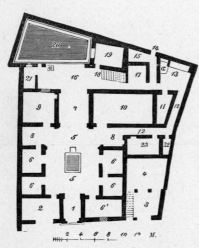

Fig. 127. — Plan of the house of the Surgeon.

1. Fauces.
5. Atrium.
7. Tablinum.
8, 8. Alae.
9, 10. Dining rooms.
13. Kitchen, with hearth (*a*).
14. Posticum.
16. Colonnade.
18. Stairway to rooms over the rear of the house.
19. Room with window opening on the garden.
20. Garden.

We pass directly from the street through the fauces (1) into the Tuscan atrium (5) at the sides of which are sleeping

274

rooms (6) and the two alae (8).   Back of the tablinum is a
colonnade (16) opening on the garden (20), which originally
had a greater length; the room at the right (19) is a later
addition, as also the smaller room at the other end (21).   The
roof of the colonnade was carried by square limestone pillars,
one of which has been preserved in its original form.

The oblong room at the right of the tablinum (10) was once
square, as (9).   Both were well adapted for winter dining rooms;
in summer, meals were undoubtedly served in the tablinum.
The room at the left of the entrance (2) was a shop, at least
in later times.   The corresponding room on the other side
(6') was retained for domestic use.

The shop at the right (3) and the back room (4), as well as
the kitchen with the adjoining rooms at the rear, used as store
closets and quarters for slaves, were a later addition; 22 is a
light court, to which the rain water was conducted from different parts of the roof.   Over these rooms was a second story
reached by stairs leading from the colonnade (18).   It may be
that this part of the house took the place of a garden in which
previously there was an outside kitchen; that the ground belonged to the house from the beginning is clear from the existence of a door between the rooms 6' and 3, afterwards walled
up, and the appearance of the unbroken party wall on this
side.

The rooms about the atrium had no upper floor, and were
relatively high; the doors measured nearly twelve feet in height,
and the ceiling of the tablinum was not far from twenty feet above
the floor.   In respect to height, this house was not unlike those
of the next period.

In the later years of the city, but before 63, the decoration
was renewed in the fourth style.   There are paintings of interest, however, only in the room at the rear (19), which had a
large window opening on the garden.   In one of the panels
here we see a man sitting with a writing tablet in his hand;
opposite him are two girls, one sitting, the other standing; the
latter holds a roll of papyrus.   This kind of genre picture is not
uncommon; the type is spoken of elsewhere (p. 467).

In another panel, which was transferred to the Naples

Museum, a young woman is represented as painting a herm of Dionysus (Fig. 128); a Cupid is holding the unfinished picture while she mixes colors on her palette. Two other maidens are watching the artist with unfeigned interest. Upon the pillar behind the herm hangs a small painting; in the vista another herm is seen, together with a vase standing on a pillar.

Fig. 128. — A young woman painting a herm.
Wall painting from the house of the Surgeon.

The room contained a third picture which is now almost obliterated. Perhaps this pleasant apartment was once the boudoir of a favorite daughter, who busied herself with painting and verse.

In the corner of the garden is an open-air triclinium (25), over which vines could be trained; there is a small altar (*l*) near by. At *n* a jet of water spurted from an opening in the wall upon a small platform of masonry; the water was perhaps conducted into the rectangular basin (*k*) opposite, the inside of which was painted blue. Only the edges of this portion of the garden, which is higher than the floor of the colonnade, were planted; steps led up to it at *f* and *g*. A hearth (*p*) was placed in the colonnade at the left, for the preparation of the viands served in the triclinium. The room at the other end of the garden (27) was connected with the street at the rear by a posticum; back of it was an open space (26) with remains of masonry (*m*), the purpose of which is not clear.

The large dining room (13) may once have belonged to the bakery; the anteroom (12) leading to it was made from one of the side rooms of the atrium. The arrangement recalls that of the dining room of which the plan is given in Fig. 119.

The appearance of the atrium in its original form may be suggested by our restoration (Fig. 130). The proportions are monumental. The treatment of the entrances to the tablinum and the alae, with pilasters joined by projecting entablatures, the severe and simple decoration (illustrated in Fig. 250), and the admission of light through the compluvium increased the apparent height of the room and gave it an aspect of dignity and reserve. At the rear we catch glimpses of the vines and shrubs at the edge of the garden; painted trees and bushes were also seen upon the garden wall.

The series of apartments entered through the room at the right of the atrium (29) present a marked contrast with the rest of the house. They are low, the eight-sided, dark-red columns of the colonnade (31), with their white capitals, being less than ten feet high; and the dark shades of the decoration, which is in the fourth style upon a black ground, give a gloomy impression to one coming from the atrium with its masses of brilliant color.

There was a small fountain in the middle of the little garden (32), the rear wall of which is covered by a painting representing the fate of Actaeon, torn to pieces by his own hounds as a penalty for having seen Diana at the bath. At first the colon-

nade had a flat roof, with an open walk above on the three
sides; but when the large dining room (35) was constructed,
the flat roof and promenade on this side were replaced by a
sloping roof over the broad entrance to the dining room.   On
the outer walls of the two sleeping rooms (33, 34) were two

Fig. 130. — Atrium of the house of Sallust, looking through the tablinum and colonnade
at the rear into the garden, restored.

paintings of similar design, Europa with the bull, Phrixus and
Helle with the ram.   The rear inner wall of 34 contained two
pairs of lovers, Paris and Helen in the house of Menelaus, and
Ares and Aphrodite. .The room at the corner of the colonnade
(36) is the kitchen; the stairway in it led to the flat roof of the
colonnade.

This portion of the house probably dates from the latter part
of the Republic; it underwent minor changes in the course of
the century during which it was used.   Previously there was in

all probability a garden on this side, into which opened a large window in the rear wall of the right ala, afterwards closed.

The changes made in the stately house of the pre-Roman time are most easily explained on the supposition that near the beginning of the Empire it was turned into a hotel and restaurant. The shop at the left of the entrance (3) opens upon the atrium as well as on the street; the principal counter is on the side of the fauces, and near the inner end is a place for heating a vessel over the fire. Large jars were set in the counter, and there was a stone table in the middle of the room. Here edibles and hot drinks were sold to those inside the house as well as to passers-by. The shop at the right of the entrance was

Fig. 131. — Longitudinal section of the house of Sallust, restored.

At the left, the fauces with the counter of the shop; then the north side of the atrium with the entrance of the left ala, the north side of the tablinum, with one of the pilasters at the entrance from the atrium; lastly, the colonnade at the back and the vine-covered triclinium in the corner of the garden.

connected with the fauces, the atrium, and a side room (16). The number of sleeping rooms had been increased by changes in several of the earlier apartments, and by the addition of a second floor reached by the stairway in room 18. The private apartments were for the use of the proprietor, and were guarded against the intrusion of the guests of the inn by the porter stationed at the entrance.

This explanation is confirmed by the close connection of the bakery with the house; and the use of the open-air triclinium is entirely consistent with it (p. 396). The arrangement of the house after it had become an inn may be seen in our section (Fig. 131).

CHAPTER XXXV

THE HOUSE OF THE FAUN

The house of the Faun, so named from the statue of a dancing satyr found in it (Fig. 248), was among the largest and most elegant in Pompeii. It illustrates for us the type of dwelling that wealthy men of cultivated tastes living in the third or second century B.C. built and adorned for themselves. The mosaic pictures found on the floors (now in the Naples Museum) are the most beautiful that have survived to modern times.

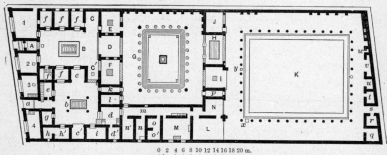

Fig. 132. — Plan of the house of the Faun.

A. Fauces of Tuscan atrium.
B. Tuscan atrium.
C, C'. Alae.
D. Tablinum.
E, F. Dining rooms.
G. First peristyle.
H. Exedra with mosaic of the battle of Alexander.
I, J Dining rooms.
K. Second peristyle.
L. Large room used as wine-cellar.
M. Kitchen.
N. Bedroom.
a. Vestibule.
b. Tetrastyle atrium.
c, c'. Alae of tetrastyle atrium.
e. Storeroom.
f, f'. Sleeping rooms.
o, o'. Bath.
q. Gardener's room.
r. Doorkeeper's room.
v. Broad niche for three statues.
1-4. Shops.

The wall decoration, which is of the first style, in the more important rooms was left unaltered to the last, and is well preserved. This decoration, however, does not date from the building of the house. In order to protect the painted surfaces against moisture, the walls in the beginning were carefully covered with sheets of lead before they were plastered. Later two doorways

were walled up, and the plastering over the apertures, which
was applied directly to the wall surface without the use of
lead sheathing, forms with its decoration an inseparable part of
that found on either side. When the original decoration was
replaced by that which we see on the walls to-day it is impossible to determine, but the change must have been made
before the first century B.C. A few unimportant rooms are
painted in the second and fourth styles.

An entire block (VI. xii.), measuring approximately 315 by
115 feet, is given to the house; there are no shops except the
four in front (Fig. 132). The apartments are arranged in four
groups: a large Tuscan atrium, B, with living rooms on three
sides; a small tetrastyle atrium, *b*, with rooms for domestic
service around it and ex-
tending on the right side
toward the rear of the
house; a peristyle, G, the
depth of which equals the
width of the large and half
that of the small atrium;
and a second peristyle, K,
occupying more than a

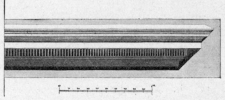

Fig. 133. — Part of the cornice over the large
front door.

third of the block. At the rear of the second peristyle is a
series of small rooms (*q–u*) the depth of which varies according to the deviation of the street at the north end of the insula.

In front of the main entrance we read the word HAVE (more
commonly written *ave*), 'Welcome!' spelled in the sidewalk
with bits of green, yellow, and white marble. The street door
here, quite exceptionally, was at the outer end of the vestibule.
It consisted of three leaves (seen in Fig. 134) and opened toward
the inside, while the double door between the vestibule and the
fauces (A on the plan) opened toward the outside; the closed
vestibule was not unlike those of many modern houses. Fragments of the lintel over the outer door, with its projecting dentil
cornice, are preserved in one of the shops (Fig. 133).

The shops with their upper floors, *pergulae*, were nine-
teen feet high. When the shutters were up they presented
a monotonous appearance (Fig. 134), but on sunny days, when

the articles offered for sale were attractively displayed, and buyers and idlers were loitering in front or leisurely passing from one to the other, shops and street alike were full of color and animation.

The floor of the fauces, as of many of the other rooms, is rich in color. It is made of small triangular pieces of marble and

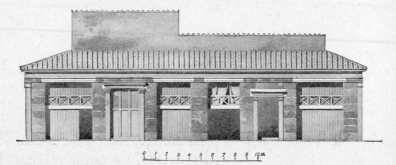

Fig. 134.—Façade of the house of the Faun, restored.

At the left, the front of a shop (1 on the plan) with its upper floor; then the large front door, two shops, the entrance of the smaller atrium and the fourth shop, which, like the second, is completely closed by shutters.

slate — red, yellow, green, white, and black. At the inner end it was marked off from the floor of the atrium by a stripe of finely executed mosaic, suggestive of a threshold (Fig. 135), now in the Naples Museum. Two tragic masks are realistically outlined, appearing in the midst of fruits, flowers, and garlands, the details of which are worked out with much skill.

Fig. 135.—Border of mosaic with tragic masks, fruits, flowers, and garlands, at the inner end of the fauces.

The walls of the fauces are ornamented in an unusual manner. The ordinary decoration of the first style is carried to the height of eight feet. Above this on either side projects a tufa shelf

about sixteen inches wide, on which is placed the façade of a
diminutive temple; that on the left is seen in Fig. 136. The
front of the cella, with closed doors, is presented in relief, but
the four columns of the portico stand free. The shelf is supported underneath by a cornice with stucco brackets in the shape
of dogs, which have now in part fallen away; the underside is
carved to represent a richly ornamented coffered ceiling.

The atrium was a room of imposing dimensions. The length
is approximately 53 feet, the breadth 33; the height, as indicated by the remains of the walls and the pilasters, was certainly not less than 28 feet. Above was a coffered ceiling.
The sombre shade of the floor, paved with small pieces of dark
slate, formed an effective contrast with the white travertine
edge and brilliant inner surface of the shallow impluvium, covered with pieces of colored marbles similar to those in the
fauces. Still more marked was the contrast in the strong colors
of the walls. Below was a broad surface of black; then a projecting white dentil cornice, and above this, masses of dark red,
bluish green, and yellow. The decoration, as usual in the first
style, was not carried to the ceiling, but stopped just above the
side doors; the upper part of the wall was left in the white.

As one stepped across the mosaic border at the end of the
fauces, a beautiful vista opened up before the eyes. From the
aperture of the compluvium a diffused light was spread through
the atrium brilliant with its rich coloring. At the rear the lofty
entrance of the tablinum attracted the visitor by its stately
dignity. Now the portières are drawn aside, and beyond the
large window of the tablinum the columns of the first peristyle
are seen (Fig. 136). The shrubs and flowers of the garden are
bright with sunshine, and fragrant odors are wafted through the
house; in the midst a slender fountain jet rises in the air and
falls with a murmur pleasant to the ear. If the vegetation was
not too luxuriant, one might look into the exedra, on the further
side of the colonnade, and even catch glimpses of the trees and
bushes in the garden of the second peristyle.

Of the rooms at the side of the atrium, one (f') was apparently the family sleeping room; places for two beds were set
off by slight elevations in the floor. This room had been care-

fully redecorated in the second style; the room opposite, the decoration of which was inferior to that of the rest, was perhaps used by the porter (*atriensis*).

The tablinum (D), like that of the house of Sallust, had a broad window opening on the colonnade of the peristyle. In the middle of this room is a rectangular section paved with lozenge-shaped pieces of black, white, and green stone; the rest of the floor is of white mosaic. The floor of each ala was ornamented with a mosaic picture. In that at the left (C) were doves pulling a necklace out of a casket — a work of slight merit.

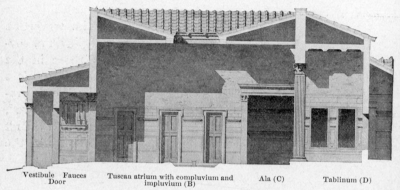

Vestibule Fauces   Tuscan atrium with compluvium and   Ala (C)   Tablinum (D)
           Door   impluvium (B)

Fig. 136. — Longitudinal section of the house of the Faun, showing the large

The mosaic picture found in the right ala is characterized by delicacy of execution and harmonious coloring. It is divided into two parts; above is a cat with a partridge; below, ducks, fishes, and shellfish. A large window in the rear wall of this ala opens into the small atrium, not for the admission of light, but for ventilation; in summer there would be a circulation of air between the two atriums.

Two doors, at the right and the left of the tablinum (seen in Fig. 138), opened into large dining rooms, one (E) nearly square, the other (F) oblong. Both had large windows on the side of the peristyle, and the one at the left also a door opening upon the colonnade. The mosaic pictures in the floors harmonized well with the purpose of the rooms. In one were fishes of various kinds, and sea monsters; in the other was the picture

— often reproduced — in which the Genius of the autumn is represented as a vine-crowned youth sitting on a panther and drinking out of a deep golden bowl.

The colonnade of the first peristyle was of one story (Fig. 136). The entablature of the well proportioned Ionic columns presented a mixture of styles often met with in Pompeii, a Doric frieze with a dentil cornice. The wall surfaces were divided by pilasters and decorated in the first style. In the middle of the garden the delicately carved standard of a marble fountain basin may still be seen.

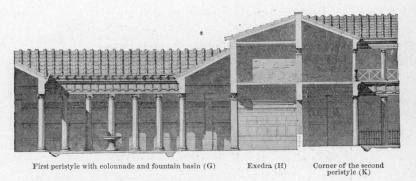

First peristyle with colonnade and fountain basin (G)   Exedra (H)   Corner of the second
                                                                                    peristyle (K)

atrium, the first peristyle, and a corner of the second peristyle, restored.

The open front of the broad exedra (H) was adorned with two columns, and at the rear was a window extending almost from side to side, opening upon the second peristyle. Between the columns of the entrance were mosaic pictures of the creatures of the Nile, — hippopotamus, crocodile, ichneumon, and ibis; and in the room, filling almost the entire floor, was the most famous of ancient mosaic pictures, the battle between Alexander and Darius.

This great composition has so often been reproduced that we need not present it here; as illustrating the style and treatment, however, we give a small section, in which the face of Alexander appears (Fig. 137). The mosaic is a reproduction of a painting made either in the lifetime of Alexander, or soon after his death. The battle is perhaps that of Issus. The left side of the picture

is unfortunately only in part preserved. At the head of the
Greek horsemen rides Alexander, fearless, unhelmeted, leading a
charge against the picked guard of Darius. The long spear of
the terrible Macedonian is piercing the side of a Persian noble,
whose horse sinks under him. The driver of Darius's chariot
is putting the lash to the horses, but the fleeing king turns with
an expression of anguish and terror to witness the death of his
courtier, the mounted noblemen about him being panic-stricken

Fig. 137. — Detail from the mosaic picture representing a battle between Alexander and
Darius.
Alexander, having thrown aside his helmet, is leading the charge upon the guard of Darius,
who is already in flight.

at the resistless onset of the Greeks. The grouping of the combatants, the characterization of the individual figures, the skill
with which the expressions upon the faces are rendered, and the
delicacy of coloring give this picture a high rank among ancient
works of art. The colors in the mosaic are necessarily more
subdued than in the original painting.

A corridor (*p*), both ends of which could be closed, led from
the first to the second peristyle. The columns here, of the
Doric order, were of brick, with tufa capitals, the shafts being
edged, not fluted. The entablature rested on a line of timbers, as
often in the buildings of the Tufa Period. At one time, as indi-

cated by the remains and shown in our restoration (Fig. 136), there must have been an upper colonnade of the Ionic order, affording access to the second story rooms on the south side ; but it seems to have been taken down and not replaced.

On either side of the exedra were two dining rooms (I, J), one open in its entire breadth upon the second peristyle, the other having a narrow door with a window beside it. The fine mosaic picture in I was found in so damaged a condition that the subject — a lion standing over a prostrate tiger — could not be made out, until a duplicate was discovered in 1885.

In the sleeping room on the other side of the corridor (N), which had been redecorated in the second style, remains of two beds were found. The room next to it (L) was the largest in this part of the house ; at the time of the eruption it was without decoration and was used as a wine cellar. A great number of amphorae were found in it, as also in both peristyles.

One of the small rooms at the rear (q) was perhaps occupied by the gardener ; the one next to it (r) was the doorkeeper's room. At v is a long, shallow niche, designed for statues. Nearer the corner were two smaller niches, each of which was ornamented in front with pilasters and a gable. These were the shrines of the household gods ; in front of them were found two bronze tripods, two bronze lamp stands, two pairs of iron tongs, a couple of common lamps, and the remains of a branch of laurel with the bones and eggs of a dove that had nested in it. A bronze statuette of a Genius was found seemingly in one of the niches.

The domestic apartments were entered by a front door between the two shops at the right (Fig. 134). The vestibule, unlike that of the other entrance, is open to the street, the fauces being narrower and deeper. The relation of the tetrastyle to the Tuscan atrium is indicated in our transverse section (Fig. 138). The alae (c, c') are here at the middle of the sides ; the one at the left served as a passageway between the two atriums. The four tufa Corinthian columns, nearly twenty feet high, are well preserved, as well as the pilasters at the entrances of the alae. A tablinum was not needed in this part of the house, and the space which it might have occupied was given

U

to the andron (*k*) and a sleeping room opening on the first peristyle (*l*).

This part of the house was much damaged by the earthquake of 63, and there are many traces of repairs, particularly in the upper rooms. The walls were simply painted in the fourth style. Two money chests stood on large flat stones in the rear corners of this atrium.

In one of the rooms at the front (*e*) there are traces of shelves; stairs at one side led to the upper rooms at the left of the atrium, the shape and size of which are indicated in Fig. 138. On the right, also, there were small chambers over

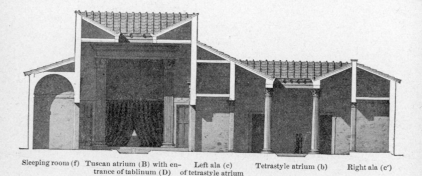

Sleeping room (f)   Tuscan atrium (B) with en-   Left ala (c)   Tetrastyle atrium (b)   Right ala (e′)
trance of tablinum (D)   of tetrastyle atrium

Fig. 138. — Transverse section of the house of the Faun, showing the two atriums with adjoining rooms.

g, *h*, and *h'*, on the same level as the second floor of the shop in front (4), and accessible only by means of the stairway in this shop; there were no other stairs in this corner of the house, and these rooms could not have been connected with chambers over other parts of the atrium, because there were no upper rooms over the fauces and the right ala (*c'*). Another stairway in *d*, partly of wood, led to chambers over *i*, *d'*, *n'*, *n*, *o*, *o'*, and part of the kitchen, M.

Bronze vessels and remains of ivory feet belonging to a bedstead were found in the double room *h*, *h'*; but it is more likely that this was used as a storeroom for discarded furniture than that members of the family slept here.

A long corridor at the end of the first peristyle (*m*) connected the rooms at the right of the small atrium with the closet (*n*), the bath (*o, o'*), the kitchen (M), and the large bedroom (N) opening on the second peristyle.   The two rooms of the bath, tepidarium and caldarium, were provided with hollow floors and walls, and were heated from the kitchen, into which the draft vents (p. 182) opened.

The kitchen is of unusual size.   A niche for the images of the household gods was placed in the wall at the left, so high up that it could only have been reached by means of a ladder. The front is shaped to resemble the façade of a small temple, and in it is a small altar of terra cotta for the burning of incense.

CHAPTER XXXVI

A HOUSE NEAR THE PORTA MARINA

THE height of the important rooms can be accurately determined in so few houses of the Tufa Period, that special importance attaches to a house on the edge of the city north of the Porta Marina (No. 13), in which not merely the three-quarter columns at the entrance of the tablinum and alae, but also the pilasters at the corners of the fauces and part of the Ionic columns of the peristyle are seen in their full height. The atrium is the best preserved of any in the large pre-Roman

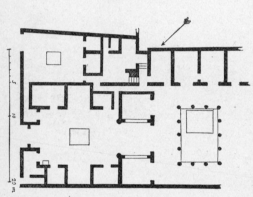

Fig. 139.—Plan of the house near the Porta Marina.

houses, and the height of the ceiling in several of the adjoining rooms is clearly indicated. The house lies about seventy paces north of the Strada della Marina, on the last street leading to the right. It is without a name and is seldom visited.

Neither the decoration, renewed in the second style and without paintings, nor the arrangement of the rooms (Fig. 139) requires extended comment. There are two atriums, the smaller with the domestic apartments being at the left and entered directly from the street. The fauces of the other are of unusual width, being about two fifths of the width of the atrium. The alae are at the middle of the sides, as in the house of Epidius Rufus and the smaller atrium of the house of the Faun. At the sides of the tablinum are large windows opening into two dining rooms, which are entered from the peristyle.

More than a third of the plot enclosed by the peristyle is taken up by a deep rectangular basin for fish.   At the rear are apparently other rooms, adjusted to the slope of the ground, which, however, have not yet been excavated.

It will, perhaps, be easier to appreciate the stately character of the pre-Roman atriums if we give a few of the dimensions which were used in making our restoration (Fig. 140).

The atrium is 41 by 29 feet.   The tablinum measures 13 feet 9 inches between the three-quarter columns which stand, in place of the usual pilasters, at the entrance; it is thus half as wide as the atrium.   The height of the tablinum at the entrance

Fauces   Ala   Tablinum   Peristyle
Vestibule   Atrium   Fish pond

Fig. 140. — Longitudinal section of the house near the Porta Marina.

is 18 feet 6 inches; according to the proportions given by Vitruvius it should be 15 feet 4 inches.

The alae and fauces also exceed the dimensions presented by the Roman architect, the former being $12\frac{2}{3}$ feet wide and $16\frac{1}{4}$ feet high, while the height of the broad fauces, $17\frac{1}{2}$ feet, is only a trifle less than that of the tablinum.

The height of the walls of the atrium is easily determined with the help of the data before us; and the arrangement of the roof over the fauces, atrium, tablinum, and colonnade of the peristyle must have been very similar to that shown in our restoration.   The entablature seen over the entrance of the left ala is restored in accordance with the architectural forms commonly used in the period when the house was built.

Both the three-quarter columns and the pilasters present a peculiarity of construction found also in other houses, but not easy to explain.   The former appear as half-columns on the side of the tablinum, but present only three fourths of their breadth on the side of the atrium.   The pilasters at the entrances of the alae and fauces have, on the inside, a good proportion, the breadth being about one eighth of the height; but on the outside, toward the atrium, they are much more slender.

A well designed scroll pattern appears in the black and white mosaic floor of the fauces, which, as often in Pompeian houses, slopes gently toward the street.   The floor of the atrium is made of black mosaic with pieces of colored marble arranged in rows, and white stripes at the edges.   The base of a shrine for the household gods stands against the right wall.   In the first room at the right was an alcove for a bed opposite the door; the ceiling of the alcove, in the form of a vault, was lower than that of the rest of the room.

CHAPTER XXXVII

THE HOUSE OF THE SILVER WEDDING

AMONG the more interesting of the large houses excavated in the last decade is the house of the Silver Wedding, which marks the limit of excavation in the fifth Region (V. ii. *a* on Plan VI). The main part was cleared in 1892 (Fig. 8); and in April, 1893, in connection with the festivities with which the Silver Wedding of the King and Queen of Italy was celebrated, a special excavation was made in one of the rooms, in the presence of their Majesties and of their imperial guests, the Emperor and Empress of Germany. Portions of the house are still covered, the façade, the inner end of the oecus, and the greater part of an extensive garden on the left side.

Notwithstanding the extent of the house — the greatest length is not far from 150 feet, the breadth of the excavated portion 130 — and the number of apartments, the plan is simple (Fig. 141). From the fauces (*a*) we pass into a tetrastyle atrium (*d*), the largest of its kind yet discovered, with alae on either side and a high tablinum (*o*). Back of this is a Rhodian peristyle, at the rear of which is an exedra (*y*) with sleeping rooms at the right and the left (*x, z*). Opening into the rear of the peristyle on one side is the oecus (4), on the other a long dining room (*w*).

Another series of apartments lay between the peristyle and the garden at the right (2), a kitchen (*s*), and a bath (*t–v*). In front of the garden and extending to the street is a small house (*a–ι*) which had been joined to the larger establishment; it was connected with this by a small door under the stairs in the corner of the atrium (*β*), which opened into a side room (*e*) of the large atrium.

The essential parts of the house date from the Tufa Period. Alterations were made from time to time in the course of the two centuries during which it was occupied, but they were not so extensive as to obscure the original plan. The most obvious changes were those affecting the wall decoration.

In the small rooms at the right of the atrium are traces of the decoration of the first style, which was in vogue when the house was built. Toward the end of the Republic almost the whole interior was redecorated in the second style, but without paintings. Brilliant blocks and panels dating from this renovation may still be seen upon the upper part of the walls of the atrium and on those of the oecus, the exedra, the two bedrooms next to the exedra, and the front part of the long apodyterium.

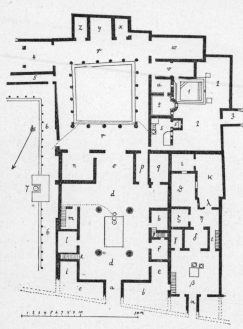

Fig. 141. — Plan of the house of the Silver Wedding.

a. Fauces.
d. Tetrastyle atrium.
n. Dining room.
o. Tablinum.
p. Andron.
r. Peristyle.
s. Kitchen.
t-v. Bath. (v. Apodyterium. u. Tepidarium. t. Caldarium.)
w. Summer dining room.
x, z. Sleeping rooms.
y. Exedra.

1. Open-air swimming tank, in a small garden (2).
3. Corridor leading to another house and to a side street.
4. Oecus.
6. Garden, partially excavated.
7. Open-air triclinium.
a-ι. Fauces, atrium, and other rooms of separate dwelling connected with the larger house.

Afterwards a few rooms were done over in the third style, of which scanty remains are found.

Lastly, after the fourth style had come into vogue, but before 60 A.D. — as shown by an inscription on a column of the peristyle — a large part of the house was redecorated in the fourth style, including the tablinum, the andron and the room at the right (q), the peristyle, the long dining room (w), and the inner portion of the apodyterium. The lower part of the walls of the atrium were also painted over, but with designs and coloring that harmonized well with the decoration of the second style above. In this house the history of Pompeian wall decoration can be followed from the century after the Second Punic War to the middle of the first century of our era, from the time of Cato the Elder to that of Claudius and Nero. There are few paintings, however, and they are not of special interest.

In marked contrast with the atriums in the house of the Faun and the other houses which we have examined, the atrium here had a relatively large compluvium (Fig. 142); all parts of the room must have been brilliantly lighted. In summer some kind of protection against the sun was a necessity. It was probably afforded by hanging curtains between the columns; on the side of each column, facing the corner of the atrium, is a bronze ring through which a cord might have been passed to use in drawing the curtains back and forth. The large compluvium with its supporting columns suggests the arrangement of the Corinthian atrium.

The dimensions of the atrium are monumental. The length is approximately 54 feet, the breadth 40; and the Corinthian columns of tufa coated with stucco, are $22\frac{3}{4}$ feet high.

At the rear of the impluvium is a fluted cistern curb of white marble (seen in Fig. 8). In the impluvium near the edge is the square pedestal of a fountain figure, which threw a jet into a round marble basin in front.

The doors of the rooms at the sides of the atrium were originally more than thirteen feet high; those which we now see are comparatively low. The height was reduced because a second floor was placed in the rooms, thus making low chambers, which were reached by three stairways, one (g) at the right of the atrium, the other two (k and m) on the opposite side. The upper rooms were lighted by small windows, part of which opened into the atrium, others upon the garden on the left side of the house. These changes were completed before the atrium received its decoration in the second style. There was no second story over the alae, the tablinum, or the rooms about the peristyle. In the left ala was once a large window opening on the garden, but it was afterwards walled up.

The curtain fastenings on the pilasters at the front of the tablinum have been referred to in another connection (p. 250). The arrangement of the rooms at the sides is not unlike that in the house of Sallust; one, *n*, retained its original form; the other was divided up into an andron (*p*), with a bedroom (*q*) at one side.

The peristyle is remarkably well preserved. We find not only the columns in their full height, but also, except on the north side, large portions of the entablature, with its stucco ornamentation intact, supported on a line of planks placed upon the columns at the time of excavation; and the decoration of the walls retains much of its brilliancy of coloring.

Fauces   Tetrastyle atrium   Ala   Tablinum

Fig. 142. — Longitudinal section of

The colonnade of this peristyle has been mentioned elsewhere as illustrating the Rhodian form (p. 254). The difference in height between the colonnade in front and on the other three sides was accentuated in the decoration. On the walls in front are large red panels separated by architectural designs on a yellow background; the walls under the lower part of the colonnade were painted with black panels, the designs of the narrow intermediate sections being on a white background. The lower third of the columns in front was yellow; at the sides and rear, dark red, like that on the lower part of the high columns in the atrium. Thus a pleasing contrast was made between the portions of the colonnade designed to receive the sunshine, particularly in winter, and the shadier parts; and the higher front served as an intermediate member between the lofty atrium with its stately tablinum and the lower rear division of the house.

The ornamentation of the architrave retains no trace of the decorative forms in vogue at the time when it was constructed. The surface, moulded in stucco, is divided into sections, corresponding with the capitals and intercolumniations, as in the colonnade of the Stabian Baths (Fig. 84); in these sections are small figures of birds and animals and other suitable designs, the effect being heightened by the use of color.

That the decoration of the peristyle received its present form before the earthquake is evident from an inscription scratched upon the plaster of one of the columns on the north side:

Rhodian peristyle   Entrance to oecus   Exedra

the house of the Silver Wedding.

Nerone Caesare Augusto
Cosso Lentulo Cossi fil[io] co[n]s[ulibus]
VIII Idus Febr[u]arias
Dies Solis, Luna XIIIIX, nun[dinae] Cumis, V nun. Pompeis,—

'In the consulship of Nero and of Cossus Lentulus the son of Cossus,' that is 60 A.D.   The dates given in the rest of the inscription are difficult to explain, and the reading of the number after *Luna* is uncertain.   The memorandum seems to indicate that the eighth day before the Ides of February in this year was the market day at Cumae, being Sunday and the sixteenth day after the New Moon ; and that the market day at Pompeii came five days later.   The inscription is the earliest yet found in which a day of the week is named in connection with a date.

The garden plot enclosed by the peristyle was watered by means of two jets at the front corners, fed by pipes under the floor. In the middle is a slight elevation on which were found two crocodiles, a huge toad, and a frog of a whitish glazed earthenware, apparently made in Egypt. The figures are about sixteen inches long.

Each of the bedrooms at the rear had an alcove for a bed, the ceiling being arranged as in that of the house of the Centaur (p. 256); a distinction between the two parts of the room was made also in the wall decoration and in the floor, of black and white mosaic. The frescoing on the walls of the sleeping rooms presents a brilliant variety of colors; the decoration of the exedra is in yellow. One of the bedrooms has a small side door (p. 255). In the large dining room at the right (w) the place for the table is indicated by an ornamental design in the mosaic floor; in the oecus (4) the part of the room designed for the table and couches is distinguished from the rest by a difference in the decoration both of the floor and of the wall.

In the oecus, the excavation was made from which the house received its name. The peristyle had already been cleared, and the volcanic débris had been, for the most part, removed from the front part of the oecus, leaving a layer at the bottom about two feet deep. The King and Queen of Italy, with the Emperor and Empress of Germany and a small suite, stationed themselves in the corner of the peristyle opposite the opening of the oecus; when all was ready a line of workmen proceeded to draw back the loose fragments of pumice stone, exposing the floor to view. Here nothing was found except the bronze fastenings of the large doors; but a more fruitful outcome followed a similar search in a room of a small house adjoining the oecus on the south, in which several vessels of bronze were brought to light.

The bath is unusually complete for a private house, comprising a long, narrow apodyterium (v), an open-air swimming tank in the garden (1), a tepidarium (u), and a caldarium (t). Steps led down into the swimming tank at the corner nearest the door of the apodyterium, and also on the side furthest from the house; on the same side a jet fell into it from a marble standard adorned with a lion's head.   If we imagine a thick growth of shrubs and flowers about the tank, we have the setting which explains the tasteful decoration of the frigidarium in the Stabian Baths (p. 185) and in the Baths near the Forum.

The pavement of the apodyterium is especially effective, being composed of small bits of black, white, dark red, green, and yellow marble and stone ; near the rear wall a place for a couch is left white.

The caldarium and the side of the tepidarium next to it were provided with hollow walls ; a hollow floor extended under both rooms.   In the left wall of the tepidarium is the bronze mouth of a water pipe ; perhaps in winter a cold bath was taken here rather than in the swimming tank.   In the caldarium the niche for the labrum remains ; the bath basin probably stood opposite the entrance, where it could be easily heated from the kitchen.

Above the broad hearth of the kitchen (s), which stands against the wall adjoining the garden, are the vestiges of a painting of the two Lares ; near them a serpent is seen coiled around an altar, on which is a large pine cone.   At the end next the caldarium is a depression in the floor, for convenience in building a fire to heat the bath rooms.   In the corner is a foundation of masonry to support the vessel in which water was warmed for the bath.

The colonnade at the left of the house (6), with its slender eight-sided columns, seems to have been thrown down by the earthquake of 63, and removed.   In the place of four of the columns an open-air triclinium was made, like that in the house of Sallust.   It is well preserved, and shows an interesting peculiarity of construction.   When the table was not in use, a jet of water would spring from the foundation of masonry supporting the round top.   The water was conveyed by a lead pipe, and at the rear of the colonnade one may still see the stopcock by which the flow was regulated.

The stairway at the left of the small atrium (a) led to rooms over the front of the house.   Over the rooms at the rear, a bedroom (γ), a central room (δ) taking the place of the tablinum, and a corridor (ε), was a dining room, the front of which was supported by columns (p. 269), the stairway being in the corridor; fragments of the tufa columns are lying on the floor. At the back of the house was originally only the small sleeping room (ζ) with a simple decoration in the first style, and a colonnade (η) with Doric columns opening on the garden (κ). Later the colonnade was turned into an apartment, and two rooms were built at the left, a dining room (ϑ) and a bedroom (ι).

In the front of one of the rooms is an unusually well preserved niche for the images of the household gods, ornamented with stucco reliefs and painted in the last style. On the rear wall stands Hercules, with the lion's skin hanging from his left arm, his club on the left shoulder. In his right hand he holds a large bowl above a round altar; at the left is a hog ready to be offered as a victim.

the plan.   Behind the pedestal is a round cistern curb; another
jet rose in the middle of the impluvium.

The apartment at the right of the tablinum (20) was a dining
room.   Of the smaller rooms about the atrium, three (6, 8, and
12) were sleeping rooms for members of the family; some of
the others were so poorly decorated as to prompt the suggestion
that they were intended for slaves.   That next the stairs (14)
was a storeroom; the traces of the shelving are easily distinguished.   Under the stairs was a low room (16), perhaps used
for a similar purpose; the small double room (17) was also low,
and used as a sleeping room.

The domestic apartments were reached by the andron (18).
In the kitchen (21) is a broad hearth (*b*); a dim light was fur-

Fig. 144.— Façade of the house of Epidius Rufus, restored.

nished by narrow windows.   The little room at the entrance of
the kitchen (*a*) was perhaps a storeroom; the closet, as often,
was in the corner of the kitchen.

At the opposite end of the colonnade is the gardener's room
(23).   The main part of the garden (24), as indicated by the
arrangement of the ground, was used for vegetables; the small
flower garden at the rear (25) was on a higher level.

In the house originally there was no second floor.   In the
Roman period, apparently near the end of the Republic, a large
upper room — probably a dining room — was built over the
kitchen; and there may have been one or two small storerooms
at the head of the stairway which was built in one of the side
rooms of the atrium.

x

Traces of the first and third decorative styles are found in the atrium; but the most interesting remains are those of the last style. The alae and several rooms were redecorated shortly before the destruction of the city. The dining room (20) contains a series of paintings illustrating the contest between Apollo and Marsyas; they are skilfully displayed in a light architectural framework on a white ground. On the wall at the left (at a) Apollo is seen moving rapidly forward, striking with his right hand a large cithara which hangs from his left shoulder. Opposite him (at b) is Marsyas, playing the double flute; on the intervening panels (d, e) are the Muses, who are acting as judges in the contest of skill. The painting at c seems to relate to Apollo, but the subject has not been explained.

There were no shops in the front of this house, but in one respect our restoration of the façade (Fig. 144) can not be taken as indicating the appearance of such houses in general. Here the front line was set back several feet from that of the adjoining houses on either side, and the space thus gained was given to a terrace or ramp about four feet high, mounted by steps at either end. The elevation of the front entrance above the sidewalk and the placing of the approaches at the ends of the ramp gave the house an appearance of seclusion.

CHAPTER XXXIX

THE HOUSE OF THE TRAGIC POET

In the "Last Days of Pompeii" the house of the Tragic Poet is presented to us as the home of Glaucus. Though not large, it was among the most attractive in the city. It received its present form and decoration not many years before the eruption,

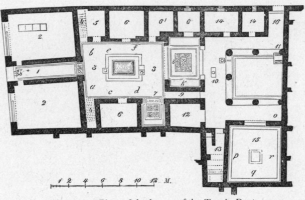

Fig. 145. — Plan of the house of the Tragic Poet.

1. Fauces.	5. Porter's room.	8. Tablinum.	12, 14. Sleeping rooms.
2, 2. Shops.	6, 6. Sleeping rooms.	9. Andron.	13. Kitchen.
3. Atrium.	6'. Storeroom.	10. Peristyle.	15. Dining room.
4, 4. Stairways to upper floor.	7. Ala.	11. House shrine.	16. Posticum.

apparently after the earthquake of 63, and well illustrates the arrangements of the Pompeian house of the last years.

The house received its name at the time of excavation, in consequence of a curious misinterpretation of a painting — now in the Naples Museum — which was found in the tablinum. The subject is the delivery to Admetus of the oracle which declared that he must die unless some one should voluntarily meet death in his place. On one side sits Admetus, with his devoted queen Alcestis; opposite them is the messenger who is reading the oracle from a roll of papyrus. The excavators thought that the scene represented a poet reciting his verses; and since they found, in the floor of the tablinum, a mosaic picture in which an actor is seen making preparations for the stage, they concluded that the figure with the papyrus in the wall painting must be a tragic poet.

The plan (Fig. 145) presents slight irregularities; yet in essential points the arrangement of rooms does not differ mate-

Fig. 146. — View of the house of the Tragic Poet, looking from the middle of the atrium through the tablinum toward the shrine at the end of the peristyle.

At the right, the andron. In the foreground, a cistern curb, at the rear of the impluvium.

rially from that which we have found in the houses of the pre-Roman time. As our section (Fig. 147) shows, all the parts of the house are comparatively low; the ceiling of the atrium and of the large dining room at the rear (15) were only a few feet higher than the colonnade of the peristyle. The entrances of the ala — here there is but one — and of the tablinum are not adorned with pilasters; plain wooden casings were used instead. The second story rooms are not an afterthought but a part of the architect's design; the stairways (4) leading to them are symmetrically placed at the sides of the atrium. There was no upper floor, however, over the fauces, the atrium, or the tablinum. To a modern visitor this dwelling would have seemed more homelike and comfortable than the monumental houses of the earlier time.

The large shops (2) are both connected with the house by doors opening into the fauces (1). They were doubtless the proprietor's place of business. In one of them gold ornaments were found, but we should scarcely be warranted in assuming from this fact that the master of the house was a goldsmith.

In the floor of the fauces, immediately behind the double front door, was a dog, attached to a chain, outlined in black and white mosaic, with the inscription, *cave canem*, 'Beware of the dog!' The picture is now in the Naples Museum. The black and white mosaic is well preserved in the atrium, the tablinum (Fig. 146), and the dining room opening on the peristyle, as well as in the fauces.

The purpose of the various rooms is in most cases easy to determine. The first at the left of the atrium (5) was the room of the porter, *atriensis*. The three rooms marked 6 were sleeping rooms, as were also 12 and 14 opening on the peristyle; 6' was a storeroom, 13 the kitchen. There was a colonnade on three sides of the peristyle; against the wall at the rear stands the shrine of the household gods (seen in Fig. 146) in which was found a marble statuette of a satyr carrying fruits in the fold of a skin hanging in front of him.

The decoration of the large dining room (15) is especially effective. In the front of the room is a broad door opening into the colonnade of the peristyle; each of the three sides contains three panels, in the midst of a light but carefully finished architectural framework. In the central panels are large paintings: at *p*, a young couple looking at a nest of Cupids; at *q*, Theseus going on board ship, leaving behind him the beautiful Ariadne; and at *r* a composition in which Artemis is the principal figure. In four of the smaller panels are the Seasons, represented as graceful female figures hovering in the air; the others present youthful warriors with helmet, shield, sword, and spear, all well conceived and executed with much delicacy.

The atrium, unlike most of those at Pompeii, was rich in wall paintings. Six panels, more than four feet high, presented a series of scenes from the story of the Trojan war, as told in the "Iliad." These were united with the decorative framework in such a way as to make a harmonious and pleasing whole; the main divisions of the right wall of the atrium, as well as of the fauces and tablinum, are indicated in Fig. 147.

In arranging the pictures, the decorators had little regard for the order of events. The subjects were the Nuptials of Zeus and Hera (at *a* on the plan); the judgment of Paris (*b*) — though this is doubtful, as the picture is now entirely obliter-

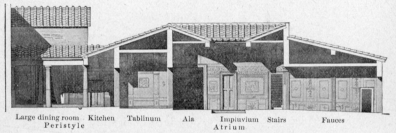

Large dining room   Kitchen   Tablinum   Ala   Impiuvium   Stairs   Fauces
      Peristyle   Atrium

Fig. 147. — Longitudinal section of the house of the Tragic Poet, restored.

ated; the delivery of Briseis to the messenger of Agamemnon (*c*); the departure of Chryseis (*d*), and seemingly Thetis bringing arms across the sea to Achilles (*f*). Of the painting at *e* only a fragment remained, too small to make it possible to recognize the subject. The fragment at *f*, in which were seen a Triton, two figures riding on a sea horse, and a Cupid on a dolphin, is now entirely faded. Half of the painting in which Chryseis appears was already ruined at the time of excavation; the other half was transferred to the Naples Museum, together with the paintings that were best preserved, the Nuptials of Zeus and Hera, and the sending away of Briseis.

The two pictures last mentioned are among the best known of the Pompeian paintings, and have often been reproduced. In the first we see Zeus sitting at the right, while Hypnos presents to him Hera, whose left wrist he gently grasps in his

right hand as if to draw her to him.   Hera seems half reluc-
tant, and her face, which the artist, in order to enhance the
effect, has directed toward the beholder rather than toward
Zeus, is queenly in its majesty and power.   The scene is
located on Mt. Ida.   In the background stands a pillar, on
which are three small figures of lions ; below at the side are
two pipes, cymbals, and a tambourine, all sacred to the potent

Fig. 148. — The sending away of Briseis.
Wall painting from the house of the Tragic Poet.

divinity of Mt. Ida, Cybele.   Three youths, crowned with garlands, appear in the lower right hand corner of the picture ;
they are perhaps the Dactyli, demons skilled in the working of
metals who followed in the train of Cybele.

A higher degree of dramatic interest is manifested in the
other painting, which we present in outline (Fig. 148).   In the

foreground at the right, Patroclus leads forward the weeping Briseis. In the middle Achilles, seated, looks toward Patroclus with an expression of anger, and with an impatient gesture of the right hand directs him to deliver up the beautiful captive to the messenger of Agamemnon, who stands at the left waiting to receive her. Behind Achilles is Phoenix, his faithful companion, who tries to soften his anger with comforting words. Further back the helmeted heads of warriors are seen, and at the rear the tent of Achilles.

The scene is well conceived. Yet in both this picture and the one previously described, the composition seems to lack depth and perspective. The artist is remarkably skilful in portraying facial expression, and foreground details; his limitations are apparent in the handling of groups. We have the feeling that the first designs were not made freely with brush or pencil, but that the artist was here translating into painting designs which he found already worked out in reliefs. The original paintings, of which these are copies, very likely go back to the fourth century B.C.

Another painting worthy of more than passing mention was found on a wall of the peristyle (at *o*), and removed to the Naples Museum. The subject is the sacrifice of Iphigenia, who was to be offered up to Artemis that a favorable departure from Aulis might be granted to the Greek fleet assembled for the expedition against Troy (Fig. 149).

At the right stands Calchas, deeply troubled, his sheath in his left hand, his unsheathed sword in his right, his finger upon his lips. The hapless maid with arms outstretched in supplication is held by two men, one of whom is perhaps Ulysses. At the left is Agamemnon, with face averted and veiled head, overcome with grief. Beside him leans his sceptre, and on a pillar near by we see an archaic statue of Artemis with a torch in each hand, a dog on either side. Just as the girl is to be slain, Artemis appears in the sky at the right, and from the clouds opposite a nymph emerges bringing a deer, which the goddess accepts as a substitute.

In this painting, also, though the style is entirely different from that of the others, we perceive the limitations of the artist

in the treatment of the background. Nevertheless the bold-
ness of the conception, and the skill manifested in the handling
of several of the figures, seem to point to an original of more
than ordinary merit.

Fig. 149.—The sacrifice of Iphigenia.   Wall painting.

Not far from 400 B.C. the sacrifice of Iphigenia was made
the subject of a painting by Timanthes, in which the maiden
was represented as standing beside the altar.   We are told that
the artist painted Calchas sorrowful, Ulysses more sorrowful,
Ajax lamenting, and Menelaus in sorrow so deep that deeper
sorrow could not be expressed; finding it impossible to portray
the grief of the father, Agamemnon, Timanthes represented
him with veiled head.

The veiled Agamemnon appears in our painting, and the figure of Calchas perhaps reflects the conception of Timanthes. For the rest, it is difficult to establish a relation between the two pictures; even if we did not know that Iphigenia, in the painting of Timanthes, stood beside an altar, we could scarcely believe that a great painter would have represented her thus awkwardly carried. Undoubtedly the Pompeian painting, or its original, is indebted to the masterpiece of the Greek artist; but the decorative painter has adapted this to suit his purpose, omitting the figures, the facial expression of which was most difficult to reproduce, and at the same time attempting to heighten the effect by making more prominent the helplessness and terror of the victim.

CHAPTER XL

THE HOUSE OF THE VETTII

THE house of the Vettii, excavated in the years 1894–1895, bears the same relation to the other houses built in the Roman period that the house of the Faun does to those of the earlier

Fig. 150. — Exterior of the house of the Vettii, restored.

time; it is the most important representative of its class. It was situated in a quiet part of the city, and was not conspicuous by reason of its size; its interest for us lies chiefly in its paintings and in the adornment of the well preserved peristyle.

The relationship between the two owners, Aulus Vettius Restitutus and Aulus Vettius Conviva (p. 498) is not known. They were perhaps freedmen, manumitted by the same master;

Conviva, as we learn from a painted inscription, was a member of the Brotherhood of Augustus.

The exterior of the house (Fig. 150) was unpretentious. The main entrance was on the east side, and there was a side door near the southeast corner; elsewhere the street walls were unbroken except by small, square windows, part of which were in low second story rooms.

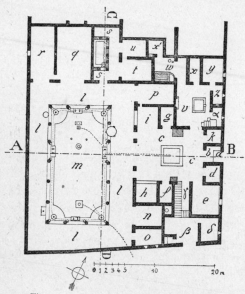

Fig. 151. — Plan of the house of the Vettii.

a. Vestibule.
b. Fauces.
c. Atrium.
h, i. Alae.
l. Colonnade of the peristyle.
m. Garden.
n, p. Dining rooms.
q. Room with the Cupids and Psyches.
s. Small peristyle.
t. Dining room.
u. Bedroom.
v. Side atrium.
w. Kitchen.
x'. Cook's room.
γ. Corridor leading to side rooms (β, δ) and posticum.

The vestibule (Fig. 151, a), as in the house of Epidius Rufus (p. 242), was connected with the fauces (b) by a large double door and also by a small door at the right. The atrium (c) is without a tablinum; at the rear it opens directly on the peristyle. One of the alae (h) at the time of the eruption was used as a wardrobe. At the sides of the atrium were two money chests; the one at the right is seen in Fig. 152.

Opening on the peristyle are three large apartments (n, p, q), and two smaller rooms (o, r). A door at the right leads into a small side peristyle (s, shown in Fig. 153), with a quiet dining room (t) and bedroom (u).

The domestic apartments were near the front of the house. At the right of the principal atrium is a small side atrium (v) without a separate street entrance. Grouped about it were rooms for the slaves and the kitchen (w) with a large hearth (Fig. 120). Beyond the kitchen is a room for the cook (x').

At the rear of the small atrium is the niche for the household gods (Fig. 122).

The corridor at the left of the principal atrium (γ) led to an unimportant room (β) with a door opening on a side street. In this corridor there was a stairway to the second story, which extended over this corner of the house (above *e*, *f*, *h*, *n*, *o*, β, δ). Along the front also were low chambers, over the fauces and the small rooms on either side (*d*, *k*), and over the rooms adjoining the small atrium (*x*, *y*, *z*).

In the accompanying sections two restorations of the interior are given. In the first (Fig. 152) we are looking toward the right side of the atrium and the inner end of the peristyle; the depth of the peristyle more than equals that of the atrium, together with the vestibule and fauces. The difference in height between the atrium and the peristyle, as in the house of the Tragic Poet, is much less than in the houses built in the pre-Roman period; and the corners of the alae were protected by simple wooden casings, altogether unlike the stately pilasters of the olden time.

The transverse section (Fig. 153) presents the long side of the peristyle next to the atrium, with the side of the small peristyle at the north end. The extent of the house is greater measured across the two peristyles (along the line C–D on the plan) than from front to rear. Of the three entrances from the atrium into the peristyle, that in the middle is broader and higher than the other two, which are not much wider than ordinary doors; the arrangement of the openings is similar to that in houses having a tablinum open toward the peristyle with an andron on one side, and on the other a room with a door corresponding with the door of the andron.

The columns of the peristyle are well preserved (Fig. 154). They are white, with ornate capitals moulded in stucco and painted with a variety of colors. Part of the entablature also remains; the architrave is ornamented with an acanthus arabesque in white stucco relief on a yellow background.

The roof of the greater part of the colonnade has been restored, and the garden has been planted with shrubs in accordance with the arrangement indicated by the appearance

of the ground at the time of excavation. Nowhere else in
Pompeii will the visitor so easily gain an impression of the
aspect presented by a peristyle in ancient times. The main

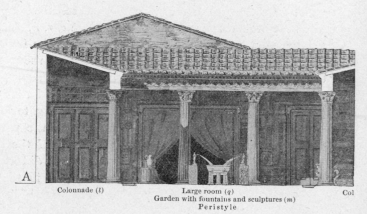

Colonnade (*l*)   Large room (*q*)   Col
Garden with fountains and sculptures (*m*)
Peristyle

Fig. 152. — Longitudinal section

part of the house was searched for objects of value after the
eruption, but the garden was left undisturbed, and we see in

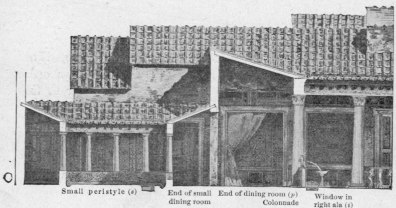

Small peristyle (*s*)   End of small   End of dining room (*p*)   Window in
                             dining room   Colonnade   right ala (*i*)

Fig. 153. — Transverse section of the house of the

it to-day the fountain basins, statuettes, and other sculptures
placed there by the proprietor.

In each corner of the colonnade is a round fountain basin

(indicated on the plan), at each side an oblong basin, all of
marble. Jets fell into them from statuettes standing on pedestals beside the columns; there were two figures for each side

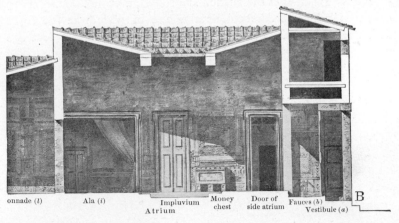

onnade (*l*)   Ala (*i*)   Impluvium   Money   Door of   Fauces (*b*)   B
                                          Atrium   chest   side atrium   Vestibule (*a*)

of the house of the Vettii, restored.

basin, one each for those at the corners. The two statuettes
at the inner end of the colonnade (Fig. 155) are of bronze;

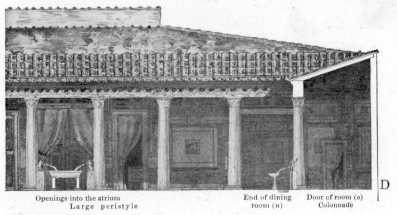

Openings into the atrium   End of dining   Door of room (*o*)   D
        Large peristyle   room (*n*)   Colonnade

Vettii, restored, showing the two peristyles.

they represent a boy with a duck, from the bill of which the
water spurted. The rest are of marble, and not of special
interest. Among them are a Bacchus and two satyrs. The

water pipes were so well preserved that it has been found possible to place them in repair, and they are now ready for use   There were also two fountains in the garden.

Near the middle of the garden is a round, marble table. Three others stand under the colonnade, one of which, at the right near the inner end, is particularly elegant. The three feet are

Fig. 154. — Base, capital, and section of the entablature from the colonnade
of the peristyle.

carved to represent lions' claws; the heads above are well exe-cuted, and there are traces of yellow color on the manes.   On two pillars in the garden are double busts, the subjects of which are taken from the bacchic cycle. One represents Bacchus and a bacchante (Fig. 247), the other Bacchus and Ariadne; there are traces of painting on the hair, beard, and eyes.

The wall paintings of this house are the most remarkable yet

discovered at Pompeii.   Although the decoration of which they
form a part is throughout of the fourth style, they fall into two
groups, an earlier and a later, distinguished by differences in
composition and handling that are easily perceived.

The earlier paintings are found in the atrium (c), the alae
(h, i), and the large room at the end of the peristyle (q).   At
the time when they were painted the left ala (h) was connected
with the room behind it (n) by a door, and had a large window

Fig. 155. — Peristyle of the house of the Vettii, looking south from the colonnade
at the north end.

opening on the peristyle like that in the other ala (seen in Fig.
153).   Afterwards both window and door were walled up and
the ala was turned into a wardrobe.   After this change had
been made, as the remains of the masonry show, the earthquake
of 63 threw down a part of the wall between the ala and the
peristyle.   The earlier paintings, then, must have been placed
upon the walls before the year 63, in the reign of Claudius or
the earlier part of the reign of Nero.

The later pictures are on the walls of the fauces (b), the large
apartment at the left of the atrium (e), the colonnade of the

Y

peristyle (*l*), the two dining rooms opening on the peristyle
(*n*, *p*), and the small peristyle (*s*) with the adjoining rooms (*t*, *u*);
to the same class belongs also the painting of the Genius with
the Lares in the side atrium (*v*), which, aside from this, contains no pictures. The remaining rooms present nothing of
interest.

The paintings of the first group are characterized by refinement in the choice of subjects, fertility in the composition, firm-
ness of touch in the drawing, and exquisite finish in even the
smallest details. The colors used are simple and harmonious,
violent contrasts being avoided. A number of these pictures
show the hand of a true artist, whose work has been found in
no other house, and the system of decoration is the most effective of its kind in Pompeii.

The decoration of the walls painted after the earthquake is
not unlike that found in other houses upon walls of the fourth
style. The designs are sketchy and without painstaking in the
handling of details; the lines are coarse, the colors sometimes
crude. The pictures in the panels are by different painters,
some of whom were not without skill, yet none far above the
average. One of the decorators had a fondness for representing mythological scenes by moonlight, manifesting a taste little
short of barbarous.

The contrast between the earlier and the later decoration is so
marked that it seems impossible to explain except on the assumption of a change of owners. We may well believe that about
the middle of the first century this was the home of a family of
culture and standing, who secured for the decoration of it the
best artist that could be obtained, bringing him perhaps from
Rome or from a Greek city. But within a score of years afterwards the house passed into the hands of the Vettii, freedmen,
perhaps, whose taste in matters of art was far inferior to that of
the former occupants, and a number of rooms were redecorated.

The excellent preservation of a large part of both the earlier
and the later decoration gives the house the appearance of an
art gallery. To describe fully and interpret all the paintings
would require a small volume. The limitations of space make
it possible to present here only the more important; we com-

mence with those in the large room at the right of the peristyle,
which are the most interesting of the entire series.

This apartment (*q*) may have been used either as a dining
room or as a sitting room.   The scheme of decoration is indicated in Fig. 156, which presents the
division of the end wall; the side
walls had five large panels instead of
three.

The ground of the base is black.
The stripe separating the base from
the main part of the wall is red, except the small sections (4, 4), which
have a black ground; the vertical
stripes between the panels are black,
and the same color appears in parts of
the border above.   The ground of the
panels is cinnabar red.   The paintings

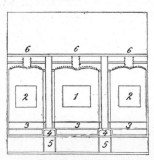

Fig. 156. — Scheme of wall division
in the large room opening on
the peristyle.

in the central panels have not been preserved; in those at the
sides (2) are floating figures.   The upper division of the wall (6)
is filled with an architectural framework upon a white background, against which many figures, skilfully disposed, stand out
with unusual distinctness.

The floating figures in the side panels differ from those found
elsewhere in the choice of subjects.   Here instead of satyrs and
bacchantes we find gods and heroes.   In one panel is Poseidon
with a female figure, perhaps Amymone; in another, Apollo with
Daphne.   Bacchus and Ariadne also appear, and Perseus with
Andromeda.

The figures in the upper part of the wall at the end of the
room belong to the bacchic cycle, — Silenus, satyrs, and bacchantes.   Of those at the sides, one, near the right-hand corner,
represents a poet with a roll of papyrus against his chin, the
open manuscript case, *scrinium*, at his feet; opposite him sits a
maiden clothed in white, drinking in his words.   A comic mask
on the left wall seems to suggest a writer of comedy, and the
scene reminds one of the letter of Glycera to Menander, in
Alciphron: " What is Athens without Menander, what Menander
without Glycera? Without me, who make ready your masks, who

lay out your costume, and then stand behind the scenes pressing my finger tips into the palms of my hands till the applause breaks forth. Then all a-trembling I breathe again, and enfold you, godlike poet, in my arms."

The figures in which we are specially interested, however, are not those in the upper or middle division of the wall, but those in the black stripes (3), less than nine inches wide, under the panels, in the narrow sections (4) and in the corresponding sections of the base.

In each of the sections at the bottom is a standing figure. In those of the end wall (5) are a satyr and a bacchante; in the two nearest the middle of each side wall are Amazons, in the rest female figures with implements of sacrifice. The Amazons,

Fig. 157. — Psyches gathering flowers.
Wall painting in the house of the Vettii.

armed with battle-axe and shield, are full of life; they are distinguished by the colors of their mantles and their Phrygian caps.

In the narrow sections on the end walls (4), and all but four of the others, were Psyches gathering flowers. Only a part of the scenes are preserved; in each are three figures, grouped with a pleasing variety and rendered with singular delicacy of touch. In one, the Psyches are sprightly children; in another, young girls (Fig. 157); and in a third we see a lady sitting at ease and plucking the flowers close at hand, while two maids gather the blossoms beyond her reach.

The two narrow sections nearest the middle panel of each side wall contained mythological scenes, of which three are preserved. The subjects are taken from the cycle of myths relating to Apollo and Artemis. In one of the pictures both the divinities appear. Apollo has just slain the Python, which lies coiled about the Omphalos, the sacred symbol of the god as the giver of oracles at Delphi. His bow and quiver are hanging upon a column in the background, and he moves forward with vigorous step singing the Paean with an accompaniment upon the cithara. At the right, Artemis, with a quiver and long hunting spear, leans upon a pillar looking at her brother. Nearer the Omphalos are a priest and a female attendant, with a bull intended for sacrifice; the relation of these to the rest of the scene is not clear.

The companion picture takes us to a sanctuary dedicated to Artemis. At the left a gilt bronze image of the goddess, in hunting costume, stands upon a pillar, to the side of which a bow, quiver, and boar's head are fastened. On one side of the round altar in the middle is a white hind, sacred to the goddess; on the other, moving toward it with a sword in the uplifted right hand, is a kingly figure, the face turned with a wild and threatening look toward a frightened attendant; another attendant, back of the hind, seems not yet to have noticed the sacrilegious intruder. The composition is full of dramatic power; the subject can be none other than the slaying of the hind of Artemis by the impious Agamemnon.

The third of these small paintings presents a scene not infrequently met with on Pompeian walls, Orestes and Pylades at Tauris in the presence of King Thoas, and of Iphigenia, who is now a priestess of Artemis. The conception is akin to that of the painting in the house of the Citharist (Fig. 175), but the picture is partially obliterated.

The long stripe below the panels is preserved in more than half its length, on the end wall (3), on that at the right, and on the short sections of the front wall; there is also a fragment on the left side. It contains a series of charming pictures representing Cupids and Psyches. Some of the little creatures are engaged in sports, others are celebrating a festival, while others still are busying themselves with the manifold work of everyday life. The execution is less careful than in the small mythological pictures; yet the figures are so full of life, their movements are so purposeful, and their bearing so suggestive that we seem to

catch the expression of the tiny faces.   The Cupids and Psyches,
whether playing the part of children or of men and women in
elegant attire, whether garland makers or vinedressers or smiths,
are always Cupids and Psyches still; we instinctively recognize
them as such, not by reason of outward attributes so much as
by their bearing.   Prosaic daily toil has nowhere been more
happily idealized.

The Cupids at the right of the entrance are playing with a
duck.   One holds the duck under his arm ready to let it go;
the other stretches out his hands to catch it as it tries to escape.
The group on the other side are throwing at a wooden mark.

Fig. 158. — Cupids making
Wall painting in the

One is setting up the target.   Two are making ready to throw,
one of them being mounted on the back of a companion; the
successful contestant in such games was called "the king," the
loser, "the ass," because he had to carry the others upon his
back.   A fifth stands ruefully beside the target, awaiting his
turn to carry the victor.

Among the most attractive groups are those of the flower
dealers, at the end of the right wall near the entrance.   First
we see the gardener leading to market a goat laden with roses;
his little son trudges along behind the animal, carrying a basket
of roses suspended from a stick on the left shoulder.   Next is
the dealer, who stands behind a broad marble table covered
with garlands; he is handing two to a youth who already has

several, while a Psyche near by is placing the garlands in a
basket.   Beyond these, workmen are making garlands, which
hang in profusion from a wooden frame.   At the extreme left
is a lady asking the price.   One of the workmen holds up
two fingers, signifying two asses.   The price of a wreath is
given in a graffito as three asses (p. 487).

In the following scene Cupids appear as makers and sellers
of oil (Fig. 158).   At the right is the oil press.   It stands upon
a square stone, the upper surface of which contains a semicircular incision to catch the oil and carry it to a round vessel standing in front.   The two sides, each with a broad vertical opening,

and selling oil.
house of the Vettii.

are securely fastened by a crosspiece at the top.   The ends of
four horizontal boards are fitted to the openings, in which they
move up and down.   The olives are
placed under the lowest board; in the
spaces between the others, and between the upper board and the crosspiece, thick wooden wedges are driven.
As the workmen drive in the wedges
with heavy mallets, the pressure upon
the olives is increased, and the oil is
forced out.   The arrangement may
be more plainly seen in Fig. 159, from

Fig. 159. — Oil press.   From a wall
painting found at Herculaneum.

a wall painting at Herculaneum, in which a similar press appears.

At the left of the press is a large kettle resting on a tripod. The oil is being stirred as it is heated; a similar kettle appears in the scene in a shop presented in the other part of the picture. Further on are two figures beside a deep vessel, but the process represented is not clear.

The rest of the picture relates to the selling of oil. In the background is a cupboard, with a statuette — perhaps of a divinity — on the upper shelf. In front is an open chest resting on four legs. Both the cupboard and the box contain bottles and jars of various shapes and sizes for holding oil; a Cupid

Fig. 160. — Cupids
Wall painting in the

has just taken one up. On the top of the chest is a roll of papyrus with a pair of scales; oil was sold by weight. A memorandum on the wall of an adjoining house reads: *XIII. K. Fe. oli. p. DCCCXXXX*, — 'January 20, 840 pounds of oil.'

The central figure of the group at the left is the lady who has come to make a purchase. A cushioned seat has been placed for her, with a footstool; the maid stands motionless behind, a large fan resting on the right shoulder. The proprietor holds in his right hand a spoon containing a sample which he has just taken from the jar under his arm; the lady seems to be testing the quality in her hands. The article sold is doubtless the fine perfumed oil, not the common variety.

Hardly less animated are the scenes in which Cupids take
the place of goldsmiths (Fig. 160).   At the right is the furnace,
adorned with the head of Hephaestus, the patron divinity of
workers in metals.   In front is a Cupid with a blowpipe and
pincers.   Behind it another is working with a graver's tool upon
a large gold vessel.   The pose, suggesting at the same time
exertion and perfect steadiness, is rendered with remarkable
skill.

Next is a figure at a small anvil; then the counter for the sale
of jewellery, which is displayed in three open drawers.   Be-

as goldsmiths.
house of the Vettii.

hind the case containing the drawers a large and a smaller pair
of scales are seen.

The first two figures in the other half of the picture represent
a lady purchaser, seated, and the proprietor, who weighs out
an object with a small pair of scales.   The left hands of both
point to the balance; they are deeply interested in the weigh-
ing.   Lastly, we see two figures at an anvil.   Nothing could be
more natural than the pose of the one at the left, holding the
metal upon the anvil for his companion to strike, yet drawing
back as far as possible in order to avoid the sparks.

The processes of the fullery also are illustrated, — treading
the clothes in vats, carding, inspection of the cloth to see if the

work is properly done, and folding the finished garments for delivery to the owners.

Three of the pictures — two on the end wall and one on the left side — relate to wine.

The first is a vintage scene (Fig. 161), of which only a part is distinct. At the left is a Cupid gathering grapes, from vines trained to run from tree to tree. The press is worked on a different principle from the one shown in Fig. 158. Here two Cupids are turning a windlass by means of long levers. The windlass is connected by a pulley with a press beam above; as the end of this is gradually lowered, the pressure upon the grapes underneath is increased.

The triumph of Bacchus is presented in another picture,

Fig. 161. — Vintage scene: Cupids gathering and pressing grapes.
Wall painting in the house of the Vettii.

which is fortunately in a better state of preservation. At the head of the procession is a bacchante, riding on a panther. Bacchus sits in a four-wheeled chariot drawn by goats; the coachman is a satyr. Behind the triumphal car is Pan, dancing and playing the double flute; last comes a vine-crowned Cupid, dancing, with a large mixing bowl upon his shoulder. The skill shown in the pose of the dancing figures is especially noteworthy; they stand lightly erect, seeming not to feel their weight or the exertion of rapid movement.

In the last of this series, upon the left wall, Cupids appear as wine dealers; the part of the picture that has been preserved is shown in Fig. 162. The rustic bearing of the seller, at the left, is in pleasing contrast with the free and graceful carriage of the well-bred buyer, to whom he is handing a sample of the wine in a cup. At the right two servants are drawing another

sample from an amphora; one tips the amphora so cautiously
that the other, who is holding the bowl, presses the neck gently
with his left hand in order to make the slender stream flow
faster.

Rapidity of movement reaches a climax in the middle picture
of the right wall, which represents the games of the Circus.
The scene is laid in the country; each goal is marked by three
trees. Antelopes take the place of horses, and the groups are
conceived with wonderful realism. The tiny, fluttering garments of the drivers display the colors of the four parties, —
green, red, white, and blue.

Fig. 162. — Cupids as dealers in wine.
Wall painting in the house of the Vettii.

Two of the pictures on the end wall are so damaged that it is
not easy to make out the details. One of them, like that just
described, presents a purely Roman subject — the festival of
Vesta (Fig. 163). Cupids and Psyches are reclining at ease
about a serving table in the shape of a deep platter with two
handles, on which drinking vessels are seen; in the background
are two asses, sacred to Vesta (p. 98). Some, at least, of the
Cupid pictures could not have been taken from Greek originals.

In the atrium also there was a black stripe containing Cupids
similar to those already described, but the figures are not so well
preserved. The most interesting scene represents a sacrifice to

Fortuna. Cupids appear also riding and driving. Some are mounted on goats and engaged in a contest. One stands on a crab, guiding the ungainly creature with reins and plying the whip; another is similarly mounted on a lobster. A few are in chariots, the chariot in one case being drawn by two dolphins.

In each division of the wall of the atrium near the bottom is the half-length figure of a child, painted on a dark red ground. The children are busied with vessels of all kinds, apparently intended for sacrifice. The seriousness of their task, the importance which they attach to their helpfulness, is finely expressed in the faces, which are individualized in the manner of a true artist.

We may dismiss the later paintings of the house with few words. In the fauces (*b*) are small monochrome panels contain-

Fig. 163. — Cupids celebrating the festival of Vesta.
Wall painting in the house of the Vettii.

ing a pair of deer, a cock fight, vases, and a wallet with a herald's staff, attributes of Mercury, who perhaps had a place among the Penates of the house.

In the room at the left of the atrium (*e*) is a painting of Cyparissus, the youth beloved of Apollo, with his wounded deer on the ground near him; in another part of the room is the wrestling match between Pan and Eros. Among the figures seen in the architectural framework of the upper division of the wall is Zeus, sitting on his throne, represented as a youth, un-bearded; Leda with the swan also appears, and Danaë holding out her robe to catch the golden rain.

The direction of the owner's tastes is perhaps indicated by a painting in the peristyle, at the middle of the wall under the colonnade at the left. It contains a portrait, probably of an author; near by is a manuscript case with rolls of papyrus.

The paintings in the two dining rooms opening on the peristyle, *n* and *p*, are in a better state of preservation than those of any other part of the house. In the first room, *n*, the simple and restful decoration surrounding the large pictures is in striking contrast with the pictures themselves, one of which is placed at the middle of each of the three walls. Here we see the infant Hercules strangling the serpents, there Pentheus and the Maenads about to tear him in pieces; the subject of the third painting is the punishment of Dirce, the treatment being not unlike that of the sculptured Farnese group in the Naples Museum.

The decorative effect of the other room, *p*, is more harmonious. The divisions of the wall space, the relation of the three principal paintings to the decorative design, and the distribution of ornament are indicated in our illustration (Plate VIII); but no reproduction can do justice to the richness of the coloring.

The painting in the middle panel at the right brings before us Bacchus with his train as they come upon the sleeping Ariadne. On the left wall opposite is Daedalus, pointing out the wooden cow that he has made to Pasiphae, who hands to him a golden arm band. The subject of the third picture is here met with for the first time at Pompeii — the punishment of Ixion.

The tragedy of the scene (Fig. 164) is plainly suggested, but not forced upon the beholder; we see, at the left, only half of the ever revolving wheel to which the wretched victim is bound. The other figures are more prominent and, with one exception, convey no suggestion of pain or sympathy in either pose or expression of face. Nearest the wheel is Hephaestus, who has just fastened Ixion upon it; his pincers, hammer, and anvil are lying upon the ground in the corner. In front of him is Hermes, who, in obedience to the command of Zeus, brought the offender to the place of punishment.

A sad-faced female figure with veiled head sits in the foreground — a personification of the spirit of one who has died, a shade introduced to indicate that the place of punishment is the Underworld. The left hand is involuntarily raised with the shock that the thought of the victim's suffering brings ; the face has been thought by some to resemble that often given to the Madonna.

The two figures at the right of the picture are of the upper world, not directly connected with the main action, yet well con-

Fig. 164. — The punishment of Ixion.
Wall painting in the house of the Vettii.

ceived and skilfully introduced. Nearer the foreground Hera sits enthroned, her sceptre in her left hand; behind her stands Iris, faithful messenger, who points out to her the well deserved fate of him who dared to offer an affront to the queen of heaven.

CHAPTER XLI

In the houses described in the preceding chapters the distribution of the rooms is characterized by a certain regularity, which makes it possible to indicate the arrangements by reference to an ideal or normal plan. A wide departure, however, is occasionally noted; and by way of illustration three houses of unusual plan will be briefly presented here, first a house without an atrium, then one having an atrium but no compluvium, and, lastly, a large establishment built on terraces at different levels.

I. THE HOUSE OF ACCEPTUS AND EUHODIA

Sometimes a few rooms of a large house were cut off from the atrium and used as a separate dwelling; the original plan in such cases is easily determined. The number of houses built without an atrium in the beginning is exceedingly small. Among

Fig. 165.— The house of Acceptus and Euhodia.

a. Colonnade.
b. Garden.
c. Kitchen.
d. Bedroom.
f. Dining room.
g. Garden.
i. Bedroom with places for two beds.

the pleasantest was the modest dwelling of Acceptus and Euhodia, on the south side of the double Insula in the eighth Region (VIII. v.-vi. 39); the names are taken from a couple of election notices painted on the front, in which they appear together.

From the street one passed directly under a colonnade (Fig. 165, *a*) in two stories, facing a small garden (*b*), from which it

335

was separated by a low wall. At one end of the garden was an open-air triclinium (*k*), which still remains. The rest of the plot, used as a flower garden, was profusely ornamented; five heads of herms, a frog and other objects of marble were found in it, besides a couple of alabaster basins and five statuettes of Egyptian divinities made of glazed pottery. In the corner of the colonnade, between the garden and the entrance, is a small hearth, conveniently placed for serving the open-air triclinium; in the opposite corner at the left the excavators found the remains of a cupboard, together with vessels of bronze, glass, and clay. At the further end of the colonnade one passed into another small garden (*g*).

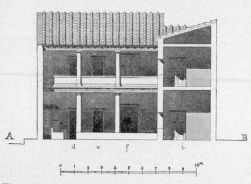

Fig. 166. — Longitudinal section of the house of Acceptus and Euhodia, restored.

A bedroom (*d*) opened on the colonnade near the entrance. A corridor (*e*) led to the kitchen (*c*) behind it. Beyond the corridor is the dining room (*f*). Another sleeping room (*i*) with places for two beds is entered through a kind of anteroom (*h*) at the rear of the house.

The rooms of the second story corresponded closely with those underneath, and were entered from the second story of the colonnade; the stairs, partly of wood, started in the kitchen. The appearance of the house as one looked from the garden at the right toward the colonnade may be inferred from our restoration, which gives a longitudinal section (Fig. 166); the letters under the section refer to the rooms as they are indicated in the plan.

The house was decorated in the fourth style. On the south wall of the kitchen there is a painting of Fortuna, with the usual attributes, a cornucopia and a rudder resting on a ball. The Genius and the Lares nowhere appear, and as a lotus blossom is painted on the forehead of the goddess, who is thus conceived of as a form of Isis, we may suppose that Acceptus and his wife were adherents of the Egyptian cult.   Besides the statuettes of Egyptian divinities there was found in the garden the foot of a marble table with a Greek inscription " of Serapion," an Egyptian name.   Acceptus and Euhodia may have come from Alexandria and thence have introduced into Pompeii this type of house, so unlike the native form.   The Latin name of Acceptus does not stand in the way of this explanation, for he was probably a freedman, who in Egypt may have had a Roman master.

II. A House without a Compluvium

The accompanying plan (Fig. 167) shows the arrangement of a small house on the north side of Nola Street in the fifth Region (V. v. 2).   The problem of lighting the atrium (*e*), the roof of which sloped toward the back, was met in a simple way.

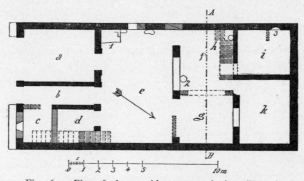

Fig. 167.— Plan of a house without a compluvium (V. v. 2).

a. Shop.   *b.* Fauces.   *e.* Atrium.   *f.* Light court.   *k.* Dining room.
1. Hearth.   2. Cistern curb.

At the rear a light court (*f*) was constructed, which furnished light and air by means of broad windows, not only to the atrium, but also to the adjoining room *g* and indirectly to the dining room *k*, which had a window opening on *g*.

This arrangement, however, is in part the result of later changes.   Originally the room marked *g* belonged to the court, *f*, and the house consisted of two parts, separated by a narrow area.   The kitchen was then in the low room (*i*), above which

z

was a correspondingly low chamber, the height of the two rooms being only equal to that of the dining room (*k*).   In later times,

however, the hearth was moved to the corner of the atrium (1), the smoke being let out through a small window in the wall.   A stairway, partly of wood, led to the upper rooms at the front of the house.   Along the street ran a stone bench, protected by a roof projecting over it.

Fig. 168. — Transverse section of the house without a compluvium.

At the left, light court (*f*), with stairs (*h*) leading to an upper room over *i*.   At the right, room *g*, with the window opening into the dining room *k*.

The water from the roofs fell into the light court *f*, and was collected in a cistern.   We give a transverse section across *f* and *g* (Fig. 168), showing the arrangement of the roofs, doors, and window at the rear.

On the wall of *g* is scratched the inscription, *Fures foras, frugi intro*, — 'The thieves are outside, the honest folk within.'

III. The House of the Emperor Joseph II

A good example of a house extended over terraces at different levels may be seen on the edge of the hill west of the Forum Triangulare (VIII. ii. 39), that of the Emperor Joseph II, casa dell' Imperatore Giuseppe II.   The name was given in commemoration of a visit of this emperor to Pompeii, in 1769, when a special excavation in his honor was made in a part of the house.

The uppermost of the three terraces on which the house is built (Fig. 169, 1) is at the level of the street (Vico della Regina, Plan VI), the lowest (3) in part occupies the place of the old city wall ; the middle terrace is adjusted to the intervening slope. The arrangement of the stairways between the terraces and the distribution of the rooms may be more easily understood from an inspection of the plan in connection with the key below than from description.

There was a second story over a part of the rooms on the upper terrace, as indicated by the stairways at *e* and *n* and in

near the basins was found the skeleton of a man who at the time of the eruption had taken refuge in this room and probably died of hunger. The appearance of the room at the time of excavation is shown in a sketch published by Mazois (Fig. 170).

The door near the corner, seen in the illustration, led outside the city. The proprietor of the house perhaps had a special permit enabling him to leave or enter the city at any time without surveillance; none of the other houses along the edge of the city have a private entrance of this kind.

CHAPTER XLII

THE houses accorded a detailed description in the previous chapters are few in comparison with the number of those worthy of special study. He alone who has wandered day after day among the ruins, returning again and again to explore the parts of the city which are rarely seen by the hasty visitor, can realize what a wealth of interesting material lies behind the barren walls lining the streets on either side.

The location of the houses mentioned incidentally is given in Plan VI, at the end of the volume. Such are, the house of Caecilius Jucundus, on Stabian Street (V. i. 26), the tablinum of which contains one of the most beautiful specimens of wall decoration yet discovered, in the third style; the house of Lucretius, on the same street (IX. iii. 5), with a little garden behind the tablinum adorned with quaint sculptures; the house of the Hunt on Nola Street (VII. iv. 48), so named from the large hunting scene on the wall at the rear of the garden; and further down on Nola Street (IX. vii. 6) the extensive house with two atriums and a large peristyle, excavated in 1879, eighteen centuries after the destruction of the city, and hence called the house of the Centenary, casa del Centenario.

In the same block with the house of the Hunt, opposite that of the Faun, is the house of the Sculptured Capitals, casa dei Capitelli Figurati (VII. iv. 57). It received its name from the figures carved in the tufa capitals of the pilasters at the entrance, one of which is shown in Fig. 171; the stucco with which the surface was coated has now fallen off. Such figures are not infrequently met with in pilaster capitals of the Tufa Period, the subjects being always taken, as here, from the bacchic cycle; the satyr at the left is well rendered. The plan of the house is

simple, like that of other houses of moderate size dating from
the pre-Roman time.

Near the west end of Nola Street is the house of Pansa,
which occupies the whole of the sixth Insula of Region VI.
Although of approximately the
same size as the house of the
Faun, and built in the same
period, it contained fewer large
rooms ; its proportions were
less impressive, its finish less
elegant. The walls present
many evidences of repairs and
alterations, but of the wall decoration nothing remains.

Fig. 171. — Capital of pilaster at the entrance
of the house of the Sculptured Capitals.

The plan (Fig. 172) is of interest on account of its regu-
larity. It well illustrates the extent to which, at Pompeii, rooms
not required for household purposes were utilized as shops and
small separate dwellings, which were rented to tenants, and
doubtless formed an important source of income.

The vestibule and fauces have been mentioned previously
43). The living rooms are grouped about a single atrium
a large peristyle (9). A colonnade at the rear of the
ces the garden, which, as indicated by the appearance
ound at the time of excavation, was used for vegetables.
n the colonnade is the gardener's room (a).

nt were shops, one of which (35) was connected
e and served as the proprietor's place of business;
was used as a salesroom for the bakery, which
oms numbered 28–34. On the same side of
hree small two-story dwellings, one of which
dows opening into an adjoining room (12)
the peristyle ; it was doubtless occupied
d with the household. The dwellings on
B, C) were larger. Fiorelli thought that
d to Alleius Nigidius Maius (p. 479); the
s given to it from an election notice painted

There is a remarkable group of houses near the north end of
Mercury Street.   The first in importance is the house of Castor
and Pollux (VI. ix. 6), which is so named from the figures of
the Dioscuri, holding their horses by the bridle, painted on the
walls of the principal fauces.   Between the two atriums, one of
which is of the Corinthian type, lies a large peristyle ; and behind
the Corinthian atrium is a garden with a colonnade in front.
The decoration of the house is especially effective ; that of the
larger tablinum was by one of the best artists who worked at
Pompeii.   The paintings in the two central panels of this room

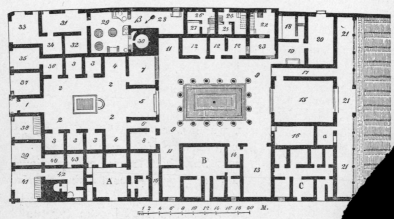

Fig. 172. — Plan of the house of Pansa.

1. Fauces.	15. Oecus.
2. Atrium.	19. Kitchen.
4, 4. Alae.	20. Room for a wagon.
5. Tablinum.	21. Colonnade opening on the
6. Andron.	garden.
9. Peristyle.	22-23. Small dwelling with second
10. Passage leading to posticum.	story, connected with the
13. Dining room.	house.

24-25, 26-27. Tv
rate dwe
28-34. Baker
30. O
35, 37-40.
41. Shop
A, B, C.
i

are often mentioned ; on the right wall
Achilles among the daughters of Lyco
quarrel between Achilles and Agamem
tion of Venus Pompeiana shown in Fig. 4
   Next beyond the house of Castor and
Centaur (VI. ix. 3), which received its name
which Hercules, Deianira, and Nessus appea

bedroom in this house is shown in Fig. 117. The rest of the insula belongs to the large house of Meleager, named from a picture representing Meleager and Atalanta. The walls contained numerous mythological pictures, part of which were transferred to the Naples Museum; those left on the walls have suffered from exposure to the weather.

The house of Apollo also (VI. vii. 23), on the opposite side of the street, is noteworthy on account of its decoration, in the last style; the god appears in a series of paintings. Two houses in the next insula, on the south, have in their gardens fountain niches veneered with bright mosaics, the casa della Fontana Grande (VI. viii. 22) and the casa della Fontana Piccola (VI. viii. 23).

At the middle of the tenth Insula, in the same Region, is the house of the Anchor (VI. x. 7), so called from an anchor outlined in the black and white mosaic of the fauces. The peristyle here presents an interesting peculiarity of construction. The level of the street at the rear of the house was below that of Mercury Street. Instead of filling up the lot so as to raise the garden to the height of the front part, the builder

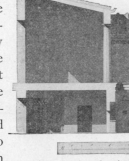

Fig. 173.—Section showing a [...] house of the An[...]

constructed a kind of basement under the co[...] style, the floor of which was thus adjusted [...] floors in the front rooms; the garden and t[...] ment were on the same level as the street [...] colonnade was higher on the north than [...] sides (Fig. 173). The effect of the whole [...] pleasing. Whether the projections seen in t[...] the level of the garden, are pedestals or sm[...] determined. The niches at the front end we[...]

(1[...]). 2[...] ([...]) and [...] h[...]use fa[...] o[...] the gr[...] opening o[...] In the fr[...] with the hou[...] another (33) [...] occupied the [...] the house were [...] (22—23) containe[...] of the house an[...] by some one con[...] the other street [...] this Insula belo[...] name of Pansa v[...] on the front.

were three in number.   In the middle niche was a diminutive
temple; the other two had the form of an apse, and contained
fountain figures.

Houses were sometimes enlarged at the expense of neighboring dwellings, which, in some cases, were destroyed to the

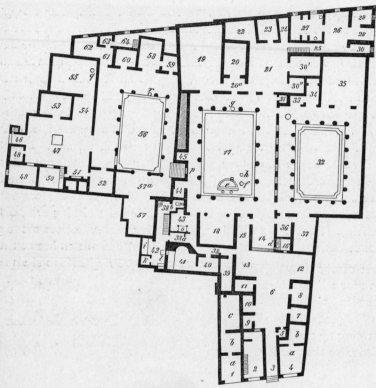

Fig. 174.— Plan of the house of the Citharist.

6. West atrium with connecting rooms, entered   42. Kitchen.
    from Stabian Street.
17, 32. Peristyles belonging with the west atrium.   47. North atrium, entered from the continuation
40, 41. Bath — tepidarium and caldarium.   of Abbondanza Street.
                                                  56. Peristyle belonging with the north atrium.

foundations, in others remodelled or incorporated with slight
change.   An example is the house of the Citharist, which fills
the greater part of the third Insula in Region I, on the east side
of Stabian Street.   A bronze statue of Apollo playing the
cithara, found in the middle peristyle (Fig. 174, 17), gave its

name to the house.   It is apparently a faithful copy of a Greek
masterpiece at Sparta, and is now in the Naples Museum.   The
house is sometimes referred to as that of Popidius Secundus.

There are two atriums (6, 47) and three peristyles (17, 32, 56).
A large part of the house, the west atrium (6), with the connect-

Fig. 175. — Orestes and Pylades before King Thoas.
Wall painting from the house of the Citharist.

ing rooms and the two peristyles, 17 and 32, was built in the
Tufa Period, in the place of several older houses.   The rooms
east of the two peristyles, and the north atrium (47) and peristyle (56), with the adjoining rooms, were added in Roman times,
probably near the end of the Republic ; the house was afterwards
decorated in the second style.   Remains of the third and fourth
styles also are found in some parts of the house.   The better
apartments are grouped about the peristyles ; the rooms about

the atriums were turned over to the slaves or used for domestic purposes.

In the large room (35) opening on the south peristyle were two paintings of unusual merit, both of which were transferred to the Naples Museum. The subject of one was the finding of the deserted Ariadne by Bacchus ; in the other Orestes and Pylades appear as captives before Thoas, the king of Tauris (Fig. 175).

At the right of the picture sits Thoas, looking at the captives, his sword lying across his knees, his hands resting upon the end of his sceptre. Behind him stands a guard with a long spear in the right hand. Another guard with two spears stands behind Orestes and Pylades, whose hands are bound. Orestes, upon whose head is a wreath of laurel, looks downward, an expression of sadness and resignation upon his finely chiselled features. Pylades is not without anxiety, but is alert and hopeful. Between the two groups is an altar on which incense is burning. In the background Iphigenia is seen moving slowly forward ; the head is entirely obliterated. It is unfortunate that the painting is so badly preserved. The faces of the two youths are individualized with remarkable skill, and the picture here used as the centre of a decorative framework of the fourth style is evidently a copy of a masterpiece.

angle with the street. The orientation of the building was determined by an abrupt descent in the ground, which runs across
the middle and divides it into two parts. The front part, the
rooms of which are numbered on the plan (Fig. 176), is a few
feet above the level of the street at the entrance. The rear portion, as may be seen from our section (Fig. 177), is considerably
lower; on the plan the rooms of this portion are designated by
letters. From traces of the second style of decoration found in
two of the rooms, and from the character of the masonry, we
infer that the villa was built in Roman times, but before the
reign of Augustus.

In front of the door was a narrow porch (Fig. 177). The
door opened directly into the peristyle (3 on the plan), in the
middle of which was a garden. At the left is a small triangular
court (17) containing a swimming tank (ζ) and a hearth (ϵ) on
which a kettle and several pots were found; the Romans partook of warm refreshments after a bath. The wall back of the
swimming tank was in part decorated with a garden scene, not
unlike those in the frigidariums of the two older public baths.
Over the tank was a roof supported by two columns, and on the
other two sides of the court there was a low but well proportioned colonnade.

The arrangements of the bath were unusually complete, comprising an apodyterium (19), a tepidarium (20), and a caldarium
(21), from which the tepidarium was warmed by means of an
opening in the wall; the caldarium had a hollow floor and walls,
and was heated from the kitchen (22). In the tepidarium were
found four panes of glass about $10\frac{1}{2}$ inches square, together
with the remains of the wooden frame in which they were set.
The caldarium, like those of the public baths, had a bath basin
and a semicircular niche for the labrum.

A small oven stands on one end of the hearth in the kitchen,
and a stone table is built against the wall on the long side. The
room in the corner (23) was used as a reservoir for water, which
was brought into it by means of a feed pipe and thence distributed through smaller pipes leading to the bath rooms and other
parts of the house.

At the left of the peristyle is a passage (15) leading to a garden which has not yet been excavated. The only apartment of special interest in this portion of the house is the semicircular sleeping room (14) built out into the garden. It faced the south, and had three large windows; it was separated from the rest of the house by an anteroom, *procoeton* (13), at one end of which is a small division (β) designed for the bed of an attendant. In the semicircular room are an alcove for a bed (γ) and a stationary wash bowl of masonry (δ). The plan is similar to that of a bedroom in Pliny's villa at Laurentum. Another sleeping room (9) was provided with both a large and a small door (p. 255).

The large room (8) at the rear of the peristyle may be loosely called a tablinum; it could be closed at the rear. Back of the

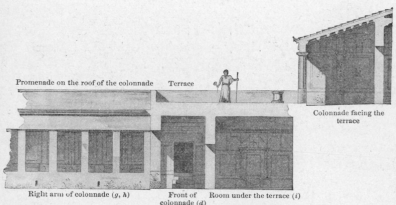

Promenade on the roof of the colonnade   Terrace

Colonnade facing the terrace

Right arm of colonnade (*g, h*)   Front of   Room under the terrace (*i*)
                                       colonnade (*d*)

Fig. 177. — Longitudinal section of

tablinum was originally a colonnade (26), which was later turned into a corridor, with rooms at either end; the original form is assumed in our restoration. Beyond the colonnade was a broad terrace (28) extending to the edge of the garden. It commanded a magnificent view of Stabiae, the coast in the direction of Sorrento, and the Bay. Connected with it was an unroofed promenade over the colonnade (*e, f, g, h*) surrounding the large garden below. A rectangular room (27, indicated on the plan but not in the restoration) was afterwards built on the terrace.

Members of the family could pass into the lower portion of the villa by means of a stairway, at *b*; the slaves could use a

long corridor (*a*), which was more directly connected with the
domestic apartments. The flat roof of the quadrangular colonnade (*e, f, g, h*) was carried on the outside by a wall, on the
inside by square pillars (Fig. 177). The rooms (*i, k*) opening
into the front of the colonnade were vaulted, and the decoration,
in the last style, is well preserved; the ceiling of the corner
rooms (*l, m*) is flat, and the decoration of one of them (*l*) is
noteworthy; green and red stars are painted on a white ground.
In the narrow space between *i* and *c* a cistern was built, from
which water could be drawn by means of a faucet in front.

At the opposite corners of the colonnade were two airy garden
rooms (*n, o*). Outside of the left arm (*e, f*) was a broad walk

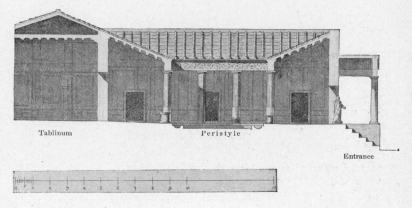

Tablinum   Peristyle

Entrance

the villa of Diomedes, restored.

(*u*), at the upper end of which were steps leading to the garden
above.

The garden enclosed by the colonnade was planted with trees,
charred remains of which were found at the time of excavation.
In the middle was a fish pond (*r*), in which was a fountain.
Back of it was a platform, over which vines were trained on a
framework supported by six columns, making a pleasant arbor
in which meals were doubtless often served.

The door at the rear of the garden led into the fields. Near
it were found the skeletons of two men. One of them had a
large key, doubtless the key of this door; he wore a gold ring

2 A

on his finger, and was carrying a considerable sum of money —
ten gold and eighty-eight silver coins. He was probably the
master of the house who had started out, accompanied by a
single slave, in order to find means of escape.

The floor of the three sides of the colonnade was a few feet
higher than that of the front. Underneath was a wine cellar,
lighted by small windows in the wall on the side of the garden;
it contained a large number of amphorae.

At the time of the eruption many members of the family
took refuge in the cellar. Here were found the skeletons of
eighteen adults and two children: at the time of excavation the
impressions of their bodies, and in some instances traces of
the clothing, could be seen in the hardened ashes. Among the
women was one adorned with two necklaces and two arm bands,
besides four gold rings and two of silver. The victims were
suffocated by the damp ashes that drifted in through the small
windows. According to the report of the excavations, fourteen
skeletons of men were found in other parts of the house, together with the skeletons of a dog and a goat.

KEY TO PLAN IV

A. COURT.

   1, 5. Cistern curbs.

   2. Wash basin of masonry.

   3. Lead reservoir from which water was conducted to the reservoir in the kitchen supplying the bath.

   4. Steps leading to the reservoir.

B. KITCHEN.

   1. Hearth.

   2. Reservoir containing water for the bath.

   3. Stairway to rooms over the bath.

   4. Entrance to cellar under the inner end of the first wine press, in which were the fastenings of the standard of the press beam.

C–F. BATH.

   C. Furnace room.

   D. Apodyterium.

   E. Tepidarium.

   F. Caldarium.

H. STABLE.

J. TOOL ROOM.

K, L. SLEEPING ROOMS.

N. DINING ROOM.

M. ANTEROOM.

O. BAKERY.

   1. Mill.

   2. Oven.

P. ROOM WITH TWO WINE PRESSES.

   1, 1. Foundations of the presses.

   2, 2, 2. Receptacles for the grape juice.

   3. Receptacle for the product of the second pressing.

   4. Holes for the standards of the press beams.

   5, 5. Holes for the posts at the ends of the two windlasses used in raising and lowering the press beams.

   6. Pit affording access to the framework by which the windlass posts were tied down.

Q. CORRIDOR.

   1. Wine vats.

R. COURT FOR THE FERMENTATION OF WINE.

   1. Channel for the fresh grape juice coming from P.

   2. Fermentation vats, *dolia*.

   3. Lead kettle over a fireplace.

   4. Cistern curb.

S. ROOM — USE UNKNOWN.

T. THRESHING FLOOR.

U. OPEN CISTERN FOR THE WATER FALLING ON THE THRESHING FLOOR.

V–V. SLEEPING ROOMS.

W. ENTRANCE TO CELLAR UNDER THE INNER END OF THE SECOND WINE PRESS; see B. 4.

X. ROOM WITH HAND MILL.

Y. ROOM WITH OIL PRESS.

   1. Foundation of the press.

   2. Hole for the standard of the press beam.

   3. Entrance to cellar with appliances for securing the press beam.

   4. Holes for the windlass posts.

   5. Hole affording access to the fastenings of the windlass posts.

   6. Receptacle for the oil.

Z. ROOM CONTAINING THE OLIVE CRUSHER.

CHAPTER XLIV

THE VILLA RUSTICA AT BOSCOREALE

Less than two miles north of Pompeii, near the village of Boscoreale, a farmhouse was excavated in 1893–94 on the property of Vincenzo de Prisco. In the last century similar buildings were brought to light in the vicinity of Castellammare, but they were covered up again. Especial importance attaches to this villa rustica, both on account of the extreme rarity of examples of the type and because of the character of the remains, which makes it possible to determine the arrangements with certainty.

The living rooms, the stable, and the rooms used for the making of wine and oil were all under one roof. The size of the building is not so great as might have been assumed from the variety of purposes which it served; the enclosed area, exclusive of the threshing floor, measures about 125 by 80 feet. The plan (Plan IV) is regular, the principal entrance being near the middle of the southwest side.

The entrance was wide enough for carts and wagons, which were kept in the court (*A*). Along three sides of the court ran a colonnade, over which at the front were upper rooms; the roof on the left side and the rear rested on columns connected by a parapet. Under the colonnade at the further corner is a cistern curb (1), on one side of which is a large wash basin of masonry (2); on the other is a pillar supporting a small reservoir of lead (3). The reservoir, reached by means of steps (4), was filled from the cistern.

In a Roman farmhouse the kitchen was the large, central room (p. 247). Vitruvius recommends that it be placed on the warmest side of the court; and in our villa rustica it lies at the north corner (*B*) where, in winter, it would receive the full benefit of the sunshine. The hearth (1), on which remains of fire were found, stands in the middle of the room; in the wall at one side is a niche, ornamented to resemble the façade of a diminutive temple, in which were placed the images of the household gods.

A large door in the right wall of the kitchen opened into the stable (*H*). Near it was a stairway (3) leading to upper rooms; in the corner was a pit (4) affording access to a small cellar in which the standard of the press beam in the adjoining room (*P*, 4) was made fast. In the opposite corner was a reservoir of lead (2) standing on a foundation of masonry; it received water from the reservoir in the court (*A*, 3) and supplied the bath. On the same side of the room is the entrance to the bath and to the closet (*G*).

The arrangements of this bath are in a better state of preservation than those of any other Roman bath yet discovered; the

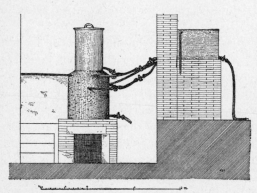

tank and reservoir with the connecting pipes may now be seen at Pompeii in the little Museum near the Forum fitted up for the exhibition of the objects found in this villa. The bath rooms comprised an apodyterium (*D*), a tepidarium (*E*), and a caldarium (*F*) with a

Fig. 178. — Hot water tank and reservoir for supplying the bath in the villa rustica at Boscoreale.

bath basin at one end and a labrum in a semicircular recess at the other. The bath was heated from a small furnace room (*C*). Over the hot air flue leading from the furnace into the hollow space under the floor of the caldarium was a water heater in the form of a half cylinder similar to the one found in the Stabian Baths (p. 188). The tepidarium, as well as the caldarium, had a hollow floor and walls.

Over the furnace stood a round lead tank, the lower part of which was encased in masonry; the pipes connecting it with the reservoir in the corner of the kitchen and with the bath rooms were found in place, and are shown in Fig. 178. The middle pipe supplied the tank with cold water; the flow could be regulated by means of a stopcock. The lower pipe started from the reservoir, but before reaching the tank was divided, the left arm leading into the tank, the other into the bath basin. As there were stopcocks in the main pipe and in the arm entering the tank, by adjusting these the bath basin could be supplied with either hot or cold water through a single pipe. The upper pipe was divided in the same way, one arm leading to the labrum. In the public baths there was a separate tank for lukewarm water ; here a moderate temperature was obtained by mixing hot and cold water.

At the bottom of the tank (seen at the right) is a short bib-cock used when the water was drawn off. On the side of the reservoir we see the end of the feed pipe leading from the reservoir in the court ; at the right is a supply pipe which probably led to a cold bath.

On the same side of the court with the kitchen and the bath is a tool room (*J*), in which were found remains of tools ; several sickles were hanging on the walls. Next are two sleeping rooms (*K, L*), the latter being perhaps the bedroom of the overseer, *villicus*, which, according to Varro, should be near the entrance. A short passage between these rooms leads to the bakery, with a single mill (1) and an oven (2). The large apartment in the corner (*N*) is a dining room, which is separated from the court by an anteroom (*M*).

The oblong room at the southeast side of the court contained appliances for making wine. At each end was a large press (1) with a raised floor. The presses were operated on the same principle as that previously described (p. 330), and though the woodwork has perished, it is easy to understand the arrangements from the depressions in which the posts were set.

At the rear of each press was a strong standard (4, 4), to which the inner end of the heavy press beam was attached. In front stood two posts (5–5), to which were fitted the ends of a horizontal windlass. By means of a pulley and a rope passed around the windlass, the outer end of the press beam could be raised or lowered. When it was lowered in order to increase

the pressure on the grapes, the standard to which the inner end
was attached would be pulled out of the ground unless firmly
braced.   Under the rear of each press was a small cellar, in
which was placed a framework for holding the standard in place.
One was entered from a pit in the corner of the kitchen (*B*, 4),
the other from a similar depression in a small separate room (*W*).

The grape juice ran into round vats (2, 2) sunk in the ground.
In front of the first press are two, in front of the second only
one ; an oblong basin of masonry at one corner (3) here takes the
place of the other round vat.   The oblong vat could be filled
also from the first press by means of a lead pipe under the floor.
The round vats were for the pure juice of the first pressing.
Into the other was conducted the less copious product of the
second pressing ; the remains of the grapes, after the juice had
ceased to flow, were drenched with water and again subjected to
pressure.

In Pliny's "Natural History" (xiv. 136) we read that in Campania the best wine underwent fermentation in the open air,
exposed to sun, rain, and wind.   This villa supplies an interesting confirmation of the statement ; the round fermentation vats
fill a large court (*R*), the walls of which are pierced with openings in order to give readier access to the wind.   Along one side
runs a channel of masonry about three feet above the ground,
protected by a narrow roof ; thence the grape juice was distributed to the vats.   During the vintage season, the inner end
of the channel was connected with the press room by means
of a temporary pipe or channel entering the wall above the
oblong basin (*P*, 3).

The surface of this court is higher than that of the rest of the
building ; instead of excavating in order to set the large earthen
vats in the ground, the proprietor filled in with earth around
them.   In one corner is a lead kettle (3) with a place for building
a fire underneath ; perhaps wine was heated in it.   The vats in
the court seem not to have been used exclusively for wine.   In
one were found remains of wheat, in another of millet.   Other
vats stood in the passageway on the side of the court (*Q*, 1).

Three of the small rooms toward the rear were sleeping rooms
(*V–V*).   In another (*X*) was found a hand mill.   At the end of

the passageway was a double room containing the appliances
for making oil, a press (in *Y*) and a crusher (in *Z*).   The press
was like the wine press described above, only much smaller, with
a raised floor (1), a standard for the press beam (2), a pit for
bracing the standard of the press beam (3), two posts at the
ends of the windlass (4, 4), a pit from which a crosspiece connecting these posts could be reached, and a vat (6) at one side
for receiving the oil.   This vat, for some reason not understood,
was divided into two parts by a partition in the middle.

Fig. 179. — Olive crusher.

The olive crusher, *trapetum*, now in the Museum at Pompeii
mentioned above, is shown in the accompanying illustration
(Fig. 179).   It was designed to separate the pulp of the olives
from the stones, which were thought to impair the flavor of the
oil.   It consists of a deep circular basin of lava, so hollowed
out as to leave in the centre a strong standard of the stone,
miliarium.   In the top of this standard was set an iron pin,
on which was fitted a revolving wooden crosspiece (shown in
Fig. 179, restored).   This carried two wheels of lava, having the
shape of half a lens, which travelled in the basin.   The wheels
were carefully balanced so that they would not press against
the side of the basin and crush the stones of the olives.

In the long room *S* remains of bean straw and parts of a wagon were found, but the purpose of the room is not indicated. South of it is the threshing floor (*T*), the surface of which is raised above the ground and covered with Signia pavement. The water that fell upon the threshing floor was conducted to a small open cistern (*U*). As the establishment was not connected with an aqueduct, rain water was carefully saved.

For at least a part of the year the proprietor of the villa probably lived in it. So elaborate a bath would not have been built for the use of slaves, and in the second story was a modest but comfortable series of apartments, apparently designed for the master's use. In the farmhouses in the vicinity of Rome and Naples to-day rooms over the domestic apartments or the quarters of the tenant are frequently reserved for the use of the owner.

In a place where such a find would least have been anticipated — the oblong vat in the room of the wine presses — was made one of the most remarkable discoveries of treasure in modern times. Here a man had taken refuge, and with his skeleton were found, besides more than a thousand gold coins, six gold bracelets, a gold chain nearly thirty inches long, and the beautiful silver table service afterwards presented by Baron Rothschild to the Louvre. We can hardly believe that so costly a set of silverware was used in this farmhouse. More likely it belonged in a wealthy country seat nearer the mountain; the man who had fled with it, when unable to go further, sought shelter here.

CHAPTER XLV

HOUSEHOLD FURNITURE

MUCH less large furniture has been found at Pompeii than is ordinarily supposed. In not a single sleeping room has a bed been preserved; and in only one of all the dining rooms have sufficient remains of the dining couches been found to make it possible to reconstruct them. Beds, couches, chairs, and tables

Fig. 180. — Dining couch with bronze mountings, the wooden frame being restored.

were ordinarily of wood, which crumbled away, leaving slight traces. Reference has been made elsewhere to the marble tables standing in the atrium, and occasionally in other parts of the house. Tables of bronze are infrequently met with, while bronze chairs are almost as rare as bronze couches.

Wood was not a suitable material for many classes of smaller articles, and these, made of bronze, clay, glass, or stone, are found in great numbers.   Such are the lamps, the bronze lamp stands, the kitchen utensils, the table furnishings, and the toilet articles of bronze, ivory, or bone.

The wooden frame and end board of one of the dining couches just mentioned was completely charred, but the form was clearly

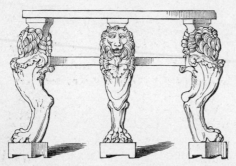

Fig. 181. — Round marble table.

indicated, and the wood-work has been restored (Fig. 180).   The couch is now in the Naples Museum, as are also the other articles of furniture illustrated in this chapter.

The half figures on the front of the end board, shown more plainly in the detail at the left of the illustration, were cast; the rest of the mounting was *repoussé* work.   The bronze on the side toward the table was inlaid with silver.   The end boards were placed at the head of the up-per couch and the foot of the lower one (p. 258); the middle couch did not have a raised end.   The mattress rested on straps stretched across the frame.   The dining room in which the couches were found adjoins the tablinum of a house in the seventh Region (VII. ii. 18).

The carved marble supports of a gartibulum are shown in Fig. 116; a complete table of a plainer

Fig. 182. — Carved table leg, found in the second peristyle of the house of the Faun.

type is seen in Plate VII.   An example of a round marble table, found in 1827 in a house near the Forum, is presented in Fig. 181.   The three legs are carved to represent those of lions, a lion's head being placed at the top of each.   A table of similar design was found in the peristyle of the house of the Vettii, with traces of yellow color on the manes of the lions.

Among the best examples of ornamental carving is the marble table leg in the form of a sphinx, found in the second peristyle of the house of the Faun (Fig. 182). The figure is well conceived, and the technical handling is much above the average of excellence.

Small tables or stands of bronze supported by three slender legs were called tripods. The top was flat, but not infrequently surrounded by a deep rim, making a convenient receptacle for light objects. The rim of the example shown in Fig. 183 is ornamented with festoons and bucrania, while the upper parts of the legs are modelled to represent winged sphinxes. This stand was not found in the temple of Isis, as is often stated, but probably in Herculaneum.

The bisellium, the 'seat of double width,' was a chair of simple design without a back, used in the Theatre and Amphitheatre by members of the city council and others upon whom the "honor of the bisellium" had been con-

Fig. 183. — Bronze stand with an ornamented rim around the top.

ferred. The remains of one with bronze mountings have been restored. The restoration, however, does not seem to be correct in all particulars, and instead of presenting it we may refer the reader to the somewhat conventional bisellium carved on the tomb of Calventius Quietus (Fig. 232).

The lamps are found in a great variety of forms. The essential parts are the body, containing the oil, which was poured in

through an opening in the top, and the nozzle with a hole for the wick (Fig. 184). Hand lamps were usually provided with a handle, hanging lamps with projections containing holes through which the chains could be passed.

Fig. 184.— Lamps of the simplest form, with one nozzle.

The opening for the admission of oil was often closed by an ornamental cover (Figs. 187, 188). In front of it, near the base of the nozzle, was frequently a much smaller orifice through which a large needle could be inserted to pick up the wick when it had burned out and sunk back into the oil, and air could be admitted when the cover was closed.

The material of the lamps was clay or bronze. The bronze lamps were more costly and ordinarily more freely ornamented. Those of clay were left

Fig. 185.— Lamps with two nozzles.
At the left, a hanging lamp; at the right, a hand lamp.

unglazed, or covered with a red glazing like that of the Arretian ware; lamps with a greenish glaze are occasionally found.

The light furnished by the wicks was dim and smoky. A more brilliant light was obtained by increasing the number of

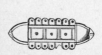

Fig. 186. — Lamps with more than two nozzles.

nozzles. Lamps with two nozzles are often found. These were sometimes placed at one end, the handle being at the other; sometimes in the case of hanging lamps, at opposite ends, as in the example shown in Fig. 185.

Lamps with several nozzles are not infrequently met with. The shape is often circular, as in two of the examples pre-sented in Fig. 186, one of which had six wicks, the other twelve. Sometimes a more ornamental form was adopted. Lamps having the shape of a boat are not uncommon; the one represented in Fig. 186 was provided with nozzles for fourteen wicks.

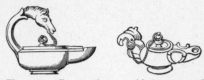

Fig. 187.—Bronze lamps with ornamental covers attached to a chain.

The hanging lamps were sometimes made with a single nozzle, as the curious one having the shape of a mask shown in Fig. 189, at the left; sometimes with two nozzles (Fig. 185). Bronze hanging lamps with three arms, each of which contained a place for a wick, are occa-sionally found; an ex-ample is given in Fig. 189, at the right. Still more elaborate are those with a large num-ber of nozzles, as the one represented in the same illustration, which had nine wicks.

Fig. 188.—Bronze lamps with covers ornamented with figures.

The name of the maker is often stamped upon the bottom of the lamp, sometimes in the nominative case, as PULCHER, in the example given in Fig. 184, more often in the genitive and in an abbreviated form.

The variety displayed in the ornamentation of lamps was as great as that manifested in the forms. Ornament was applied to all parts, — the body, the handle, the cover, and even the nozzle. The covers of the two bronze lamps shown in Fig. 188 are adorned with figures. On one is a Cupid struggling with a goose. The chain attached to the right hand of the figure on the other is fastened to a hooked needle for pulling out the wick.

The object of which we give a representation in Fig. 190, often erroneously classed as a lamp, is a nursing bottle, *biberon*.

Fig. 189. — Three hanging lamps.
The one at the left and the middle one are presented in two views.

The material is clay, and the figure of a gladiator is stamped on it, symbolizing the hope that the infant will develop strength and vigor. On some bottles of this kind the figure of a thriving child is seen, on others a mother suckling a child.

Three kinds of supports for lamps may be distinguished ac-

Fig. 190. — A nursing bottle.

cording to their size : lamp standards, which stood on the floor and ranged in height from $2\frac{1}{2}$ to 5 feet ; lamp holders, not far from 20 inches high, which were placed on tables ; and small lamp stands, also used on the table. The general term *candelabrum* was originally applied to candle holders containing several candles (*candelae*). Such candle holders have been found in Etruscan graves, but the candelabra met with at Pompeii were all designed to carry lamps.

The lamp standards, of bronze, are often of graceful proportions and ornamented in good taste. The feet are modelled to represent the claws (Fig. 191) or hoofs of animals. The slender shaft rises sometimes directly from the union of the three legs at the centre, sometimes from a round, ornamented disk resting on the legs. Above the shaft is usually an ornamental form, a sphinx, as in our illustration, a head, or a vase-like capital sustaining the round flat top on which the lamp rested. Occasionally the shaft is replaced by a conventional plant form.

Adjustable standards also occur; the upper part slides up and down in the hollow shaft of the lower part, so that the height can be changed at will.

The bronze lamp holders were sometimes designed to support a single lamp (Fig. 192). Frequently the main part divides into two branches, each of which sustains a small round disk for a lamp; often the arms or branches were designed to carry hanging lamps. The example shown in Fig. 193 is from the villa of Diomedes.

In the lamp holders conventional plant forms are more frequently met with than in the standards. The trunk of a tree with spreading branches is especially common (Fig. 194).

The lamp stands, which resemble diminutive bronze tables, are found in a pleasing variety of form and ornament. The top is sometimes a round disk resting on a single leg supported by three feet; sometimes, as in the example presented in Fig. 195, the legs are carried to the top, and the intervening spaces are utilized for ornamentation.

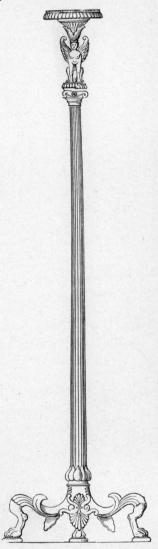

Fig. 191. — Lamp standard, of bronze.

Fig. 192. — Lamp holder for a
hand lamp.

Fig. 193. — Lamp holder for hanging
lamps.

Fig. 194. — Lamp holder in the form
of a tree trunk.

Fig. 195. — Lamp stand, of bronze.

The lamp seen in this illustration is the same as that shown more clearly in Fig. 188, at the right.

Kitchen utensils of bronze and red earthenware have been found in great quantity; table furnishings more rarely. A group of typical examples is presented in Fig. 196. The forms are so similar to those of the utensils found in modern households that few words of explanation are needed.

Fig. 196. — Bronze utensils.

a. Kettle mounted on a tripod ready to be placed on the fire.	*c, d*. Pails.	*k*. Pitcher.	*s*. Pastry mould.
b, g, h, l. Cooking pots.	*e*. Ladle.	*m*. Kitchen spoon.	*q, u*. Wine ladles.
	f. Dipper.	*n, v*. Table spoons.	*r*. Two-handled pan.
	i, t. Baking pans for small cakes.	*o, p*. Frying pans.	

The pastry mould (*s*) is of good size and neatly finished, and must have left a clear impression. Besides the two types of table spoons illustrated here (*n, v*) a third is represented by examples found at Pompeii, the *cochlear*, which had a bowl at one end and ran out into a point at the other. The point was used in picking shellfish out of their shells, the bowl in eating eggs.

The two long ladles were used in dipping wine out of the mixing bowl into the cups. The ancients ordinarily drank their wine mingled with water; for mixing the liquids they used a large bowl of earthenware or metal, which was often richly ornamented. The mixing bowl presented in Fig. 197 was found in a house on Abbondanza Street, near the entrance of the building of Eumachia. It is in part inlaid with silver, and nearly twenty-two inches high.

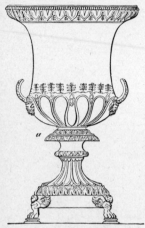

Fig. 197. — Mixing bowl, of bronze in part inlaid with silver.

Hot water was often preferred for mixing with wine, and small heaters of ornamental design were sometimes used upon the table. The ancient name for these utensils is *authepsa*, 'self-cooker'; the appropriateness of it is apparent from an example found at Pompeii, in which the coals of fire were entirely concealed from view.

Fig. 198. — Water heater for the table, view and section.

This heater (Fig. 198) has the form of an urn. In the middle is a tube, the bottom of which is closed by a diminutive grate; the arrangement is shown in the section at the right. In this tube the coals were placed, and when the water in the urn was hot, it could be drawn off by means of a faucet at the side. Back of the faucet is a small vertical vent tube.

In some cases the appearance of a heater was more suggestive of its purpose. One (Fig. 199) has the form of an ordinary brazier, the water being heated in the hollow space about the

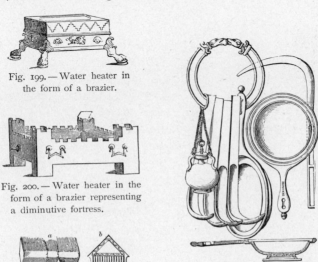

Fig. 199.— Water heater in the form of a brazier.

Fig. 200.— Water heater in the form of a brazier representing a diminutive fortress.

Fig. 202.— Combs.

Fig. 201.— Appliances for the bath.

fire pan. In another instance (Fig. 200) the brazier is ornamented with towers and battlements like those of a diminutive fortress; the faucet can be seen in our illustration, on the left side.

An interesting group of toilet appliances for the bath was found in the Baths north of the Forum (Fig. 201). Hanging from a ring were an unguent flask, four scrapers (*strigiles*), and a shallow saucer with a handle in which the unguent was poured out when it was to be applied. One of the scrapers is repeated in a side view at the right, and both side and front views of the unguent saucer are given.

Small articles of toilet are discovered in a good state of preservation. The forms in most cases do not differ greatly from those to which we are accustomed.

The fine comb seen in Fig. 202 *a* is of bone; the two coarse combs (Fig. 202 *b* and Fig. 206 *d*) are of bronze.

Fig. 203. — Hairpins. Underneath, two small ivory toilet boxes.

Fig. 204. — Glass box for cosmetics.

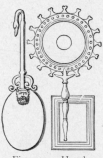

Fig. 205. — Hand mirrors.

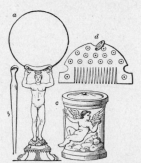

Fig. 206. — Group of toilet articles.

a. Standing mirror.   *c.* Ivory box for cosmetics.
b. Ear cleaner.   *d.* Bronze comb.

The ends of the hairpins were often ornamented with figures. The specimens shown in Fig. 203 are of ivory. The designs in which female figures appear are in keeping with the use, but the ornamentation for the most part seems excessive.

The toilet boxes, of glass or ivory, were used for a variety of purposes. Of those presented in our illustrations, one (Fig. 203, at the right) probably contained perfumed oil. The round glass box (Fig. 204) was used for cosmetics, as was also the ivory box seen in Fig. 206, the outside of which is carved in low relief.

The mirrors were of metal, highly polished. The one seen in Fig. 206 was designed to stand upon a dressing case; the other three (Fig. 205) are hand mirrors. The frame of the rectangular mirror is modern; whether or not this had a handle is not clear.

Fig. 207. — Gold arm band.

.Jewellery of gold and silver, cups of silver, and other small objects wrought in the precious metals have now and then been found. A characteristic example of the jewellery is the large gold arm band in the form of a serpent, with eyes of rubies, which was found in one of the houses (Fig. 207). It weighs twenty-two ounces; to judge from the size, it must have been intended for the upper arm.

PART III

TRADES AND OCCUPATIONS

CHAPTER XLVI

THE TRADES AT POMPEII.— THE BAKERS

In antiquity there was no such distinction between trades and professions as exists to-day. In the Early Empire all activity outside the field of public service, civil and military, or the management of estates, was considered beneath the dignity of a Roman; the practice of law, which had received its impulse largely from the obligation of patrons to protect their clients, was included among public duties. The ordinary work of life was left mainly to slaves and freedmen. Not only the trades, as we understand the term, but architecture and engineering, — in antiquity two branches of one occupation, — the practice of medicine, and teaching, were looked upon as menial. A Roman of literary or practical bent might manifest an interest in such vocations, but it was considered hardly respectable actively to engage in them.

This attitude of mind, especially toward the higher occupations, is only explicable in the light of the social conditions then existing. Men who kept slaves of every degree of intelligence and training, and were at all times accustomed to command, were not disposed to hold themselves in readiness to do another's bidding, excepting in the service of the State alone; and work committed to slaves and freedmen naturally came to be considered unworthy the employment of a gentleman. The freemen of the same craft were often united in guilds or corporations, for the administration of certain matters of mutual interest; but nothing is known in regard to the activities of such organizations at Pompeii.

In a city as large as Pompeii, all the occupations corresponding to the needs of daily life must have been represented. The remains of the appliances and products of labor are of the most varied character, sometimes far from satisfactory, raising more difficulties than they solve; yet often revealing at a glance the ancient methods of work, and casting light upon the economic background of Greek and Roman culture. The excavations have brought before us three sources of information, inscriptions, paintings, and the remains of buildings or rooms used as workshops.

The inscriptions refer to more than a score of occupations; from farming to innkeeping, and from hairdressing to goldworking. Most of them are election notices, in which the members of a craft unite, or are exhorted to unite, in recommending a certain candidate for a municipal office. These are painted in red letters on the walls along the streets, and are much alike, though some are fuller than others. The simplest form contains only three words, as *Trebium aed. tonsores*, — 'The barbers recommend Trebius for the office of aedile.' The more elaborate recommendations may be illustrated by the following: *Verum aed. o. v. f.* (for *aedilem, oro vos, facite*), *unguentari, facite, rog[o]*, — 'Do make Verus aedile, perfumers, elect him, I beg of you.' The whole craft of goldsmiths favored the election of Pansa: *C. Cuspium Pansam aed. aurifices universi rog[ant]*, — 'All the goldsmiths recommend Gaius Cuspius Pansa for the aedileship.'

The recommendations of the fruit sellers are particularly conspicuous. On one occasion they joined with a prominent individual in the support of a ticket: *M. Holconium Priscum II vir. i. d. pomari universi cum Helvio Vestale rog.*, — 'All the fruit sellers, together with Helvius Vestalis, urge the election of M. Holconius Priscus as duumvir with judiciary authority.' There may have been some special reason why the fruiterers wished to keep in favor with the city authorities, and so took an active part in the elections; the dealers in garlic (*aliari*) also had a candidate.

Among the representatives of other employments that joined in the support of candidates were the dyers (*offectores*), cloak-cutters (*sagarii*), pack-carriers (*saccarii*), mule-drivers (*muliones*), and fishermen (*piscicapi*). The inscription in which reference is made to the gig-drivers is mentioned elsewhere (p. 237).

The paintings in which we see work going on are numerous. By far the most pleasing are those in which the workmen are Cupids, busying themselves with the affairs of men. Several pictures of this kind have already been described (pp. 97, 326–331); but we ought to add to those mentioned two scenes from Herculaneum, often reproduced, in which Cupids are represented as carpenters and as shoemakers.

Among the more important paintings in which the figures of men appear are those which picture the life of an inn and those that present the processes of cleaning cloth; both groups are reserved for later discussion. In a house in the ninth Region (IX. v. 9) a stuccoer is pictured at work putting the finishing touches on a wall with a smoothing tool, and in the house of the Surgeon an artist is seen painting a herm (Fig. 128).

In only a few instances are the remains of workshops sufficiently characteristic to indicate their purpose. Among the most impressive, to the visitor at Pompeii, are the ruins of the bakeries, with their large millstones (Fig. 208). Equally important, also, are the remains of the fulleries, and of a large tannery, which, as well as those of the inns and winecrooms, will be discussed in separate chapters.

A few out of the hundreds of shops opening on the streets contain remains of the articles exposed for sale. The discovery of charred nuts, fruits, and loaves of bread in the market stalls north of the Macellum has already been noted (p. 96). We know the use of other shops from the remains of paints found in them. The arrangements of such places of business were discussed in connection with those of the Pompeian house.

Several establishments which contain large lead kettles set in masonry, with a place for a fire underneath, have been identified as dyehouses. In the case of one on Stabian Street (VII. ii. 11), the identification seems complete. Nine such kettles stand in the peristyle, which has a direct connection with the street; in a closet were numerous bottles, part of which contained coloring materials. There was formerly a painting on the

wall of the entrance, representing a man carrying on a pole
an object which had the appearance of a garment fresh from
the dye.

On the opposite side of the street is the election notice:
Postumium Proculum aed. offectores rog[*ant*], — 'The dyers
request the election of Postumius Proculus as aedile.' The
house on which this inscription is painted (IX. iii. 2) contains
three kettles similar to those already mentioned; the dyers of

Fig. 208. — Ruins of a bakery, with millstones.

both establishments may have united in supporting the candidacy of Proculus.

A potter's workshop, with two ovens, is located outside the
Herculaneum Gate, where the streets divide opposite the villa
of Diomedes (Plan V, 29–30). The ovens, which are not large,
have an upper division, in which were placed the vessels to be
baked, and a firebox underneath, the floor above being pierced
with holes to let the heat through. The vault of one of the ovens
is constructed of parallel rows of jars fitted into one another.

There was a shoemaker's shop on the northwest corner of

Insula VII. i opening upon two streets. It is connected with the entrance hall of the adjoining house (No. 40), and in the middle is a small stone table. The identification rests upon the discovery here of certain tools, particularly leather-cutters' knives with a crescent-shaped blade; there was also an inscription on the wall, making record of some repairing done 'July 14, with a sharp-cornered knife (*scalpro angulato*) and an awl.' Apparently the porter of the house (*ostiarius*) was at the same time a cobbler, as frequently in Italy to-day.

On the same wall is another scribbling: *M. Nonius Campanus mil. coh. VIIII pr. > Caesi,* — 'Marcus Nonius Campanus, a soldier of the ninth praetorian cohort, of the century led by Caesius.' The name of the centurion, M. Caesius Blandus, is scratched twice on the columns of the peristyle in the same house. Captain and private may have come from Rome in the escort of an emperor. Perhaps the centurion was quartered in this house; the soldier, waiting to have his shoes mended, scratched his name upon the wall.

The better houses were so freely adorned with statuettes and other ornaments of marble that there must have been marble-workers in the city. The workshop of one was found, in 1798, on Stabian Street, near the Large Theatre. It contained various pieces of carving, as herms, table feet, and table tops; there was also an unfinished mortar, together with a slab of marble partly sawed, the saw being left in the cut.

Signs of shops are not often seen in Pompeii, but two or three may be mentioned. In the wall of a shop-front in the block containing the Baths north of the Forum, there is a terra cotta plaque with a goat in relief, to indicate the place of a milk dealer; and not far away we find a sign of a wineshop, a tufa relief of two men carrying between them an amphora hung from a pole supported on their shoulders.

Not all such reliefs, however, are signs of shops. Near the Porta Marina (at the northwest corner of Insula VII. xv), a tufa block may be seen near the top of the wall, showing a mason's tools in relief; above it is the inscription, *Diogenes structor*, 'Diogenes the mason.' This is not a sign — the inscription can hardly be read from below; it is, moreover, on the

outside of a garden wall, with no house or shop entrance near
it.   It is rather a workman's signature; Diogenes had built the
wall, and wished to leave a record of his skill.

In antiquity the miller and the baker were one person.   We
rarely find in Pompeii — and then only in private houses — an
oven without mills under the same roof.   There were many
bakeries in the city.   The portion already excavated contains
more than twenty, each of them with three or four mills; bread
was furnished, therefore, by a number of small bakeries rather
than by a few large establishments.

The appearance of a bakery to-day, with its mills and its large
oven, may be seen in Fig. 208.   The arrangements can more

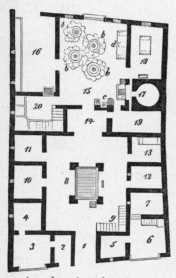

easily be explained, however, from
the plan of another establishment,
one of the largest, in the third Insula of Region I (Fig. 209).   Entering from the street through the
fauces, we find ourselves in an atrium
of simple form (8) with rooms on
either side; the tablinum (14) is here
merely an entrance to the mill room
(15).   In the corner of the atrium
is a stairway leading to a second
story, which was particularly needed
here, because the living rooms at the
rear were required for the bakery;
the floor of the second story was
supported by brick pillars at the
corners of the impluvium, joined by
flat arches.

Fig. 209. — Plan of a bakery.

8. Atrium.	17. Oven.
15. Mill room.	18. Kneading room.
16. Stable.	19. Storeroom.

The four mills (*b*), were turned
by animals; the floor around them
is paved with basalt flags like those
used for the streets.   In the same room, at *d*, are the remains
of a low table; at *c* there is a cistern curb, with a large earthen
vessel for holding water on either side, while the wall above is
ornamented with a painting representing Vesta, the patron god-

dess of bakers, between the two Lares. On one side of the oven (17) is the kneading room (19), on the other the storeroom (18). The room at the left (16) is the stall for the donkeys that turned the mills.

The mills of Pompeii, with slight variations, are all of one type ; if there were water-mills on the Sarno, no trace of them has been found. The millstones are of lava (p. 15). The lower stone, *meta*, has the shape of a cone resting on the end of a cylinder, but the cylindrical part is in most cases partially concealed by a thick hoop of masonry, the

Fig. 210.— A Pompeian mill, without its framework.

top of which was formed into a trough to receive the flour, and was covered with sheet lead (Fig. 210). A square hole, five or six inches across, was cut in the top of the cone, in which was inserted a wooden standard ; this supported a vertical iron pivot on which the frame of the upper millstone turned.

The shape of the upper millstone, *catillus*, may best be seen in Fig. 211. It was like a double funnel, the lower cavity being fitted to the cone of the lower millstone, while that in the upper part answered the purpose of a hopper. The two cavities were connected at the centre by an opening similar to that of an

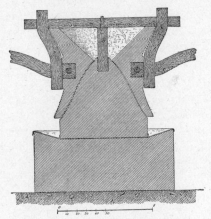

Fig. 211.— Section of a mill, restored.

hourglass, which left room for the standard and allowed the grain to run down slowly, when the *catillus* was turned, to be ground between the two stones. The flour ran out at the base of the cone and fell into the trough, ready to be sifted and made into bread.

The upper millstone was nicely balanced over the lower, the surface of which it touched but lightly; it could not have rested on the under stone with full weight, for in that case the strength of a draft animal would not have sufficed to move it. The stones could be set for finer or coarser grinding by changing the length of the standard.

The arrangement for turning the mill was simple. In shaping the upper millstone, strong shoulders were left in the narrowest part (Fig. 210), on opposite sides. In these square sockets were cut, in which the ends of shafts were inserted and firmly fastened by round bolts passing through the shoulders (Fig. 211). The shafts were tied to the ends of the crossbeam above by curved vertical pieces of wood, or by straps of iron, which were let into grooves in the stone and so made firm. The crosspiece above, which turned on the pivot in the end of the standard, was sometimes of iron, sometimes of wood with an iron socket fitting the pivot. The framework must necessarily have been exceedingly strong. One of the mills at Pompeii has lately been set up with new woodwork, and grinds very well.

Fig. 212. — A mill in operation. Relief in the Vatican Museum.

The smaller mills were turned by slaves, the larger by draft animals. Men pushed on the projecting shafts, but animals wore a collar which was attached by a chain or rope to the end of the crosspiece at the top. The links of the chain running to the crossbeam are distinctly shown in a relief in the Vatican Museum (Fig. 212), in which a horse is represented turning a mill. Blinders are over the eyes of the horse, which seems also to be checked up in order to prevent eating. A square hopper rests on the crossbeam, and the miller is bringing a measure of wheat to pour into it. On a shelf in the corner of the room is a lamp.

The ovens were not unlike those still in use in many parts of
Europe. They were shaped like a low beehive, generally with
some kind of a flue in front to make the fire burn inside while

they were being heated. The oven in the
bakery described above, however, has a
special device for saving as much heat as
possible (Fig. 213); it is entirely enclosed
in a smoke chamber (*b*), with two openings above (*d*) for the draft. Fires were
kindled in such ovens with wood or charcoal; the latter was probably used here.
When the proper temperature for baking

Fig. 213.—Section of bake
oven.

had been reached, the ashes were raked out (in Fig. 213, *e* is an
ashpit), the loaves of bread shoved in, and the mouth closed to
retain the heat. A receptacle for water stands in front of our
oven (*f*), a convenience for moistening the surface of the loaves
while baking. The front of the oven (at *c*) was connected with

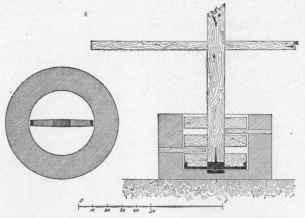

Fig. 214. — Kneading machine, plan and section.

the rooms on either side, as may be more clearly seen by referring to Fig. 209. In the kneading room (18), where were found
remains of a large table and shelves, the loaves were made ready,
and could be passed through one opening to the front of the
oven; the hot loaves could be conveniently passed through the
other opening into the storeroom (19).

In many establishments a machine was used for kneading; the best example is in a bakery on the north side of Insula xiv in Region VI. Such kneading machines are seen also in ancient representations of the baker's trade, as in the reliefs of the tomb of Eurysaces, near the Porta Maggiore at Rome.

The dough was placed in a round pan of lava a foot and a half or two feet in diameter. In this a vertical shaft revolved, to the lower part of which two or three wooden arms were attached (three in Fig. 214); the one at the bottom was strengthened by an iron crosspiece on the under side, the projecting centre of which turned in a socket below. The side of the pan was pierced in two or three places for the insertion of wooden teeth, so placed as not to interfere with the revolution of the arms. As the shaft was turned, the dough was pushed forward by the arms and held back by the teeth, being thus thoroughly kneaded. Modern kneading machines are constructed on the same principle, but have two sets of teeth on horizontal cylinders revolving toward each other.

CHAPTER XLVII

THE FULLERS AND THE TANNERS

THE work of the ancient fuller was twofold, to make ready for use the cloth fresh from the loom, and to cleanse garments that had been worn. As the garments used by the Romans were mainly of wool, and needed skilful manipulation to retain their size and shape, they were ordinarily sent out of the house to be cleansed; in consequence the trade of the fuller was relatively important. In the part of Pompeii thus far excavated we find two large fulleries and one smaller establishment that can be identified with certainty; and there were doubtless many laundries, with less ample facilities, the purpose of which is not clearly indicated by the remains. The following account of the processes employed relates exclusively to woollen fabrics.

At the time of the destruction of Pompeii, soap, a Gallic invention, was only beginning to come into use; the commonest substitute was fuller's earth, *creta fullonia*, a kind of alkaline marl. For raising the nap, teasel does not seem to have been used, as with us, but a species of thorn (*spina fullonia*) the spines of which were mounted in a carding tool resembling a brush (*aena*); the skin of a hedgehog also was sometimes utilized for this purpose.

The fulling of new cloth involved seven or eight distinct processes, — washing with fuller's earth, or other cleansing agents, to remove the oily matter; beating and stretching, to make the surface even; washing and drying a second time, for cleaning and shrinking; combing with a carding tool to raise the nap, brushing in order to make it ready for clipping, and shearing to reduce the nap to proper length; then, particularly in the case of the white woollens so commonly used, bleaching with sulphur fumes; and finally, smoothing in a large press. The process of cleaning soiled garments was more simple.

A series of paintings in the largest of the fulleries, on the west side of Mercury Street, picture several of these processes with great clearness. They were on a large pillar at the front end of the peristyle, from which they were removed to the Museum at Naples; they supplement admirably the scenes of the Cupids' fullery in the house of the Vettii, mentioned in a previous chapter (p. 329).

Fig. 215.—Scene in a fullery: treading vats.

In the first picture (Fig. 215), the clothes are being washed. They are in four round treading vats, which stand in niches formed by a low wall. One of the workmen is still treading his allotment, steadying himself by resting his arms on the walls of the niche at both sides; the other three have finished treading and are standing on the bottom of their tubs, rinsing the garments before wringing them out.

The next scene (Fig. 216) is threefold. In the foreground at the left sits a richly dressed lady, to whom a girl brings a garment that has been cleaned; that

Fig. 216.—Scene in a fullery: inspection of cloth; carding; bleaching frame.

the woman is not one of those employed in the fullery is evident from her elaborate headdress, necklace, and bracelets. In the background a workman dressed in a tunic is carding a large piece of cloth. Near by another workman carries on his shoulders a bleaching frame, over which garments were spread to receive the fumes of the sulphur; he holds in his left hand the pot in which the brimstone was burned. An owl, symbol of Minerva, who was worshipped by fullers as their patron divinity, sits upon the frame; and the man underneath has on his head a wreath of leaves from the olive tree, which was sacred to the same goddess.

In the third picture a young man hands a garment to a girl; at the right a woman is cleaning a carding tool. The fourth (Fig. 217) gives an excellent representation of a fuller's press, worked by two upright screws; it is so much like our modern presses as to need no explanation. The festoons with which it is adorned are of olive leaves.

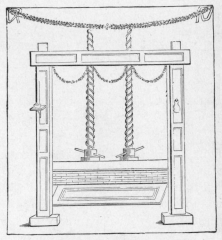

Fig. 217. — A fuller's press.

With these pictures before us, it will be easy to understand the plan of the fullery on the west side of Stabian Street, opposite the house of Caecilius Jucundus (Fig. 218). It was excavated in 1875. The building was not originally designed for a fuller's establishment, but for a private house, and part of the rooms were retained for domestic use, as the well preserved kitchen (*d*), and some of the other rooms opening off from the atrium (*b*). The furniture of the atrium — a table in front of the impluvium, with a pedestal for a fountain figure, and a marble basin to receive the jet — is like that of the house the interior of which is shown in Plate VII.

The fuller's appliances are found in the shop next to the entrance (21), and in the peristyle (*q*). In the former are the foundations of three treading vats, and on the opposite side an oblong depression in which the press was placed. The peristyle contains three large basins of masonry for soaking and rinsing the clothes. A jet of water fell into the one next the rear wall (3), from which it ran into the other two through holes in the sides. Along the wall is a raised walk (4) on a level with the top of the basins, into which the workmen descended by means of steps. At the ends of this walk are places for seven tread-ing vats, five in one group, two in the other. The wall above is

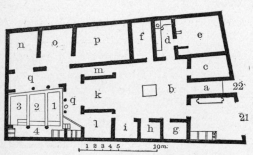

Fig. 218. — Plan of a fullery.

decorated with a long sketchy painting, in which the fullers are seen engaged in the celebration of a festi-val, — doubtless the Quinquatrus, the feast of Minerva ; the cele-bration is followed by a scene before a magis-trate, resulting from a fight engaged in by the celebrants. A mass of fuller's earth was found in the passage at *m*.

From the receipts found in the house of Caecilius Jucundus, it appears that this thrifty Pompeian, in the years 56–60 A.D., rented a fullery belonging to the city. In view of the nearness of this establishment to his house, it seems likely that he was in charge of the business here. At the time of the eruption, however, the enterprise was in the hands of Marcus Vesonius Primus, who lived in the house next door (No. 20), where a por-trait herm, dedicated to him by his cashier (*arcarius*), stands in the atrium ; the house is often called the house of Orpheus. from the large painting on the rear wall of the garden.

To judge from the election notices painted on the front of the fullery and on the houses at either side, Primus must have taken an active interest in local politics. He was an ardent partisan, as witness this inscription : *Cn. Helvium aed. d. r. p.* (for *aedi-lem, dignum re publica*) *Vesonius Primus rogat,* — 'Vesonius Primus urges the election of Gnaeus Helvius as aedile, a man

worthy of public office.' The endorsement of Gavius Rufus is
even stronger : *C. Gavium Rufum II vir. o. v. f. utilem r. p.*
(*duumvirum, oro vos, facite, utilem rei publicae*) *Vesonius Primus
rogat*, — 'Vesonius Primus requests the election of Gaius Gavius
Rufus as duumvir, a man serviceable to public interests; do
elect him, I beg of you.'

In one of the shorter recommendations, Primus names his
occupation : *L. Ceium Secundum II v. i. d. Primus fullo
ro[gat]*, — 'Primus the fuller asks the election of Lucius Ceius
Secundus as duumvir with judiciary authority.' On one occasion he united with his employees in favoring a candidate for
the aedileship : *Cn. Helvium Sabinum aed. Primus cum suis
fac [it]*, — 'Primus and his household are working for the election of Gnaeus Helvius Sabinus as aedile.'

The fullery on Mercury Street, like that just described, had
been made over from a private house, built in the pre-Roman
period. Among other changes, the columns of the large peristyle were replaced by massive pillars of masonry supporting a
gallery above for the drying of clothes. At the rear are four
square basins, the two larger of which are about six feet across ;
the water passed from one to the other as in the basins of
Primus's fullery. In the corner near the last basin are six rectangular niches for treading vats, separated by a low wall, the
purpose of which is clear from Fig. 215. There is a vaulted
room at the right of the peristyle, with a cistern curb, a large
basin of masonry, and a stone table. Here a substance was
found which the excavators supposed to be soap, but which was
doubtless fuller's earth, like that found in the establishment on
Stabian Street.

There were naturally fewer tanners than fullers ; and so far
only one tannery has been discovered. That is a large establishment, however, filling almost an entire block near the Stabian Gate (Ins. I. iii), excavated in 1873. Like the two larger
fulleries, it occupied a building designed for a house. The
appliances of the craft are found in only a small part of the
structure; they relate to two processes, — the preparation of
the fluids used for tanning, and the manipulation of the hides.

The mixture for the tan vats was prepared in a tank under a colonnade opening on the garden. It could be drawn off through two holes in the side into a smaller basin below, or conducted by means of a gutter running along the wall to three large earthen vessels.

The vats, fifteen in number, are in a room formerly used as an atrium (Fig. 219). They are about 5 feet in diameter, and

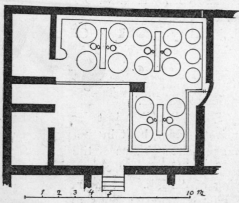

from 4 to about 5½ feet deep; they were built of masonry, and plastered; two holes were made in the side of each to serve as a convenience in climbing in and out. Between adjacent pairs of pits was an oblong basin about twenty inches deep, lined with wood. On either side of this was a large earthen jar, sunk in the earth; a

Fig. 219. — Plan of the vat room of the tannery.

small, round hole between the basin and each jar seems to mark the place of a pipe tile, connected with the former at the bottom. The large pits were for ordinary tanning; the oblong basins were probably used in making fine leather (*aluta*), a process in which alum was the principal agent, the chemicals being placed in the jars on either side, and supplied to the basins through the pipe tiles.

In the same building four tools were found, similar to those used by tanners at the present time. One was a knife, of bronze, with a charred wooden handle on the back of the blade; two were scraping irons, with a handle on each end; and there was another iron tool with a crescent-shaped blade.

The garden on which the colonnade opened contains an open-air triclinium. The table was ornamented with a mosaic top, now in the Naples Museum, with a characteristic design (Fig. 220). The principal motive is a skull; below is a butterfly on the rim of a wheel, symbols of the fluttering of the disembodied

soul and of the flight of time. On the right and on the left are the
spoils that short-lived man leaves behind him, — here a wanderer's
staff, a wallet, and a beggar's tattered robe; there, a sceptre,
with a mantle of royal purple. Over all is a level, with the

Fig. 220. — Mosaic top of the table in the garden of the tannery.

plumb line hanging straight, symbolic of Fate, that sooner or
later equalizes the lots of all mankind. The thought of the
tanner, or of the earlier proprietor of the house, is easy to
divine: *Mors aurem vellens, Vivite, ait, venio,*

> 'Death plucks my ear, and says,
> "Live !" for I come.'

CHAPTER XLVIII

INNS AND WINESHOPS

WINESHOPS, *cauponae*, were numerous in Pompeii, and the remains are easily identified. Like the Italian *osterie*, they were at the same time eating houses, but the arrangements for drinking were the more conspicuous, and give character to the ruins. The Roman inn, *hospitium*, or simply *caupona*, was a wineshop with accommodations for the night, provision being also made in most cases for the care of animals. Keepers of inns, *caupones*, are frequently mentioned in Pompeian inscriptions, sometimes in election notices, more often in graffiti.

Several inns have been identified from signs and from scribblings on the walls within. At the entrance of one (west side of Ins. IX. vii) is painted *Hospitium Hygini Firmi*, 'Inn of Hyginius Firmus.' The front of the 'Elephant Inn' (west side of Ins. VII. i) was ornamented with the painting of an elephant in the coils of a serpent, defended by a pygmy. The name of the proprietor is perhaps given at the side : *Sittius restituit elephantu*[*m*], 'Sittius restored the elephant,' referring no doubt to the repainting of the sign. Evidently the owner, whether Sittius or some one else, was anxious to rent the premises ; below the elephant is the painted notice : *Hospitium hic locatur — triclinium cum tribus lectis,* — 'Inn to let. Triclinium with three couches.' The rest of the inscription is illegible.

The plan of another inn in the same region (west side of VII. xii) well illustrates the arrangements of these hostelries (Fig. 221). The main room (*a*), which probably served as a dining room, is entered directly from the street. At one side is the kitchen (*h*); six sleeping rooms (*b–g*) open upon the other sides. But the landlord did not provide merely for the entertainment of guests from out of town ; he endeavored to attract local patronage also, by means of a wineshop (*n*), which opened

upon the street and had a separate dining room (*o*).   A short
passage (*i*) led from the main room to the stalls (*k*), in front of
which was a watering trough.   The vehicles were probably
crowded into the recess at *m*, or the front of *a*.
The two side rooms (*l* and *p*) were closets.

The walls of several of the rooms contain
records of the sojourn of guests.   C. Valerius
Venustus, 'a pretorian of the first cohort, en-
rolled in the century of Rufus,' scratched his
name on the wall of *c*, to which also an affec-
tionate husband confided his loneliness : 'Here
slept Vibius Restitutus all by himself, his heart
filled with longings for his Urbana.'   Three
players and their friend Martial passed a night
together in the same apartment.   In the next
room (*d*) a patriotic citizen of Puteoli left a

Fig. 221. — Plan of an
inn.

greeting for his native town : 'Well be it ever with Puteoli, col-
ony of Nero, of the Claudian line ; C. Julius Speratus wrote this.'
This city, as we learn from Tacitus, received permission from
Nero to call itself Colonia Claudia Neronensis.   Lucifer and
Primigenius, two friends, spent a night in room *f*, Lucceius
Albanus of Abellinum (Avellino) in *g*.

The arrangement of rooms here is so unlike that of an ordinary house that the building must have been designed at the
beginning for a tavern.   Sometimes a dwelling was turned into
an inn, as in the case of the house of Sallust, which, as we have
seen, in the last years of the city must in part at least have
been used as a hostelry.

Inns near the gates had a paved entrance for wagons, inter-
rupting the sidewalk.   A good example is the inn of Hermes, in
the first block on the right as one came into the city by the Stabian Gate (Fig. 222).   On either side of the broad entrance (*a*),
are winerooms (*b, d*).   Behind the stairway at the right, which
leads from the street to the second story, is a hearth with a
water heater.   On the wall at the left was formerly a painting
with the two Lares and the Genius offering sacrifice ; below was
the figure of a man pouring wine from an amphora into an
earthen hogshead (*dolium*), and beside it was written *Hermes*,

apparently the name of the proprietor. The wagons stood in the large room at the rear (f), with which the narrow stable (k) is connected; in one corner is a watering trough of masonry. On the ground floor were only three sleeping rooms (e, g, and h),

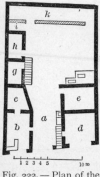

Fig. 222. — Plan of the inn of Hermes.

but there were upper rooms at the rear, reached by a flight of stairs in f; these were probably not connected with the upper rooms of the front part, which, having a street entrance, may have been rented separately.

The Pompeian inns were doubtless fair representatives of their class in the different Roman cities. Those of Rome must have been numerous, but are rarely mentioned, and innkeepers are generally referred to in terms of disrespect. The ordinary charges seem to have been low, and the accommodations were of a corresponding character. Owing to the universal custom of furnishing private entertainment to all with whom there existed any ground of hospitality, places of public entertainment tended to become the resorts of the vicious.

The wineshop of which the plan is here given (Fig. 223) is on the east side of Mercury Street, at the northwest corner of Ins. VI. x. It was designed not only for the accommodation of guests who would go inside to partake of refreshments, but also for the sale of drinks over the counter to those who might stop a moment in passing. This is evident from the arrangement of the main room (a), which has a long counter in front, with a

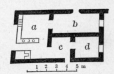

Fig. 223. — Plan of a wineshop.

series of small marble shelves arranged like stairs on one end of it, for the display of cups and glasses; on the other is a place for heating a vessel over a fire. Large jars are set in the counter, in which liquids and eatables could be kept. In the corner of the room, at the right as one enters, a hearth is placed. In view of the provision for heating water, we are safe in calling this a *thermopolium*, a wineshop which made a specialty of furnishing hot drinks. The passage at the rear of the hearth (c)

is connected with a small room (*d*) and also with the adjoining
house, which may have been the residence of the proprietor,
or may have been used for lodgings.

The long room with an entrance from the side street (*b*, now
walled up) was in-
tended for the use of
those who preferred to
eat and drink at their
leisure. The walls are
decorated with a series
of paintings presenting
realistic scenes from
the life of such places.
We see the guests eat-
ing, drinking, and play-
ing with dice. Some
are standing, others sit-
ting on stools; it is the

Fig. 224.—Scene in a wineshop. Wall painting.

kind of public house that Martial calls a 'stool-ridden cookshop,'
in which couches were not provided, but only seats without
backs.

In one of the scenes (Fig. 224) four men are drinking, about
a round table, while a boy waits on them; two of the figures
have pointed hoods like those
seen to-day in Sicily and some
parts of Italy. Strings of
sausage, hams, and other eatables hang from a pole suspended under the ceiling.

Some of the figures in the
pictures are accompanied by
inscriptions. Thus by the
side of a guest for whom a
waiter is pouring out a glass
of wine is written: *Da fri-*
dam pusillum, 'Add cold water — just a little.' In a similar
connection we read, *Adde calicem Setinum*, 'Another cup of
Setian!' The Setian wine came from a town in Latium at the

Fig. 225. — Delivery of wine. Wall painting.

foot of the hills bordering the Pontine Marshes, now Sezze ; we
infer that our wineshop sold not merely the products of neighboring vineyards, but choice brands from other regions as well.
Wines from the locality were probably brought to town in amphorae ; the delivery of a consignment from a distance is shown
in a separate scene (Fig. 225), in which amphorae are being
filled from a large skin on a wagon ; the team of mules is meanwhile resting, unharnessed, the yoke hanging on the end of the
pole.

The pictures present the life of a tavern from the point of
view of the landlord ; but occasionally we have a suggestion
of the other side, as in the following couplet, the faulty spelling
of which we can forgive on account of its pithiness : *Talia te
fallant utinam me[n]dacia, copo, Tu ve[n]des acuam et bibes
ipse merum,*—

> 'Landlord, may your lies malign
>   Bring destruction on your head !
> You yourself drink unmixed wine,
>   Water sell your guests instead.'

The wineshop in which this graffito is found (I. ii. 24) is
larger than that on Mercury Street, and has several dining
rooms.   Connected with it is a garden with a triclinium, once
shaded by vines, which calls to mind the invitation of the bar-
maid in the Copa : —

> 'Here a garden you will find,
>   Cool retreat, with cups and roses,
> Lute and pipe, for mirth designed,
>   Bower that mask of reeds encloses.

> 'Come, weary traveller, lie and rest
>   'Neath the shade of vines o'er-spreading,
> Wreath of roses freshly pressed
>   On your head its fragrance shedding.'

All the pictures found in Pompeian wineshops bear out the
inference, based upon numerous allusions in classical writers,
that such places everywhere were in the main frequented by
the lower classes ; among the adjectives applied to taverns by
the poets are 'dirty,' 'smoky,' and 'black.'   They were haunted
by gamblers and criminals, and the life was notoriously immoral.

KEY TO THE LEFT SIDE

24. Villa of Diomedes.

16–23. Tombs — Group III.
   16. Unfinished tomb.
   17. Tomb of Umbricius Scaurus.
   18. Round tomb.
   19. Sepulchral enclosure.
   20. Tomb of Calventius Quietus.
   21. Sepulchral enclosure of Istacidius Helenus.
   22. Tomb of Naevoleia Tyche.
   23. Triclinium Funebre.

5–15. So-called Villa of Cicero.

1–4 a. Tombs — Group I.
   1. Sepulchral niche of Cerrinius Restitutus.
   2. Sepulchral bench of A. Veius.
   3. Tomb of M. Porcius.
   4. Sepulchral bench of Mamia.
   4 a. Tomb of the Istacidii.

A. Herculaneum Gate.
C. Bay Road.

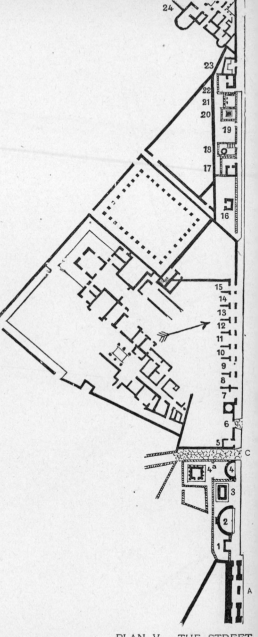

PLAN V.—THE STREET

OF TOMBS.

PART IV

THE TOMBS

CHAPTER XLIX

POMPEIAN BURIAL PLACES. — THE STREET OF TOMBS

THE tombs of Pompeii, like those of Rome, were placed in close array along the sides of the roads that led from the city gates. Only a few have been uncovered; how many still lie concealed under the mantle of volcanic débris that rests upon the plain, no one has yet ventured to conjecture. The tombstone of a magistrate of one of the suburbs was found at Scafati, a mile and a half east of the ancient town; and others have been brought to light on the east, south, and west sides. The most interesting and best known tombs are those of the Street of Tombs, in front of the Herculaneum Gate; but important remains have been found also near the Stabian and Nocera gates, and burial places of a humbler sort lie along the city wall near the Nola Gate.

Most of the tombs thus far excavated belong to the Early Empire, having been built between the reign of Augustus and 79 A.D. Two or three date from the end of the Republic; and a small corner of an Oscan cemetery has been uncovered on the northwest side of the city. Remains of skeletons were found only in the Oscan graves; the Roman burial places were all arranged with reference to the practice of cremation, the ashes being deposited in urns.

The tombs present so great a variety of form and construction that it is impossible to classify them in a summary way, or to dismiss them with the presentation of two or three typical examples. The character of the monument varied not merely accord-

397

ing to the taste and means, but also according to the point of
view or religious feeling of the builder.   Some deemed it more
fitting that the ashes of the dead should be covered over with
earth; others preferred to place them in a conspicuous tomb
that would please the eye and impress the imagination of the
beholder.   To many the matter of paramount importance seemed
to be the provision for the worship of the dead, the arrangement
of the tomb so that offerings could easily be made to the ashes.
Others still desired to have the sepulchre convenient for the living, who at times would gather there, and tarry near the resting
place of the departed.   And there were not a few who attempted,
in the construction of a monument, to accomplish at the same
time several of these ends.   The architectural designs were suggested by the form of an altar, a temple, a niche, a commemorative arch, or a semicircular bench, *schola*.

On account of this diversity of aim and of type, it will be most
convenient to study the tombs in topographical groups, com-
mencing with those at the northwest corner of the city.

The highway that passes under the Herculaneum Gate runs
almost directly west, descending with a gentle grade.   Above it
on the north side is the ridge formed by the stream of lava on
the end of which the city lay; here, before the eruption, were
sightly villas.   Below, to the south, was the sea, not so far away
as now, over the shimmering surface of which the traveller, as
he rode along, could catch charming glimpses of the heights
above Sorrento and of Capri.   A short distance from the gate
on the left, a branch road, which for convenience we may call
the Bay Road, led directly to the sea.   Another branch, on the
right, followed the direction of the city wall; further from the
gate on the same side, a third, which may be designated as
the Vesuvius Road, ran off from the highway in the direction
of the mountain.   The highway itself, so far as excavated, has
been named the Street of Tombs.

The tombs that have been uncovered here are distributed in
four groups.   The first, on the left side, extends from the gate
to the Bay Road; it comprises Nos. 1–4 *a* on Plan V.   The
second, on the right (Nos. 1–9), includes the tombs between the

gate and the beginning of the Vesuvius Road. The third group, on the left, lies between the ruins of the villa to which the name of Cicero has been attached and the villa of Diomedes; the tombs are numbered on the plan 16–23. The monuments of the fourth group occupy the tongue of ground at the right between the highway and the Vesuvius Road (33–43). The street fronts of the two villas by which the continuity of the series of tombs on both sides is interrupted, appear to have been used as inns; the sidewalk was here shaded by colonnades supported by pillars, and there were small rooms opening toward the street.

At the further end of the villa on the right (10–28) is the potter's workshop (29–30), mentioned in a previous chapter (p. 378). Beyond this are the Oscan graves (31–32), several of which have been explored. In them were found rough stone coffins, made of slabs and fragments of limestone, containing remains of skeletons together with small painted vases, of the sort manufactured in Campania in the third and second centuries B.C. Two coins were found, in separate graves, with Oscan legends that have not yet been deciphered; apparently they were from Nola. The burial places lie close together, and evidently belong to a cemetery for people of humble station; there are no headstones to mark the graves. This is the only place at Pompeii in which painted vases have been found.

A narrow strip of land on each side of the road belonged to the city, and burial lots therein were granted by the municipal council to citizens who had rendered public service. Others, however, might obtain lots by purchase; private ownership may be assumed unless the gift of the city is indicated in the inscription. The location of several tombs — 1, 3, 4, 6 on the right, 3 on the left — shows that the direction of the street near the gate was changed after sepulchral monuments had begun to be erected.

An interesting inscription referring to the municipal ownership of land was found at the further corner of the Bay Road: *Ex auctoritate imp. Caesaris Vespasiani Aug. loca publica a privatis possessa T. Suedius Clemens tribunus causis cognitis et mensuris factis rei publicae Pompeianorum restituit,* — 'By virtue

of authority conferred upon him by the Emperor Vespasian
Caesar Augustus, Titus Suedius Clemens, tribune, having investigated the facts and taken measurements, restored to the city
of Pompeii plots of ground belonging to it which were in the
possession of private individuals.'

To judge from the location of the inscription, the land which
the military tribune sent as commissioner by Vespasian gave
back to the city, must have been at the sides of the Bay Road.
A marble statue of a man dressed in a toga and holding a scroll
in his hand, was found near by. It was probably a portrait of
Suedius Clemens, and may have stood in a niche in the villa of
Cicero.

There is an implied reference to the Bay Road also in another
inscription which was found out of its proper place, in the court
of the adjoining inn : THERMAE · M · CRASSI · FRUGI · AQVA ·
MARINA · ET · BALN · AQVA · DVLCI · IANVARIVS · L — ' Bathing
establishment of Marcus Crassus Frugi. Warm sea baths and
freshwater baths. (Superintendent) the freedman Januarius.'
We learn from Pliny the Elder that M. Licinius Crassus Frugi,
who was consul in 64 A.D., and was afterwards (in 68) put to
death by Nero, owned a hot spring which gushed up out of the
sea. This spring, then, was at Pompeii, and was utilized for
baths. The inscription is at the same time an advertisement
and a sign directing people down the Bay Road to the bath
house.

A general view of the Street of Tombs is given in Plate IX.
It is taken from the high ground beyond the fourth group, as
one looks toward the Herculaneum Gate. The rugged mass of
Monte Sant' Angelo looms up in the distance; at the right the
trees skirting the edge of the excavations form an effective background. The beauty of the surroundings, especially on a summer morning, the associations of the street, its deserted appearance, and the unbroken, oppressive stillness give rise to mingled
feelings of pleasure and sadness in the visitor.

We commence our survey with the first group of tombs
at the left as one passes out from the Herculaneum Gate.
Close by the gate is the tomb of Cerrinius Restitutus (1 on
the plan, left side). It is simply a low vaulted niche, having

seats at the sides. Against the rear wall stood a marble tombstone, with a place for a carved portrait; in front of it was a
small altar under which doubtless was placed the urn containing the ashes. Both altar and tombstone have the inscription:
M. Cerrinius Restitutus, Augustalis, l. d. d. d. (for *loco dato decurionum decreto*), — 'Marcus Cerrinius Restitutus, member of the
brotherhood of Augustus. Place of burial granted by vote of
the city council.' The tomb here was designed as a structure to
which relatives might repair on anniversary days in order to
make offerings to the dead.

The remains of the other tombs in the first group are shown

Fig. 226. — Sepulchral benches of Veius and Mamia; tombs of Porcius and the Istacidii.

in the accompanying illustration (Fig. 226). We notice first two
large semicircular benches. That at the left (2 on the plan)
marks the resting-place of Veius. It is of tufa, and nearly
twenty feet wide at the front. The ends are modelled to represent winged lion's paws, the carving of which is full of vigor
and may be compared with that of the lion's paws in the Small
Theatre (Fig. 65). The statue that once stood at the rear, on a
high pedestal, has disappeared, but the inscription remains:
*A. Veio M. f. II vir. i. d. iter. quinq. trib. milit. ab populo ex
d. d.*, — 'To the memory of Aulus Veius, son of Marcus, twice
duumvir with judiciary authority, quinquennial duumvir, military
tribune by the choice of the people. (Erected) by order of the
city council.' The city not only gave a burial place, but built

2 D

the tomb as well. The cinerary urn was probably placed in the earth in the narrow unwalled space behind the bench.

This monument was intended at the same time to do honor to the dead and render service to the living. Here, on feast days of the dead, relatives could gather and partake of a commemorative meal; but at all times the inviting seat and conspicuous statue served to maintain that friendly relation with the living, the desire for which so often finds expression in Roman epitaphs. The portrait and inscription made it seem as if Veius himself offered a friendly greeting to those that passed by, and was greeted by them in turn as they looked upon his face and read his name.

The other bench (4) was evidently built by the heirs of a priestess, Mamia, upon a lot given by the city. The inscription appears in large letters on the back of the seat: *Mamiae P. f. sacerdoti publicae; locus sepultur[ae] datus decurionum decreto,*— 'To the memory of Mamia, daughter of Publius Mamius, priestess of the city. Place of burial granted by order of the municipal council.' In this instance, also, the cinerary urn was probably buried in the earth behind the bench. A certain delicacy in the modelling of the lion's paws seems to indicate for this monument a somewhat later date than that of the monument to Veius, — possibly the end of the reign of Augustus, or the reign of Tiberius. The date of erection is not given in the case of any Pompeian tomb.

Between the two benches we see a lava base and the core of a superstructure; they belong to the tomb of Marcus Porcius. The name is known from a boundary inscription which appears on two small blocks of lava at the corners of the lot in front: *M. Porci M. f. ex dec. decret. in frontem ped. xxv, in agrum ped. xxv,* — '(Lot) of Marcus Porcius son of Marcus, granted by order of the city council; twenty-five feet front, twenty-five feet deep.'

This Porcius may have been one of the builders of the Small Theatre and the Amphitheatre, or a son of that Porcius, whose name appears on the altar of the temple of Apollo. The tomb was in the form of an altar; the terminal volutes at the top, of travertine, have been preserved. The sides were of tufa blocks,

which may have been carried off for building purposes after the
tomb was damaged by the earthquake of 63.   The interior was
made hollow to save expense ; there was no sepulchral chamber,

Fig. 227. — The tomb of the Istacidii, restored.

the ashes being placed in the earth under the monument.   This
tomb is the oldest of the group.

The conspicuous monument of the Istacidii (4 a) stands behind
the tombs of Mamia and Porcius, at the left of the Bay Road.
It is raised upon a narrow terrace, enclosed by a balustrade of

masonry, and has the appearance of a temple, with half-columns
at the sides.   The remains of the lower story alone are seen in
Fig. 226; above this was a circular structure formed by columns
supporting a roof, under which were placed statues of members
of the family (Fig. 227).   The lower story contains a sepulchral
chamber, entered by a door at the rear; in the middle of the
chamber is a massive pillar reaching to the vaulted ceiling.   The
decoration of the room is simple, of the third style.   On one side
is a large niche, for two urns, those of the head of the family
and his wife; the other three sides contain ten smaller niches.

The principal inscription of the tomb has not been found, but
a number of names are preserved on the commemorative stones
set up in the plot of ground about it.   These stones are of a
peculiar type, met with elsewhere only at Capua and Sorrento;
we shall call them bust stones.   The outline resembles that of
a human head and neck terminating below in a pillar, but the
front was left smooth, and an inscription was cut or painted on
the bust.   Difference of sex was indicated by the treatment of
the hair; an example may be seen in Fig. 230.   The bust stones
of men are generally larger than those of women; those of children are still smaller, the size perhaps varying with the age.

The bust stones here may refer to those whose ashes were
deposited in urns in the tomb, or to others whose urns were
buried in the plot of ground in which it stands.   From them we
learn that the head of the family was Numerius Istacidius, and
that he had a daughter, Istacidia Rufilla, who was a priestess.
Representatives of two other families, the Melissaei and the
Buccii, are named on similar stones found in a plot connected
with that of the Istacidii at the rear.   The three families were
perhaps closely connected by intermarriage.   The bust stone
of one of the Melissaei, Gnaeus Melissaeus Aper, duumvir in
3–4 A.D., stood in the same enclosure with those of the Istacidii.

Only one of the nine tombs in the second group (2) bears a
name.   In the case of two (3 and 4) the superstructure has
completely disappeared, leaving only the lava bases in place.
Another (5) has not been excavated; the front of the burial lot
has been cleared, but the monument, lying further back, is still
covered.

The first tomb lies in the angle between the highway and the branch road along the wall, which was evidently laid out after the monument was erected. It has the form of an altar, and must have resembled in appearance the tomb of Porcius on the opposite side of the street. Here, however, there is a sepulchral chamber in the base, entered by a low, narrow passage, which was closed until 1887 by a block of stone. In corners of this chamber two cinerary urns, in lead cases, were found covered with earth and with the remains of a funeral pyre — bits of wood and iron nails used in building the pyre, together with pieces of a richly carved ivory casket and broken perfume vials of terra cotta. Among the fragments of bone in each urn was a coin of Augustus. Though the ashes of the dead were here placed in a burial vault, it was nevertheless considered important to cover them with earth. It was not thought necessary, however, to leave the vault accessible for the performance of sacred rites in honor of the dead; the entrance, securely closed, was only to be unsealed for the admission of new urns.

The next tomb (2) is of an entirely different type from any of those previously described. It is an unroofed enclosure, entered by a door at one end. As we learn from the inscription, it was built in honor of Terentius Felix by his widow, the city furnishing the burial lot and a contribution of two thousand sesterces (about $90) toward the expense: *T. Terentio T. f. Men. Felici maiori aedil[i] ; huic publice locus datus et sest. MM. Fabia Probi f. Sabina uxor,* — 'To the memory of Titus Terentius Felix the Elder son of Titus, of the tribe Menenia, aedile. The place of burial was given by the city, with two thousand sesterces. His wife, Fabia Sabina, daughter of Probus Fabius, (built this monument).' Pompeians who were Roman citizens were enrolled in the tribe Menenia.

The cinerary urn of Felix was of glass. It was protected by a lead case and placed in an earthen jar, which was buried in the earth under a small altar or table of masonry against the wall on the left as one enters. Here also was a tombstone, with the inscription, 'To the elder Terentius'; he probably left a son with the same name. In the urn, or near it, were found two coins, one of Augustus, the other of Claudius, deposited to

pay the fare of Charon. The right side of the enclosure was
set off by a low wall; here several urns belonging to other
members of the household were buried. Shells of oysters and
other shellfish were found in the main room, remains of a
banquet in honor of the dead; the libations were poured upon
the earth above the urns. The plan of this tomb closely re-

Fig. 228. — View of the Street of Tombs.

At the left, the Bay Road and remains of the so-called villa of Cicero; at the right, Garland tomb, foundation of the tomb of the Blue Glass Vase, and semicircular niche.

sembles that of the enclosure in front of the Doric temple in
the Forum Triangulare (p. 133).

Of the remaining tombs of the second group, two are prominent, and may readily be distinguished in the accompanying
illustration (Fig. 228), the so-called Garland tomb (6 on the
plan), and the roofed semicircular niche at the end (9). The
Garland tomb has the shape of a temple, with pilasters instead
of columns, between which hang festoons of leaves and flowers.
It is solid; the cinerary urn was probably placed underneath.

The form of the second story cannot be determined. The material is tufa, coated with white stucco, and the monument is one of the oldest in the series, dating from the end of the Republic.

Adjoining the Garland tomb is a simple sepulchral enclosure (7) with an entrance from the street. Between this and the roofed niche we see in Fig. 228 the travertine base of a tomb, like those seen in Plate IX, at the right; the altar-shaped superstructure has disappeared (8). This is called the tomb of the Blue Glass Vase. The base contains a sepulchral chamber, entered by a door at the rear. Here three urns, two of glass and one of terra cotta, were found, standing in niches. On the floor were several statuettes, a couple of small figures of animals, and a mask with a Phrygian cap, — all of terra cotta.

In beauty of material, harmony of design, and skill of workmanship, one of the glass urns, which gave the name to the tomb and is now preserved in the Naples Museum, ranks with the finest examples of its class in the world. Among specimens of ancient glass it stands second only to the famous Portland vase in the British Museum, which was found in a tomb near Rome. The urn has the form of an amphora; the support seen at the bottom (Fig. 229) is modern. It is decorated with reliefs cut in a layer of pure white on a background of dark blue. Near the bottom is a narrow band, showing goats and sheep in pasture. Resting on this are two bacchic masks, on opposite sides of the vase; vines laden with clusters rise in graceful arabesques above the masks, dividing the body of the vase into two fields, which present scenes from the vintage.

One of these scenes is reproduced in Fig. 229. The vintage is interpreted as a festival of Bacchus. Above is a festoon of fruits and flowers. At the sides are two boys on elevated seats, one playing the double flute, the other holding a Pan's pipe in his hands, ready to take his turn; the grapes are gathered and pressed to an accompaniment of Bacchic airs, the two players following each other with alternate strains. A third boy, treading the grapes in a round vat, shakes the thyrsus in honor of the Wine-god, while a companion empties in fresh bunches. The scene is full of action; no reproduction can do justice to the delicacy and finish of the original.

A bench of masonry runs along the inner wall of the semi-circular niche (9), which is covered by a roof in the form of a

Fig. 229. — Glass vase with vintage scene, found in the tomb of the Blue Glass Vase.

half dome and opens upon the street as do the large unroofed monuments of Veius and Mamia. A blank marble tablet was placed in the gable; the builder of the monument, who was doubtless living at the time of the eruption, preferred to leave it to his heirs to add the memorial inscription, but the disaster interfered with the fulfilment of his wishes. It was probably intended to bury the cinerary urn either in the floor of the niche or in the ground at the rear. The effect of the double series of pilasters at the corners, placed one upon the other without an intervening entablature, and of the fantastic stucco decoration of the gable, is not unpleasing, although the designs are far from classical; the tiles shown in the illustration are modern. The inner wall is painted in red and black panels; the vaulted ceiling, from which the stucco has now fallen, was moulded to represent a shell.

Both the niche and the tomb of the Blue Glass Vase seem to have belonged to the adjoining villa. The stucco decoration of the villa in its main features is identical with that of the niche; and the plot of ground behind the tombs is connected by a gateway with a garden of the villa (12 on the plan), which was too richly adorned to have been intended for the use of the occupants of the inn. In the middle of the garden was a pavilion supported by four mosaic columns (now in the Naples Museum), similar to that in the garden of the villa of Diomedes, and to others belonging to city houses. A mosaic fountain niche was made in the rear wall facing the entrance from the street, and in two corners were short columns on which were placed small figures, — on one a boy with a hare, in marble, on the other a frog of glazed terra cotta.

Nevertheless, the garden seems to possess a distinctly sepulchral character. Besides the entrances from the tombs and from the street, there was a third, which led into a court of the villa, with which the peristyle and living rooms were connected by a passageway; in the corner of the court nearest the garden, and facing the entrance from the street (15), was an elaborate domestic shrine, dedicated, as shown by the symbolical decoration, to Apollo, Bacchus, Hercules, and Mercury. The relation of the garden with the living rooms of the villa was only indirect; and we conclude that it was intended for gatherings and sacred rites in honor of the dead. Relatives could partake of the sepulchral banquet under the pavilion.

The tombs of the third group, as may be seen from Plate IX,

form a stately series. The prevailing type is that which was in
vogue at the time of the destruction of the city — a high base,
with marble steps at the top leading up to a massive superstructure in the form of an altar, faced with marble. The
burial plot was enclosed by a low wall. In the base of the tomb
was a sepulchral chamber, entered by a door in the rear or at
one side; it was now the custom for relatives to enter the burial
vault when they wished to pour libations on the ashes.

The first of the series (16 on the plan, seen in Plate IX next
to the cypress) was unfinished at the time of the eruption.
Part of the marble veneering had not yet been added, the walls
of the sepulchral chamber were in the rough, and there were
no urns in the five niches designed for their reception. In the
burial plot surrounding the tomb, however, a marble bust
stone was found (Fig. 230) with the inscription, *Iunoni Tyches
Iuliae Augustae Vener*[*iae*], —
'To the Genius of Tyche, slave
of Julia Augusta, — of the cult
of Venus.'

Fig. 230. — Bust Stone of Tyche, slave of
Julia Augusta.

The reference is plainly to a
female slave of Julia, the daughter of Augustus; how her ashes
came to be deposited here it is
not worth while, in default of
information, to conjecture. In
sepulchral inscriptions of women
Iunoni sometimes takes the
place of *genio* in men's epitaphs.
Tyche was seemingly a member
of a sisterhood for the worship of Venus, to which, as to the
organization of the 'Servants of Mercury and Maia,' and of the
'Servants of Fortuna Augusta,' slaves were admitted.

The tomb of Umbricius Scaurus (17) is conspicuous by reason of its size and noteworthy on account of its decoration.
The inscription on the front of the altar-shaped superstructure
gives interesting details in regard to the man the memory of
whom is here perpetuated: *A. Umbricio A. f. Men. Scauro, II
vir i. d.; huic decuriones locum monum*[*enti*] *et sest*[*ertios*] *MM*

in funere et statuam equestr[am] in foro ponendam censuerunt.
Scaurus pater filio, — 'To the memory of Aulus Umbricius
Scaurus son of Aulus, of the tribe Menenia, duumvir with judiciary authority. The city council voted the place for a monument to this man and two thousand sesterces toward the cost
of the funeral; they voted also that an equestrian statue in his
honor should be set up in the Forum. Scaurus the father to
the memory of his son.'

Why these honors were conferred upon Scaurus, who probably became a duumvir early in life and died soon after his
term of office, is not clear. The upper part of the base of the
tomb in front was adorned with stucco reliefs — now for the
most part gone — in which gladiatorial combats and a venatio
were depicted; but a painted inscription along the edge of one
of the scenes indicates that the show thus commemorated was
given by another man, *N. Fistius Ampliatus; Munere [N. Fis]ti*
Ampliati die summo. Perhaps the last two words mean that
'on the last day' the younger Scaurus, a relative or friend of
Ampliatus, shared the cost of the exhibition under some such
arrangement as that between Lucretius Valens and his son
(p. 216). If this be the correct explanation, it is evident that
Scaurus could have given no shows in the Amphitheatre during
his duumvirate, else the father would have taken pains to mention the fact in the inscription. His term of office may have
come after the year 59, when such exhibitions were prohibited at
Pompeii for ten years (p. 214).

The gladiatorial scenes, if space permitted, would merit a
detailed presentation — they are so full of human interest.
Two gladiators are fighting on horseback, the rest on foot.
The vanquished with uplifted thumbs are mutely begging for
mercy. The plea of some of them is heeded by the populace;
in other groups we see the victor preparing to give the death
thrust. Beside each gladiator was painted his name, school,
and number of previous combats, as in a programme; and
letters were added to give the result of this fight. One com-
batant, who was beaten and yet by the vote of the audience
permitted to live, died on the sand from his wounds. We see
him resting on one knee, faint from loss of blood; the letter M

beside his name, for *missus*, is followed by the death sign Θ, the first letter of the Greek word for death, ΘΑΝΑΤΟΣ.

The animals shown in the venatio are mainly wild boars and bears, but we recognize also a lion and a bull. Lions were doubtless much more rarely seen in such exhibitions at Pompeii than at Rome.

As more attention came to be given to the outward appearance of tombs, less was bestowed upon the adornment of the sepulchral chamber. So in the tomb of Scaurus the burial vault is low, cramped, and with plain white walls. A massive pillar, as in the tomb of the Istacidii, supports the vaulted ceiling. It is pierced by two openings, forming four niches, two on each side. Three of these, when the tomb was opened, were closed by panes of glass, and there were traces of a curtain that hung over the one opposite the entrance. There were fourteen other niches in the walls at the sides.

No name is associated with the third tomb (18 on the plan) which, as shown by Plate IX, is simply a large cylinder of masonry, the top of which probably had the shape of a truncated cone ; the material is brick, with a facing of white stucco lined off to give the appearance of blocks of marble. The base is square ; the enclosing wall is adorned with miniature towers. The structure illustrates in its simplest form the type of the massive tomb, or mausoleum, found at Rome ; we are at once reminded of the imposing monument of Caecilia Metella on the Appian Way, and of Hadrian's Mausoleum in the city.

A blank tablet was placed by the builder on the front of the enclosing wall to receive an inscription after his death. The heirs, however, preferred to put the memorial on the tomb itself, where the place of an inscription is plainly seen, the slab itself having disappeared. The sepulchral chamber is in the superstructure ; it was decorated with simple designs in the fourth style on a white ground. There were only three niches, perhaps for father, mother, and child ; the urns were let into the bottoms of the niches, as often in the Roman columbaria.

One of the miniature towers on the enclosing wall is ornamented with a relief presenting a singular design ; a woman in mourning habit is laying a fillet on a skeleton reclining on a

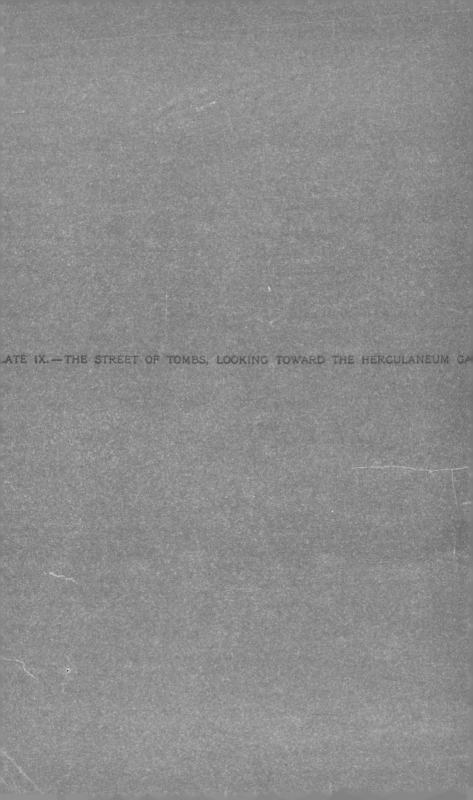

ATE IX.—THE STREET OF TOMBS, LOOKING TOWARD THE HERCULANEUM GA

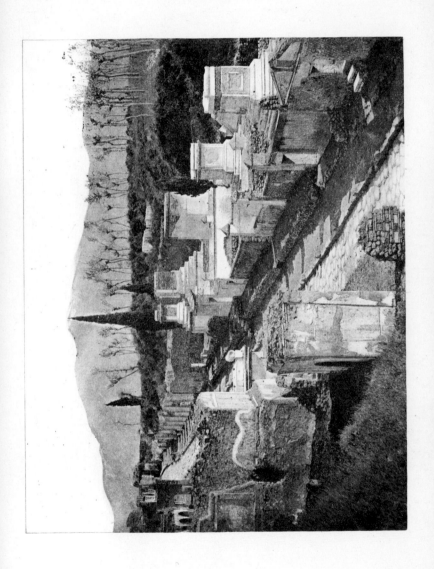

heap of stones (Fig. 231). The scene may be interpreted as symbolizing the grief of a mother for a dead son.

There is only a simple tombstone in the burial lot (19) beyond the round monument. Next comes the beautiful tomb of Calventius Quietus (20), which may be seen in Plate IX, as well as the tomb of Naevoleia Tyche (22; further to the right). Between these two is a walled enclosure (21) without a door, in which are three bust stones. The largest stone bears the name N. Istacidius Helenus; in front of one of the others a small jar was set to receive offerings for the dead. On the front of the enclosing wall is a tablet on which the names of N. Istacidius Januarius and of Mesonia Satulla appear with that of Helenus; they were all freedmen of the Istacidii (p. 404).

Fig. 231. — Relief, symbolic of grief for the dead.

The monuments of Quietus and of Tyche are the finest examples of the altar type at Pompeii. Both are ornamented in good taste, but the carvings of the former are more delicate, while the motives of the latter are more elaborate. Quietus was a man of some prominence, as we see from the epitaph: *C. Calventio Quieto Augustali; huic ob munificent[iam] decurionum decreto et populi conse[n]su bisellii honor datus est,* — 'To the memory of Gaius Calventius Quietus, member of the Brotherhood of Augustus. On account of his generosity the honor of a seat of double width was conferred upon him by the vote of the city council and the approval of the people.'

At the Theatre and the Amphitheatre, Quietus had the privilege of sitting on a bisellium, as if he were a member of the city council. Below the inscription is a representation of the 'seat of double width,' shown in Fig. 232. The square footstool at the middle implies that the seat was intended for a single person. The ends of the tomb were ornamented with finely carved reliefs of the civic crown, which was made of oak leaves and awarded to those who had saved the life of a Roman citizen (Fig. 233). As the inscription does not record any deed of valor, it may be that the crown is used here merely as a decorative device.

Though the monument of Quietus was built in the last years of the city, when such structures were generally provided with

Fig. 232. — Front of the tomb of Calventius Quietus, with bisellium.

sepulchral chambers, it has no burial vault, and the enclosing wall is without a door. It is perhaps a cenotaph, a monument erected in honor of a man whose remains were interred elsewhere; it is also possible that Quietus had no relatives who wished to have an accessible sepulchral chamber in order to make libations to his ashes, and that for this reason the monument was made solid, the urn being buried in the earth underneath. The small turrets on the enclosing wall are adorned with reliefs; among them Oedipus solving the riddle of the Sphinx, and Theseus after the slaughter of the Minotaur. The suggestion is obvious: he who is commemorated here had solved the riddle of existence, had found an exit from the labyrinth of life.

Around the front and sides of the tomb of Naevoleia Tyche runs a border of acanthus arabesques, forming panels in which reliefs are placed. The border in front is interrupted at the middle of the upper side by the portrait of Tyche; the lower half of the panel is devoted to a ceremonial scene in which offerings appear to be made to the dead, while in the upper half, under the portrait, we read the inscription: *Naevoleia L. lib-[erta] Tyche sibi et C. Munatio Fausto Aug[ustali] et pagano, cui decuriones consensu populi bisellium ob merita eius decreve-*

*runt. Hoc monumentum Naevoleia Tyche libertis suis liberta-
busque et C. Munati Fausti viva fecit,* — 'Naevoleia Tyche,
freedwoman of Lucius Naevoleius, for herself and for Gaius
Munatius Faustus, member of the Brotherhood of Augustus
and suburban official, to whom on account of his distinguished
services the city council, with the approval of the people, granted
a seat of double width. This monument Naevoleia Tyche built in

Fig. 233. — End of the tomb of Naevoleia Tyche, with relief of a ship entering port;
beyond, end of the tomb of Calventius Quietus, with the civic crown.

her lifetime also for the freedmen and freedwomen of herself and
of Gaius Munatius Faustus,' who was seemingly her husband.

The bisellium of Faustus is shown in one of the end panels;
in the other we see a ship sailing into port (Fig. 233). The
helmsman has taken his hands from the steering paddles, the
sailors are furling the sail, and the vessel is gliding into still
water. The scene is symbolical of death, — the entrance of the
soul after the storms of life into a haven of rest. The thought
is expressed by Cicero with deep feeling in his essay on Old

Age: 'As for myself, I find the ripening of life truly agree-
able; the nearer I come to the time of death, the more I feel like
one who begins to see land and knows that sometime he will
enter the harbor after the long voyage.'

The sepulchral chamber of this tomb has a large niche opposite the entrance; the urn standing in it apparently contained
the cinerary remains of two persons, Tyche and Faustus.   Other
urns were found in the smaller niches in the walls and on the
bench of masonry along the sides.   Three were of glass, protected by lead cases; one of them is shown in Fig. 234.   They
contained ashes and fragments of bone, with remains of a liquid
mixture, which was shown by chemical analysis to have consisted

Fig. 234. — Cinerary
urn in lead case.

of water, wine, and oil.   Lamps were found on
the bench, one for each urn, and there were
others in a corner; they were used on anniversary days to light the chamber.

The last monument consists of a walled enclosure, with a table and couches of masonry
like those often found in the gardens of private houses (Fig. 235).   In front of the table
is a small round altar for libations.   This was
a place for banquets in honor of the dead, *triclinium funebre ;* a tomb designed to serve the
convenience of the living, like the niche of Cer-

rinius Restitutus and the benches of Veius and Mamia.   The
walls were painted in the last style.

Over the entrance in front we read: *Cn. Vibio Q. f. Fal. Sa-
turnino Callistus lib.*, — 'Callistus the freedman erected this monument in memory of Gnaeus Vibius Saturninus son of Quintus,
of the tribe Falernia.'   As Saturninus did not belong to the
tribe Menenia, he was very likely not a native of Pompeii.
His ashes were probably placed in an urn and buried in the
earth between the altar and the entrance.

There is every reason to suppose that the series of tombs
on the south side of the highway is continued beyond the villa
of Diomedes; but it has not yet been found possible to carry
the excavations further in that direction.

The tombs of the fourth group present no new types of

design or construction. Several of them are of interest, however, on account of peculiarities of arrangement. At the time
of the eruption two of the monuments (33, 35) were in process
of building ; it is impossible to tell what form they were to have.
A third (36) had been commenced on a large scale, but apparently the money of the heirs gave out, and little pyramids were
set up at the corners of the walled enclosure, the urns being
buried in the earth.

Fig. 235. — Sepulchral enclosure with triclinium funebre.

Two of the monuments were erected for children (40, 41).
They stand near together on the high ground in the angle
formed by the Vesuvius Road. They are small vaulted niches,
ornamented with reliefs in white stucco, most of which has fallen
off. The urn in each was placed in the earth under the bottom
of the niche, with a small pipe tile leading to the surface,
through which libations could be poured down upon it. A
tablet is set in the sustaining wall at the side of the street below
the larger niche (41), with the simple inscription, *N. Velasio
Grato, vix*[*it*] *ann. XII*, — 'To the memory of Numerius Vela-
sius Gratus, who lived twelve years.' The inscription belong-

2 E

ing to the other niche was even more simple, giving no first
name : *Salvius puer vixit annis VI,* — ' The boy Salvius lived six
years.'

One tomb (34) is noteworthy on account of its door. This
has the appearance of a double door, but it is made of a single
slab of marble, and swings, like an ordinary Roman door, by
means of pivots which are fitted into sockets in the threshold
and lintel. It was also provided with a lock. The exterior
of the tomb was unfinished ; the reticulate masonry still lacked
its facing of more costly material. The sepulchral chamber,
however, contained several cinerary urns ; one of them, of
alabaster, was in a large niche facing the entrance, and a gold
seal ring, with the figure of a deer in an intaglio, was found
in it among the ashes and fragments of bone. There were
also several lamps, a small altar of terra cotta, and a few glass
perfume vials. Two amphorae, of the sort used for wine, stood
against the sides of the chamber ; such were sometimes utilized
as repositories for ashes.

One of the volutes of the well preserved travertine tomb of
M. Alleius Luccius Libella (37) is seen in Plate IX. The monument has the shape of an altar, and is apparently solid. It was
erected by the widow, Alleia Decimilla, priestess of Ceres, in
memory of her husband, who was duumvir in 26 A.D., and of
a son of the same name, who was a member of the city council
and died in his eighteenth year. The burial plot was given by
the city. As no opening was left in the monument, Decimilla
evidently planned to have her ashes deposited in another tomb,
perhaps that of her father's family.

The remaining four tombs are of the same type ; the idea is
that of a temple, the columnar construction being suggested
not by projecting half-columns, as in the tomb of the Istacidii,
but by more or less prominent pilasters at the corners and on
the sides. Two of the tombs (38 and 39) stand where the
tongue of land between the highway and the Vesuvius Road
begins to descend to the level of the pavement.

The remains of the tomb of Ceius Labeo (38) are shown in
Plate IX (in the foreground, at the left). The appearance of
this monument was somewhat like that of the Istacidii ; there

was a second story, the roof of which was supported entirely by columns; between these, statues of members of the family were placed, of both men and women, some of marble, others of tufa coated with stucco. The high base, or podium, was ornamented with stucco reliefs, which have almost entirely disappeared; above, in front, were two portrait medallions.

The large sepulchral chamber can be seen in the plate. The floor was more than six feet below the surface of the ground. A vaulted niche in the rear wall was connected with the outside by means of a small opening at the top, through which libations could be poured or offerings dropped upon the urn below. In the vicinity of the monument was found the inscription : *L. Ceio L. f. Men. Labeoni iter*[*um*] *d. v. i. d. quin*[*quennali*] *Menomachus l*[*ibertus*], — 'Menomachus the freedman built this tomb in memory of Lucius Ceius Labeo son of Lucius, of the tribe Menenia, twice duumvir with judiciary authority, also quinquennial duumvir.'

There were bust stones in the plot belonging to this monument, and also about the adjoining tomb (39); the names of those whose ashes were deposited under the stones, in part, at least, seem to have been painted upon the base of Labeo's tomb, but they were illegible at the time of excavation. The adjoining tomb (39) is without a name, but was built after that erected in honor of Labeo.

The tombs at the end of the fourth group (42, 43) belong to one household. In the sustaining wall along the highway a sepulchral tablet of tufa is seen with the inscription : *Arriae M. f. Diomedes l*[*ibertus*] *sibi suis*, — 'Diomedes, a freedman, for Arria, daughter of Marcus Arrius, for himself and for his family.' On the elevation directly above is his tomb, the end of which is seen in Plate IX (in the foreground). It bears the inscription : *M. Arrius Ɔ. l. Diomedes sibi suis memoriae, magister pag*[*i*] *Aug*[*usti*] *Felic*[*is*] *suburb*[*ani*], — 'Marcus Arrius Diomedes, freedman of Arria, magistrate of the suburb Pagus Augustus Felix, in memory of himself and his family.'

The abbreviation Ɔ. l. takes the place of *Gaiae libertus*, 'freedman of Gaia,' the letter C, which stands for Gaius, being reversed; Gaia is used, as in legal formulas, to show that the

person referred to is a woman.   The slave Diomedes, after receiving his freedom, was entitled to the use of the family name,
and was known as Marcus Arrius Diomedes.   His mistress, as
Roman ladies generally, was called not by a first name, but by
the feminine form of the family name, Arria, which was as
plainly suggested to a Roman reading the name Arrius followed
by the symbol as if it had been written in full.

On the front of the tomb we observe in stucco relief two
bundles of rods, *fasces*, with axes, having reference to the official
position of Diomedes as a magistrate of a suburb.   The axes
are quite out of place.   Suburban officers did not have the
' power of life and death ' ; the lictors of such magistrates carried
bundles of rods without axes.   The vain display of authority
reminds one of the pompous petty official held up to ridicule
by Horace in his Journey to Brundisium ; it suggests also the
rods and axes painted on the posts at the entrance of the dining
room of Trimalchio, in Petronius's novel.   The tomb was constructed without a burial vault, but there were two bust stones
near by with names of freedmen of Diomedes.

The monument to Arria (43) lies further back ; it fronts on
the Vesuvius Road.   Diomedes found a way to reconcile happily
his own love of display with his duty to his former mistress ; he
built a larger monument for her, but chose for his own the more
conspicuous position.   The small sepulchral chamber of Arria's
tomb contained nothing of interest and is now walled up.

CHAPTER L

No part of the highway leading from the Nola Gate has yet
been excavated. In the year 1854, however, excavations were
made for a short distance along the city wall near this gate, and
thirty-six cinerary urns were found buried in the earth. In or
near them were perfume vials of terra cotta with a few of glass.
Here in the pomerium, the strip of land along the outside of the
walls, which was left vacant for religious as well as practical
reasons, the poor were permitted to bury the ashes of their dead
without cost. In some cases the place of the urn was indicated
by a bust stone; often the spot was kept in memory merely by
cutting upon the outside of the city wall the name of the person
whose ashes rested here.

There was another cemetery of the poor a short distance
southwest of the Amphitheatre, south of the modern highway.
It lay along a road which branched off from the highway leading to Stabiae and ran east in the direction of Nocera. Sepulchral remains were found here in 1755–57, and again in 1893–94,
when further explorations were made. They consist of cinerary
urns, buried in the earth, with small glass perfume vials in or
near them, and a bust stone to mark the spot. A few of the
stones are of marble and bear a name; the great majority are
roughly carved out of blocks of lava, and if a name was painted
on the front it has disappeared.

Of special significance, in connection with these burial places,
is the arrangement for making offerings to the dead. In order
that libations might be poured directly upon the cinerary urns,
these were connected with the surface of the ground by means
of tubes. In one instance a lead pipe ran from above into an
opening made for it in the top of the lead case inclosing an urn.

More often the connection was made by means of round tiles;
in the case of one urn, three tiles were joined together, making a
tube five feet long.   The upper end of the libation tube did not
project from the ground, but was placed just below the surface
and covered with a flat stone; over this was a thin layer of
earth, which the relatives would remove on the feast days of the
dead.   Pagan antiquity was never able to dissociate the spirit of
the dead from the place of interment; the worship of ancestors
was in no small degree the product of local associations.

In the vicinity of these remains is a sepulchral monument of
modest dimensions, which, as we learn from the tablet over the
entrance, was erected by Marcus Petasius Dasius in memory of
his two sons, Severus and Communis, and of a freedwoman
named Vitalis.   There was no floor in the burial chamber;
the urns were placed in the earth and marked by bust stones,
among which was one set up for Dasius himself, with the
initials M. P. D.

The Stabian Road has been excavated for but a short distance
near the gate.   The only monuments completely cleared are two
large, semicircular benches, like those of Veius and Mamia
(p. 401).   At the rear of each is a small sepulchral enclosure in
which the urns were buried.   The memorial tablet belonging
to the monument nearest the gate has disappeared, but two
boundary stones at the corners of the lot bear the inscription :
M. Tullio M. f. ex d[ecurionum] d[ecreto], — 'To Marcus Tullius
son of Marcus, in accordance with a vote of the city council.'
The Tullius named was perhaps the builder of the temple of
Fortuna Augusta (p. 126).

The inscription of the second bench, like that of Mamia, is
cut in large letters on the back of the seat : M. Alleio M. f.
Men. Minio, II v. i. d.; locus sepulturae publice datus ex d. d., —
'To the memory of Marcus Alleius Minius son of Marcus, of
the tribe Menenia, duumvir with judiciary authority.   The place
of burial was given in the name of the city by vote of the municipal council.'

A third bench, close to the second, lies under a modern house
and has not been uncovered.   Further from the gate a rectangular seat, probably belonging to the same series of monuments,

was discovered in 1854; it was built in memory of a certain
Clovatius, duumvir, as shown by a fragment of an inscription
that came to light at the same time. From still another
tomb are reliefs with gladiatorial combats, now in the Naples
Museum.

With the exception of those near the Herculaneum Gate, the
most important tombs yet discovered at Pompeii are in a group
beyond the Amphitheatre, excavated in 1886–87. They are six
in number, and lie close together on both sides of a road which
ran east from the Nocera Gate, bending slightly to the north
(Fig. 236). This road was not in use in the last years of the
city; the stones of the pavement and sidewalk had been removed. The monuments, however, were large and stately,
erected by people of means, and the ruins are characteristic and
impressive. The tombs were built of common materials, stucco
being used on exposed surfaces instead of marble. The simplicity of construction, and the shapes of the letters in the election notices and other inscriptions painted on them, suggest a
relatively early date, which is confirmed by the age of the coins
found in the urns; the
monuments belong to the
early decades of the Em-
pire.

The first tomb at the
right (No. 1 on the plan)
was built in the form of
a commemorative arch,
with pilasters at the corners. Above was a low
cylinder surmounted by
a truncated cone, on which
stood a terminal member
in the shape of a pine cone,
found near by. The cine-
rary urn was buried in the
earth below an opening in

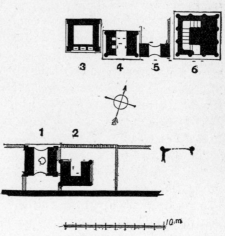

Fig. 236.— Plan of the tombs east of the Amphitheatre.

the floor of the passage under the arch (shown in the plan). No
name appears in connection with this monument.

Another monument of the arch type, that of Mancius Diogenes, is seen on the opposite side of the street (5; Fig. 238).
The structure is shallow, the vaulted opening low.   On the top
of the arch were three niches, in which stood three travertine
statues; two of these, both of women, have been preserved,
and are of indifferent workmanship.   A marble tablet was
placed in front, over the vault, with the inscription, *P. Mancio
P. l[iberto] Diogeni ex testamento arbitratu Manciae P. libertae*

Fig. 237. — View of two tombs east of the Amphitheatre.
That at the left is No. 3 on the plan; the next is No. 4.

Dorinis, — 'To the memory of Publius Mancius Diogenes, freedman of Publius Mancius; (the monument was erected) in accordance with the terms of his will, under the direction of Mancia
Doris, freedwoman of Publius Mancius.'

There is a curious ambiguity in this inscription; we cannot
tell whether Doris, seemingly the wife of Diogenes, was manumitted by the Publius Mancius who gave him his freedom, or
by Diogenes himself after he had gained his freedom and
was entitled to use the name Publius Mancius.   Four bust
stones stood in front of the tomb and two at the rear,

arranged as indicated on the plan; those in front are seen in our illustration.

The tomb at the left of that just described (4; Fig. 237) is of interest as showing the result of an attempt to blend the arch type with that of the temple. A passage roofed with a flat vault runs through the middle of the first story. The second story had the appearance of a diminutive temple with four Corinthian columns in front. The niche representing the cella was of the full width of the tomb, and occupied two thirds of the depth; the other third was given to the portico. Four statues of tufa coated with stucco that were found here probably stood under the portico or in the intercolumniations, where they would best be seen from below; three were statues of men, the fourth of a woman.

The arrangement of the five bust stones in the vaulted passage is indicated on the plan. The three nearest the street entrance bear the name of a freedman, *L. Caesius L. l. Logus*, — 'Lucius Caesius Logus, freedman of Lucius Caesius,' and of Titia Vesbina and Titia Optata, both evidently freedwomen manumitted by a lady named Titia. We are probably safe in assuming that the two inmost stones, without names, are those of Caesius and Titia, husband and wife, who gave Logus, Vesbina, and Optata their freedom, and built the monument. It was not necessary to place the names of the builders upon the commemorative stones, because they were doubtless given in the memorial tablet in front, which has disappeared. Coins of Augustus and Tiberius were found in the urns.

One tomb (2) has the form of a niche, resembling those of the two children near the end of the Street of Tombs (p. 417), but larger and more costly than they. The corners are embellished with three-quarter columns, which have Doric flutings and composite capitals. On the walls at the entrance we see, modelled in stucco, doorposts with double doors swung back. Two marble bust stones, the places of which are indicated on the plan, show where the urns of the two most important members of the family, Apuleius and his wife Veia, were buried; their names doubtless appeared in an inscription on the front of the monument. In one of the urns was found a coin of

Tiberius of the year 10 A.D. The other was enclosed in a lead case, and a lead libation tube was extended from the ashes through both covers to the surface.

The names of Apuleius and Veia are obtained from two other bust stones, in front of the niche. One reads, *Festae Apulei f[iliae] vix[it] ann[os] XVII*, — 'To the memory of Festa, daughter of Apuleius, who lived seventeen years.' The other

Fig. 238. — Two other tombs east of the Amphitheatre.
Nos. 5, 6 on the plan.

has simply *Conviva Veiae vix. ann. XX*, — 'Conviva, slave of Veia, lived twenty years.' An as of the time of the Republic was found in the urn of Conviva; and a square tile, the upper end of which was closed by a piece of marble, served as a libation tube for the urn of Festa.

The two remaining tombs are of the temple type, one (3; Fig. 237) having pilasters at the corners, the other half-columns at the corners and on the sides (6). The first has a vaulted sepulchral chamber, entered from the rear. On the inside of the wall next the street are three low niches, the top of which is nearly on a level with the sidewalk; each of them con-

tained an urn. Directly over the inner niches, in the outside
of the wall and opening toward the street, are three other
niches, shown in the illustration, in the bottom of which were
libation tubes leading to the urns below. Relatives could
thus pour their offerings of wine or oil upon the urns without entering the sepulchral chamber. Lava bust stones were
placed against the back of the outer niches. The hair on
one of them is treated in a manner to indicate that a woman
is represented. The entrance of the tomb was closed by a
large block of lava. On account of the arrangement for offering libations from the outside, it was not necessary to make
the burial vault easy of access.

The entrance to the other tomb (6; Fig. 238) was in front,
and closed by a block of travertine. It led, not to a sepulchral
chamber, but to a stairway by which one ascended to the second
story. Here statues were placed, but the exact form of the
upper part cannot be determined. The finding of five tufa
capitals suggests that the second story may have been a columnar structure, like that of the tomb of the Istacidii; when the
excavations are carried further east enough other fragments
will perhaps be found to make a complete restoration possible.
One of the statues is of a man holding a roll of papyrus in his
hand, with a round manuscript case, *scrinium*, at his feet.

Among the inscriptions painted on these tombs were two,
relating to gladiatorial combats, which have already been mentioned (p. 215). One of the election notices, oddly enough,
refers to a candidate for an office in Nuceria: *L. Munatium
Caeserninum Nuceriae II vir. quinq. v. b. o. v. f.* (for *duumvirum
quinquennalem, virum bonum, oro vos, facite*), — 'Make Lucius
Caeserninus quinquennial duumvir of Nuceria, I beg of you,
he's a good man.' As long as the relations of the Pompeians
and Nucerians were friendly, the highway between the two
towns was doubtless much travelled by the citizens of both
places.

If the visitor pauses to think of the religious feeling which
the ancients manifested generally in relation to their burial
places, it gives something of a shock to see notices even of a
semi-public character painted in bright red letters upon tombs.

All such inscriptions, however, are surpassed in ludicrous incongruity with the purpose of the monument by the following advertisement regarding a stray horse : *Equa siquei aberavit cum semuncis honerata a. d. VII Kal. Septembres* (corrected into *Decembres*), *convenito Q. Deciu*[*m*] *Q. l. Hilarum . . . L. l. . . . chionem, citra pontem Sarni fundo Mamiano,* — 'If anybody lost a mare with a small pack-saddle, November 25, let him come and see Quintus Decius Hilarus, freedman of Quintus Decius, or . . . (the name is illegible), freedman of Lucius, on the estate of the Mamii, this side of the bridge over the Sarno.' The two freedmen were very likely in partnership, working a farm belonging to the family, one representative of which we have already met, Mamia the priestess (p. 402).

A more serious desecration of burial places, after offerings to the dead ceased to be made by relatives, or a family became extinct, was probably not uncommon. Different families had different gods, and those of one household were quite independent of those of another. Ordinarily a man had no reason to fear or respect the gods of his neighbor; notwithstanding the associations of worship connected with tombs, the general feeling toward them was very different from that manifested toward temples, where local divinities or the great gods were worshipped. The most stringent regulations of the emperors could not prevent the ransacking of the tombs about Rome for objects of value, and the removal of their materials of construction for building purposes. The superstructure of two of the monuments near the Herculaneum Gate had disappeared apparently before the destruction of the city, and of the tomb of Porcius only the core remained.

PART V

POMPEIAN ART

CHAPTER LI

ARCHITECTURE

In the preceding pages the principal buildings of Pompeii have been described, and reference has been made to many works of art. We shall now offer a few observations of a more general nature in regard to the remains of architecture, sculpture, and painting.

The different periods in the architectural history of the city have been defined in a previous chapter. The most significant of these, from every point of view, is that which we have called the Tufa Period, which corresponds roughly with the second century B.C. Its importance is chiefly due to the fact that it records for us a phase of architectural development, a style, of which only slight traces are found elsewhere, — in the East. It is the last offshoot of untrammelled Hellenistic art in the field of construction; the architecture of the following period was still derived from Hellenistic sources, but was dominated by Roman conceptions, and received from Rome the impulse that determined the direction of its development. The remains of the Tufa Period at Pompeii furnish materials for a missing chapter in the history of architecture.

As we have seen, the stone preferred in this period for all purposes was the gray tufa. Where used for columns, pilasters, and entablatures, it was covered with stucco; in plain walls it appeared in its natural color. Unfortunately, the covering of stucco is preserved in only a few cases; the best example is presented by an Ionic capital in the first peristyle of the house of the Faun. The stucco was generally white, but color was sometimes

employed, as in the Corinthian columns and pilasters of the
exedra in the same house, which are painted a deep wine red.

No other period of Pompeian art shows in an equal degree
the impress of a single characteristic and self-consistent style,
alike in public buildings, temples, and private houses, in the
interior decoration as well as in the treatment of exteriors.
The wall decoration of the first style is simply the adaptation
of tufa construction to decorative use. The motives are identical. The forms are the same, but these naturally appear in a
freer handling upon interior walls, the effect being heightened
by the use or imitation of slabs of marble of various colors.

This style throughout gives the impression of roominess and
largeness. It is monumental, especially when viewed in contrast with the later architecture of Pompeii. No building erected
after the city became a Roman colony can be compared, for
ample dimensions and spatial effects, with the Basilica. In the
same class are the temples of Jupiter and Apollo, with the impressive two-storied colonnades enclosing the areas on which
they stand; the contrast with the later temples, as those of
Fortuna Augusta and Vespasian, is striking. All the more important houses of this period are monumental in design and proportions, with imposing entrances, large and lofty atriums, and
high doors opening upon the atrium; the shops in front also
were high, and in two stories.

In point of detail, the architecture of the Tufa Period reveals
less of strength and symmetry than its stately proportions and
modest material would lead us to expect. The ornamentation
is a debased descendant of the Greek. It is characterized by
superficial elegance, together with an apparent striving after
simplicity and an ill-concealed poverty of form and color.
Though the ornamental forms still manifest fine Greek feeling,
they lack delicacy of modelling and vigor of expression. They
are taken from Greek religious architecture, but all appreciation
of the three orders as distinct types, each suited for a different
environment, has disappeared. In consequence, we often find
a mixture of the orders, a blending of Doric, Ionic, and Corinthian elements; and still more frequently do we meet with a
marked departure from the original proportions.

Thus in the court of the temple of Apollo and in the first peristyle of the house of the Faun we see Ionic columns supporting a Doric entablature; in the house of the Black Wall, Doric columns with an Ionic entablature.   The Doric architrave,

contrary to rule, appears divided into two stripes, not only in the colonnade of the Forum, where the stripes represent a difference of material, but also in the house of the Faun, where the architrave is represented as composed of single blocks reaching from column to column (p. 51).   In

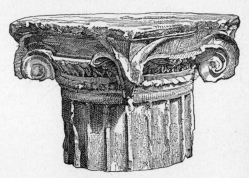

Fig. 239. — Four-faced Ionic capital.   Portico of the Forum Triangulare.

the Palaestra (p. 159), and in many private houses, the Doric column was lengthened, in a way quite out of harmony with the original conception, in order to make it conform to the prevailing desire for height and slender proportions.   The shaft nowhere appears with the pronounced entasis and strong diminution characteristic of the type, and the capital has lost the breadth and graceful outline of the Greek Doric.

The Ionic columns in the cella of the temple of Jupiter (p. 65) are of the Greek type, with volutes on two sides; elsewhere

Fig. 240. — Capital of pilaster. Casa del duca d'Aumale.

we find only the so-called Roman Ionic, with four volutes, a type that appears in several well defined and pleasing examples.   One of these, a capital from the portico at the entrance of the Forum Triangulare, is shown in Fig. 239.   The deep incisions of the egg-and-dart pattern, which give the egg almost the appearance of a little ball, is characteristic; it is found only at Pompeii, and there not after the Tufa Period.   A still freer handling of the Ionic is seen in the capital of a pilaster in the casa del duca d'Aumale (Fig. 240).

The Corinthian capital appears in the usual forms, but the
projecting parts are shallow, on account of the lack of resisting
qualities in the stone.   The best examples are the capitals of the
columns and pilasters of the exedra in the house of the Faun.
The workmanship here is fine, the realistic treatment of the
acanthus leaves being especially noteworthy.   An interesting
series of variations from the normal type is seen in the capitals
of the pilasters at house entrances; we have already met with
a striking example of this series, ornamented with projecting
busts of human figures (Fig. 171).   The design is often so fantas-

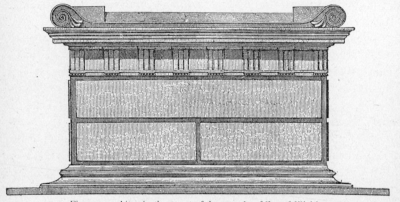

Fig. 241. — Altar in the court of the temple of Zeus Milichius.

tic that the essential character of the Corinthian capital seems
entirely lost sight of.

The entablatures of the temples built in the Tufa Period, as
of those erected in later times, have all perished.   The entablatures of the colonnades, however, are at least in part well preserved in a number of instances, and are of two types, the
Doric, characterized by the use of triglyphs, and the Ionic, distinguished by the dentils of the cornice.

Both types are found also in the wall decoration, the first
rarely, the second very frequently.   On the altar of the temple
of Zeus Milichius, which is of tufa coated with stucco, the Doric
entablature appears in association with the characteristic decoration of the first style, the imitation of large blocks of marble ;
on the top are terminal volutes of Ionic origin, as generally

upon Roman altars and altar-shaped tombs (Fig. 241). On walls decorated in the first style, however, only Ionic entablatures are seen, — sometimes even twice upon the same wall. From this we infer that in the temple construction of the Tufa Period, the simple and elegant Ionic entablature was the prevailing type.

Notwithstanding its free adaption of Greek forms, the Tufa Period availed itself very sparingly of polychrome decoration for architectural members. The stucco of the Ionic capital in the house of the Faun is white ; white likewise are most of the capitals of pilasters found in the houses, and also the numerous Ionic cornices on the walls.

There are, nevertheless, scanty traces of the application of color. In the wall decoration of the house of Sallust we find a Doric frieze with the metopes painted red. The frieze under the Ionic cornices on the walls also is usually made prominent with color, — red, yellow, or blue ; and a red frieze is seen in the peristyle of the house of the Black Wall, above the pilasters of the garden wall. The lower stripe of the painted architrave in the house of the Faun, already referred to, is yellow.

It seems probable that in some cases color was applied to the projecting figures of the peculiar capitals used in houses ; at the time of excavation, traces of coloring were distinctly seen upon those belonging to the alae of the house of Epidius Rufus (p. 303). The exposed capitals at the entrances (Fig. 171), if originally painted, would naturally have lost all traces of the coloring before the destruction of the city, unless it were from time to time renewed. Notwithstanding these exceptions, we must conclude that the stucco coating upon public buildings and temples was generally white, in the case of capitals and cornices as well as of the shafts of columns and outside walls ; colors were used to a limited extent, upon friezes and perhaps other parts of entablatures.

The architectural remains of the half century immediately succeeding the Tufa Period, between the founding of the Roman colony at Pompeii and the establishment of the Empire, present nothing specially characteristic outside of the peculiarities of construction mentioned in chap. 6.

2 F

In the earlier years of the Empire, the Pompeians, as Roman
subjects everywhere, commenced to build temples and colonnades of marble. The style, which was distinctively Roman, can
be studied to better advantage elsewhere; the remains at Pompeii are relatively unimportant, and the chief points of interest
have been mentioned in connection with our study of individual
buildings.

The stylistic development of Roman architecture in the next
period, — the gradual transition from the simplicity of the Augustan Age to the more elaborate ornamentation of the Flavian
Era, — is marked by two opposing tendencies, one conservative,
holding to the traditions of marble construction, the other re-

Fig. 242. — Capitals of columns, showing variations from typical forms.
A. Ornate Doric, from the house of Sallust.   B. Modified Corinthian.   C. Fantastic Corinthian.

actionary. The latter tendency manifests itself so strongly at
Pompeii that it merits special comment.

First in the East, it appears, men wearied of seeing the ornamental forms of the Greek religious architecture repeated over
and over again in every kind of building, and attempted to
break away from them entirely. The reaction reached Italy in
the earlier years of the Empire, and began to exert an influence
upon ornamental forms, especially of domestic architecture, at
the time when the third style of wall decoration was coming
into vogue.

At Pompeii, this revolt from tradition affected not only the
ornamentation of private houses, but also that of public buildings, as the Stabian Baths, and even of temples, as those of
Apollo and Isis, rebuilt after the earthquake of the year 63.

Greek forms were replaced by fantastic designs of every sort,
worked in stucco. The capitals of columns and pilasters retained a semblance of Doric and Corinthian types, but were
adorned with motives from many sources; the variety of form
and treatment can best be appreciated
by inspecting the examples shown in
our illustrations (Figs. 242, 243, 244).

The entablatures no longer retained
the ancient division of architrave, frieze,
and cornice, but were made to represent
a single broad stripe, sometimes, however, with a projecting cornice; this
stripe was ornamented with stucco reliefs, and was frequently painted in
bright colors. Sometimes the decora-

Fig. 243. — Capital of pilaster,
modified Corinthian type.

tive theme is taken from a vine, as in the entablature of the
portico in front of the temple of Isis (Fig. 75) and that of the
peristyle of the house of the Vettii (Fig. 154). In some cases
the stripe is divided into vertical sections; the broad sections correspond with the intercolumniations, the narrow ones with the

Fig. 244. — Capitals of pilasters, showing free adaptations of the Corinthian type.

spaces above the columns ; and the ornamental design is varied
accordingly, as in the palaestra of the Stabian Baths (p. 192),
the court of the temple of Apollo (Fig. 31), and the peristyle
of the house of the Silver Wedding. In many instances the
background is white, frequently part of the details of ornament
as well; but colors were freely used, particularly red, blue, and
yellow, in all parts of the entablature.

The lower third of the columns also was painted a bright red
or yellow — a treatment that would have been abhorrent to the

taste of the Tufa Period.   The desire for variety and brilliancy
of color increased, and was more pronounced in the years immediately preceding the eruption than at any previous time.

Consistently with this change in the standard of taste in regard to details, the Pompeians no longer had pleasure in the
ample dimensions of the olden time.   Houses were not now
*built with high rooms, great doorways, and lofty columns as
in the Tufa Period.   The rooms were smaller and lower, and
also, we may add, more homelike.   But curiously enough, the
columns were often made thick as well as short, doubtless
in order to afford more space for the display of color on the
capitals and the lower part of the shaft.

Roman public and religious architecture in most cities still
adhered to the forms of marble construction, a suggestion of
which we find in the white walls of the temple of Isis ; but the
lower third of the columns in the colonnade about this temple
was painted red, and the entablature was no doubt ornamented
with colored designs, as was that of the temple of Apollo.   The
best preserved example of this last phase of Pompeian architectural ornamentation is in the semicircular vaulted niche at the
right of the Street of Tombs.

Thus we see accomplished at Pompeii, in less than two centuries, a complete revolution in matters of taste, so far as relates
to architecture.   An entirely new feeling has been developed.
The beauty of contour and of symmetrical proportion found in
the Greek architecture had no charm for the Pompeian of the
later time ; its place had been usurped by a different form of
beauty, that produced by the use of a variety of brilliant colors in
association with forms that were intricate, and often grotesque.

PLATE X.—ARTEMIS. COPY OF AN ARCHAIC WORK

PLATE 5.   AN EMUS. COPY OF AN ARCHAIC WORK

DIANA
POMPEI

411.

CHAPTER LII

SCULPTURE

THE open squares and public buildings of Pompeii were peopled with statues. The visitor who walked about the Forum in the years immediately preceding the eruption, saw on all sides the forms of the men of past generations who had rendered service to the city, as well as those of men of his own time.

Besides the five colossal images of emperors and members of the imperial families, places were provided in the Forum for between seventy and eighty life size equestrian statues; and behind each of these was room for a standing figure. Whether all the places were occupied cannot now be determined, but from the sepulchral inscription of Umbricius Scaurus (p. 410) it is clear that as late as the time of Claudius or Nero, there was yet room for another equestrian figure. Statues were placed also in the Forum Triangulare and occasionally at the sides of the streets.

In the portico of the Macellum were twenty-five statues; the sanctuary of the City Lares contained eight, while the portico of the Eumachia building furnished places for twenty-one. But only one of the hundreds of statues erected in honor of worthy citizens has been preserved, that of Holconius Rufus, the re-builder of the Large Theatre; the figure was dressed in the uniform of a military tribune, and stood on Abbondanza Street near the entrance to the Stabian Baths. With this, perhaps, the unknown portrait statues in the temple of Fortuna Augusta should be classed, as well as that of the priestess Eumachia.

The statue of Eumachia is an interesting example of the ordinary portrait sculpture of the Early Empire (Fig. 245). The pose is by no means ungraceful, the treatment of the drapery is modest and effective. The tranquil and thoughtful

437

face is presented realistically, yet without offensive emphasis of
details.   The statue is not a masterpiece; nevertheless, it gives
us a pleasant impression of the lady whose generosity placed
the fullers under obliga-
tion, and affords an in-
sight into the artistic
resources of the city.

Fig. 245. — Statue of the priestess Eumachia.

A number of portrait
statues belonging to se-
pulchral monuments were
found when the tombs
east of the Amphitheatre
were excavated (chap. 50).
Most of them are of tufa
covered with stucco; the
rest are of fine-grained
limestone. From the aes-
thetic point of view they
are valueless.

Sculptured portraits of
a different type were set
up in private houses. Relatives, freedmen, and even
slaves sometimes placed
at the rear of the atrium,
near the entrance of the
tablinum, a herm of the
master of the house.   At
each side of the square
pillar supporting the bust,
there was usually an arm-
like projection (seen on
the herm of Cornelius Rufus, Fig. 116), on which garlands were
hung upon birthdays and other anniversary occasions. Both the
herm of Rufus and that of Vesonius Primus previously mentioned
(p. 388) are of marble; the bust belonging to the herm of Sorex
(p. 170) is of bronze.

The most striking of the portrait herms is that of Lucius

Caecilius Jucundus (Fig. 246), which was set up in duplicate, for the sake of symmetrical arrangement, in the atrium of his house on Stabian Street. The pillar is of marble; the dedication reads *Genio L[ucii] nostri Felix l[ibertus]*, — 'Felix, freedman, to the Genius of our Lucius.'

The bust, of bronze, is modelled with realistic vigor. There is no attempt to soften the prominent and almost repulsive features by idealization. We see the Pompeian auctioneer just as he was, a shrewd, alert, energetic man, with somewhat of a taste for art, and more for the good things of life, — a man who would bear watching in a financial transaction.

Houses were adorned also with heads and busts of famous men of the past, — poets, philosophers, and statesmen. An extensive collection of historical portraits was discovered at Herculaneum, but Pompeii thus far has not yielded many examples. In a room in one of the houses was found a group of three

Fig. 246. — Portrait herm of Caecilius Jucundus.

marble heads, about one half life size, representing Epicurus, Demosthenes, and apparently the Alexandrian poet Callimachus, whose works were particularly valued in the time of the Early Empire. The identification of the third head is not certain, but whether Callimachus or some other poet is intended, the group reveals the direction of the owner's literary tastes; he was interested in philosophy, oratory, and poetry.

Two portrait busts of distinguished men, which evidently belong together, were found in another house, laid one side. In the Naples Museum they bear the names of Decimus Brutus and of Pompey, but both identifications are erroneous; the features in neither case agree with the representations upon coins. The faces, as shown by the physiognomy and the treatment of the hair, are those of Romans of the end of the Republic or the beginning of the Empire. Recently a new identification has

Fig. 247. — Double bust, Bacchus and bacchante. Garden of the house of the Vettii.

been proposed which has much in its favor. It rests chiefly upon the resemblance of one of the busts to the mosaic portrait of Virgil, discovered in 1896 at Susa, in Africa. The full, round face of the other agrees very well with what we know of the appearance of Horace. It may be that we have here a pair of poets, the two most prominent of the Augustan Age.

Frequently the gardens of the peristyles, as those of the houses of the Vettii and of Lucretius, were profusely adorned with sculptures of all kinds. We find in them statuettes, herms, small figures of animals, and diminutive groups. Figures derived from the myths of the bacchic cycle, Bacchus, Silenus, satyrs, and bacchantes, are particularly common. The artistic value is slight; among the best examples is the double bust, with Bacchus on one side and a bacchante on the other, found in the garden of the house of the Vettii (Fig. 247).

Characteristic among these sculptures are the figures designed for the adornment of fountains; a number of them are exhibited in the Museum at Naples. Bacchic figures are met with most frequently. A good example is the marble Silenus in the garden

of the house of Lucretius; the water spurts from the opening in
the wineskin which the old man carries.   The design of the
small bronze satyr in the peristyle of the house of the Centenary
is more pleasing; an opening in the wineskin, held under the
left arm, cast a jct against the outstretched right hand in such a
way that the water was thrown back upon the satyr's body.

Fountains were adorned also with genre groups and animal
forms.   We have already noticed the two bronze groups in the
peristyle of the house of the Vettii, each representing a boy
holding a duck, from the bill of which sprang a jet of water
(Fig. 155).   The largest collection of animal forms was about
the basin in the middle peristyle of the house of the Citharist;
it comprised two dogs, a boar, a lion, a deer, and a snake, each
throwing a jet into the basin below.   The fountain jets, however, were not in all cases so closely related to the ornamental
pieces.   A number of those in the house of the Vettii sprang
from lead pipes near the figures.   The familiar bronze statue of
the seated fisherman, in the Naples Museum, belonged to a fountain, in which the jet was thrown forward, not from the figure,
but from the mouth of a mask projecting from the stump on
which the fisherman sits.

Of the statues of divinities set up for worship in the temples,
there are unfortunately but few remains.   The most important
fragment is the head of Jupiter, discussed in a previous chapter
(Fig. 22).   Three wretched terra cotta statues of the gods of the
Capitol were found, as we have seen, in the temple of Zeus Milichius; and mention has been made also of the herms and other
specimens of sculpture in the courts of the temples of Apollo
and Isis, and in the Palaestra.   More numerous than any other
class of sculptures, however, are the small bronze images of
tutelary divinities preserved in the domestic shrines.   These
are of interest rather from the light which they shed on the
practices of domestic worship than from their excellence as
works of art, and it seems unnecessary to add anything here to
what has already been said in regard to them in the chapter
dealing with the arrangements of the Pompeian house.   But
occasionally there were large domestic shrines, in which statues
of merit were placed; among these are two worthy of mention.

In the corner of a garden belonging to a house in the first Region (I. ii. 17) is a shrine faced with white marble, in which was a small marble statue of Aphrodite, partly supported by a figure commonly identified as Hope, *Spes*. The carving is in no way remarkable, but the statue is of interest on account of the well preserved coloring applied to the eyes, hair, and dress. The group is now in the Naples Museum.

A more important example, from the aesthetic point of view, is the statue of Artemis, of one half life size, shown in Plate X. It was found in a house near the Amphitheatre which was excavated in 1760 and covered up again. It is a careful copy, made in the time of Augustus, of a Greek masterpiece produced in the period of the Persian Wars. The original was probably the Artemis Laphria mentioned by Pausanias. This was a work of Menaechmus and Soedas, two sculptors of Naupactus. Previous to the battle of Actium it stood in a sanctuary in Calydon, whence it was removed by Augustus, who presented it to the colony founded by him at Patras.

The goddess appears in this statue as a huntress, moving forward with a firm but light step; the bow in the left hand has disappeared. The copyist was remarkably successful in impressing upon his work the gracious and pleasing character of the original; the later archaic Greek art, in spite of its conventions, is full of human feeling. The copy preserved also the coloring of the model; but the tinting of the Roman colorist was probably less delicate than that of the Greek limner who added the polychrome decoration to the marble original. The hair was yellow. The pupils of the eyes were brown, the eyelashes and eyebrows black. The rosettes of the diadem were yellow, and the border of the outer garment was richly variegated in tints of yellow, rose color, and white. Traces of rose-colored stripes are visible also about the openings of the sleeves, on the edge of the mantle at the neck, and on the border of the chiton.

Besides the bronze statues of Apollo and Artemis already mentioned (pp. 88, 346), three others of those found at Pompeii are worthy of more than passing notice, — the dancing satyr from which the house of the Faun received its name, the

remarkable beauty. The face wears an expression of childlike innocence and pleasure. The head leans forward in the attitude of listening; the index finger of the right hand is extended, and the graceful pose is that of one who catches the almost inaudible sound of a distant voice.

The name Narcissus, given to the figure by Fiorelli immediately upon its discovery, is surely wrong; that unhappy youth did not reciprocate the love of the nymph Echo, and could not have been imagined with so cheerful a face. The figure has also been called Pan, from a myth in which Pan and Echo appear together; but the characteristic attributes are lacking, and the rough god of the shepherds would not have been represented in so lithe and graceful a form.

This beautiful youth, with an ivy crown upon his head and elaborate coverings for the feet, and with the skin of a doe hanging over his shoulder, is none other than Dionysus himself. The mirthful god of the vine is not playing with his panther — the base is too small to have been designed for two figures, and the attitude of listening is not consistent with this interpretation. The youthful divinity has fixed his attention upon some distant sound, — the cries of the bacchantes upon some mountain height, or the laughter of naiads in a shady glen.

Had the ruins of Pompeii not been systematically searched, after the disaster, for works of art and other objects of value, they would have yielded a far richer store of sculptures. But while the specimens recovered add little to our knowledge of types, they give a new insight into the application of the sculptor's art in antiquity to the beautifying of the surroundings of everyday life.

CHAPTER LIII

PAINTING.— WALL DECORATION

THE inner walls of houses and public buildings at Pompeii were plastered, and usually decorated with colors; only storerooms, kitchens, and apartments designed for the use of slaves were left in the white. Outer walls were as a rule plastered, except when built of hewn stone, a kind of construction not employed after the Tufa Period. Stucco was occasionally used on façades of ashlar work where special ornamentation seemed to be needed, as at the entrance of the house of the Faun; and in later times, now and then, a front with reticulate or brick facing was left unplastered. Previous to the time of Augustus the stucco coating of outer walls ordinarily remained uncolored. Afterwards color was employed, but only to a limited extent, as in the addition of a dark base to a wall the rest of which remained white.

The painting upon Pompeian walls, as shown by the painstaking investigations of Otto Donner, was fresco, that is, executed in water colors upon the moist stucco of a freshly plastered surface. The method of preparing the wall was less elaborate than that recommended by Vitruvius, who advises the use of seven coats of plaster, first a rough coat, then three of sand mortar and three of stucco made with powdered marble, each coat being finer than the one preceding. In the better rooms, however, we find upon the walls at least one, often several, layers of sand mortar, and one or more coats of marble stucco; the entire thickness of the plastering varies from two to three inches. In unfinished or neglected rooms walls are sometimes found with a single coat of sand mortar. Occasionally powdered brick was used in the stucco as a substitute for marble dust.

Plastering so thick as that ordinarily used must have remained moist for a considerable length of time, much longer than the plastering of our day; yet it could not have retained its moisture long enough to complete the painting of an entire wall as one piece. Walls which are elaborately decorated sometimes show traces of a seam, where a moist section was laid on next to one that had already become partially dry. When the decorative design included pictures, usually the divisions and borders and other decorative elements were finished rapidly while the surface was moist; then a square or round hole was cut where a picture was to be inserted, and filled with fresh stucco, on which the picture was painted. In this way a carefully executed painting could be set in a wall already dry.

In the last years of the city pictures were sometimes painted on the dry surface of a wall that had previously received its decorative framework; some of the figures seen in the middle of the large panels furnish examples of this method of work. A size of some kind must have been used in such cases, but chemical analysis thus far has failed to determine its nature. The distemper painting was much less durable than the fresco, the colors of which became fixed with the hardening of the wall.

Sometimes, as in the house of Lucretius, the place of paintings upon stucco was taken by paintings upon wood, the wooden panels being let into the wall. As these panels were thin and lacked durability, we may perhaps believe that the paintings which they contained were of inferior quality.

The artistic value of Pompeian painting varies from the routine work of indifferent decorators to pictures of genuine merit, such as those found in the house of the Tragic Poet, the house of the Vettii, and the house of Castor and Pollux. Viewed as a whole, the wall decoration has a peculiar interest for us; it not only richly illustrates the application of painting by the ancients to decorative uses, but also affords a striking example of the evolution of decorative designs from simple architectural motives to intricate patterns, in which the scheme of coloring is hardly less complicated than that of the ornamental forms.

The four styles of wall decoration were briefly characterized in the Introduction, in connection with our survey of the periods of construction. It now remains to illustrate these by typical examples and to trace their inner connection. We are here concerned only with the decorative designs, or ornamental framework of the walls; the paintings, which formed the centre of interest in the later styles, are reserved for consideration in a separate chapter.

The development of ancient wall decoration came comparatively late, after the art of painting, in the hands of the Greek masters, had reached and passed its climax. Yet we know almost nothing in regard to the earlier stages. Apparently the system which we find at Pompeii originated in the period following the death of Alexander the Great, and received its impulse of development from the contact of Greece with the Orient. But whatever the origin, from the time to which the earliest specimens at Pompeii belong — the second century B.C. — to the destruction of the city, we can trace an uninterrupted development, which, nevertheless, comes to an end in the latter part of the first century A.D.

The decline is characterized by increasing poverty of design, with feeble imitation of past styles. Just as it is setting in, however, extant examples become rare. Some specimens of the wall decoration of later times, as of the period of the Antonines and the reign of Septimius Severus, are preserved, but they are isolated and not sufficient in number to enable us to follow the stages of the decline. Thus it happens that the only period in the history of ancient wall decoration in regard to which we have the materials for a full and satisfactory study, is the period exemplified in the remains at Pompeii, the chronological sequence of which extends over two centuries.

The oldest houses, those belonging to the Period of the Limestone Atriums (p. 39), have preserved no traces of wall decoration beyond the limited application of white stucco.

The remains of the decoration of the Tufa Period are fairly abundant, and are well preserved on account of the excellent quality of the stucco to which the colors were applied. They belong to the first or Incrustation Style. A good example has already been given, the end wall of a bedroom in the house of the Centaur (Fig. 117); we present here, for more detailed examination, the left wall of the atrium in the house of Sallust (Fig. 250).

Notwithstanding the lack of color in our illustration, the divisions of the wall are plainly seen — a dado, painted yellow; a relatively low middle division, the upper edge of which is set off by a projecting cornice; and an upper part reaching from the first cornice, which appears in three sections on account of the doors, to the ceiling. The surface of the main part of the wall is moulded in stucco to represent slabs or blocks with bevelled edges, which are painted in imitation of different kinds of marble. Above the high double doors opening into rooms connected with the atrium, frames of lattice-work for the admission of air and light have been assumed in our restoration.

The dado in the Incrustation Style is generally treated as a separate member; in rare instances the imitation of marble blocks is extended to the floor. It has a smooth surface and is painted a bright color, usually yellow; there is no suggestion of the practice of later times, which gave a darker color to the base than to the rest of the wall. This independent handling is undoubtedly to be explained as a survival from a previous decorative system, in which the lower part of the wall, as at Tiryns, was protected by a baseboard; the conventional yellow color with which it is painted, as in the case of the lower stripe of the Doric architrave in the house of the Faun (p. 51), is a reminiscence of the use of wood. The upper edge of the dado was ordinarily distinguished by a smooth, narrow projecting band or fillet.

The blocks moulded in slight relief upon the main part of the wall are of different sizes. In our illustration we see first a series of three large slabs, which are painted black. Above these are three narrow blocks of magenta. The rest present a considerable variety of size and color, until we reach those just under the cornice, which again are all of the same shade, magenta.

The cornice in this style is always of the Ionic type, with dentils. In many cases, as that of the bedroom in the house of the Centaur, it serves as an upper border for the decoration, the wall above being unpainted. Sometimes, however, the

2 G

imitation of marble is carried above the cornice, the wall surface being divided to represent smoothly joined blocks without bevelled edges, or painted in plain masses of color separated by a narrow white stripe, as in the atrium of the house of Sallust. Above these brilliant panels we see in Fig. 250 a second cornice of simple design ; the wall between this cornice and the ceiling was left without decoration.

This system made no provision for paintings ; their place was taken in the general scheme of decoration by elaborate mosaic

Fig. 250. — Wall decoration in the atrium of the house of Sallust. First or Incrustation Style.

pictures upon the floor. The taste of the age evidently preferred representations in mosaic ; otherwise the painting of pictures upon the walls, which was brought to so high a degree of perfection by Polygnotus and his contemporaries, would not have been abandoned.

The Incrustation Style, as exemplified at Pompeii, is in a secondary stage; it must have been worked out originally in genuine materials, at a time when walls were actually veneered, to a certain height, with slabs of various kinds of marble, cut and arranged to represent ashlar work ; above the cornice marking the upper edge of the veneering, the surface was left in the white. The use of different varieties of marble points

to an active commercial intercourse between the countries about
the Mediterranean Sea, such as first became possible after the
conquests of Alexander. So characteristic a style, requiring
the use of costly materials, could only have been developed in
an important centre of wealth and culture.

In view of all the circumstances, we are probably safe in
concluding that the Incrustation Style originated in Alexandria,
in the third century B.C. From Alexandria it spread to other
cities of the East and West, stucco being used in imitation of

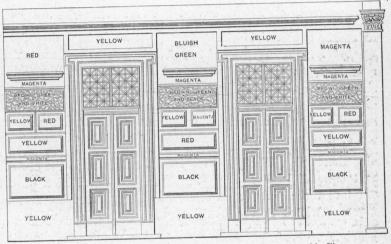

Fig. 251.— Distribution of colors in the section of wall represented in Fig. 250.

marble, where marble could not be procured; scanty remains
similar to those at Pompeii, and of approximately the same
period — the second century B.C. — have been found at Per-
gamon, on the island of Delos, and lately in Priene. This style
represents for us the wall decoration of the Hellenistic age. It
is characterized by the same poverty of form and obvious striving after simplicity which we have noticed in the architecture of
the Tufa Period. The projecting cornice above the body of the
wall is always of the same type; yet the second century B.C.
enjoyed a rich heritage of architectural forms, and lack of variety in this and other details of ornamentation was due, not to
dearth of materials, but to the prevailing taste.

The earliest known example of the decoration of the second or Architectural Style, is on the walls of the Small Theatre, which was built soon after 80 B.C. The style remained in vogue till the middle of the reign of Augustus; it may be loosely characterized as the wall decoration of the first century B.C. It shows an interesting development from simpler to richer and more complex forms. The more elaborate and finished designs are not so well exemplified at Pompeii as in Rome, where two beautiful series have been found, both dating from the earlier part of the reign of Augustus. One series is in the so-called house of Livia or Germanicus on the Palatine. The other was found in a house on the right bank of the Tiber, excavated in 1878; the paintings were removed to the new Museo delle Terme. The specimen shown in Plate XI, however, is from a Pompeian wall; the room in which it was found opens off from the peristyle of a house in the fifth Region (V. i. 18).

The oldest walls of the second style closely resemble those of the first, with this characteristic difference: the imitation of marble veneering is no longer produced with the aid of relief; color alone is employed, upon a plane surface, as in the cella of the temple of Jupiter (Fig. 20). The earlier division of the wall into three parts is retained, but the painted cornice, no longer restricted to the dentil type, appears in a variety of forms. The base also is treated with greater freedom. Frequently it is painted in strong projection, as if the rest of the wall above it were further from the eye, while upon the shelf thus formed are painted columns reaching to the ceiling and seemingly in front of the main part of the wall; such columns and pillars, with Corinthian capitals, are seen in Plate XI, at the right and the left.

Thus the designs of this style at first comprised only simple elements, a wall made up of painted blocks or panels with a dado painted in projection supporting columns that seemed to carry an architrave on which the ceiling rested; there is an excellent example in the house of the Labyrinth, on the walls of a room at the rear of the garden. But the designs gradually became more complex, partly through the differentiation of the simple elements, partly through the introduction of new motives, until

PLATE XI. — SPECIMEN OF WALL DECORATION. SECOND OR
ARCHITECTURAL STYLE

a complete architectural system was developed. This system differs from that of the fourth style, which is also architectural, in that it adheres in the main to actual or possible structural forms, while those of the fourth style are fantastic in their proportions and arrangement.

In this process of development two clearly defined tendencies become manifest, one affecting the treatment of the upper division of the wall, the other the elaboration of a characteristic motive which now first appears, a framework for the principal painting ; for architectural designs are well adapted for the display of pictures, and wall paintings now begin to have a prominent place in Pompeian decoration.

The upper division tends more and more to be represented as an open space, behind the plane of projection in which the main part appears. Thus in Plate XI we see on either side a silver vase with fruits and vine leaves, standing on the cornice of the main wall, in the open. Often the upper space is painted blue, as if one caught a glimpse of the sky above the wall ; sometimes the outline of a wall further beyond is seen, or columns in the rear connected with those in front by a decorative framework ; and not infrequently small architectural designs, in perspective, rest upon the cornice where the vases are shown in our plate. But in all the designs of this style, complex as well as simple, the threefold division of the wall carried over from the first style is retained ; very often the distinction between the base, main wall, and upper portion is emphasized by painting them so that they seem to be in three planes of projection.

The ornamental framework for the painting, consistently with the architectural character of the decoration as a whole, is generally conceived as a pavilion projecting from the wall ; so in Plate XI, where we see two columns sustaining a roof, upon the front of which winged figures stand, each with a hand extended upward to the entablature of the large pillars at the sides. The design of the pavilion is suggested by that of a shrine, such a shrine as the one in the apse of the sanctuary of the City Lares (Fig. 40).

This conception is here borne out by the subject of the painting, which represents a statue of Dionysus resting, ivy-crowned,

with a thyrsus in his left hand ; the right hand is thrown grace-
fully over the head, and at the feet of the god the lifelike figure
of a panther is seen.   The round high pedestal supporting the
group is in the open, and the background affords a charming
vista among the trees.

This framing of the principal painting led further to the
division of the body of the wall vertically into three sections,
a broad central section, included within the outline of the
pavilion, and two panels, one at each side.   The arrangement
is well illustrated in our plate, the side panels of which are
adorned with painted statues of tastefully draped figures, one of
them holding a lyre.   The later styles of decoration retained
this symmetrical division of the wall space, which made prominent the picture of greatest interest without detracting from the
finish of the decorative setting ; but in the fourth style it is often
obscured by the intricacy of the designs.

The third style came into vogue during the reign of Augustus,
and was prevalent until about 50 A.D.; we shall call it the
Ornate Style, from its free use of ornament.   It was developed
out of the second style in the same way that the second style
was developed out of the first; but the transition was not accomplished at Pompeii, which, like the provincial cities of our
day, received its fashions from the great centres.

The characteristics of the Ornate Style, as regards both the
main design and the ornamentation, may easily be perceived
from the example presented in Fig. 252, especially if this is
viewed in contrast with the specimen of the preceding style
shown in Plate XI.   The architectural design has now lost all
semblance of real construction.   Columns, entablatures, and
other members are treated conventionally, as subordinate parts
of a decorative scheme ; they are, with few exceptions, reduced
to narrow bands or stripes of color dividing the surface of the
wall.   The elaborate border of the central painting suggests
a pavilion, yet the projecting base, which in the second style
gave this design its significance, is lacking.   Hardly less noteworthy is the treatment of the upper portion of the wall. Fanciful architectural forms and various ornaments stand out against
a white background, suggestive of the open sky; yet in our

example, as often in this style, there is no organic connection between the decoration of the main part of the wall and that of the ceiling.

Every part of the framework of the third style is profusely ornamented. Among the ornamental forms are many of Egyptian origin, as figures of Egyptian priests, sistrums, sphinxes, and creatures of the Nile, whence we infer that this style was developed in Alexandria. Early in the reign of Augustus, in consequence of the relations with Egypt following the battle of Actium, a new impulse may well have been given to the introduction into Italy of Alexandrian art.

The specimen of the third style shown in Fig. 252 is from the beautiful decoration of the house of Spurius Mesor, portions of which are well preserved. The base of our specimen consists of two parts, a lower border and a broad stripe of black divided into sections of different shapes and sizes by lines of light color. In the small sections ornaments are seen painted in delicate shades, two of them being faces.

The large painting presents a mythological scene, but the subject is not clear. The priestess seems to be performing a ceremony of expiation in order to free from the taint of some crime the young man who, with a wreath on his head and a sword, pointed downward, in his right hand, bends over the hind just slain as a sacrifice. The colors are subdued and effective; the painting from the technical point of view is among the best found at Pompeii.

Around the painting are narrow black stripes separated by white lines; in the broader stripe underneath, between the columns, are two light blue birds upon a dull red ground. The small squares in the flat cornice above are of many colors, shades of green, pink, and brown predominating. The broad panels on either side of the painting are of the color often called Pompeian red; they have an ornamented border, and a small winged figure in the centre. The stripe below these shows vases and other ornaments on an orange-yellow ground; that above, interrupted by the cornice over the painting, is black, with various ornaments, as baskets of fruit, sistrums, and geese, painted in neutral colors. Among the ornaments of the upper

Fig. 252. — Specimen of wall decoration. Third or Ornate Style.
From the house of Spurius Mesor.

part of the wall, festoons of leaves, vines, vases, parrots, and griffins can be distinguished, painted in light shades of brown, blue, green, and yellow.

The effect of the Ornate Style, with its symmetrical forms and variety of detail, is pleasing; but the free use of neutral tones gives the walls a somewhat cold and formal appearance when we bring into contrast the warm coloring of the next period.

The fourth or Intricate Style first appears about the middle of the first century A.D. It started, as did the third, with the symmetrical division of the wall developed in the second style; it differs from the third in that it always retained a sense of architectural form. The columns are often fluted, as in a specimen in the Naples Museum (Fig. 253). The entablatures and coffered ceilings, light and airy as they often seem, have nevertheless a suggestion of reality; we know that architectural forms are presented, and not mere stripes of color. Yet the difference between the fourth and the second style is no less apparent. In the latter the architectural designs are not inconsistent with real construction; in the former the imagination of the designer had free scope, producing patterns so fantastic and intricate that the fundamental idea at the basis of the wall divisions seems entirely lost sight of at times.

The preference for architectural forms was carried so far that between the large panels of black, red, or yellow, vertical sections of wall were left which were filled with airy structures on a white background; the parts represented as nearest the beholder were painted yellow, those further back were adorned with all the colors of the rainbow, thus forming a kind of color perspective (Fig. 254). The designs of the main part were extended into the upper division, and frequently the whole wall appears as an intricate scaffolding, partially concealed by the large panels; these sometimes have the appearance of tapestries hanging suspended from the scaffolding, and are so treated, as in the case of the curtains shown in Plate XII. The fundamental conception of the decorative system is lost when the background of the upper part and of the airy scaffoldings is no longer left white, but painted the same color as the rest of the wall, so that the effect of distance and perspective is obscured. Occasionally, also, the architectural framework of the upper portion of the wall has no connection with that of the main part.

The ornaments of the fourth style were taken largely from the domain of plastic art. Groups of statuary as well as single figures appear either upon projecting portions of the architectural framework, as in Fig. 253, or in the background. They

Fig. 253.—Specimen of wall decoration.   Fourth style.

are frequently painted yellow, suggesting the gilding applied to ancient statues, particularly those of bronze, and present a striking contrast to the masses of strong color in the large panels and the brilliant shades of the architectural designs. They are in harmony with the taste of the period, which, as we have seen, manifested a fondness for ornamentation in stucco relief, the effect of which was heightened by the free use of color.

The large panels contained paintings of various sizes, sometimes copies of masterpieces, more often a simple floating figure or a Cupid; groups are also found, as Cupid and Pysche, or a satyr with a bacchante. The appearance of a picture worked in tapestry is given by a border just inside the framework of the panel, as in several of the landscapes of the wall shown in Plate XII.

The fourth style cannot have been derived from the third. It is organically related with the second, out of which it was developed by laying stress on precisely that element, the architectural, the suppression of which gave rise to the third style

of decoration. The most reasonable explanation of the relations
of the four styles, briefly stated, is this : —

The Incrustation Style, a direct offshoot of Hellenistic art, was
prevalent in eastern cities, where it was naturally followed by the
Architectural Style ; this may have been developed at one centre
or, in different phases, at different centres contemporaneously.

Fig. 254.— Specimen of wall decoration. Fourth style.
In the middle panel, mythological scene in which Hercules is the principal figure ; in each
of the panels, a satyr and a bacchante.

At some prominent centre, probably Alexandria, the Architectural Style passed over into the Ornate Style, which was
introduced into Italy in the reign of Augustus and remained in
vogue till the middle of the first century A.D.

Meanwhile, at some other centre of culture, possibly Antioch,
the Architectural Style, by an equally natural course of develop-

ment, had passed over into the Intricate Style, which was first
brought to Pompeii about 50 A.D. and remained in fashion till
the destruction of the city.

The earthquake of the year 63 threw down some buildings
and made necessary the thorough-going repair of many others.
Between that year and 79, more walls were freshly decorated,
probably, than in any previous period of equal length in the
history of the city. For this reason, examples of decoration in
the Intricate Style are much more numerous than might have
been expected from the length of time that it was in vogue;
they give the prevailing cast to the remains of painting in the
ruins, and this style is ordinarily thought of when Pompeian
wall decoration is referred to. The complex designs and brilliant colors form a decorative scheme which is often most effective, although the system of the third style reveals a finer and
more correct taste.

If no remains of the two earlier styles had survived to modern
times, the antecedents and relations of the other two could not
possibly be understood. But with the first two in mind, we are
able to see clearly how the most complex forms of the later
decoration may be reduced, in last analysis, to simple elements.
Even in the example of the Intricate Style given in Plate XII,
we find a suggestion of the threefold division of the wall into
base, main part, and upper part, which was so prominent in the
Incrustation Style; and also an elaborate structural form at the
middle of the wall recalling the pavilion framework of the second style, with a symmetrical arrangement of the architectural
designs on either side, suggesting the panels at the sides of the
principal painting.

The slabs of colored marble in the Incrustation Style are represented by panels for pictures or ornamental forms of all shapes
and sizes; and the architectural designs, so simple at the beginning, have by almost imperceptible changes and additions become decorative patterns so varied and intricate that taken by
themselves they give no hint of their origin.

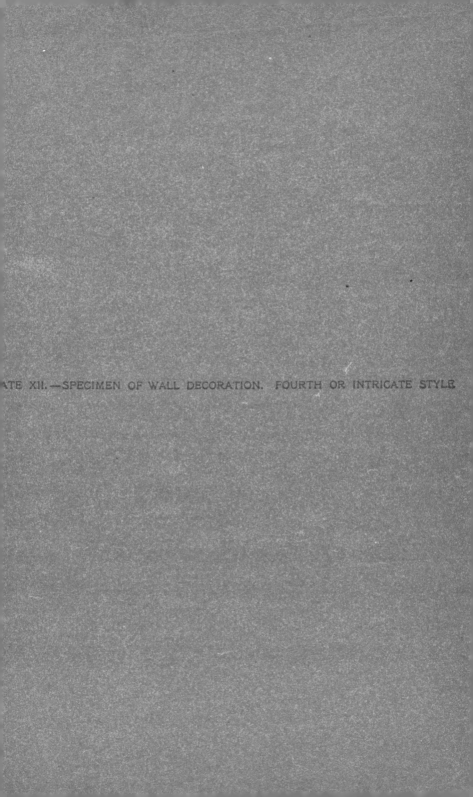

ATE XII.—SPECIMEN OF WALL DECORATION. FOURTH OR INTRICATE STYLE

CHAPTER LIV

THE PAINTINGS

THE hanging of pictures upon the walls seems not to have been in vogue at Pompeii during the period to which the remains belong. The system of decoration left no room for framed paintings, and no traces of any such have been discovered. The paintings which have been preserved at Pompeii, not merely the small groups and single figures introduced to enliven the design, but the large compositions as well, all formed a part of the wall decoration.

The number is relatively large. In the catalogue by Helbig, published in 1868, there are nearly two thousand entries, including a few paintings from Herculaneum and other Campanian sites. The supplement compiled by Sogliano in 1879 records more than eight hundred pictures brought to light in the preceding decade. We are probably safe in estimating the whole number of Pompeian paintings still in existence, or known from description, as about thirty-five hundred.

In all this wealth of examples, however, it is not possible to find any evidence of a progressive development either in composition or in technique. There are indeed slight differences, mainly in regard to technical handling and color scheme, which distinguish the paintings found in the decoration of the third style from those of the other two styles in which paintings appear; but, on the other hand, the distinction between those of the second and those of the fourth style is much less marked.

The period from 80 B.C. to 79 A.D. was as little creative in the field of painting as in that of sculpture. No new types appear, no improvements are worked out; the painter, as the sculptor, was an eclectic, who drew upon the creations of the past as suited his fancy, and contented himself with copying or imitating. In the adaption of paintings to decorative use the artist reproduced either entire compositions or single motives which seemed to answer his purpose. The general preference was for paintings of the Hellenistic age, after the death of Alexander; yet examples of earlier styles are occasionally found, as the Sacrifice of Iphigenia (Fig. 149) and the dramatic scene in which Orestes and Pylades appear before King Thoas (Fig. 175).

New discoveries and the progress of research will sometime, perhaps, make it possible to present a general survey of the Pompeian paintings from the historical and critical point of view. No such comprehensive treatment is yet possible, however, and we must content ourselves with offering a few observations in regard to the distribution of the paintings among the different decorative styles and the classes of subjects represented.

The Incrustation Style, as previously remarked, left no place for paintings upon the walls. Nevertheless, in isolated cases, we find a simple pictorial representation upon the surface of one of the blocks painted in imitation of marble, as if the veins of the stone had run into a shape suggestive of an object, as a vase or a bird; in one instance, curiously enough, a wrestling match is outlined, between Hercules and Antaeus. In the Tufa Period the desire for paintings was satisfied by the mosaic pictures upon the floor.

The earlier walls of the second style in this respect resemble those of the first; the examples in the house of the Labyrinth have no paintings. The later walls, however, are rich in pictures, but those of Pompeii are not so abundantly adorned as those in Rome (p. 452). The elaborate painting shown in the pavilion frame in Plate XI is exceptional among the Pompeian remains of this style.

The great majority of the paintings are found upon walls of the third and fourth styles. On the older walls of the third style, as we have seen, the principal painting appears in a frame, the design of which is taken from that of the conventional pavilion of the second style. In later examples the close relation between the picture and the frame is no longer maintained; the frame simply encloses a large panel of uniform color, in the middle of which a relatively small picture is seen. This arrangement was carried over into the fourth style, but the conception of a pavilion frame is entirely lost sight of ; the painting is in the middle of a large panel of brilliant color, around which the architectural framework is extended. A Pompeian room well decorated in either of the later styles contained four of these prominent paintings, in case there was no door at the middle of one of the sides ; if a door interfered, there were only three.

Paintings were also placed in the divisions of the wall at the right and the left of the central panel. In Plate XI we noticed a single figure on either side of the pavilion, but such additions are rare in the second style. In the third style the side panels are uniformly adorned with paintings. In Fig. 252 the small figure in the middle of the panel at the left is a Cupid ; frequently a flying swan is seen, or a landscape lightly sketched in monochrome on the ground of the panel. Sometimes the painting is set off by a separate frame ; if this is round, a bust is usually represented. Groups of two figures were preferred for the side panels of the fourth style, the favorite subject being a satyr and a bacchante, as in Fig. 254 ; these sometimes appear as busts, but are more often represented as floating figures.

Characteristic of the fourth style, in respect to the distribution of paintings, is the use of single figures and simple compositions to add life to the fantastic architectural designs in the upper part of the wall and in the divisions between the large panels. Here we may see satyrs and bacchantes, young girls and solemn-visaged men with implements of sacrifice; the figures appear in great variety of type and subject. Sometimes groups are broken up, and the elements of a mythological scene, as that of Admetus and Alcestis, are distributed as single figures in the architectural framework.

At the time of the eruption the fondness for pictorial representations was increasing, and they were being introduced into every part of the decoration, including the frieze of the main part of the wall, the use of which in this way commenced in the time of the third style (Fig. 252), and the stripe below, between the main part of the wall and the base (Fig. 254);

how elaborate this intermediate decoration might become we have already seen in the case of the house of the Vettii.

Frequently in the fourth style the lower part of the architectural framework separating two large panels appears to be closed, as in Plate XII, by a narrow panel, above which a painting is seen. The pictures found in these places often represent still life. Seafights are also a favorite subject; such may be seen in the temple of Isis, the Macellum, and one of the rooms in the house of the Vettii. Generally on the walls of the fourth style, wherever there is available space, we find small pictures in great variety, the most common being landscapes, simply painted, with the use of few colors.

It is by no means easy to make a satisfactory classification of Pompeian paintings according to subject. Nevertheless, with a few exceptions, they may be roughly grouped in four general classes, mythological paintings, genre paintings, landscapes, and still life. Most of the large and important pictures belong to the first class. The mythological paintings will therefore be discussed at somewhat greater length; the other three classes will require only a brief characterization.

Fig. 255. — A fruit piece, Xenion.

The still-life paintings represent all kinds of meat, fish, fowl, and fruits. According to Vitruvius, this kind of picture was called Xenion. The reason given for the name recalls a curious custom of ancient Greece. When a guest, *xenos*, was received into a Greek home, says this writer, he was invited to sit at the table for one day. After that provisions were furnished to him uncooked, and he prepared his own meals. A portion of unprepared victuals thus came to be called *xenion*, 'the stranger's portion,' and the name was afterwards transferred to pictures in which such provisions appear. A fruit piece, now in the Naples Museum, is shown in Fig. 255.

Landscapes are numerous and of all sizes. Occasionally a garden wall is covered with a single large painting, in which villas, gardens, roads, and harbors are realistically presented. Such pictures belong to a class of landscapes that originated in Italy; the name of the artist who first painted them is probably Sextus Tadius, but the reading of the passage of Pliny the Elder, in which the name occurs, is uncertain. The finest example, however, is not at Pompeii, but in the villa of Livia, at Prima Porta, near Rome, the decoration of which has by some been attributed to Tadius (or Ludius) himself. The examples found at Pompeii all belong to the time of the fourth style, and are quite unlike the paintings of the Villa of Livia.

Fig. 256. — A landscape painting.

Large landscapes sometimes have a place in the principal panels of the walls. These are all of Hellenistic origin, and are found almost without exception in the decoration of the third style. They generally represent a quiet nook of woodland, with high cliffs; in the foreground is a shrine — perhaps more than one — with figures of men sacrificing or coming to offer worship.

The great majority of the landscapes, however, are introduced into various parts of the decoration outside of the large panels, and are quite small. In them we see little shrines or villas by the seaside; a river with a bridge on which a traveller appears crossing the stream; or buildings on an island or peninsula in the edge of a body of water, as in Fig. 256. Often they are

2 H

simply light sketches; now and then one of these small landscapes is painted in a peculiar tint, as if the scene were represented by moonlight.

The genre paintings are of special importance on account of
the light they shed on the life and customs of the ancients. A
number have already been described or illustrated in the chapter

Fig. 257. — Group of musicians, one of whom is tuning a lyre.

on the house of the Vettii, and in the part devoted to the trades
and occupations. To these we should add the picture of an
artist in the house of the Surgeon (Fig. 128), and the scenes
from the life of the Forum (Figs. 16, 17).

Here belong also the groups in which figures are seen with
a roll of papyrus or a writing tablet, suggestive of literary pur-
suits, and figures with musical instruments. A group of mu-

sicians is shown in Fig. 257, in which are four women, one of whom is tuning a couple of stringed instruments to sound in unison.

In the same class are included two small painted busts not infrequently met with, that of a girl with a writing tablet in her left hand holding the end of a stylus against her lips, as if pondering what to write, and that of a young man with one end

Fig. 258. — Paquius Proculus and his wife.

of a roll of papyrus, in which he has been reading, under his chin. A Pompeian baker, Publius Paquius Proculus, brought these two ideal busts into one painting, substituting for the faces of the youth and maiden those of himself and his wife (Fig. 258). The portraits are realistic, but the faces are not unattractive; that of Proculus seems more kindly and ingenuous than the face of Caecilius Jucundus (Fig. 246).

Two ideal painted busts have recently been found, each of a youth with a roll of papyrus. Their chief interest lies in the fact that each roll is provided with a narrow tag or label, of the sort that the Romans called *index*, on which the names *Plato* and *Homerus* can be plainly read. The two types of face well correspond with the trend of taste suggested by the titles: the delicate features and upturned gaze of the one indicate a poetic temperament; the other has a high forehead and an air of meditation, appropriate for a student of philosophy.

The mythological paintings rarely present rapid movement. To the few exceptions belong the two familiar pictures placed opposite each other in the tablinum of the house of Castor and Pollux, Achilles among the daughters of Lycomedes on the island of Scyros, and the quarrel between Achilles and Agamemnon. Only part of the latter painting is preserved, but both are strong compositions, and are repeated on other walls.

Scenes of combat, the interest of which lies in the display of physical force, are still more infrequently met with, and seem out of harmony with the prevailing taste. Two pictures from Herculaneum represent Hercules putting forth his strength; in one he is struggling with the Nemean lion, in the other carrying the Erymanthian boar. The few paintings of this kind at Pompeii are badly preserved. In two of them Meleager appears, engaged in combat with the boar; in another we see Achilles before the walls of Troy with drawn sword in one hand, with the other grasping by the hair Troilus, an effeminate Trojan youth, attired in Oriental fashion, who mounted on his horse is vainly trying to escape; a fourth represents a combat between a heavy-armed warrior and an Amazon. But such paintings are the more conspicuous by reason of their rarity, and those that have thus far been discovered are all found upon walls of the third style.

A much larger number of mythological compositions represent a moment of dramatic interest, the artist relying for his effect upon the bearing and facial expression of the persons appearing in the scene. The interest is purely psychological, and several of the pictures that have been preserved give us an exceedingly favorable idea of the ability of ancient painters to express emotion, especially when we remember that these paintings are merely decorative copies of masterpieces the originals of which in most cases had probably never been seen by the workmen who painted the copies on the walls.

Among the more familiar examples is the face of Orestes in the painting found in the house of the Citharist (Fig. 175), and that of Io, watched by Argus, in the Macellum. Emotion is expressed with even greater skill in the face of Io in a·painting of the temple of Isis. The goddess welcomes the wanderer to Egypt after her long season of suffering; the traces of the suffering are clearly seen, yet are illumined by the ineffable and serene joy of final deliverance.

One of the most beautiful specimens of ancient painting is a fragment, badly preserved, in the tablinum of the house of Caecilius Jucundus. The composition probably represented Priam turning back toward Troy with the body of Hector, which he had just ransomed. In the fragment, shown in Fig. 259, we see the aged Hecuba, together with a daughter or maidservant, looking with unutterable anguish from an upper window down upon the scene. The gray-haired

Fig. 259. — Hecuba with a younger companion looking from an upper window as Priam brings back the body of Hector.

queen, whose features still retain much of their youthful beauty, gazes upon the dust-stained body of her son with grief too deep for tears.

In the majority of paintings the subjects of which are taken from myths the characters are represented either in a relation of rest, not suggestive of intense emotion, or in a lasting situation of dramatic interest, which is devoid of momentary excitement and does not suggest the display of evanescent feeling. The situation is sometimes cheerful, sometimes calculated to arouse sympathy; if the characters were not mythological, the scenes might pass for those of everyday life. Thus we see Narcissus

looking at the reflection of his face in a clear spring in the forest; Polyphemus, on the seashore, receiving from the hands of
a Cupid a letter sent by Galatea; and Apollo playing on the lyre
for Admetus, while the herd grazes around him.

To the same series of cheerful or idyllic pictures belong the
Selene bending over the sleeping Endymion; Paris and Oenone
on Mt. Ida, Paris cutting the name of his sweetheart in the bark
of a tree; and Perseus with Andromeda looking at the reflection
of the head of Medusa in a pool. With these we may class
also the representations of Bacchus as he moves along with his
rollicking band and suddenly comes upon the sleeping Ariadne;
and Hercules with Omphale, sometimes sitting in woman's attire
beside her and spinning, sometimes staggering in his cups or
lying drunk upon the ground while she stands or sits near him.

Examples of a pathetic situation are equally abundant. We
find Aphrodite caring for the wounded Adonis, and Cyparissus
grieving over the dead stag. The pathos of the scene, however,
is not always so obviously suggested. The familiar painting of
Europa represents the maiden playfully sitting upon the bull,
which one of her girlish companions is caressing. The situation, from one point of view, is idyllic, yet it brings to mind the
unhappy fate of the girl, borne far away from home over the
sea to a distant land, and the effect is heightened by giving
her a wonderfully beautiful form.

Not infrequently a similar result is produced by placing figures
of incongruous type in sharp contrast; so in the oft-repeated
composition in which the beautiful Thetis in elegant attire sits
in the workshop of Hephaestus, looking at the shield which the
rough and grimy smith is finishing for Achilles. In another
composition Pasiphaë is seen in the shop of Daedalus, who is
building the wooden cow; and a similar idea of contrast must
have been present in the mind of the artist who painted Danaë
after she had been cast ashore in a chest on the island of Seri-
phus, sitting on the beach with little Perseus in her lap, while
two fishermen standing near make inquiry concerning her strange
fate.

The symmetrical arrangement of the paintings in a Pompeian
room could hardly have failed to influence the choice of com-

positions for the principal panels, especially in cases in which mythological scenes were to be represented. Sometimes, though not so frequently as might have been expected, pictures were grouped according to subject. We have already noticed the relation of two paintings, in the house of Castor and Pollux, in which Achilles is the principal figure. The first of these, Achilles among the daughters of Lycomedes, is found in a room of another house in a group of three; one of the companion pieces represents Thetis in the smithy of Hephaestus looking at the weapons which are being made for Achilles, while in the other she is seen riding over the sea on a Triton, bringing them to her son. There is another group of three pictures related by subject in a room in the house of the Vettii; they belong to the Theban cycle, and represent the infant Hercules strangling the serpents, the death of Pentheus, and the binding of Dirce.

Similarity of scene and of treatment influenced the selection of paintings for a room much more often than unity of subject. A good illustration is the pair of pictures several times found together, one of which represents Polyphemus on the beach receiving from a Cupid a letter written by Galatea; in the other Aphrodite is seen on the seashore fishing, with Cupids all about her. The suggestion of Love is common to both paintings, but the juxtaposition of the two as counterparts is due to the similarity of scene. Opposite the picture of Europa referred to above, is a Pan playing on his pipe, with nymphs around him; the two pictures, which appear in a room of the third style, from the decorative point of view form an effective pair.

A sleeping room of the same style — though in respect to grouping no difference between the styles is apparent — offers an interesting example of a double group. The four principal paintings form two pairs. In one pair we see, on one side, Hercules in the garden of the Hesperides approaching an altar around which three maidens are standing; on the other, a shrine of Artemis in a forest with three worshippers drawing near, one of whom brings a garland. The two pictures harmonize in the character of the scenery and in the arrangement of the figures.

The effectiveness of the other pair as a decorative counterpart can be seen in our illustrations; the subject of one of the

paintings is the fate of the pipes which Athena cast aside
(Fig. 260), and of the other the fall of Icarus (Fig. 261).

In the first of the two pictures we have one of the few extant
examples of a kind of painting associated with the name of
Philostratus, in
which different
scenes representing
the successive stages
of an action are
united in one compo-
sition.

Fig. 260. — Athena's pipes and the fate of Marsyas.

In the foreground
at the left sits
Athena, with her
shield on the ground
beside her, playing
the double pipe; a
nymph in front ris-
ing from the surface
of a stream holds up
a mirror in which the
goddess may see re-
flected the beauty of
her face.

The next two
scenes lie just across
the brook. At the
foot of the cliff sits
the divinity of the
country, Phrygia, in
which the story of
Marsyas is localized.

Above, at the left, we see the satyr with a shepherd's crook in
his left hand blowing a Pan's pipe; he has not yet espied the
pipes thrown away by Athena.

At the right he appears again, near the tree, having found
the pipes discarded by the goddess and picked them up. Lastly,
in the middle of the background, we see him playing the pipes

in the presence of the Muses, who are serving as judges in the contest of skill between the satyr and Apollo.

The final scene with the flaying of Marsyas, which was sometimes represented in sculpture, and appears also in several Pompeian paintings, is here omitted.

The inner connection of the other picture is not so clear. It is perhaps a confused form of a composition in which Icarus, lying on the ground after his fall, was the central figure; the local divinities and natives of the region were looking upon the body of the hapless youth with pity; while Daedalus, hovering in the air above, was trying to find the spot where he had fallen.

Our artist, however, thinking to heighten the effect, represented Icarus as plunging head-long through the air,

Fig. 261. — The fall of Icarus.

with the result shown in the illustration; neither Daedalus nor the figures in the foreground seem yet to have become aware of the catastrophe.

We have found two other paintings, the composition of which was evidently altered by the decorative painter in order to make the effect more striking, — the nuptials of Zeus and Hera on

Mt. Ida, and the sacrifice of Iphigenia, both from the house of the Tragic Poet. Such changes make plain the essentially decorative character of the great majority of the Pompeian paintings.

PART VI

THE INSCRIPTIONS OF POMPEII

CHAPTER LV

IMPORTANCE OF THE INSCRIPTIONS. — MONUMENTAL
INSCRIPTIONS AND PUBLIC NOTICES

THE inscriptions discovered at Pompeii number more than six thousand. They cover a wide field, ranging from commemorative tablets put up at public expense to the scribblings of idlers upon the plastered walls. It would be an exaggeration to say that they contribute to our knowledge of antiquity much that is new; their value lies rather in the insight which they give into the life of the city and its people.

In one respect the evidence derived from inscriptions, though often of the most fragmentary character, is especially satisfactory. We feel that we are handling original documents, without the intervention of that succession of copyists which stands between the author of a Greek or Roman masterpiece and the modern reader. The shapes of the letters and the spelling are just as they were left by the stonecutter or the scribbler; the various handwritings can still be as plainly distinguished on the charred tablets of Caecilius Jucundus as though the signatures were witnessed only yesterday. Through the inscriptions we are brought into contact with the personality of the Pompeians as in no other way.

The inscriptions may be classified either according to the subject matter or according to the form in which they appear, whether cut in stone, or painted, or scratched upon a smooth surface with a stylus. No detailed classification need be given here; it will be sufficient for our purposes to discuss the main divisions briefly under four heads, — monumental inscriptions and

475

public notices, graffiti, and inscriptions relating to business
affairs.

Monumental inscriptions include those which are cut in hard
material and are intended to be read by all who see them.
They are found at Pompeii chiefly in or upon public buildings,
on pedestals of statues and on sepulchral monuments. They
are characterized by extreme brevity. A few are in the Oscan
language, the rest are in Latin. The more important examples
have been presented in the preceding pages in connection with
the monuments to which they belong. A list of them is given
in the Index under "Inscriptions."

The public notices are painted upon the walls along the sides
of the streets, ordinarily in a bright red color; a few are in
black. The most important are the election notices, in which
a candidate is recommended for a public office. These are
about sixteen hundred in number, and the names of more than
a hundred different candidates appear in them.

The election notices fall into two classes, distinguished both
by the style of writing and by the manner of expression, —
earlier, from the time of the Republic, and later, belonging to
the Imperial period. The shapes of the letters in those of the
former class are irregular, and bear the mark of an unpractised
hand. The later notices, on the contrary, have a more finished
appearance; they are executed in a kind of calligraphic style
that suggests the employment of skilled clerks who made the
painting of electoral recommendations a part of their business.
We have already met with the name of one painter of notices
who signed his work, Aemilius Celer (p. 217). His house has
been discovered, near the northeast corner of the ninth Region;
it was identified by means of an inscription painted on the outside : *Aemilius Celer hic habitat*, — 'Aemilius Celer lives here.'

The language of the earlier recommendations is of the simplest. We find the name of the candidate with no suggestion
of praise excepting occasionally the letters *v. b.*, for *virum
bonum*, 'good man.' The name of the office is given in an
abbreviated form, but that of the person who makes the recommendation nowhere appears. In one example the elements of

the common formula *o. v. f.*, for *oro vos, facite*, are given almost in full: *M. Marium aed. faci., oro vos,* — 'Make Marcus Marius aedile, I beg of you.' The following notice appears on Stabian Street in letters nearly 8 inches high: P · FVR · II · V · IB · O · IF, that is *Publium Furium duumvirum, virum bonum, oro vos, facite,* — 'Make Publius Furius duumvir, I beg of you; he's a good man.'

Some of the later election notices are almost equally brief, presenting merely the name of the candidate, the office for which he is recommended, and the formula *o. v. f.*, as in this instance: *Herennium Celsum aed[ilem] o. v. f.,* — 'Make Herennius Celsus aedile, I beg of you.' Occasionally even the formula is omitted, and we have simply the name of the candidate and of the office, both invariably in the accusative case, as *Casellium aed.*, which appears in several places, and *M. Holconium Priscum II. vir. i. d.*

More frequently the recommendation includes a reference to the good qualities of the candidate. Sometimes he is simply styled 'a good man,' as in the earlier notices; but the most common formula in this connection is *d. r. p.*, for *dignum re publica*, 'worthy of public office.' In some instances the characterization is more definite. More than one candidate is affirmed to be 'an upright young man' (*iuvenem probum*), or 'a youth of singular modesty' (*verecundissimum iuvenem*). In regard to one aspirant for office we are informed that 'he will be the watch-dog of the treasury' — *hic aerarium conservabit*.

The names of those who make the recommendations often appear in the later notices. Now and then individuals assume the responsibility, as Vesonius Primus (p. 388), or Acceptus and Euhodia (p. 335). The candidate's neighbors are sometimes represented as favoring his election; so in the case of Claudius Verus: *Ti. Claudium Verum II. vir. vicini rogant,* — 'His neighbors request the election of Tiberius Claudius Verus as duumvir.' This Verus must have been either a very popular man or an energetic candidate; electoral recommendations are painted on all sides of his house — the extensive establishment in the ninth Region known as the house of the Centenary.

The class of election notices in which we find the members of a craft united in the support of a candidate has been sufficiently illustrated in another connection (p. 376). To these we may add a recommendation found on a wall facing the temple of Isis : *Cn. Helvium Sabinum aed. Isiaci universi rog[ant]*, — 'The worshippers of Isis, as a body, request the election of Gnaeus Helvius Sabinus as aedile.' A suburb also might have a candidate, as in the following instance : *M. Epidium Sabinum aed. Campanienses rog.*, — 'The inhabitants of the Pagus Campanus ask for the election of Marcus Epidius Sabinus as aedile.'

Sometimes all those who are engaged in an occupation are urged to support a candidate. 'Innkeepers, make Sallustius Capito aedile,' we read in one notice. In others, various classes of citizens having a common bond, as the ballplayers, and the dealers in perfumes, are exhorted to work for the election of a candidate presumably favorable to their interests. In one instance there is a direct appeal to an individual, involving a pledge of future support : *Sabinum aed[ilem], Procule, fac, et ille te faciet*, — 'Proculus, make Sabinus aedile, and he will do as much for you.'

In view of the deep interest in the municipal elections, revealed by these notices, it is not surprising to find that the support of a candidate by a man of unusual prominence was extensively advertised. In three different parts of the city the attention of voters was directed to the fact that Suedius Clemens, the commissioner sent by Vespasian to decide the ownership of certain plots of ground (p. 399), favored the election of Epidius Sabinus as duumvir. One of the notices reads : *M. Epidium Sabinum II. vir. iur. dic. o. v. f., dignum iuvenem, Suedius Clemens sanctissimus iudex facit vicinis rogantibus*, — 'At the request of the neighbors, Suedius Clemens, most upright judge, is working for the election of Marcus Epidius Sabinus, a worthy young man, as duumvir with judiciary authority. He begs of you to elect this candidate.'

So public a method of pressing a candidacy put a formidable weapon into the hands of the candidate's enemies, and the form of a recommendation was sometimes used against an office seeker with telling effect. *Vatiam aed. furunculi rog.*, — 'The sneak thieves request the election of Vatia as aedile,' we find conspicuously painted on a wall on Augustales Street. According to other notices near by, 'The whole company of late drinkers' (*seribibi universi*) and 'all the people who are asleep' (*dormientes universi*) favored the candidacy of the same unhappy Vatia. The last notice which we shall present in this connection may have been painted on the order of the girl who appears in it: *Claudium II. vir. animula facit*, — 'His little sweetheart is working for the election of Claudius as duumvir.' The reference is probably to the Tiberius Claudius Verus mentioned above.

The other kinds of public notices are represented by relatively few examples. Of special interest are the announcements of gladiatorial combats, which were discussed in a previous chapter (p. 215). Next in importance are perhaps the advertisements of buildings to rent. One of these, relating to the Elephant Inn, has already been mentioned (p. 392). We present here two others, which have to do with large properties. The first, which has now disappeared, was painted on a wall in the sixth Region, at the south end of the third Insula. It reads as follows : —

INSULA ARRIANA
POLLIANA CN. ALLEI NIGIDI MAI
LOCANTUR EX K[alendis] IULIS PRIMIS TABERNAE
CUM PERGULIS SUIS ET CENACULA
EQUESTRIA ET DOMUS. CONDUCTOR
CONVENITO PRIMUM, CN. ALLEI
NIGIDI MAI SER[vum].

'To rent, from the first day of next July, shops with the floors over them, fine upper chambers, and a house, in the Arrius Pollio block owned by Gnaeus Alleius Nigidius Maius. Prospective lessees may apply to Primus, slave of Gnaeus Alleius Nigidius Maius.'

The word *equestria*, translated 'fine,' is used colloquially with *cenacula*, in the sense 'fit for a knight.' The Insula named after Arrius Pollio was thought by Fiorelli to be the so-called house of Pansa, across the street from the block on which the advertisement was found. The identification may be correct, but a notice painted in so prominent a place might refer to a block in any part of the city.

The following inscription was found in the last century near the Amphitheatre, on a wall of the extensive establishment named from it the villa of Julia Felix : —

IN PRAEDIS IULIAE SP. F. FELICIS
LOCANTUR
BALNEUM VENERIUM ET NONGENTUM, TABERNAE, PERGULAE,
CENACULA EX IDIBUS AUG. PRIMIS IN IDUS AUG. SEXTAS, ANNOS
CONTINUOS QUINQUE
S. Q. D. L. E. N. C.

'To let, for the space of five years, from the fifteenth day of next August to the fifteenth day of the sixth August thereafter, the Venus bath, fitted up for the best people, shops, rooms over shops, and second story apartments in the property owned by Julia Felix, daughter of Spurius Julius.'

The bath may have received its name from Venus Pompeiana. The word *nongentum* is difficult to understand. The interpretation given is based upon a passage of Pliny the Elder, from which we understand that in colloquial language the knights were known as 'the nine hundred.' A bath 'of the nine hundred' would then be one designed to attract the patronage of the best people. The seven letters at the end of the inscription have not yet been satisfactorily explained.

Advertisements of articles lost or found are also met with. A notice in regard to a stray horse, painted on one of the tombs east of the Amphitheatre, is given on p. 428. On the east side of Insula VIII. v.–vi. we read : —

VRNA AENIA PEREIT · DE · TABERNA
SEIQVIS · RETTVLERIT DABVNTVR
HS LXV · SEI · FVREM
DABIT · VND . . .

'A copper pot has been taken from this shop. Whoever brings it back will receive 65 sesterces. If any one shall hand over the thief ' . . . (the rest of the inscription is illegible).

CHAPTER LVI

THE GRAFFITI

THE graffiti form the largest division of the Pompeian inscriptions, comprising about three thousand examples, or one half of the entire number; the name is Italian, being derived from a verb meaning 'to scratch.' Writing upon walls was a prevalent habit in antiquity, as shown by the remains of graffiti at Rome and other places besides Pompeii, a habit which may be accounted for in part by the use of the sharp-pointed stylus with wax tablets; the temptation to use such an instrument upon the polished stucco was much greater than in the case of pens and lead pencils upon the less carefully finished wall surfaces of our time. Pillars or sections of wall are covered with scratches of all kinds, — names, catchwords of favorite lines from the poets, amatory couplets, and rough sketches, such as a ship, or the profile of a face. The skit, occasionally found on walls to-day,

> 'Fools' names, like their faces,
> Are always seen in public places,'

has its counterpart in the couplet preserved as a graffito both at Pompeii and at Rome : *Admiror, paries, te non cecidisse ruinis, Qui tot scriptorum taedia sustineas,* —

> 'Truly 'tis wonderful, Wall, that you have not fallen in ruins,
> Forced without murmur to bear the taint of so many hands.'

Of a similar vein is a Greek line scratched upon a wall on the Palatine hill in Rome : 'Many persons have here written many things; I alone refrained from writing.'

Taken as a whole, the graffiti are less fertile for our knowledge of Pompeian life than might have been expected. The people with whom we should most eagerly desire to come into direct contact, the cultivated men and women of the ancient city, were not accustomed to scratch their names upon stucco or to confide their reflections and experiences to the surface of a wall. Some of the graffiti, to judge from the height at which we find them above the floor, were undoubtedly made by the hands of boys and girls; for the rest, we may assume that the writers were as little representative of the best elements of society as are the tourists who scratch or carve their names upon ancient monuments to-day. Nevertheless, we gain from these scribblings a lively idea of individual tastes, passions, and experiences.

A few graffiti have reference to events, as the siege of Sulla, in 89 B.C. (p. 234). The most interesting historical examples are those which relate to the conflict between the Pompeians and the Nucerians, in the year 59 A.D. (p. 214). An ardent Pompeian wrote : *Nucerinis infelicia,* — ' Down with the Nucerians!' From a scribbling by a partisan of the other side it appears that the inhabitants of Puteoli sympathized with the Nucerians, while those of Pithecusae — the island of Ischia — favored the Pompeians : *Puteolanis feliciter, omnibus Nucherinis felicia, et uncu*[*m*] *Pompeianis* [*et*] *Pitecusanis,* — ' Hurrah for the Puteolaneans, good luck to all Nucerians; a hook for the Pompeians and Pithecusans!' The hook referred to in this connection was that used by executioners and the attendants of the Amphitheatre in dragging off the dead. Another Pompeian wrote : *Campani, victoria una cum Nucerinis peristis,* — ' Campanians, you were conquered by the same victory with the Nucerians.' The Campani were not the inhabitants of Campania, but of the suburb called Pagus Campanus.

Two inscriptions, attesting the presence of members of the Praetorian Guard in Pompeii, have been previously mentioned (pp. 379, 393). Another praetorian left his name in a house of the eighth Region (VIII. iii. 21): *Sex. Decimius Rufus milis coh*[*ortis*] *V pr*[*aetorianae*] *Ɔ Martialis,* — ' Sextus Decimius Rufus, a soldier of the fifth praetorian cohort, of the century led by Martialis.' To the same division of the army probably belonged a centurion of the first rank, Q. Spurennius Priscus, whose name was found in a house of the first Region (I. iii. 3). The first, fifth, and ninth praetorian cohorts, mentioned in the graffiti, may have come to Pompeii with different emperors, or on different occasions with the same emperor; it is unlikely that the three were united to form a single escort.

Graffiti are sometimes useful for the identification of buildings; so in the case of the Basilica and of several inns. The dated examples throw some light on the age of the stucco on which they are found. They are for the most part late, and afford little help in determining the time of commencement of the various decorative styles; but in several cases they indicate a later limit clearly. In this way we learn that the decoration of the Basilica, in the first style, was finished before October 3, 78 B.C. — how long before we cannot tell; and that in 37 B.C. the plastering of the Small Theatre was already on the walls, decorated in the second style. The gladiatorial graffito in the house of the Centenary (p. 220) proves that the decoration of the room in which it is found — a late example of the second style — was finished before November, A.D. 15. A dated inscription of the reign of Nero is given in the chapter on the house of the Silver Wedding (p. 299).

Several hundred graffiti present merely the name of the scribbler, sometimes with the addition *hic fuit*, — 'was here,' or simply *hic;* as, *Paris hic fuit, Sabinus hic.*

A large number contain a greeting, perhaps in some cases intended for the eye of the person mentioned, as *Aemilius Fortunato fratri salutem,* — 'Aemilius greets his brother Fortunatus.' In this as in other examples it is interesting to note that one brother is designated by the gens name, the other by the cognomen. Sometimes the greeting is the reverse of cordial, as in this instance: *Samius Cornelio, suspendere,* — 'Samius to Cornelius: go hang yourself.' Hardly less naïve is the message to a friend who has died: *Pyrrhus Chio conlegae sal[utem]: moleste fero, quod audivi te mortuom; itaq[ue] vale,* — 'Pyrrhus to his chum Chius: I'm sorry to hear that you are dead; and so, Good-by.'

The most prominent theme of the graffiti is love, which is constantly reappearing, in prose scribblings and in snatches of verse. The verse form is usually the elegiac distich. Some of the lines are taken from the poets; others were made up for the occasion, and not a few couplets were adapted from quotations, as if the would-be versifier found original composition more difficult than he had anticipated.

Several distichs extol the power of love, as the following, which, taken from some unknown poet, is found in several places : *Quisquis amat, valeat, pereat qui nescit amare ; Bis tanto pereat quisquis amare vetat :* —

> 'Good health be with you, lovers all ;
> Who knows not how to love, be cursed ;
> But oh may double ruin fall
> On him who sets out love to worst!'

A similar thought finds expression in a single line, perhaps also a quotation : *Nemo est bellus nisi qui amavit mulierem,* — 'He who has never been in love can be no gentleman.'

Not all the Pompeians, however, viewed the matter so seriously. To the first line of the couplet just quoted a scribbler of a cynical turn in one instance joined a parody, to the effect that those who are in love may well avoid the use of hot baths, on the principle that 'the burnt child dreads the fire,' — *Nam nemo flammas ustus amare potest.*

The uselessness of interference with the course of love is also made prominent. In this distich, apparently from some poet, the scribbler seems to have made a slight change to meet a specific case, substituting *obiurgat* for *custodit* or some similar word : *Alliget hic auras, si quis obiurgat amantes, Et vetat assiduas currere fontis aquas,* —

> 'Whoever has a mind
> To hinder lovers' way,
> Let him go zephyrs bind
> Or running waters stay.'

Ancient lovers nevertheless had their fears, and the following couplet, which is no doubt borrowed from a poet, appears also, in a slightly different form, on a wall in Rome : *Si quis forte meam cupiet violare puellam, Illum in desertis montibus urat Amor,* —

> 'If any man shall seek
> My girl from me to turn,
> On far-off mountains bleak
> May Love the scoundrel burn.'

Of extant elegiac poets Ovid, Propertius, and Tibullus are quoted or paraphrased. Among the quotations is the familiar couplet of Propertius : *Nunc est ira recens, nunc est discedere tempus; Si dolor afuerit, crede, redibit amor,* —

> ' Now is it time to depart,
> Now anger freshly burns;
> When one ceases to feel the smart,
> Believe me, love returns.'

If it was written by a lover after a quarrel, reconciliation was not far off. Another discouraged suitor perhaps consoled himself by writing on the wall of the Basilica this distich from Ovid's "Art of Love," the form of which differs slightly from that given in the manuscripts : *Quid pote tam durum saxso aut quid mollius unda ?   Dura tamen molli saxsa cavantur aqua,* —

> ' What is so hard as rock, or what can be softer than water ?
> Hard rocks nevertheless by water are worn away.'

Amatory inscriptions often have the form of a message or greeting to a loved one, as in this example : *Victoria, vale, et ubique es; suaviter sternutes,* — ' Health to you, Victoria, and wherever you are may you sneeze sweetly,' that is, may good luck follow you. Often the greeting is more ardent, as that to Cestilia : *Cestilia, regina Pompeianorum, anima dulcis, vale,* — ' Cestilia, queen of the Pompeians, sweet soul, greeting to you.' Sometimes the lover avoided writing the lady's name : *Pupa quae bella es, tibi me misit qui tuus est; vale,* — ' Maiden who are so beautiful, he who is yours sent me to you; good-by.' Now and then we find an inscription of this class that leaves an unfavorable impression. The following is repeated several times on the outside of a house in the first Region : *Serenae sodales sal[utem],* — ' Greeting to Serena, from her companions ! '

Spurned lovers also confided their woes to graffiti, sometimes adding an appeal to the obdurate one, as in this wretched couplet, which can scarcely have been taken from a poet; the play upon words in the last clause was apparently intentional : *Si quid amor valeat nostei, sei te hominem scis, Commiseresce mihi, da veniam ut veniam,* —

'If you a man would be, —
   If you know what love can do, —
   Have pity, and suffer me
   With welcome to come to you.'

It was probably a lover in straits who scratched on the wall a
line of the Aeneid (IX. 404) as a prayer to Venus : *Tu, dea, tu
praesens nostro succurre labori,* —

'Thou, goddess, with thy present help
   Our sore distress relieve.'

Another unsuccessful suitor found the lines of a single poet
inadequate to express his feelings, and joined together a couplet
from Ovid (Am. I. viii. 77–78) and one from Propertius (IV. v.
47–48) in order to voice his complaint against a miserly mistress
who barred her door upon all except wealthy lovers. But the
climax is reached in four lines of irregular verse in which the
rejected lover proposes to vent his anger on the goddess of
love herself : 'All lovers, come! I purpose to break the ribs of
Venus and to smash the small of her back with clubs ; if she can
bore a hole in my tender breast, why can I not break her head
with a cudgel?' From the psychological point of view the
complete identification of the goddess with a statue representing her is noteworthy.

Occasionally a pair of lovers left on a wall a record of a meeting ; thus, *Romula hic cum Staphylo moratur,* — ' Romula tarried
here with Staphylus.'   Staphylus, however, was apparently a
flirt ; in the house of Caecilius Jucundus a similar meeting with
another maiden is recorded on a column of the peristyle : *Staphi-
lus hic cum Quieta.*   But Staphylus does not seem to have gained
the confidence of the fair sex to the extent that another Pompeian
gallant did, of whom we find it written : *Restitutus multas de-
cepit saepe puellas,* — 'Restitutus has many times deceived many
girls.'

The names of husband and wife are sometimes joined together,
as in a room of a house in the ninth Region : *L. Clodius Varus,
Pelagia coniunx ;* there is a similar example in a house ruined
by the earthquake of the year 63, *Ba[lbus] et Fortunata, duo
coiuges.*

We find a pleasing instance of marital affection in a graffito in which a lonely wife sends a greeting to an absent husband and other relatives : *Hirtia Psacas C. Hostilio Conopi coniugi suo manuductori et clementi monitori et Diodot[a]e sorori et Fortunato fratri et Celeri suis salutem semper ubique plurimam, et Primigeniae suae salutem*, — 'Hirtia Psacas at all times and in all places sends heartiest greeting to Gaius Hostilius Conops, her husband and guide and gentle adviser, and to her sister Diodota, her brother Fortunatus and her Celer ; and she sends a greeting to her Primigenia, too.' The names of both husband and wife are Greek, *psaças* signifying ' dewdrop,' and *conops* ' gnat.'

Many happenings are chronicled on the walls ; and there are memoranda of every description. The programmes of gladiatorial combats have already been mentioned (p. 217). One man records the result of a trip to Nuceria, where he won at the gaming table — without cheating, he takes pains to add — a sum amounting to $130 : *Vici Nuceriae in alia* (for *alea*) ✗ *DCCCLVS, fide bona*, — 'At Nuceria, I won 855.5 denarii by gaming, fair play.'

Another Pompeian counted the steps as he walked up and down the colonnade at the side of his garden (in the house VII. ii. 41) for exercise ; he recorded 640 paces for ten turns back and forth.

In the peristyle of a house in the first Region the advent of young pigs, or of puppies, is noted : *XV K[alendas] Nov-[embres] Puteolana peperit mascl[os] III, femel[as] II*, — 'On October 17 Puteolana had a litter consisting of 3 males and 2 females.'

The inscriptions relating to business transactions are reserved for another chapter. We may notice here, however, that memoranda of accounts were sometimes scratched on walls, usually containing only the figures indicating measure or price, as in the shops on the south side of the Macellum. The following is from a bakery in the first Region (I. iii. 27): *Oleum, l[ibra], a[ssibus] IV ; palea a. V ; faenum a. XVI ; diaria a. V ; furfure a. VI ; viria I a. III ; oleum a. VI*, — 'Oil, a pound, 4 asses ; straw, 5 asses ; hay, 16 asses ; a day's wages, 5 asses ; bran, 6 asses ; one wreath for the neck, 3 asses ; oil, 6 asses.'

The value of the as varied; in the Early Empire it was nearly equivalent to 1½ pence, or 3 cents.

Children scratched upon walls the alphabet that they were learning. The frequent quotations from Virgil, generally incomplete, are likewise an echo of lessons at school, where this author was carefully studied; we find very often the beginnings of lines at the opening of a book, as *Arma virumque cano*, or *Conticuere omnes.* The first word of the poem of Lucretius, *Aeneadum*, also occurs several times.

Occasionally gnomic quotations are found, in most cases, perhaps, from writers of comedy. Among them is the well-known maxim, *Minimum malum fit contemnendo maximum,* — 'The smallest evil, if neglected, will reach the greatest proportions.' A proverb more concrete in its form of statement is the following : *Moram si quaeres, sparge milium et collige,* — 'If you want to waste your time, scatter millet and pick it up again.'

CHAPTER LVII

INSCRIPTIONS RELATING TO BUSINESS AFFAIRS

THE most important inscriptions relating to business transactions are the receipts, discovered in 1875, which formed a part of the private accounts of L. Caecilius Jucundus (p. 439). They were written on wax tablets, which were carefully packed in a wooden box. The box, which was in the second story of the house, crumbled to pieces when the ash about it was removed; but the tablets, 127 in number, still retained their shape and were taken to the Naples Museum. The wood of the tablets had turned to charcoal, but the writing has been for the most part deciphered. One receipt dates from 15 A.D., another from the year 27; the rest belong to the decade immediately preceding the earthquake, 52–62 A.D. The documents are of the greatest interest as casting light on the business methods of antiquity.

Most of the tablets are triptychs. The three leaves were tied at the back so as to open like the leaves of a book, making six pages (Fig. 262). The average height is about 5 inches, the width varies from 2 to 4 inches. Pages 1 and 6 served as covers, being left smooth and without writing. Pages 2, 3, and 5 were hollowed out, leaving a polished surface with a raised rim around it. On this surface a thin layer of wax was spread, in which the letters were made with a stylus; the writing could be easily read because the wood, which was of a light color, showed through wherever a scratch was made in the wax coating.

Two pages facing each other, 2 and 3, were devoted to the receipt. Page 4, as shown in Fig. 263, was not hollowed out but was divided into two parts by a broad, flat groove running across the middle. When the document was ready to be sealed, the first two leaves were brought together and tied by a thread

which passed around the middle, the ends meeting in the groove
on page 4. In this groove at convenient distances melted wax
was then dropped, on which the witnesses, ordinarily seven in
number, impressed their seals. The names of the witnesses
were written with pen and ink in a line with the seals, parallel
with the sides of the page, sometimes at the right, as in Fig. 263,

Fig. 262. — Tablet with three leaves, opened so as to show the receipt and part of the
memorandum on page 5, restored.

sometimes divided, the first name and the gens name being at
the left of the seal, the cognomen at the right.

This arrangement made it impossible to consult the receipt
without cutting the thread or disturbing the seals of the witnesses. To meet the difficulty a memorandum, which was practically a duplicate receipt, was placed on page 5; this could be
read at any time.

The difference in form between the receipt, on pages 2 and 3,
and the memorandum will be plain from the examples. The
receipt, with few exceptions, is simply a record of an oral ac-

knowledgment in the presence of witnesses that a sum of money was received, *accepti latio*. In nearly all the tablets this acknowledgment and the names of the witnesses, on page 4, are in the same handwriting, which must have been either that of Jucundus himself or of his secretary. It did not matter who wrote the receipt; in case of a dispute the seals of the witnesses would alone be sufficient to prove its genuineness. The memorandum, however, was ordinarily in a different hand,

Fig. 263. — Tablet, restored, with the two leaves containing the receipt tied and sealed, and with the signatures of the witnesses at the right of the seals.

either that of the person who gave the receipt, or of some one authorized to write for him. As it was not under the seals of witnesses, the handwriting might become a matter of importance if any question should arise in regard to the document.

The entire tablet, with its receipt, memorandum, and names and seals of witnesses was called *perscriptio*, 'entry of account.' This word appears ordinarily on the edge of the tablet, with the name of the person who gave the receipt in the genitive case.

Nearly all the tablets record transactions connected with auction sales, the person whose effects were thus disposed of giving

Jucundus a receipt in full for the proceeds of the sale less a commission, *mercede minus*. A few contain receipts for rent which Jucundus paid for the use of property belonging to the city — a fullery (p. 387), the rent of which altogether amounted to 1652 sesterces, about $75 ; a pasture, for the use of which he paid 2675 sesterces, about $130; and a piece of arable land, *fundus*, on which he paid 6000 sesterces, about $300, in rents.

We present an example of both classes of receipts. The first, which we may call Tablet A, was given by a lady, Umbricia Januaria, for the proceeds of an auction sale; it is dated December 12, A.D. 56. The other, Tablet B, is the receipt for the rent of public pasture land and belongs to the year 59 A.D.

TABLET A

Title

Perscriptio Umbriciae Januariae, 'Entry of account of Umbricia Januaria.'

Receipt. Pages 2 and 3

HS n. CC | כככ ∞ XXXVIIII, quae pecunia in stipulatum L. Caecili Iucundi venit ob auctionem Umbriciae Ianuariae mercede minus persoluta habere se dixit Umbricia Ianuaria ab L. Caecilio Iucundo.

Act[um] Pompeis pr[idie] id[us] Dec[embres] L. Duvio, P. Clodio cos.

'Umbricia Januaria declared that she had received from L. Caecilius Jucundus 11,039 sesterces, which sum came into the hands of L. Caecilius Jucundus by agreement as the proceeds of an auction sale for Umbricia Januaria, the commission due him having been deducted.

'Done at Pompeii on the twelfth day of December, in the consulship of Lucius Duvius and Publius Clodius.'

Names of the Witnesses. Page 4

The seals of the witnesses, nine in number, appear in the groove at the middle of the page. The names are in the genitive case, as if dependent on *sigillum*, 'seal.'

Q. Appulei Severi.
M. Lucreti Leri.
Ti. Iuli Abascanti.
M. Iuli Crescentis.
M. Terenti Primi.

M. Epidi Hymenaei.
Q. Grani Lesbi.
T. Vesoni Le. . . .
D. Volci Thalli.

'Seal of Quintus Appuleius Severus, Marcus Lucretius Lerus, Tiberius Julius Abascantius, M. Julius Crescens, M. Terentius Primus, M. Epidius Hymenaeus, Q. Granius Lesbus, Titus Vesonius Le. . . . , D. Volcius Thallus.'

MEMORANDUM. Page 5

L. Duvio Avito, P. Clodio Thrasea cos., pr. id. Decembr. D. Volcius Thallus scripsi rogatu Umbriciae Ianuariae eam accepisse ab L. Caecilio Iucundo HS n. $\overline{XI}$ xxxix ex auctione eius mercede minus ex interrogatione facta tabellarum [signatarum]. Act. Pompeis.

'On December 12, in the consulship of Lucius Duvius Avitus and Publius Clodius Thrasea, I, Decimus Volcius Thallus, having examined the tablets put under seal, at the request of Umbricia Januaria declared in writing that she had received from L. Caecilius Jucundus 11,039 sesterces as the proceeds of an auction sale after deducting his commission. Done at Pompeii.'

Tablet A gives the ordinary form of the receipt and the memorandum. There are occasional variations. A few tablets have only two leaves and four pages. In such cases, the leaves are tied and sealed in the same way as the first two of the triptych, but only half of the fourth page is left for the signatures of the witnesses; the memorandum is written on the other half with pen and ink, and so appears on the outside of the tablet.

In two of the older tablets, dated 27 and 54 A.D., the memorandum, as the receipt, is a record of an oral acknowledgment; it may be that this was the proper legal form in use to the end of the reign of Claudius. In a few of the later examples, as Tablet B, the receipt as well as the memorandum has the form of a voucher in the handwriting of the person who receives the money, or his agent.

TABLET B

RECEIPT. Pages 2 and 3

L. Veranio Hupsaeo, L. Albucio Iusto duumviris iure dic[undo] XIIII K[alendas] Iulias Privatus coloniae Pompeian[orum] ser[vus] scripsi me accepisse ab L. Caecilio Iucundo sestertios mille sescentos septuaginta quinque nummos, et accepi ante hanc diem, quae dies fuit VIII idus Iunias, sester[tios] mille nummos, ob vectigal publicum pasqua [for *pasquorum*].

Act[um] Pom[peis] Cn. Fonteio C. Vipstano cos.

'On June 18, in the duumvirate of L. Veranius Hypsaeus and L. Albucius Justus, I, Privatus, slave of the colony of Pompeii, declared in writing that I had received from L. Caecilius Jucundus 1675 sesterces, and previous to this day, on June 6, I received 1000 sesterces, as rent for the public pasture.

'Done at Pompeii in the consulship of Gnaeus Fonteius and Gaius Vipstanus.'

NAMES OF THE WITNESSES. Page 4

In the groove in the middle of the page are four seals. As the receipt was given for the city, the witnesses were the two duumvirs and the slave Privatus, who received the money. The name of Privatus appears twice with seal, under that of each duumvir. In antiquity municipalities, as well as individuals, owned slaves.

L. Verani Hypsaei
Privati, c. c. V. C. ser. (for *colonorum coloniae Veneriae Corneliae servus*)
L. Albuci Iusti
Privati, c. c. V. C. se.
Chirographum Privati c. c. V. C. ser.

'Seal of Lucius Veranius Hypsaeus; Privatus, slave of the citizens of the colony of Pompeii; L. Albucius Iustus; Privatus, slave of the citizens of the colony of Pompeii.

'Autograph of Privatus, slave of the citizens of the colony of Pompeii.'

MEMORANDUM. Page 5

L. Veranio Hupsaeo L. Albucio Iusto d[uumviris] i[ure] d[icundo] XIV K. Iul. Privatus c. c. V. C. ser. scripsi me acce-

*pisse ab L. Caecilio Iucundo HS ∞ DCLXXV et accepi ante hanc
diem VIII idus Iunias HS ∞ nummos ob vectigal publicum
pasquorum.*

Act. Pom. C. Fonteio C. Vips. cos.

The language of the memorandum is so nearly identical with
that of the receipt that it is unnecessary to add a translation.

A considerable number of the amphorae found at Pompeii
bear inscriptions, generally written with a pen in black ink,
but sometimes painted with a brush in red or white. Most
of them contained wine. The percentage of Greek inscriptions
is large, an evidence of the strength of the Greek population in
the region about the city.

The wine underwent fermentation in large round vats of
baked clay, *dolia*, which stood in the wine cellar of the villa,
cella vinaria, or in a court (p. 358); from these the amphorae
were filled. The vats containing the common wines were ordinarily emptied before the next vintage, when they were needed
for the new wine, but the better sorts were allowed to remain in
the dolia for a longer time. The wine of one Pompeian amphora was left in the vat till after the harvest of the second year:
*C. Pomponio C. Anicio cos., ex fund[o] Badiano, diff[usum] id.
Aug., bimum,* — 'Consulship of Gaius Pomponius and Gaius
Anicius. From the Badian estate. Poured (into amphorae)
August 15. Two years old.' In what year Pomponius and
Anicius were consuls we do not know.

The earliest amphora of which the date is certain was filled
in 25 A.D.: *Cn. Len[tulo] Masinio cos. fund.* The place from
which it came, however, is not so easily determined, since *fund.*
may refer to the town of Fundi, or stand for *fundus,* 'estate,'
the name that followed having been obliterated. The names
of two such estates were lately recovered from amphorae in the
house of the Vettii, *fundus Satrianus* and *fundus Asinianus.*

In addition to the product of Italian vineyards the Pompeians
used also imported wines from the coast of Asia Minor and the
islands near by. One dealer, M. Fabius Euporus, kept wine
from Cnidus, *Cnidium.* Wine from the island of Cos is fre-

quently mentioned, as in this inscription: *Coum vet*[*us*] *P. Appulei Bassi*, — 'Old Coan of Publius Appuleius Bassus.'

Different kinds of wine were sometimes designated by characteristic names. A certain Greek, M. Pomponius Teuponius, produced a brand which he called 'Frenzy Wine' (Λύττιος), as if so strong that it would make the drinker frantic. Another Greek, Timarchus, named one of his wines 'White Drink,' Λευκουνάριον.

An amphora in the house of the Vettii was labelled *Gustaticium*, 'Breakfast Drink'; it no doubt contained *mulsum*, a kind of mead made by mixing honey with wine, which the ancients drank with the first meal of the day. The word *mulsum* occurs on another amphora discovered previously.

Fruits and other edibles of all kinds were kept in amphorae. On one was written: *Oliva alba dulce* (for *olivae albae dulces*) *P. C. E.*, — 'White sweet olives of P. C. E.'; the name cannot be determined from the initials. On other amphorae the words for bean meal (*lomentum*), honey, and lentils appear, the last being designated by the Greek word.

A large number of small jars contained the fish sauces, — *garum*, *liquamen*, and *muria*, — of which the ancients were so fond; reference has already been made to Umbricius Scaurus (p. 15), who seems to have had several establishments for the making of the sauces, conducted by slaves, freedmen, and perhaps by members of his family.

The best quality of *garum*, which was probably a thick preparation, a kind of fish jelly, was designated by the letters *g. f.*, for *garum — flos*, 'garum blossom,' as in the following inscription: *g*[*arum*] — *f*[*los*] *scombr*[*i*] *Scauri ab Eutyche Scauri*, — 'Scaurus's tunny jelly, blossom brand, put up by Eutyches, slave of Scaurus.' We frequently find *liquamen optimum*, 'best liquamen.'

The *muria* was apparently a fish pickle, certain parts of the fish, or certain varieties, being preserved in brine. According to Pliny the Elder some fish sauces were prepared in a special way, to be used by the Jews on fast days; two of these, as already noted, appear in the inscriptions upon Pompeian jars, *garum castum* and *muria casta*.

In these inscriptions upon jars of various sizes the name of
the proprietor is sometimes given, in the genitive case, as *M.
Caesi Celeris*, — 'Of M. Caesius Celer.' The name of the man
to whom the consignment is made is put in the dative, as *Albucio Celso*.

The name of the consignor sometimes follows that of the
consignee, as *liquamen optimum A. Virnio Modesto ab Aga-
thopode*, — 'Best liquamen, for Aulus Virnius Modestus, from
Agathopus.'

An inscription similar to that just mentioned, on an amphora
found in the house of Caecilius Jucundus, illustrates the extent
to which family pride might assert itself in the naming of children : *Caecilio Iucundo ab Sexto Metello*, — 'To Caecilius Jucundus from Sextus Metellus.' The sender and the recipient were
both sons of Lucius Caecilius Jucundus. According to common
usage, one of the sons would have received the name Lucius
Caecilius Jucundus, after the father ; while the other would have
been called Lucius Caecilius, with a cognomen derived perhaps
from the name of the mother. But the prosperous Pompeian
wished to suggest a relationship with the distinguished family
of the Caecilii Metelli, so he named one son Sextus Caecilius
Jucundus Metellus, and the other Quintus Caecilius Jucundus,
the name Quintus being common in the family of the Caecilii
Metelli. The names of the two sons are found together in an
election notice : *Q. S. Caecili Iucundi*, — 'Quintus and Sextus
Caecilius Jucundus.'

Besides the seals which were used in signing documents the
Romans had stamps, *signacula*, which they impressed upon
various articles as a means of identification or as an advertisement.[1] Impressions of such stamps are found upon bricks and
other objects of clay, and in one or two instances upon loaves
of bread. Several charred loaves in the Naples Museum have

[1] The stamps of various kinds, as well as the mason's marks upon stone, are given
in the tenth volume of the *Corpus Inscriptionum Latinarum;* examples found since
this volume was issued are recorded in the Roman *Mittheilungen* and the *Notizie
degli Scavi*. Painted inscriptions and graffiti are published in *C. I. L.* IV. The
receipts of Caecilius Jucundus are given in the first part of the Supplement to this
volume (1898); the second part of the Supplement will contain the inscriptions found
on walls and amphorae since 1871.

2 K

the stamp : [C]*eleris Q. Grani Veri ser.*, — '(Made by) Celer, slave of Quintus Granius Verus.'

The names upon stamps appear regularly in the genitive case, as *N. Popidi Prisci*, spelled backward on the stamp, so that the letters appear in the right order in the impression. Since the time of Fiorelli many houses have been named from the stamps found in them ; in this way the two houses of the Vettii were identified, two stamps being found with the names of Aulus Vettius Restitutus and Aulus Vettius Conviva.

CONCLUSION

CHAPTER LVIII

SIGNIFICANCE OF THE POMPEIAN CULTURE

THE ideals of a nation — the true index of its culture — find expression alike in its laws, its literature, its art, and the environment of daily life. They are a common heritage, which one generation passes on to another with its own increment of change, and their influence extends as far as that of the people whose spirit is manifested in them. Thus it happens that the conditions of culture found in a single city, unless that city, as Athens, had an independent development as a state, are not isolated but are determined in the main by general movements and tendencies, and are reproduced, with local differences, in all places having the same racial and political connections. The local element was more pronounced and more characteristic in ancient than in modern cities; yet, unless the surroundings were exceptionably favorable, we should not be warranted in expecting to find in a small city an isolated development of special significance in art or taste. Pompeii forms no exception to the rule.

The situation of Pompeii was unfavorable to the growth of an indigenous culture. Founded by Samnites, a primitive folk, it lay in the overlapping edges of two great zones of influence, Greek and Roman. It was a small town, which never rose to the dignity even of a provincial capital. It was a seaport, which through marine traffic kept in touch with other cities, especially those of the East, from which fashions of art, religion, and life travelled easily westward. The political institutions of the Pompeians were at first those which they shared in common with the Samnite and Oscan cities of the mountains and the Cam-

499

panian plain, later those imposed upon them by the forceful and levelling administration of Rome. The literature which they read, as we learn from quotations scratched upon the walls, consisted of the Greek and Roman writers of their own or previous periods; not a single line of an Oscan drama or poem has been found. Their art was a reproduction of designs and masterpieces produced elsewhere, — at first under Hellenistic, later under Roman influence, — on a scale commensurate with the limited resources of the place. Finally the countless appliances of everyday life, from the fixed furniture of the atrium to articles of toilet, were not rare and costly objects such as were seen in the wealthy homes of Rome or Alexandria, but those of the commoner sort everywhere in use. Any one of fifty cities might have been overwhelmed in the place of Pompeii, and the results, so far as our knowledge of the ancient culture in its larger aspects is concerned, would not have been essentially different.

The representative rather than exceptional character of the remains at Pompeii make them either of less or of greater value, according as we look at them from different points of view. If we are seeking for the most perfect examples of ancient art, for masterpieces of the famous artists, we do not find them. Many of the Pompeian paintings appeal to modern taste; yet it would be as unfair to judge of the merits of ancient painting from the specimens which are worked into the decorative designs of Pompeian walls as it would be to base an estimate of the value of modern art upon chromos and wall papers. For the noblest creations of ancient art in any field we must look not to provincial towns, but to the great centres of population and of political administration, where genius found encouragement, inspiration, and adequate means. No large city, fortunately for its inhabitants, was visited by such a disaster as that which befell the Campanian town; and the wealth of artistic types at Pompeii bears witness to the universality of art in the Greco-Roman world.

Since these remains are so broadly typical, they are invaluable for the interpretation of the civilization of which they formed a part. They shed light on countless passages of Greek and

Roman writers. Literature, however, ordinarily records only that which is exceptional or striking, while here we find the surroundings of life as a whole, the humblest details being presented to the eye.

Pompeii, as no other source outside the pages of classical authors, helps us to understand the ancient man.

KEY TO PLAN VI

The names of only the more important streets are given on Plan VI. Among the names omitted are those of the continuations of Nola Street, which it is more convenient to regard as a single thoroughfare extending without change of name across the city.

The more important buildings of each Region are given in the order of the Insulae.

Region I

INSULA

i. 5. Inn.
   8. Inn of Hermes.
ii. 24. Wineshop.
    28. House with a grating over the impluvium.
iv. 5. House of the Citharist — casa del Citarista.
v. 2. Tannery.

Region V

INSULA

i. 7. Casa del Torello di Bronzo.
   18. Casa degli Epigrammi.
   26. House of L. Caecilius Jucundus.
   28. House of M. Tofelanus Valens.
ii. 1. Casa della Regina Margherita.
    4. Casa del Triclinio.
    a. House of the Silver Wedding — casa delle Nozze d' Argento.
v. 2. House with a covered atrium.

Region VI

INSULA

Ins. Occidentalis, 1. Inn.
i. 7. House of the Vestals — casa delle Vestali.
   10. House of the Surgeon casa del Chirurgo.
   13. So-called custom-house.
ii. 4. House of Sallust — casa di Sallustio.
    6. Bakery.
    14. House of the Amazons — casa delle Amazoni.

iii. 3. Bakery.
     7. So-called Academy of Music — Accademia di Musica.
    20. Wineshop.
v. 3. House of Neptune — casa di Nettuno.
vi. 1. House of Pansa — casa di Pansa.
vii. 18. House of Adonis — casa di Adone.
     20. Casa dell' Argenteria.
     22. Inn.
     23. House of Apollo.
     25. Casa del Duca d' Aumale.
viii. 5. House of the Tragic Poet — casa del Poeta Tragico.
      20. Fullery.
      22. Casa della Fontana Grande.
      23. Casa della Fontana Piccola.
ix. 2. House of Meleager — casa di Meleagro.
    3. House of the Centaur — casa del Centauro.
    6. House of Castor and Pollux — casa di Castore e Polluce.
x. 1. Wineshop.
   7. House of the Anchor — casa dell' Ancora.
   11. Casa del Naviglio.
xi. 10. House of the Labyrinth — casa del Laberinto.
xii. House of the Faun — casa del Fauno.
xiii. 6. House of M. Terentius Eudoxus.
xiv. 20. House of M. Vesonius Primus, often called the house of Orpheus—casa di Orfeo.
     22. Fullery.
     30. House of Laocoon — casa di Laocoonte.

xiv. 35. Bakery with kneading machine.
43. Casa degli Scienziati.
xv. 1. House of the Vettii.
9. House with atrium in two stories.

REGION VII
INSULA
i. 8. Stabian Baths.
25. House of Siricus.
40. House of Caesius Blandus.
45. Elephant Inn.
ii. 11. Dyehouse.
16. House of M. Gavius Rufus.
18. House of C. Vibius.
20. House of Popidius Priscus.
22. Bakery.
45. House of the Bear — casa dell' Orso.
iii. 29. House of M. Spurius Mesor.
iv. 1. Temple of Fortuna Augusta.
48. House of the Hunt — casa della Caccia.
51. House of the Colored Capitals — casa dei Capitelli Colorati, also called the house of Ariadna — casa d' Arianna.
56. Casa del Granduca di Toscana.
57. House of the Sculptured Capitals — casa dei Capitelli Figurati.
59. House of the Black Wall — casa della Parete Nera.
v. 2. Baths.
vi. 17. Water reservoir.
vii. 5. House of Cissonius.
27. City treasury.
28. Public closet.
29–30. Market buildings.
31. Table of standard measures.
32. Temple of Apollo.
viii. Forum.
a. Capitolium.
ix. 1. Building of Eumachia.
2. Temple of Vespasian.
3. Sanctuary of the City Lares.
8. Macellum.

xii. 28. House with projecting upper story — casa del Balcone Pensile.
35. Inn.
xiv. 9. House with skeleton.
xv. 8. House with second story dining room.
Ins. Occidentalis.
13. House near the Porta Marina.

REGION VIII
INSULA
i. Basilica.
ii. 1, 3. Casa di Championnet.
6. Office of the aediles.
8. Hall of the city council.
10. Office of the duumvirs.
17–21. Terrace house, with bath.
23. Bath.
39. House of the Emperor Joseph II — casa del' Imperatore Giuseppe II.
iii. 1. Comitium.
4. House of the Wild Boar — casa di Cinghiale.
iv. 4. House of Marcus Holconius.
15. House of Cornelius Rufus.
v–vi. 39. House of Acceptus and Euhodia.
viii. The theatres and other public buildings.

REGION IX
INSULA
i. 20. House of Epidius Rufus.
22. House of Epidius Sabinus.
ii. 16. House of Balbus.
iii. 2. Dyehouse.
5. House of M. Lucretius.
10. Bakery.
25. House of L. Clodius Varus.
iv. Central Baths.
v. 11. House with triclinium of masonry and seat for the children.
vii. 6. House of the Centenary — casa del Centenario; also known as the house of Tiberius Claudius Verus.
a. Inn of Hyginius Firmus.

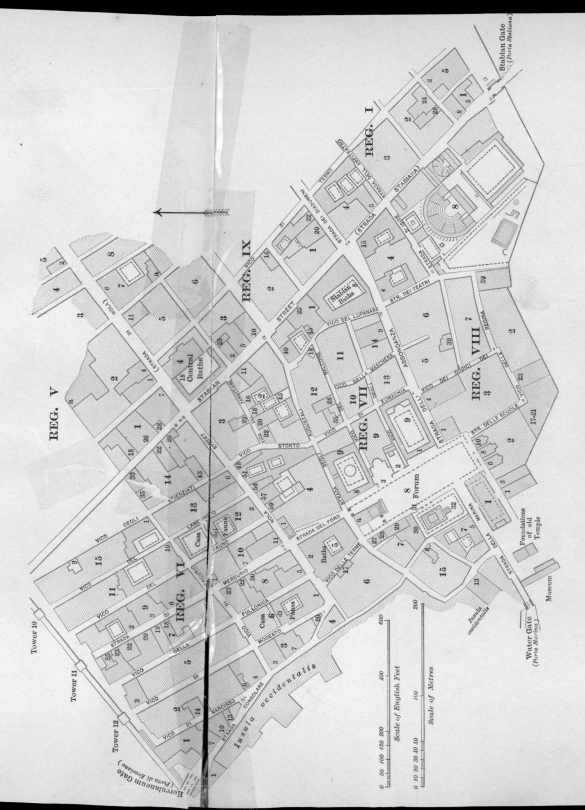

PLAN VI.—THE EXCAVATED PORTION OF POMPEII.

REG. V

REG. IX

REG. I

Tower 10

Tower 11

Tower 12

Herculaneum Gate
(Porta di Ercolano)

Stabian Gate
(Porta Stabiana)

Central
Baths

Stabian
Baths

REG. VI

REG. VII

REG. VIII

Casa
di
Fauno

Casa
di
Pansa

Casa
di
Modesto

Forum

Water Gate
(Porta Marina)

Museum

Foundations
of old
Temple

Insula occidentalis

Scale of English Feet
0 50 100 150 200   300   400   600

Scale of Metres
0 10 20 30 40 50   100   200

INDEX

Abinnerich, 18.

Acceptus and Euhodia, house of, 335–337.

accounts, memoranda of, on walls, 328, 487; of Caecilius Jucundus, 489.

Acerrae, Pompeii seaport of, 3.

Achilles, in paintings: among the daughters of Lycomedes, 344, 468, 471; delivering up of Briseis, 311; quarrel with Agamemnon, 84, 344, 468; Thetis bringing arms to, see Thetis; Troilus seized by, 468.

Actius Anicetus, actor, 142.

Admetus and Alcestis, painting, 307.

aediles, office of, 121, 123; title of, 12, 13.

Aemilius Celer, writer of notices, 217, 476.

Aeneas, statue of, 115.

Aesculapius, worshipped at domestic shrine, 266.

Agamemnon, in the sanctuary of Artemis, painting, 325; quarrel with Achilles, painting, 84, 344, 468.

Agrippina, mother of Nero, statues of, 47, 99.

alae, sanctuary of the City Lares, 102; of Pompeian house, 252–253.

Alexander and Darius, battle of, mosaic, 287–288.

Alexandria, influence of, in the development of decorative styles, 451, 455.

Alleia Decimilla, priestess of Ceres, 418.

M. Alleius Luccius Libella, tomb of, 418.

M. Alleius Minius, tomb of, 422.

Cn. Alleius Nigidius Maius, 216, 343, 479.

altar in dining room, 258.

altars, in the courts of temples: of Apollo, 86; of Isis, 168; of Doric temple, 133; temple of Vespasian, 107; temple of Zeus Milichius, 177, 432; on the sides of the streets, 227–230.

Amphitheatre, 26, 206–220.

amphorae, number of, 14; in the house of the Faun, 289; in the villa of Diomedes, 354; inscriptions upon, 495–496.

Anchor, peristyle of the house of the, 345.

andron in Pompeian houses, 254.

P. Aninius, 189.

antefixes about compluvium, 245.

Antioch, 459.

Apelles, 271.

Aphrodite, statue of, 442.

Apollo, house of, 256, 262, 267, 345; in stucco relief and in paintings, 199, 306, 323, 325, 470; statues of, 88, 134, 266, 346; temple of, 49, 80–90.

Apuleius on the worship of Isis, 163, 167, 168, 170, 175, 176.

Apuleius, tomb of, 425.

architectural periods at Pompeii, 39–44.

architecture, Pompeian, 429–436.

architraves of timber and stone, 51.

Ares and Aphrodite, painting, 280.

Ariadne, in paintings. See Bacchus, Theseus.

arm band, 373.

Arria, tomb of, 420.

M. Arrius Diomedes, tomb of, 350, 419.

Artemis, in paintings: 309; Agamemnon in sanctuary of, 325; shrine of, 471; statues of, 88, 442.

artist at work, painting, 276.

M. Artorius Primus, architect of the Large Theatre, 144.

Atella, Atellan farces, 136.

Athena and Marsyas, painting, 472.

M. Atinius, 194.

atrium of Pompeian houses, 244–249; atrium without a compluvium, 337–338.

Atticus, gladiator, 217–218.

Auctor, gladiator, 219.

Augustales, 100, 210.

Augustus Caesar, regulation of standard measures, 93; statues of, 47, 115; Vespasian compared with, 108; worship of, 14, 89–90, 104.

Auriolus, gladiator, 218.

autumn, Genius of, mosaic, 287.

L. Avianius Flaccus, 237.

bacchantes, 320, 330, 440, 458, 463.

bacchic figures in capitals of columns, 303, 343; in paintings, 323.

Bacchus, reliefs of Blue Glass Vase, 407; triumph of, 330; in paintings: 88, 348; as tutelary divinity, 230, 409; finds Ariadne, 333, 348, 470; in sculptures, 169, 319, 440.

bakery, arrangements of, 380–384.

Niraemius, 197.
Nocera. See Nuceria.
Nola, Pompeii seaport of, 3.
M. Nonius Campanus, 379.
C. Norbanus Sorex, 170.
Nuceria, Pompeii seaport of, 3.
Nucerians, conflict with Pompeians, 214, 215, 482.
nuptials of Zeus and Hera, painting, 310–311, 473.
nursing bottle, 366.

C. Occius, 197.
Octavia, statue of, 98.
M. Oculatius Verus, 150.
Odeum of Herodes Atticus, 149.
oecus in Pompeian houses, 259.
Oenone in paintings, 470.
Officiosus, gladiator, 220.
olive, culture of, about Pompeii, 14; crusher, 359; presses for making oil, 327, 359.
Omphalos, 81, 325.
Oppius Campanius, 80.
opus compositum, opus incertum, opus mixtum, 37–38; opus reticulatum, 38, 43; opus Signinum, 74, 272, 360.
Orange, masts of theatre at, 138.
Orestes and Pylades before Thoas, painting, 347–348, 462, 469.
Oscan foot, 44.
Oscan graves, 397, 399.
Oscan inscriptions, 80, 133, 134, 159, 178, 234, 236, 237.
Oscans, founders of Pompeii, 8; conquered by the Samnites, 9.
Osiris, worship of, 162 et seq.
oven, of bakery, 383.
Ovid, quoted in graffiti, 485, 486.

Pagani, 14.
Pagus Augustus Felix, 14.
paintings, number of, 461; relation to decorative styles, 462–464; classes of, 465–474.
Palaestra, 159–161.
Pansa, house of, 27, 243, 254, 260, 343–344.
Pansas, father and son, statues of, 213.
P. Paquius Proculus, 467.
Paris, 483.
Paris in paintings, 280, 470.
Pausanias, 194.
Penates, worship of, 104, 266.
Pentheus and Maenads, painting, 333, 471.
peristyle of the Pompeian house, 254.
Perseus with Andromeda, stucco relief and paintings, 173, 174, 323, 470.
St. Peter, bronze statue of, in Rome, 118.

Q. Petronius Octavus, gladiator, 220.
Phrixus and Helle, painting, 280.
Pietas Augusta, 111.
Pithecusans, 482.
Plato, 468.
Pliny the Elder, death of, 19–20.
Pliny the Younger, account of the eruption in 79, 19–22; villa of, 349.
poet, reciting, 323.
polychrome decoration, 433.
Polyclitus, doryphorus of, 161.
Polyphemus receiving a letter from Galatea, painting, 470, 471.
Pompeii, before 79, 8 et seq.; burial of, 19–23; excavation of, 25–30; government, 11–14; population, 16–18; resources, 14–16; value of remains, 499–501.
N. Pontius, 178, 236.
N. Popidius Ampliatus, 164.
N. Popidius Celsinus, 164.
V. Popidius, 50.
M. Porcius, 86.
M. Porcius, 147, 206.
M. Porcius, tomb of, 402.
portières at entrance of tablinum, 250.
Poseidon and Amymone, painting, 323.
Postumius Proculus, 378.
potter's workshop, 378.
praefects at Pompeii, 13, 14.
Praetorian Guard, 482.
Priene, 451.
priests, 14, 33.
priestesses, 14, 33, 402, 404.
Privatus, slave, 494.
procession to the theatres, 153.
Proculus, 478.
Propertius, quoted in graffito, 485, 486.
Psyches gathering flowers, painting, 324.
public buildings, location of, 33, 61, 127.
public notices. See inscriptions.
Pugnax, gladiator, 217–218.
Puteolana, 487.
Puteoli, 163, 393, 482.
Pyrrhus, 483.

Quasi-reticulate facing, 38, 42.
C. Quinctius Valgus, 147, 206.

Regions of Pompeii, 34.
rent, notices of property for, 479, 480.
Restitutus, 486.
reticulate facing, 38, 43.
Rhodian peristyle, 254, 298.
Rocca Monfina, 1, 15.
Roman foot, 44.
Romula, 486.
Romulus, statue of, 115.
rostra, 48.

A Handbook
of Greek Constitutional History

BY

A. H. J. GREENIDGE, M.A.

Lecturer and Late Fellow of Hertford College and Lecturer in Ancient History at Brasenose College, Oxford

---

12mo. Cloth. $1.25, *net*

Glasgow Herald:

"Most of the work that we have on this subject consists of translations from the German. The present author, wisely avoiding the detail of the German, traces in a judiciously brief narrative the main lines of development of Greek public law, and gives a good representation of the different types of States in the order of their development."

Yale Review:

"The special merits of Mr. Greenidge's book are these: *First*, the author has generally chosen the most significant facts, and without losing himself in detail, has made clear the salient features, the main tendencies of Greek political institutions, and, when looked at in this way, those institutions are seen to present an unexpected symmetry and logical coherence, which are the result of natural growth rather than of conscious intention. *Secondly*, the actual working of the various constitutions is presented more clearly than by larger works. And when thus presented and understood, Greek public law is seen to deserve more respect than it commonly receives."

THE MACMILLAN COMPANY

66 FIFTH AVENUE, NEW YORK